THE LOST WORLD OF
RUSSIA'S JEWS

JEWS IN EASTERN EUROPE
Jeffrey Veidlinger
Mikhail Krutikov
Geneviève Zubrzycki

Editors

THE LOST WORLD OF RUSSIA'S JEWS

ETHNOGRAPHY AND FOLKLORE IN
THE PALE OF SETTLEMENT

Abraham Rechtman

TRANSLATED BY
Nathaniel Deutsch and Noah Barrera

INDIANA UNIVERSITY PRESS

Originally published in Yiddish as *Yidishe etnografye un folklor* by Fundación IWO in Buenos Aires, Argentina. The license to publish this translation is granted by Fundación IWO, Buenos Aires.

This book is a publication of

Indiana University Press
Office of Scholarly Publishing
Herman B Wells Library 350
1320 East 10th Street
Bloomington, Indiana 47405 USA

iupress.org

© 2021 by Indiana University Press
All rights reserved

No part of this book may be reproduced or utilized in any form or by any means, electronic or mechanical, including photocopying and recording, or by any information storage and retrieval system, without permission in writing from the publisher. The paper used in this publication meets the minimum requirements of the American National Standard for Information Sciences—Permanence of Paper for Printed Library Materials, ANSI Z39.48-1992.

Manufactured in the United States of America

First printing 2021

Cataloging information is available from the Library of Congress.

ISBN 978-0-253-05694-8 (hardback)
ISBN 978-0-253-05693-1 (paperback)
ISBN 978-0-253-05692-4 (ebook)

In Memory of Shloyme Zanvil, son of Reb Aaron HaCohen Rapoport

Sh. An-sky, of blessed memory

The ninth of November 1920—the twenty-second of Marcheshvan [in the Jewish year] 5681

CONTENTS

Acknowledgments ix

A Note on Transliteration xi

Introduction 1
1. Sh. An-sky and the Jewish Ethnographic Expedition: The Participants in the Expedition 41
2. Synagogues and Prayerhouses 58
3. Headstones, Graves, and Tombs 114
4. Communal Pinkesim 168
5. Tales about Nigunim [Melodies] and Prayers 205
6. Exorcisms, Charms, and Remedies 240
7. Scribes and Scribal Writing 271

Bibliography 285

Index 293

ACKNOWLEDGMENTS

THE AUTHORS WOULD ESPECIALLY LIKE to thank Hannah Storch, Abraham Rechtman's granddaughter, and Renée Gladstone, his daughter, for so generously sharing their memories and for all of their encouragement with this project. Sadly, Renée passed away before this book could be published. As a longtime resident of the buildings, Esther Nelson Sokolsky provided valuable insights about the Sholem Aleichem Houses in the Bronx, where Abraham Rechtman lived for many years. We would also like to thank Gabriella Safran for her expert knowledge of An-sky's life and work and for her illuminating comments on the manuscript. Polly Zavadivker provided helpful observations, as did an anonymous reader. Abraham Lichtenbaum helped with matters connected to IWO in Buenos Aires. Nathaniel Deutsch would like to thank Miriam, Simi, Tamar, and Shirin for providing inspiration during the many hours devoted to the task of translation. Noah Barrera is particularly indebted to Chava Lapin and Dovid Braun, who both possess invaluable knowledge of Yiddish language and culture, and to all those who participated in a translation workshop he led at the 2015 Yiddish-Vokh, including but not limited to Simon Neuberg and Itzik Blieman. He would also like to thank Serena, Nathan, Baruch, Jessie, and Rickie for their continual support. Finally, this book could not have seen the light of day without the expert work of our editors at Indiana University Press, Dee Mortensen, Ashante Thomas, and Darja Malcolm-Clarke. Thank you.

A NOTE ON TRANSLITERATION

WE HAVE GENERALLY TRANSLITERATED YIDDISH words according to the system of the YIVO Institute for Jewish Research, though we have made exceptions for words that commonly appear in English. For Hebrew, Russian, Ukrainian, and Polish transliterations, we have followed the Library of Congress guidelines with some exceptions, and have also eliminated some diacritical marks. The numerous towns and cities mentioned in the volume are generally identified by their Yiddish names rather than their names in Polish, Ukrainian, Russian, Lithuanian, or other languages, for example, Vilna instead of Vilnius. We have employed standard English transliterations for certain Yiddish town names rather than their YIVO forms, for instance, Mezeritch rather than Mezeritsh, as in Dov Ber, the Maggid of Mezeritch.

THE LOST WORLD OF
RUSSIA'S JEWS

INTRODUCTION
Nathaniel Deutsch

"My Sun Is Already Setting in the West": Abraham Rechtman and the Publication of *Jewish Ethnography and Folklore*

In 1914, Russian police in the city of Zhitomir arrested two young Jews on suspicion of spying. Abraham Rechtman and Solomon Yudovin were native sons of the Pale of Settlement, the western reaches of the Russian Empire to which a vast majority of its Jews were restricted prior to the Revolution of 1917.[1] With a thick dark beard and sharp avian gaze, Rechtman still resembled the brilliant yeshiva student he had once been. Physically slighter and sensitive looking, Yudovin had a Chaplinesque quality that matched his artistic temperament.[2] Nearly half a century after their arrest, Rechtman, then living a world away in the Sholem Aleichem Houses in the Bronx, published a first-person account of what had transpired that day in Zhitomir: "At the end of 1914, while the First World War raged, the artist S. Yudovin and I were arrested in Zhitomir, under the suspicion that we were spies. This was a reasonable assumption since, on account of our work, we were carrying around a camera and taking photos out in the open. We were both put under arrest and the police confiscated the materials we had collected including all the photographic plates that we had in our possession."[3]

Rather than spies, however, Rechtman and Yudovin were members of the Jewish Ethnographic Expedition in Honor of Baron Naftali Hertz Gintsburg, the most ambitious—some might say quixotic—attempt ever undertaken to document Jewish life in the Russian Pale of Settlement, where more than 40 percent of the world's Jews still lived at the turn of the twentieth century.[4] Simon Dubnow, the great Russian Jewish historian, had described the Pale as a "Dark Continent . . . that lies ahead to be explored and illuminated."[5] Between 1912 and 1914, the Jewish Ethnographic Expedition set out to explore and document this vast territory, visiting approximately seventy towns or *shtetlekh* in the traditional Jewish heartland of Podolia, Volhynia (where Zhitomir was located), and Kiev provinces. Led by the socialist revolutionary, playwright, and ethnographer, Shlomo Zanvil Rapoport or, as he was better known, An-sky, the expedition took thousands of photographs; collected five hundred manuscripts, including numerous *pinkesim* (communal record books); transcribed eighteen hundred folktales, legends, and proverbs, fifteen hundred folk songs, and one thousand melodies; made five hundred recordings with an Edison wax cylinder phonograph; and purchased or acquired seven hundred objects.[6] The expedition also produced a massive life cycle questionnaire, *Dos yidishe etnografishe program* (*The Jewish Ethnographic Program*) and established a Jewish museum in Saint Petersburg where religious artifacts and other realia could be displayed.[7]

None of this mattered, of course, to the Russian police who had been trailing members of the Jewish Ethnographic Expedition for some time before they arrested Rechtman and Yudovin in Zhitomir. In their eyes, the activities of the expedition—traveling from town to town in the western borderlands of the empire, taking photographs, collecting documents, interviewing locals—must have looked like a good cover for something nefarious, especially as war clouds gathered. As Shmuel Shrayer (later Sherira), another member of the expedition, recalled: "In every town the local police monitored each new visitor with seven eyes and all the more so when several strangers showed up taking photographs, buying old artifacts, and collecting songs. On more than one occasion we had confrontations with small jackals from the provincial authority, who took an interest in us and our work and inquired after us. This was especially the case in towns near the border."[8] After being arrested, Rechtman and Yudovin sent a telegram to An-sky, who contacted Lev Shternberg, then the head of the Russian Museum of Anthropology and Ethnography and one of the collaborators on the *Jewish Ethnographic Program*. Shternberg, in turn, sent an official document vouching for the two fieldworkers. "As soon as the Zhitomir police received this document," Rechtman later wrote, "we were freed and the confiscated materials and objects were returned to us. We then packed everything that we were taking along with us and returned to Petrograd. The work of the expedition was now officially put on hiatus."[9]

Although the expedition was over, An-sky spent the next few years traveling the war-torn hinterlands of Poland, Galicia, and Bukovina on behalf of the Jewish Committee for the Relief of War Victims, distributing aid and informally continuing his ethnographic work, a period he would memorialize in his monumental Yiddish travelogue *Khurbn Galitsye* (The Destruction of Galicia). Because of his failing health (he had diabetes among other ailments), and peripatetic existence following the Russian Revolution, An-sky never published a book on the Jewish Ethnographic Expedition before his premature death, in 1920, on the outskirts of Warsaw. Instead, that task would fall to Abraham

Rechtman, who finally succeeded in publishing his extraordinary account of the expedition and its findings, *Yidishe etnografye un folklor* (Jewish Ethnography and Folklore), in 1958, more than four decades after he and Solomon Yudovin were arrested in Zhitomir for the "crime" of conducting ethnography in the Pale of Settlement.[10] During the intervening years, the territory that the expedition had sought to explore was transformed into what the historian Timothy Snyder has called "Bloodlands"—ravaged by pogroms and the Russian Civil War, transformed by Soviet rule, and then, finally, laid waste by World War II and the Holocaust. It is the remarkable Jewish civilization that thrived in this territory for centuries before being extinguished, as well as Abraham Rechtman's own youthful efforts to document its rich folk traditions before they disappeared forever, which fill the pages of the extraordinary volume that lies before you.

BIOGRAPHY

Abraham Rechtman was born in either 1888 or 1890 in Proskurov, a shtetl in the Podolia region of Ukraine, the cradle of the Hasidic movement. By the turn of the twentieth century, more than 11,000 Jews lived in the town, constituting roughly half of the overall population of 22,855 residents.[11] Like many of his contemporaries in the shtetls that formed a kind of Jewish archipelago in the Pale of Settlement, Rechtman had a traditional upbringing before setting out in other directions. Like An-sky and Dubnow before him, Rechtman received his earliest education in a cheder or traditional elementary school, where boys as young as three were introduced to the Hebrew alphabet. After they had broken with religious tradition as teenagers, An-sky and Dubnow described their own experiences in cheder as stultifying, even brutal, though both later came to praise the institution as an important vehicle for inculcating Jewish values. Looking back after more than half a century in *Jewish Ethnography and Folklore*, by contrast, Rechtman portrayed his own cheder education in nostalgic terms and praised his *melamed* [teacher], Reb Motele, for telling the kind of tales that the Jewish Ethnographic Expedition would seek to collect some two decades later, including in Proskurov itself: "Reb Motele was truly a tender-hearted, good-natured man who was always smiling. He would horse around with his grandchildren, play all sorts of tricks on them, and everyone would crack up with laughter. I still remember quite fondly how he would pinch my cheeks as he tested me and Dovid [a friend] on the weekly Torah portion.... Instead of lecturing on Torah, he used to tell beautiful, extraordinary tales and explain scripture with an incredible degree of precision.... Many of his tales, aphorisms and insights have remained in my memory to this day."[12]

During Rechtman's childhood, in the waning years of the nineteenth century, Proskurov and its environs were still heavily Hasidic and he grew up immersed in the movement's distinctive religious culture. This upbringing was good preparation for his work with the Jewish Ethnographic Expedition, since An-sky viewed Hasidim as playing a crucial role in the preservation and transmission of folk traditions that other Jews had abandoned by the beginning of the twentieth century, and, therefore, the expedition focused on towns with large Hasidic populations and strong connections to the history of the movement. Writing in the 1920s, Rechtman fondly recalled his childhood encounters with a Hasidic holy man known popularly as the Bazilier Rebbe (Yosef Dovid Shmilovitch), in Mikolayev, a shtetl near Proskurov that had roughly two thousand Jewish residents (60 percent of the total population) in the 1890s:

> I will never forget the impression that the Bazilier Rebbe made on me when I met him for the first time. I was then in the small shtetl of Nikolaev [a.k.a. Mikolayev], not far from Proskurov. I was learning in *kheyder* there and was still only a small boy. For an entire week, the shtetl was full of noise and tumult as it prepared for the arrival of the rebbe. On Friday afternoon, I remember, the rebbe arrived and when I went to greet him, he stretched out his hand and smiled. This was something—a rebbe who smiled. All the others whom I had met until him had such stern, hard, and serious faces and here suddenly is a rebbe who smiles. How I loved him then![13]

By his own account, Rechtman was so immersed in this traditional religious milieu that he did not learn Russian as a child and, instead, devoted himself completely to the "Talmud and Poskim [later rabbinic commentators]" until the age of sixteen, when he turned to secular subjects and began to write poetry and teach Hebrew.[14] According to family lore, by this point, Rechtman had also become an atheist. Nevertheless, bowing to pressure from his pious father, Rechtman reluctantly received *semikhah* (rabbinic ordination) as a teenager, after which, in a symbolic act of rebellion, he "celebrated" by eating some pork, which he promptly vomited up and swore off for the rest of his life.[15]

In 1909, Rechtman received a draft notice from the Russian military to report to duty in Starokonstantinov [Yiddish, Alt-Konstantin], a city not far from Proskurov. Either because of his fear of the czar's army or his love of Zion—or some combination of the two—Rechtman decided instead to join some thirty thousand other young Jews from the Russian Empire then emigrating to Ottoman Palestine in what would become known in Zionist historiography as the Second Aliyah. Rechtman arrived in 1910, the same year that other Russian *halutsim* [pioneers] established Degania, the first kibbutz in Palestine. While Rechtman was excited to "drain the swamps," as his granddaughter Hannah Storch later put it, his father, Avigdor, a devout Hasid who ran a general store

West, I feel that as long as my soul is within me, I must recall the little that I still remember from what was told to me then, in the few fortunate years when I had the honor of traveling with the expedition, together with the beloved Shloyme Zanvil son of R. Aaron HaCohen Rapoport, known as Sh. An-sky, may his memory be a blessing.[20]

Abraham Rechtman's journey to the United States, where he wrote these elegiac lines, began soon after the Jewish Ethnographic Expedition ended. In the final days of October 1915, after evading the Russian army once again and making his way across Siberia, Rechtman arrived in Harbin, China, then the site of a large Russian expatriate community, including thousands of Jews. After a year in Harbin, Rechtman traveled to Japan and, from there, departed for the United States. Rechtman arrived just in time to be drafted by the US military (he was initially deemed unfit to serve and then inducted right before the war ended) and to contract influenza during the global epidemic of 1918. By that point, Rechtman was living in New York City, where he anxiously followed news about the Russian Civil War, which soon engulfed his hometown of Proskurov along with many other shtetls in the former Pale of Settlement in an orgy of violence that would take the lives of at least fifty thousand Jews.[21] As Henry Abramson has written, "Violence reached virtually every Jewish settlement, and several were attacked repeatedly. A vicious massacre of Jews in Proskurov (later ironically renamed Khmel'nyts'kyi), which occurred in February 1919, was widely regarded as emblematic of these violent times."[22]

On February 15, 1919, soldiers in Semon Petlyura's army under the command of the Hetman Ivan Samosenko entered Proskurov. While a military band played, the soldiers cried out "Kill the Jews and Save the Ukraine" and began to slaughter, maim, and rape the town's Jewish residents, employing bayonets and lances in order to conserve ammunition.[23] More than fifteen hundred Jews (some estimates exceeded four thousand) were murdered and many others injured in a pogrom that became emblematic of the tidal wave of violence that swamped Jewish communities in the borderlands region of the former Russian Empire between 1919 and 1923. In its aftermath, people around the world struggled to make sense of the scale and savagery of what had taken place in Proskurov, which not only dwarfed the loss of life in previous pogroms, including the infamous Kishinev pogrom of 1903, when forty-nine Jews were murdered, but also ushered in a new and terrifying era of mass murder. As the *New York Times* put it in September 1919, "The first of a new series of events which leave the scope of ordinary pogroms and assume the character of slaughter occurred in a city which will be forever written in letters of blood on the pages of Jewish history. It happened in Proskurov."[24]

For former residents of Proskurov now living abroad, like Abraham Rechtman, the news of the pogrom was devastating. Members of the United in Proskurov, was furious with his son for becoming a Zionist and attempting to "hasten the arrival of the messiah." Renée (Reyzl) Gladstone, one of Rechtman's three children, recalled that when Rechtman told his father of his plans to emigrate, Avigdor replied, "If you go, you shouldn't arrive alive. And if you arrive alive, you shouldn't come back alive."[16] Then he recited kaddish [the mourner's prayer] for his son.

Despite Rechtman's initial enthusiasm, he spent only two years in Palestine before returning to Proskurov in 1912. According to Gladstone, soon after arriving in town, Rechtman encountered a friend of his father drawing water from a well. The two men were engaged in conversation when Avigdor glimpsed his prodigal son and, overwhelmed with emotion, came out and embraced him. Nevertheless, Rechtman's rapprochement with his father did not return him to religion or keep him in Proskurov for long. Instead, like An-sky had done years earlier, Rechtman struck out for Saint Petersburg. There he joined other young men from the Pale living illegally in the capital—since Jews required a special residency permit—who had become students at the Jewish Academy founded in 1908 by Baron David Gintsberg, a brother of Vladimir.[17] The Jewish Academy's most prominent faculty member was Simon Dubnow, who described the "student body ... [as] made up mainly of provincials, self-taught or experts, former members of yeshivahs, well versed in specialist Jewish subjects, but without sufficient background of general education."[18] Which is to say, they were a lot like Abraham Rechtman.

Between 1912 and 1914, ten students from the Jewish Academy collaborated with An-sky on either the Jewish Ethnographic Expedition, the *Jewish Ethnographic Program*, or both. In June 1913, Rechtman and two other students from the academy, Yitzhak Pikangur and Shmuel Shrayer, joined An-sky, the composer Zusman Kisselhof, and Solomon Yudovin for the second season of the expedition, remaining in the field until November of that year when muddy roads and inclement weather made it impossible to continue.[19] Once conditions improved, in 1914, Rechtman set out again with Yudovin for what would be the third and final season of the expedition, when World War I put an end to their activities. Although his work with An-sky on the Jewish Ethnographic Expedition had extended for two seasons in the field, its profound impact on Rechtman would last a lifetime. As he put it in the "Introduction" to *Jewish Ethnography and Folklore*:

> And now, almost four decades after An-sky's death, and more than forty years since the peregrinations of the expedition through Ukraine; now—when nothing remains of the homey Ukrainian shtetls; when only sacred memories survive from the loving generations of Jews and their way of life. And when I myself reflect that I am a man of seventy and my sun is already setting in the

Proskurover Relief, a landsmanshaft organization founded in New York City in 1916, quickly mobilized to smuggle material aid to the survivors, despite the dangerous conditions then prevailing on the ground.[25] They also embarked on what would become a pioneering literary endeavor: the publication of *Khurbn Proskurov* (The Destruction of Proskurov) in 1924, considered to be the first of the modern memorial books or *yizker bikher*, which would emerge as a full-blown genre in the wake of the Holocaust.[26] Among the contributors to the volume was Abraham Rechtman, who was selected by his fellow *landslayt* (compatriots) to take on the important task of writing the "Foreword," which set the tone for the rest of the book.

Drawing on a long Jewish tradition of lamentation, extending from the biblical prophet Jeremiah to the Khmelnytsky massacres of 1648 and beyond, Rechtman composed a contemporary *kinah* or dirge: "And their blood cries out to us from the depths of their graves with thousands of loud voices: Forget us not!!! Remember us from time to time. Tell about our life and death to your children and children's children, to the coming generations."[27] In some sense, Rechtman had been preparing for this role since the expedition itself. In the *Jewish Ethnographic Program*, An-sky had lamented that "our past, soaked with so much holy blood and so many tears shed by martyrs and blameless victims, sanctified by so much self-sacrifice, is disappearing and being forgotten."[28] Now, five years later, martyrdom had come to the Jews of Proskurov. Yet, this time, Abraham Rechtman was determined not to forget.

It is unclear whether any of Rechtman's own family members were murdered in the pogrom. He does not mention it in *Khurbn Proskurov* nor do any individuals with the surname Rechtman appear in the list of victims published in the volume. Nevertheless, according to a family tradition, Rechtman's father, Avigdor, died from injuries suffered during the pogrom.[29] Of the thousands of victims, Rechtman singled out only one to eulogize in detail, the Bazilier Rebbe, who had made such a powerful impression on him during his youth: "The Angel of Slaughter, who during the dark, tear-filled day of the pogrom snatched the lives of so many of our dear and beloved ones in Proskurov, did not protect the pure, holy, and kosher soul of the Bazilier Rebbe, who along with his wife and two grandchildren, were cut off from this world before their time, by a bestial, murderous hand. With his death, the entire Jewish people lost one of the pillars of Hasidism."[30]

Among the casualties of the pogrom were materials from the Jewish Ethnographic Expedition that Rechtman had left behind with his family in Proskurov for safekeeping when he emigrated. In *Jewish Ethnography and Folklore*, Rechtman described their fate: "A small apology: what I am narrating is based on the meager notes and the few photographs which miraculously remained in my possession from that time. For, in 1915, when I fled to China via Siberia, and in 1916, when I fled from China to America by way of Japan, I did not manage to take along with me the great collection of ethnographic pictures (approximately 1,500), as well as the few hundred journals containing notes on the expedition. Everything remained in my hometown Proskurov and there, during Petlyura's pogroms, vanished."[31] Despite this firsthand account, however, family lore offers a different version of what happened to the ethnographic materials that Rechtman left behind. According to this tradition, when Rechtman left Proskurov in 1915, he packed materials from the expedition in a trunk with instructions that they were "very important" and should be brought if and when family members were able to join him in the United States. Yet, when Rechtman's mother, Rivkah, and his sister, Esther, left Proskurov in the wake of the pogrom, Rivkah decided to replace her son's "stuff" with things she deemed more crucial—down-filled blankets and pillows—which Rechtman only discovered when he opened the trunk upon their arrival in New York.[32]

Rivkah and Esther Rechtman arrived shortly before the Immigration Act of 1924 severely curtailed entry to the United States from Eastern and Southern Europe. Once they were safely settled in New York City, Rechtman, then approaching middle age, was finally ready to marry, as Renée Gladstone put it, "My father wouldn't even think of getting married before bringing family over from Europe." In 1925, Rechtman wed Bronya (Binah) Zwick, a Jewish immigrant from Kalisz, Poland. A year later, Bronya gave birth to Faye (Feyga), who would be joined over the next few years by a sister, Renée (Reyzl) and brother, Avigdor. With a growing family to support, Rechtman ran his own printing company, "Oriom Press," which moved from address to address in Manhattan throughout the 1920s and early 1930s, publishing works in Hebrew, Yiddish, and English, including for the Workmen's Circle.

For the remainder of his life, Rechtman struggled financially. After closing the printing press during the height of the Great Depression, Rechtman moved to Miami Beach in the middle of the 1930s at the invitation of a friend who offered to take him on as a partner in his wholesale grocery business. Rechtman only lasted fifteen months before returning to New York City, where relatives in the fur pieces business invited him to join them as they sat and sewed pieces together to make coats. Eventually, Rechtman was able to open his own shop but, as his daughter, Renée recalled, "It was a meager, meager income. When my father died [in 1972] there was $40 in his checking account. We had nothing as far as money was concerned. We had enough to eat and shoes on our feet. My father bought books and we had music lessons. My parents were into the brain, the heart, and the soul."[33]

Though poor in material luxuries, Abraham Rechtman nevertheless enjoyed a remarkably rich cultural life. This was especially the case after the Rechtmans moved into the Sholem Aleichem Houses in the mid-1930s. Resembling a neo-Tudor castle with a beautiful interior courtyard and garden, the Sholem Aleichem Houses were built on a hill in the western Bronx overlooking the Jerome Park Reservoir. Founded by members of the Workmen's Circle (*Der Arbeter Ring*) and named after the famous Yiddish writer, the Sholem Aleichem Houses were completed in 1927. The building functioned as a cooperative until 1931, when bankruptcy brought about by the Great Depression forced a transfer to a private owner, who, following a bitterly fought rent strike, agreed to rent a majority of the units to the original residents at a reduced rate.[34]

The Sholem Aleichem Houses belonged to a wave of "labor cooperatives" or "cooperative worker housing projects" built in the Bronx and the Lower East Side by leftist Jewish organizations including the United Workers Cooperative, the Jewish National Workers Alliance (Natsionaler Yidisher Arbeter Farband), and the Amalgamated Clothing Workers of America.[35] As Richard Plunz has written, "Each cooperative had a well-defined ideology, related to the diverse currents in leftist Jewish politics."[36] The Sholem Aleichem Houses were "much less avowedly political in the normal sense of the word" than the other cooperatives, though they still housed two Yiddish-language schools run by the communist-leaning International Workers Order (IWO) and the social democratic Workmen's Circle, to accommodate the competing political leanings of its residents.[37] Renée Gladstone remembered the building being two-thirds socialist and one-third communist when she was growing up and that she and her siblings were "not supposed to play with communist children but we did anyway."[38]

Reflecting their common leftist orientation, the labor cooperatives provided childcare, educational programs, and cafeterias, and also published their own newspapers and journals. Some ran their own summer camps, had workshops, and even generated below market electricity for residents.[39] The Sholem Aleichem Houses—or *Sholem Aleykhem Hayzer*, as residents called them in Yiddish—were distinguished by their focus on culture and the arts. The building included three artist studios with north facing windows for optimal light, as well as an auditorium where numerous lectures and performances were held over the years. In the words of Richard Plunz, "Perhaps at the Shalom Aleichem Houses the cultural activities were most extensive. . . . This activity spanned four decades, into the 1960s."[40] Over the years, the Sholem Aleichem Houses have been described as a "lofty urban oasis" and a "Bronx Utopia."[41] For Esther Nelson Sokolsky, an artist and lifelong resident born in 1928, the building was "like a little shtetl," whose early residents, like Abraham Rechtman himself, were "a bunch of Eastern European Jews, every one of them an artist or intellectual trapped by circumstances in a garment factory."[42] In short, it was an ideal place for Rechtman to raise his young family and devote himself to his lifework of documenting the now lost world of Eastern European Jewry, its language, culture, and folkways.

Late Imperial Russia had produced the first generation of Jews for whom it was possible to identify primarily or even exclusively with Jewish culture rather than—or even, over and against—religion. Indeed, it was leftist Jews in Russia, like Chaim Zhitlovsky, An-sky, and the founders of the Bund, who had worked to create a secular Jewish culture that they hoped would replace supposedly moribund and politically reactionary Orthodox Judaism. In New York City, Abraham Rechtman belonged to a circle of Jews who had grown up fully literate in the traditional Jewish life of the shtetl and then left it behind, only to remain intellectually and emotionally committed to its cultural dimensions. Of course, separating the cultural from the religious aspects of Jewish practice, at least, frequently proved to be difficult if not impossible. Thus, Renée Gladstone recalled that Rechtman "never became a practicing rabbi because he never believed. We three children were brought up totally ethnically Jewish but atheistic. We celebrated all Jewish holidays with the required ceremonies and my father recited every word of the Haggadah in Hebrew and Aramaic. We spoke Yiddish in the house and among the adult residents of the *Sholem Aleykhem Hayzer*."[43] Politically, Rechtman was a "socialist, opposed to communism," and "he was a Zionist. He believed in culture. We were culturally nothing but Jews, we were nothing but Jews."[44]

Renée Gladstone remembered her father as being at the "hub of the Yiddish intelligentsia in the city."[45] In 1945, after she married a cousin of the celebrated Yiddish poet and literary critic Yankev Glatshteyn—described by the scholar Jan Schwarz as "the leading spokesperson of Yiddish culture in America"—the latter referred to Rechtman in correspondence as his "in-law and friend" (*mekhutn un fraynt*).[46] Among the many other writers and artists with whom he socialized, Rechtman was particularly close with the novelist Yosef Opatoshu, best known for his work *In poylishe velder* (*In Polish Woods*), published in 1921. Not all of Rechtman's friends were prominent intellectuals or artists, however. For example, Abraham Twersky (1908–2000), a neighbor of Rechtman in the Sholem Aleichem Houses, whose brother, Yohanan, was an accomplished Hebrew author and whose mother, Khaykele, was a remarkable woman in her own right, was later described in an obituary in *The Forward* for his son, the journalist David Twersky, as "a militant leftist garment worker who was in turn the rebellious scion of a leading Hasidic rabbinic dynasty," namely the descendants of Mordechai (Motl) of Chernobyl, who established courts throughout Ukraine during the nineteenth century.[47]

On January 7, 1953, Abraham Twersky wrote a letter of encouragement to Rechtman, who was then in the hospital recovering from an ailment.[48] The

Yiddish and Hebrew document is extraordinary for the insight it provides into a generation of Jews for whom radical politics and Hasidic tradition, seemingly irreconcilable in so many ways, could nevertheless coexist in the same individuals. From its heading, in which Twersky employed the acronym B"H for *be'ezrat hashem* (with God's help) and the Hebrew date, to the salutation "Rav [Rabbi] Rechtman," to his invocation of "the Holy One Blessed Be He," the letter reads more like it was composed by a pious Hasid or even a rebbe than by a militant leftist garment worker. This impression is only strengthened by the *brokhe* (blessing) for a *refue shleyma* [complete recovery] that Twersky offered Rechtman, with the caveat that "in this blessing of mine lies not, God forbid, my own power—but only the power of my holy ancestors—and the blessing will, with God's help, surely be fulfilled." Twersky continued by urging, "Dear Rav [Rabbi] Rechtman, get better and recover your powers so that we may once again, at your *tish* [table], drink a real Hasidic *lekhayim* [toast]!"

Unlike Glatshteyn, Opatoshu, or the great Yiddish novelist Chaim Grade, with whom he maintained a cordial correspondence, Rechtman was not a fiction writer. Instead, he focused his considerable intellectual energies on two discrete, if sometimes overlapping, areas of interest: Eastern European Jewish folk culture and the history of the Yiddish language. Renée Gladstone remembered her father as "always sitting at his desk when he wasn't entertaining Yiddish writers. He had file cards all over the place." These file cards contained Rechtman's notes for the massive project that, along with his efforts to publish *Jewish Ethnography and Folklore*, would absorb most of his scholarly attention during the years following World War II. This was the *Groyser verterbukh fun der yidisher shprakh* (Great Dictionary of the Yiddish Language), originally the brainchild of the lexicographer Nahum Stutchkoff, who had published *Der oytser fun der yidisher shprakh* (Thesaurus of the Yiddish Language) in 1950. Stutchkoff's goal was to produce an exhaustive Yiddish-Yiddish dictionary that, as Shimeon Brisman has written, would include "all the applicable synonyms, idiomatic expressions, and Jewish customs and folklore" and reflect "all classes of the Jewish people" as well as "dialectic and limited localisms."[49]

Clearly, an undertaking of this scale would require a collective effort. In 1953, therefore, YIVO established the Yiddish Dictionary Committee to coordinate the necessary research and editorial work. The committee, in turn, established a global network of "collectors," or *zamlers*, as they were called in Yiddish, to produce the wide-ranging entries. Among the approximately three hundred individuals who answered the call to serve as zamlers was Abraham Rechtman. Thus, for the second time in his life, Rechtman would participate in an extraordinary, collective, and, it would turn out, equally quixotic, effort to document the riches of European Jewish culture. With his Hasidic upbringing in Podolia, traditional rabbinic education, and ethnographic experience, Rechtman was an ideal contributor to the dictionary.

Whereas Rechtman had only fond memories of the months he spent traveling with An-sky and the Jewish Ethnographic Expedition, from the beginning of his work on the *Groyser verterbukh*, he chafed at his interactions with the project's administrators. Indeed, Stutchkoff himself quit in 1955 due to intellectual differences with Yudel Mark, who took over as coeditor along with Yehuda Yoffe. For his part, Rechtman complained about the paltry financial compensation provided to zamlers as well as the slow pace of the project. In response, the editorial staff of the dictionary praised Rechtman for his "work on the Hebrew element" and the "work that you are now undertaking in relation to *talmudishn yidish* [Talmudic Yiddish]," but also cautioned him that they were only focusing on the first letter "aleph," and that "anything that you do, you do out of your own free and good will."[50] As for increasing the paltry pay that zamlers like Rechtman received, the editorial staff stressed that "there is not a single individual among us who does not hold that what we pay our collaborators is in truth only a portion of what they should in truth receive."[51] There is a poignancy to these exchanges that reflects the shoestring budgets, competing visions, and intense emotional investments that characterized and, often, bedeviled Yiddish cultural projects in the decades following World War II. Despite these challenges, the editors of the *Groyser verterbukh* ultimately managed to publish four volumes of the dictionary (two in New York and two in Jerusalem) beginning in 1961. All were dedicated to the letter "aleph," which nevertheless comprised an estimated one-third of the entire vocabulary of Yiddish, and filled 2,333 pages, including a brief "thank you," to Abraham Rechtman.[52]

By the time the first volume of the *Groyser verterbukh* came out in print, Rechtman had already overcome another set of obstacles to publish, in 1958, his own masterwork, *Jewish Ethnography and Folklore*. During the remaining decade of his life, Rechtman continued to work on other projects. In 1962, he published an important study in the *YIVO Bleter*, documenting Jewish customs or *minhagim* connected to childhood, weddings, marriage, divorce, prayer, illness and death, Sabbath and festivals, remedies and incantations, Hasidic dance, and so on.[53] When Parkinson's eventually robbed him of the ability to write in his last years, Rechtman dictated to his daughter, Faye, and doted on his grandchildren, giving them "matzah, butter, and salt all year round," as Hannah Storch, Faye's daughter, fondly recalled.[54] Abraham Rechtman's sun finally set on February 1, 1972, twelve years after his wife, Bronya, passed away. A standing room only crowd attended his funeral, and he was buried in the Workmen's Circle cemetery in New Jersey.

PUBLICATION

From his earliest years in the United States, Abraham Rechtman devoted himself to preserving the memory of An-sky and bringing the Jewish Ethnographic Expedition to the wider world. In 1920, Rechtman published a Hebrew-language account that either served as a model for the much longer *Jewish Folklore and Ethnography*—or, more likely—was itself based on an originally Yiddish text that Rechtman later incorporated into his book. In general, the Hebrew and Yiddish versions of the same material line up closely, though there are some differences, including omissions in the former and elaborations in the latter. Of particular interest is one detail that Rechtman included in the Hebrew article but inexplicably left out of his Yiddish book, namely, a reference to a rare *pinkes* (record book) belonging to a women's society or, in his own words: "In the rich collection of *pinkesim* that the expedition collected, there exists only one from a women's society, written in Yiddish and illustrated with wonderful pictures. However, the pictures and the content are of a different sort altogether. In the same *pinkes* we found forms of different *tkhinot* [supplicatory prayers], that were composed by righteous women at various times, and *takanot* [rules] for the societies 'hakhnasat kalah' [for poor brides] and 'yoldot' [for women who have just given birth] and the like."[55] It is unclear why Rechtman did not discuss this unusual pinkes in *Jewish Ethnography and Folklore*, especially since he devoted an entire section of the book to describing pinkesim of various kinds, as well as several sections to Jewish women's folk practices.

Rechtman concluded his Hebrew article with a cri de coeur inspired by the ongoing pogroms that had already laid waste to his hometown of Proskurov and would eventually claim the lives of more than one hundred thousand Jews across the former Pale:

> And there is much, much to regret, that during the time of the war the work of the expedition stopped, stopped in the middle, or more correctly: stopped at the beginning. For that which the expedition had gathered and collected was only a tiny amount, a mere drop in the sea, compared to the great wealth, the extraordinary abundance, of folk creativity that was dispersed throughout the cities and towns of the Pale. And all of this [cultural] wealth has now gone down the drain, swept away by the bloody surges that swamped the cities of the Pale and destroyed them forever.[56]

In an autobiographical sketch that Rechtman composed in 1927, he noted that he had published articles in Hebrew and Yiddish on "Jewish folklore and the activities of the Jewish Ethnographic Expedition in Russia," under the pseudonyms "Doktor Zamler" and "Ish Yemini."[57] From the mid-1920s until after World War

II, it appears that Rechtman did not publish anything else on the expedition. Preoccupied by the need to support his young family during the trying years of the Great Depression and then by the terrible events of the Holocaust, Rechtman appears to have had little spare time or energy. Nevertheless, the expedition was never far from his mind, as Renée Gladstone recalled of this period: "I grew up with a picture of An-sky, a huge portrait, over my father's desk. He didn't really talk much about An-sky. He was too busy. But I knew that he worshipped him."[58]

In the aftermath of World War II, a number of factors, both in Rechtman's own life and in the wider world, encouraged him to focus anew on the Jewish Ethnographic Expedition. At home, all of Rechtman's children were now grown, and he was nearing retirement age. Within his circle of Eastern European Jewish émigrés, meanwhile, the Holocaust had created an intense desire to eulogize and document the now destroyed communities of their youth. In this light, Rechtman's intellectual labors during the postwar period, culminating in the publication of *Jewish Ethnography and Folklore* in 1958, should be seen as part of a much broader, transnational effort to memorialize what Abraham Joshua Heschel, in a famous 1945 speech before the YIVO annual conference in New York, referred to as *Di mizrekh-eyropeishe tkufe in der yidisher geshikhte* or "The Eastern European Era in Jewish History."[59]

On December 10, 1950, Rechtman participated as a panelist along with Jacob (Yankev) Shatzky, then in the middle of publishing his monumental, three-volume work, *The History of the Jews in Warsaw*, in a Yiddish radio program hosted by the Congress for Jewish Culture to commemorate the thirtieth anniversary of An-sky's death. Rechtman spoke at length about the expedition and his own fond memories of An-sky, who had "devoted so many years of his creative, colorful life," to "collecting and reworking the treasures of the previous generations." He concluded by calling for American Jews to continue the important work that An-sky had only just begun by creating a new ethnographic society in his honor: "And now at the thirtieth *yahrzeit* of An-sky's death, when nothing remains of the *heymish* [homey] cities and shtetls, when only memories remain of the heartfelt Jews of past generations—I, myself a Jew already over sixty, wonder whether it would not be worthwhile if here in America, the population center of the Jewish people, that here in America, such a historic-ethnographic society should be established that would carry the shining name Shloyme Zanvil HaCohen Rapaport, known as Sh. An-sky, may his memory be a blessing."[60]

In 1954, Rechtman published a Hebrew article on the Jewish Ethnographic Expedition in an issue of the Israeli folklore journal *Yeda-Am* dedicated to the ninetieth anniversary of An-sky's birth.[61] That same year, Rechtman also began to search in earnest for a publisher for a manuscript he had completed about the expedition and its findings.

On June 22, 1954, at the recommendation of their mutual friend Jacob Shatzky, Rechtman sent a letter of inquiry to L. M. Shteyn (also known as L. M. Stein), a prominent publisher of Yiddish books in Chicago.[62] Despite Shteyn's geographic distance from New York City and its many Yiddish institutions, there were good reasons for Rechtman to reach out to him, in particular. Since 1926, when he established the eponymous L. M. Shteyn Farlag, Shteyn had published numerous high-quality, aesthetically pleasing Yiddish books that were praised as a "jewel in every intelligent Jewish home."[63] Many were art books with numerous illustrations, something that appealed to Rechtman, since, as he wrote to Shteyn, his own manuscript was accompanied by numerous photos and original woodcuts related to the expedition. Others were fine literary editions by well-known Yiddish writers, among them Shmuel Niger and Yosef Opatoshu, Rechtman's close friend. Beyond these aesthetic concerns, which were particularly important to Rechtman given his own background in printing, there was an additional factor that was of equal significance: Shteyn had a reputation for heavily subsidizing the publication of his books, as Sarah Stein has written, "he was financially better off, able to fund extravagant projects at a personal loss."[64] As Shteyn himself wrote to his friend Dovid Pinski, in 1929, "So when I allow myself to lose a few thousand dollars a year for a Yiddish book, I will surely do it. I cannot tolerate regret."[65]

Unfortunately for Rechtman, by the time he contacted Shteyn, in 1954, the latter's heyday as a publisher was already past, though he continued to put out a small number of books under the imprint L. M. Stein. Besides his advancing age and the precipitous decline of the Yiddish reading public in Chicago, Shteyn's ability to publish new books was hampered in the 1950s by what Sarah Stein has described as "financial concerns: the Shteyn family, after years of funding the press and other Yiddish projects, was feeling the effects of Shteyn's generosity as a patron."[66] This background helps to explain Shteyn's response to Rechtman's inquiry. Although Shteyn expressed genuine enthusiasm for Rechtman's manuscript, writing on June 26 that "it is clear to me from your letter that this project is important," he cautioned that because of its length and illustrations, publishing it would cost "a minimum of $2500 if not more. I have undertaken the subsidy of many works and I am extremely sorry that I do not have the capital of Baron Gintsburg of yore.... My financial means do not permit me to undertake this alone. When you can organize a committee through someone, I would, with pleasure, contribute around $1250." Shteyn encouraged Rechtman to ask Jacob Shatsky for the names and addresses of people who might serve on such a committee and suggested contacting the Jewish Museum in New York for help, though, he noted, "They will certainly want to see it in English and such a work loses very much when it is not published in our *mame loshn* [mother tongue] Yiddish."[67]

There is no surviving record of how Rechtman responded to Shteyn's letter. Given his perennially precarious finances, however, we can easily imagine that he found the prospect of having to raise $1,250 disheartening at a time when the median household income in the United States was only $5,000 and the average monthly social security benefit for a man like Rechtman was $75.86 or $910 a year.[68] Financial considerations aside, any possibility of working with Shteyn came to an end in 1956, when the publisher passed away. With his own sun already setting in the West, Rechtman must have felt increasing pressure to find a different publisher for his manuscript. Therefore, in 1957, Rechtman extended his search to Buenos Aires, Argentina, at the time one of the global capitals of Yiddish literature, supporting a rich culture of bookstores, libraries, and publishing houses, as Alejandro Dujovne has documented.[69]

The most important achievement of Yiddish publishing in postwar Argentina was the series *Dos poylishe yidntum*, founded by Mark Turkow, in 1946, under the auspices of the Central Union of Polish Jews in Argentina (Tsentral-Farband fun Poylishe Yidn in Argentine). Another landmark was the *Musterverk* series launched in 1957 by Shmuel Rozhanski, the director of IWO or Instituto Cientifico Judio (the Argentine branch of YIVO founded in 1928) in Buenos Aires. As significant as these literary concerns were to Rechtman, however, he was undoubtedly attracted by another striking feature of the Buenos Aires publishing scene, especially compared to New York City: the relatively low cost of book production. Printing Yiddish books in Argentina was considerably cheaper than in the United States during the 1950s because of lower wages and less expensive prices for paper and other materials. This was particularly significant to Rechtman because he, alone, would have to bear the financial burden of publishing his manuscript. Thus, when asked why her father had published *Jewish Ethnography and Folklore* in Buenos Aires, Renée Gladstone immediately responded: "The price! You had to pay yourself to have your own book published in those days. That's where all Yiddish books were being published. My father never went down there [to Buenos Aires]. It was all done through the mail. He never sold any. Just gave them away."[70]

It is unknown whether Rechtman initially sought to have his book included in either *Dos poylishe yidntum* or the *Musterverk* series. Had he done so successfully, it is likely that the production costs of the volume would have been defrayed or even fully subsidized. After 1955, for example, many of the books published in the *Dos poylishe yidntum* series were financed by the Conference on Jewish Material Claims against Germany, including all seven books published in 1958, the same year that *Jewish Ethnography and Folklore* appeared in print.[71] Other publications in the series were subsidized by the directors of the Banco Israelita del Rio de La Plata and other philanthropists. As Jan Schwarz has written, "The strong financial support of Yiddish culture among Jewish businesspeople in Buenos Aires was a precondition for the implementation of Turcov's project."[72] Similarly, from the very beginning, Shmuel Rozhanski enlisted a South African diamond dealer and patron of Yiddish culture named Joseph Lifshitz to subsidize the *Musterverk* series.[73]

Yet, Abraham Rechtman's manuscript did not fit neatly into either *Dos poylishe yidntum* or the *Musterverk* series. The former focused almost exclusively on three categories: memorial books, diaries, and other works dedicated to the Holocaust and its aftermath, including Elie Wiesel's *Un di velt hot geshvign* ("And the World Remained Silent"), which he later transformed into *La Nuit* and, subsequently, into *Night*; memoirs and historical studies of Jewish life in prewar Poland; and poetry and fiction.[74] Meanwhile, the *Musterverk* series, as Jan Schwarz has noted, "featured the most important works of Yiddish literature from premodern times through the first half of the twentieth century."[75] *Jewish Ethnography and Folklore*, by contrast, was devoted to an ethnographic expedition into the Pale of Settlement. Rather than having his manuscript appear in one of these subsidized series, therefore, Rechtman himself had to pay IWO in Buenos Aires for the entire cost of production. Moreover, he could not rely on the extensive distribution network that *Dos poylishe yidntum*, in particular, had already built up around the globe, as Jan Schwarz has written, "An estimated quarter-million books of *Dos poylishe yidntum* had been printed and sold by 1954," in more than twenty-two countries.[76]

On December 4, 1957, IWO in Buenos Aires issued a contract to Rechtman specifying the terms of their publishing agreement. Rechtman would pay IWO $800 (US dollars) and, in return, would receive "five hundred books bound in linen."[77] In addition, Rechtman agreed to assume all financial responsibility for paying a local copy editor, Abraham (Avrom) Zak (1891–1980). Like Rechtman, Zak had grown up in a religious home in the Pale of Settlement and received a traditional Jewish education until his teens before being drawn to leftist politics and secular culture, eventually becoming an extraordinarily prolific Yiddish writer in multiple genres.[78] In short, he was an ideal person to copyedit a manuscript that drew equally on Jewish folk and elite rabbinic traditions and was written in a Yiddish style that moved easily between scholarly and popular registers. It is a testament to the difficulty of making a living as a Yiddish intellectual in 1950s Buenos Aires—even with its vibrant Yiddish literary scene— that Zak agreed to take on the assignment, writing in a letter to Rechtman dated November 7, 1957, that he would charge $150 to do the work.[79]

Altogether, the total cost of publishing the volume in Buenos Aires would be $950, or less than one half of the $2,500 that L. M. Shteyn had estimated three years earlier in Chicago. Still, it was an enormous amount of money for

Rechtman, and it is possible that he invested his entire life's savings in the project. Given these circumstances, as well as Rechtman's own professional background as a printer, perhaps it is not surprising that as soon as the volume was published in the spring of 1958, he appears to have had some second thoughts, if not quite buyer's remorse, complaining to IWO about what he considered to be the low production quality of the book. Justifiably proud of Yiddish publishing in Buenos Aires, the staff at IWO, in turn, refused to give an inch, responding in a letter to Rechtman dated June 5, 1958, that the quality of the locally published books was not inferior to those produced in North America and that "in connection with the quality of the paper, you see, you are making a mistake when you write that there is none worse. This is the same paper used by all of the local editions: by the publishing house 'Dos poylishe yidntum,' by Yidbukh [another Buenos Aires–based Yiddish publisher], by our own IWO books, and so on."[80]

RECEPTION

Notwithstanding this tense correspondence, IWO was committed enough to Rechtman's book to host a public launch party in its Buenos Aires headquarters in July 1958. In its glowing coverage of the evening, *Di Presse*, then one of Argentina's two Yiddish dailies, described *Jewish Ethnography and Folklore* as "a wonderful Yiddish book that returns us back to the . . . sources from which [Isaac Leib] Peretz drew inspiration for his folkloric stories and from which generations of Jewish poets and prose authors received their spiritual nourishment."[81] IWO also sent review copies of the book to major Yiddish publications in Argentina and elsewhere, including *Di Idishe Tsaytung*, the other Yiddish daily published in Buenos Aires, *Tsukunft*, an important Yiddish literary journal, and *Der Forverts*, the most widely circulating Yiddish daily in New York City.[82]

Abraham Rechtman's book was published exactly midpoint between two landmarks in the rediscovery of the shtetl in the years following World War II. The first, *Life Is with People*, published in 1952, was a synthetic portrait of what its original subtitle referred to as "The Jewish Little-Town in Eastern Europe," but which, by the paperback edition of the early 1960s, had become "The Culture of the Shtetl," signifying the successful introduction of the Yiddish term into the lexicon of American English. With sales of more than one hundred thousand copies, *Life Is with People* became, in the words of Steven Zipperstein, at once "the most influential of all popular renderings of Eastern European Jewry in the English language and, arguably, the book that Jewish historians of the region loathe more than any other," as it "resolutely enveloped the Eastern European Jewish past in nostalgic amber."[83] The second landmark, *Fiddler on the Roof*, was an instant hit when it premiered on Broadway in 1964, winning nine Tony awards that year and eventually introducing Anatevka, its stylized version of the shtetl, to audiences from Tel Aviv to Tokyo. Rather than drawing directly on traditional Jewish life in Eastern Europe for inspiration, however, the relationship of *Fiddler on the Roof* to the culture of the shtetl was mediated by Sholem Aleichem's already fictionalized tales of Tevye the *milkhiker* (milkman).[84]

In ways large and small, *Jewish Ethnography and Folklore* could not have been more different than these works. First and foremost, Rechtman's book appeared in Yiddish, which dramatically circumscribed its audience. Instead of a synthetic or heavily stylized portrait of shtetl life, Rechtman's work was highly nuanced and contained many locally specific details. Nor was it fundamentally driven by nostalgia—though nostalgic elements were present, especially in its "Introduction"—but by an ethnographic sensibility. In short, rather than seeking to translate traditional Eastern European Jewish folk culture into an idiom that was easily digested by mid-twentieth-century English-language audiences, Rechtman had sought to transport native Yiddish speakers from Eastern Europe back to the world of their youth and, once there, to describe a remarkably rich range of places, cultural practices, and people. Yet, Rechtman would soon discover that in the late 1950s even this target audience was not necessarily receptive to his particular approach or, at least, to the way it was packaged.

On July 13, 1958, the literary critic Moshe Shenderay warned readers of *Di Yidishe Tsaytung* in Buenos Aires not to prejudge Rechtman's book based on its title. Used to the prose fiction, poetry, and Holocaust memoirs that dominated much of Yiddish publishing in the postwar years, Shenderay worried that many readers might dismiss *Jewish Ethnography and Folklore* as inaccessibly academic. Shenderay stressed that readers would be amply rewarded if they got beyond their initial trepidation and gave the book a chance: "You take the book in hand with a certain reservation. Probably dry 'scholasticism' flaunting its 'erudition.' However, you begin to read and it creates a torrent in your state of mind with its earthy, warm, lively folk character. And you cannot put it down. You devour the book and the book swallows you up—if I may be permitted to say—with its holy Jewish simplicity, with its unmediated *yidishkayt* which heals and warms the soul." Rather than a dry academic tome, Shenderay likened *Jewish Ethnography and Folklore* to a traditional Jewish holy book, drawing on the linguistic and conceptual distinction in Yiddish between the Germanic word *bukh*, signifying a secular book, and the Hebraic word *seyfer*, or holy book. "For the first time, a Yiddish *bukh* has given me the impression of a *seyfer*. . . . And when one closes this *bukh-sefer*, one truly feels the desire to give it a kiss as one would customarily do with a *seyfer*."[85]

In contrast to their counterparts in Buenos Aires, Yiddish publications in New York City, among them *Der Forverts*, do not appear to have published reviews of *Jewish Ethnography and Folklore*.[86] This must have stung Rechtman, not only because he had devoted so much time, energy, and money to getting it published but also because he had personally contacted numerous individuals and institutions involved in the Yiddish cultural scene to publicize the book. Perhaps Shenderay's concern that potential readers might dismiss *Jewish Ethnography and Folklore* as dry "scholasticism"—or as he called it *visnshaft*—was shared by Yiddish publications in the United States, which did not have the same direct investment in the book as their Argentine counterparts. Perhaps its wonky title and, in particular, its use of the social scientific terms "ethnography," and "expedition" made the work seem too narrow or obscure to appeal to general readers.

Tony Michels has argued that during the "era of mass [Jewish] immigration to the United States, from roughly the 1880s to the 1920s, *visnshaft* was a pervasive ideal. It was in some corners almost a cult. People spoke of it as a necessity, as an imperative, as an ideal, as a goal immigrants had to learn *visnshaft*."[87] Influenced by Enlightenment values, socialist materialism, and a progressive era belief in the power of science, Yiddish publications like *Tsukunft* (the Future) and *Dos Naye Lebn* (the New Life), attracted thousands of readers by introducing them to "articles on Darwin . . . psychology, physics, astronomy, sociology, criminology, history of the United States, history of Europe, and on and on. This was the typical issue of the magazine[s]. You'd see all these articles, articles on all these subjects. And this was a new thing. This was a new thing in Yiddish." Indeed, the creation of the Jewish Ethnographic Expedition itself was to some degree an expression of the same *visnshaftlekh* spirit, albeit in the Russian Empire rather than the United States. By the time Abraham Rechtman published *Jewish Ethnography and Folklore* roughly fifty years later, however, the cultural Zeitgeist that had made *visnshaft* so popular within certain Yiddish circles in the early twentieth century no longer existed. Instead of being attracted to forward-looking titles like *Tsukunft* that explicitly emphasized the future and to articles written in a social scientific idiom, the dwindling and aging population of Yiddish readers of nonfiction was increasingly drawn to the past and to the language of memorialization and nostalgia. In this regard, the title, if not the content, of Rechtman's book must have appeared anachronistic.

Jewish Ethnography and Folklore did not receive the kind of critical attention in precisely the publications that mattered most to Rechtman. Nevertheless, he did receive written feedback from individual readers to whom he had personally provided copies of the book. Among these letters were several from individuals who had lived in towns that the Jewish Ethnographic Expedition had visited nearly half a century before. For example, in a letter to Rechtman, the Yiddish poet and editor Aleph Katz echoed Moshe Shenderay's observation that there existed a sharp contrast between the book's potentially off-putting title and its engaging style and content: "Thank you for your gift, *Jewish Ethnography and Folklore*, which has such a dry, scientific [*trukn visnshaftlekhn*] name, but is full of wonderful stories and memories, written in such a homey, delicious style. I read the book as soon as I received it and it didn't release its hold on me until the very last page." Katz was born in 1898 in Mlinov, a town in the Pale of Settlement that the Jewish Ethnographic Expedition visited in 1913, which was also the year that Katz immigrated to the United States. *Jewish Ethnography and Folklore* brought Katz back to his own youth:

> Reading your book was like taking a virtual journey back to a Volynian shtetl like my own town Mlinov. . . . Alas, I hoped that I would also come across a description of your visit to Mlinov! I am fairly certain that you were there because I remember that people in the town had talked around that time about a group of people who had photographed the tomb of Rabbi Aharon Karliner, may his memory be for a blessing, bought Torah scroll curtains and a *mizrekh* [fixture on the eastern wall of a synagogue]. My uncle Moshe, may he rest in peace, who was a professional musician, wrote down a number of nigunim [traditional melodies] for them.[88]

While Aleph Katz was just a child when the Jewish Ethnographic Expedition visited his hometown and did not have personal contact with its members, Rechtman also received a letter from a reader who was not only an adult at the time but whom he actually mentioned in the pages of *Jewish Ethnography and Folklore*. Rabbi Chaim Bick (1887–1964) hailed from the most important non-Hasidic rabbinic family in Medzhibozh, the town in which the Baal Shem Tov was active as a public religious figure. After first serving as the town rabbi in Medzhibozh from 1909 to 1925, Bick immigrated to the United States, where he became a congregational rabbi, initially on the Lower East Side and then in Brooklyn.[89] In his letter to Rechtman, Bick pointed out what he claimed were errors in the book's description of the graves in the Jewish cemetery of Medzhibozh. Moreover, he added, "Regarding the story you print (on p. 262) in my name concerning the Besht and the chazan [cantor] Mendel, I have never heard of it. And there is also an error when it comes to the name of the storyteller, who was someone other than me."[90]

Several letters must have been particularly bittersweet for Rechtman to read. Ben Dvorkin of the Yehoash Publishing Society lauded the "tremendous amount of work and knowledge" that went into the book and asked, "Reb [Mr.] Rechtman, where have you been all these years? Instead of occupying yourself with business and other such trivialities, you could accomplish so many things."[91] The writer Chaim Grade, who lived only a ten-minute walk from Rechtman in the Bronx, nevertheless sent two letters to him regarding the book. In the first, Grade wished his "dear and good friend... *a groyser yasher koyekh* [a traditional Jewish phrase of congratulations]" for producing a work that was "extremely interesting and written not only with love but also with great understanding." Later, in 1961, Grade wrote Rechtman again, "I received [a second copy of] your book from IWO when I was in Argentina... your book is a truly valuable piece of work. Alas, you don't have any luck."[92]

In addition to praising *Jewish Ethnography and Folklore* to Rechtman, Chaim Grade may have also employed it as a source when he composed his own magnum opus, *Tsemakh Atlas*—or, as it was called in English, *The Yeshiva*—in the early 1960s.[93] For example, a synagogue in Ostroh inspired the following description by Rechtman, "On the floor of the *'polish'* [foyer] was a massive iron door fastened with a large, metal lock. Beneath the door, stone stairs led to several deep underground tunnels [*gefirt tsu etlekhe tife untererdishe heyln*]."[94] Similarly, Grade writes, "The descending rungs of the synagogue's foyer [*polish*] led his imagination deeper into secret underground tunnels [*aruntergefirt tifer in geheyme untererdishe heyln*]."[95] Strengthening the possibility that Grade drew on *Jewish Ethnography and Folklore* for inspiration is another detail. Not only did Chaim Grade read Rechtman's book but so did the person whom he thanked "for his assistance in editing" *Tsemakh Atlas*—that is, Aleph Katz.[96]

Abraham Rechtman died on the cusp of the Yiddish cultural revival that began in the 1970s and would eventually include Klezmer music festivals, Yiddish-language courses, the creation of the Yiddish Book Center, the publication of a host of new works exploring various aspects of Yiddish culture, and other activities. Within this renaissance, the protean figure of An-sky would emerge as a culture hero, par excellence, and the Jewish Ethnographic Expedition as both a crucial source of information about traditional Jewish culture in Eastern Europe and perhaps the most powerful symbol of continuity between those who sought to document this culture at the beginning of the twentieth century, like Abraham Rechtman himself and those who devoted themselves to exploring it anew at the century's end. Within this new context, *Jewish Ethnography and Folklore* received a second lease on life. A growing number of scholars cited the book and a new generation of ethnographers of contemporary Jewish communities, such as Jack Kugelmass and Jonathan Boyarin, drew inspiration from Rechtman's pioneering work in the Pale of Settlement.[97] Excerpts from the book were translated into English and published in several important works on Eastern European Jewish folk culture, including Beatrice Silverman Weinreich's collection, *Yiddish Folktales* (1988); *Tracing An-sky: Jewish Collections from the State Ethnographic Museum in St. Petersburg* (1992), edited by Mariëlla Beukers and Renée Waale; and Joachim Neugroschel's *The Dybbuk and the Yiddish Imagination: A Haunted Reader* (2000).[98]

Inspired by one of the tales in *Jewish Ethnography and Folklore*, Daniel Galay, an Argentine-born composer and musician based in Israel, created a new Yiddish opera that premiered in Tel Aviv in 2007. In an interview with the *Jerusalem Report*, Galay explained his motivation, one shared by many in the Yiddish cultural revival: "In order to decide who we are and where we're going, we have to know our Jewish heritage. This was realized even a century ago, which is why An-sky set out on his mission.... Now that we're in an era of globalization it's more important than ever to recapture the essence of Yiddish.... We can live Yiddish today."[99] Both Galay's opera and his sentiment would have undoubtedly resonated with An-sky, who wrote in the "Foreword" to the *Jewish Ethnographic Program* that he hoped to generate a contemporary cultural *oyflebn*—"revival" or "renaissance"—by providing raw material and inspiration for new artistic productions.[100] As David Roskies has observed, "Just as the Written Torah was the source of all prior Jewish creativity, so the Oral Torah [i.e., Jewish folklore], this language of symbol and memory, was to become the wellspring for Jewish creative artists of the future."[101] In this way, An-sky anticipated Barbara Kirshenblatt-Gimblett's theory of "heritage," in which older cultural traditions are given a "second life" through their exhibition or performance.[102]

Yet, until now, those who have wanted access to the full text of *Jewish Ethnography and Folklore* had to read it in the original Yiddish. Even then, the book posed considerable challenges because of its complex literary style, varied subject matter, and rich lexicon of technical terms, many of them in Hebrew, Aramaic, or Slavic languages. For the first time, we have produced an English translation of Abraham Rechtman's entire book along with notes that provide the reader with relevant historical, cultural, religious, and linguistic background information. Our goal is to make this extraordinary work accessible to a much wider audience. With this in mind, let us now turn to the text itself.

STYLE, SOURCES, AND THEMES

By turns memoir, ethnographic account, folktale collection, memorial book, and chronicle, *Jewish Ethnography and Folklore* defies easy classification into a single literary genre. In its pages, Abraham Rechtman guides the reader on a nonlinear journey through space and time, moving, for example, from the Jewish Ethnographic Expedition in 1913, to Bogdan Khmelnytsky's massacres of Jews in 1648 (known as *Takh ve-Tat* in Hebrew sources), to the Sholem Aleichem Houses in the Bronx in the 1940s, to Rechtman's childhood in Proskurov during the 1890s, to a moment in the Baal Shem Tov's life in Medzhibozh in the 1700s, and so on. Similarly, Rechtman refuses to choose between the conventions of memory or history in constructing his narrative. Instead, he draws equally on both approaches to representing and reconstructing the past, revealing them to be complementary at times, competing or even conflictual, at others. The result is a beautifully strange and powerful work that channels nearly half a millennium of Eastern European Jewish life and death into a single volume; its author, a kind of literary astronaut, chronicling from a great distance the now destroyed planet he has left behind.

Unlike *Fiddler on the Roof* with its stylized shtetl or *Life Is with People* with its synthetic one, there is no shtetl, per se, in *Jewish Ethnography and Folklore*. Instead, there are multiple shtetls, those that Rechtman lived in himself and those he visited during the expedition, each with its own distinctive character and folk traditions, even if some appear in Jewish communities across an entire region and constitute elements in a common folk heritage. Nor did the shtetl itself delimit Rechtman's interest in what might be termed *the where of things*. The pages of *Jewish Ethnography and Folklore* are filled with detailed and, in some cases, unique physical descriptions of some of the most important sites where art, architecture, music, tales, medicine, and other aspects of Jewish folk culture were created and experienced in the Pale of Settlement, including synagogues, study houses, and cemeteries. In its special focus on space, *Jewish Ethnography and Folklore* differed from Abraham Joshua Heschel's now classic 1951 work *The Sabbath*.[103] Whereas Heschel emphasized the importance of time in Judaism and, in particular, the way that the Sabbath functioned as what he called "A Palace in Time," Rechtman was drawn to the spaces in which Eastern European Jewish lives—and afterlives—were experienced. Rather than a palace, however, these spaces were far more humble, even when they were holy.

Abraham Rechtman's writing style combined influences drawn from his own complex identity: renegade rabbi, ethnographic fieldworker, and lover of Hebrew and Yiddish literature. We have already seen that the editors of the *Groyser verterbukh* lauded Rechtman for his mastery of the "Hebrew element" in Yiddish and what they termed *talmudishn yidish* or Talmudic Yiddish. What they had in mind was a register of Yiddish that included numerous terms and expressions in Hebrew and Aramaic—known as *loshn koydesh* or the "holy language"—originating in the vast corpus of biblical and rabbinic literature. The fluent, at times virtuosic, use of this register characterized the speech and writing of Eastern European Jews who had received an advanced Jewish education and distinguished them from their less educated peers. Sholem Aleichem, whom Rechtman had met when the writer visited the Jewish Museum in Saint Petersburg, in 1914, famously parodied this phenomenon in his portrait of Tevye the Milkman, a simple Jew who, in an effort to appear learned, peppered his speech with misquoted passages from the Torah, Talmud, and Midrash.

Unlike Tevye, Abraham Rechtman was rabbinically educated, and he clearly took pleasure in his own ability to write in a "fine scholarly Yiddish (*perldikn lomdishn yidish*)," to borrow a phrase that he used to praise the speech of an elderly storyteller whom the Jewish Ethnographic Expedition recorded in the old-age home in Vinitse.[104] Throughout the book, Rechtman quoted—and, on a few occasions, misquoted—phrases and aphorisms from the Torah, rabbinic literature, and the Zohar, sometimes indicating their provenance but just as frequently weaving them into the narrative without any explicit citation, itself a common feature of rabbinic writing.[105]

From an ethnographic point of view, writing in this register alone would not have been adequate to depict the speech of the different socioeconomic classes within the Jewish communities of the Pale or the many non-Jews—noblemen, peasants, priests, doctors, and so on—who appear throughout *Jewish Ethnography and Folklore*. It might also have alienated potential readers of the book who, despite their native fluency in Yiddish, nevertheless lacked knowledge of certain rabbinic terms and phrases. For these reasons, Rechtman moved between different registers of Yiddish, or frequently glossed words and expressions in Hebrew with Yiddish ones and vice versa. For example, at one point Rechtman described a young man as "very handsome," first employing the standard Yiddish phrase *zeyer a sheyner* and then immediately following it with the Hebrew phrase *yefe toar*, originally used to describe the biblical figure Joseph in Genesis 39:6.[106]

When portraying Hasidic traditions, Rechtman employed a set of terms originating in the Jewish mystical tradition—*dveykes* (mystical ecstasy or cleaving), *hislayves* (spiritual rapture or enthusiasm), *gashmies* (materiality), and so on—that added yet another register to his ethnographic portrait of the Jews of the Pale. Similarly, in reconstructing the speech of non-Jews, such as "The Ukrainian peasants [who] loved to tell wondrous tales about zaddikim and holy Jews," Rechtman drew on what his granddaughter, Hannah Storch, described as his fluency in Russian, Polish, and Ukrainian to try to create linguistically authentic depictions.[107] Finally, Rechtman employed technical vocabularies connected to a wide range of highly specialized topics—synagogue construction and architecture, the scribal craft, the organization of communal societies, and so on—in an attempt to create detailed portraits of these important but understudied aspects of Eastern European Jewish life.

The shtetl is associated with Yiddish in the popular imagination for good reason—into the twentieth century, a vast majority of the Jews who were born and raised in the shtetls of the Russian and Austro-Hungarian empires spoke Yiddish as their native language. Moreover, Yiddish literature, music, and theater treated the shtetl as both a source of inspiration and a chief object of representation. Nevertheless, the culture of the Pale of Settlement was multilingual and in *Jewish Ethnography and Folklore*, Rechtman sought to convey the various forms of multilingualism that existed among Jews as well as between them and their non-Jewish neighbors. Thus, for example, Rechtman depicts Jews singing songs in Hebrew, Yiddish, and Ukrainian and, in some cases, reproduces the songs themselves in their original languages (along with a Yiddish translation, when necessary).[108] He also contrasts female Jewish exorcists and healers, who employed incantations in Yiddish and Ukrainian, with their male counterparts, whose incantations were typically in Hebrew and Aramaic, and he reproduces the incantations themselves and their Yiddish translations.[109] And, in a vivid description of a circle of Bratslaver Hasidim the expedition visited in the town of Berdichev, Rechtman notes with some wonder that "in the heat of prayer, they would mix in many Yiddish and frequently even *goyish* [non-Jewish; in this case, Ukrainian] words."[110]

The image of Hasidim suddenly breaking into Ukrainian during the height of mystical ecstasy may be surprising—less so, perhaps, to those who have more recently witnessed Bratslaver Hasidim dancing to electronic rave music in the streets of Tel Aviv—but it is only one of many examples cited by Rechtman that demonstrate the profound degree to which the Hasidic movement was rooted in its Eastern European landscape. Nor were Hasidim the only ones influenced by contact with their neighbors. Local Christian peasants not only loved telling tales about the Besht and other Hasidic holy men, according to Rechtman; they also visited the graves of certain zaddikim "weeping ... with their requests," and "would frequently go to rabbis with requests or would bring a sick child to have a 'holy rabbi' provide a blessing. Even the rich noblemen in the area would often go to the rabbi for advice in an emergency."[111] Many Jews, in turn, relied on Muslim Tatar healers, in particular, when they were sick. As Rechtman noted: "It was not uncommon for people to call a gentile exorcist or to go to a Tatar. A sick person was often transported from miles away ... a special messenger was often sent to a Tatar, so that he could exorcise the sickness in absentia. In such a case, the proxy brought the Tatar an object belonging to the sick person, such as an adult's shirt or a child's swaddling cloth. The Tatar then chanted over the object and the sick person wore it until he recovered."[112] These instances of cross-cultural exchange are the inverse of the numerous "pogroms, evil decrees, blood libels, persecutions," described by Rechtman, that also shaped the development of Jewish folk culture in the Pale—working their way into tales, songs, tombstone inscriptions, and synagogue architecture—whose traces the Jewish Ethnographic Expedition also documented extensively.[113]

One of the most important contributions of *Jewish Ethnography and Folklore* is the light it sheds on the lives of Jewish women in the Pale of Settlement.

An-sky was a pioneer in treating women as a central subject of Jewish ethnography and the expedition recorded a number of women's practices and figures that had received little documentation elsewhere. At the same time, neither An-sky nor, following in his footsteps, Abraham Rechtman, sought to present an artificially positive portrait of the lives of these women. For example, unlike some writers who had grown up in a Hasidic milieu in Eastern Europe and then left the fold, Abraham Rechtman did not apologetically assert that the Hasidic movement had produced a revolution in the lives of Jewish women or, as Shmuel Abba Horodetsky put it, "complete equality in religious life."[114] On the contrary, Rechtman accurately, perhaps even wistfully, described traditional Jewish life in the Pale of Settlement as "patriarchal" in character and his portrait of Hasidic culture stressed the central role of male figures, beginning with the Baal Shem Tov himself. And yet, following the lead of An-sky, who had included numerous questions about their lives in the *Jewish Ethnographic Program*, Rechtman demonstrated that women were significant and, in certain ways, powerful actors within the Jewish folk culture of the Pale of Settlement.

Rechtman's exposure to the diverse roles played by Jewish women in the economy and culture of the shtetl began in childhood. According to Hannah Storch, Rechtman's own mother, Rivkah, served as a "tooth puller" in her community and "may have been a healer of some sort."[115] One of the most intimate and memorable portraits drawn by Rechtman in *Jewish Ethnography and Folklore* is of a Hasidic woman and riveting storyteller whom he knew when he was a young student in Mikulayev:

> Her name was Esterke. She was my teacher's neighbor, and was a frequent guest at our *kheyder*. I can still see Esterke's small, emaciated frame standing before my eyes. She was a precious woman of just skin and bones. Her wrinkled face was radiant and her eyes were always smiling. With walking stick in hand, she took small steps, quickly moving as if she were gliding in air. She was always in a hurry to tend to people waiting for her: be it a poor woman in childbirth, an orphaned bride, or a sick person in the almshouse, and so on. I once heard that she had declared that she was already 110 years old, and that she had reached such a ripe old age, because of the Apter Rov [a Hasidic leader], who had given her a blessing that she should live until one hundred and twenty years old.... Her deep faith in the Apter's blessing left a strong impression on us children. We did not have the slightest doubt that Esterke would not only reach her promised age, but that after reaching 120, she would live even longer.[116]

Although Rechtman did not explicitly identify her as such, Esterke was a striking example of what Jews in the shtetls of the Pale commonly called a *zaddekes* or "righteous woman." Such women were highly respected in their own communities for their good deeds, acts of charity, piety, wisdom, and self-sacrifice. Although they typically did not achieve the kind of regional fame or influence that their male counterparts did, especially within the Hasidic movement, some of these women nevertheless inspired folktales of their own and were memorialized in other ways, as Rechtman observed, "In many Ukrainian towns there are also synagogues named after pious women who are the subject of numerous wonderful tales and events."[117] A good number of these Jewish women were later revered in their communities and associated with piety because of their status as martyrs. Indeed, one of the connecting threads of *Jewish Ethnography and Folklore* is violence, including sexual violence directed toward women. This was a constant from the Khmelnytsky massacres of Takh ve-Tat (1648–1649), to those of Ivan Gonta's Haidamaks in 1768, the pogroms of the early twentieth century, including in Rechtman's own shtetl of Proskurov, and the genocidal violence of the Holocaust.

While martyred women appear throughout the book, Rechtman devoted entire chapters of *Jewish Ethnography and Folklore* to several categories of Jewish women who performed important cultural functions within shtetl society. For instance, the *klogmuter*, or female professional mourner, practiced her ancient trade in the town's Jewish cemetery. To understand the significance of the klogmuter's role, it is first necessary to appreciate two factors. The first is the profound significance of the cemetery within the spiritual and social life of the Jewish communities of the Pale. Unlike today, when Jewish cemeteries are typically located far from where most Jews live and worship, Jewish cemeteries in shtetls were usually centrally located. Far from being marginal sites, therefore, cemeteries were an integral part of the Jewish community, its rituals and folklore. Second, and closely connected to the high status of the cemetery, is the great value placed on the dead, who were not viewed as out of sight and out of mind but rather as belonging to a complex web of relations, beliefs, and practices that linked the living and the deceased, the past and the present.

The professional services of the klogmuter were especially in demand during the Jewish month of Elul, when community members traditionally came to pay respects to their dead relatives. While there, visitors would pay a klogmuter to mourn on their behalf: "The female mourners would ask the name and mother's name of the deceased and then, without any special preparations, would suddenly break out into a heart rending lament hitting themselves on the head, beating at their breasts—and improvising original *tkhines* [supplicatory prayers] and other prayers. . . . The female mourners never made use of published *tkhines* or prayer books. They thought up all of their chants on the spot, so to speak—impromptu."[118] Throughout the year, klogmuters were also hired to plead with the dead to intercede on behalf of individuals suffering from illnesses and "in the case of an orphaned bride, the [women] mourners would lead her on the wedding day to the graves of her parents. They would wish her father and mother *mazel-tov*, invite them to the wedding, cry their eyes out that the devoted father and mother would not merit to accompany their dear child to the wedding canopy, list the bridegroom's merits, and beg the parents to intercede on behalf of the couple."[119]

Another category of Jewish women documented in detail by Rechtman was the *opshprekherke*, or woman exorcist or healer. It is difficult to overstate the importance of Rechtman's book for reconstructing these understudied figures, their status within their communities, the methods they used, and their incantations. Predicated on the widespread belief that medical problems were largely the result of malevolent spirits or the workings of the *eynhore* or "evil eye," such women offered both prophylactic defenses and remedies for the already afflicted:

> In every city and town of Ukraine there were old women, whom one turned to in every time of trouble; in every case of misfortune. Almost every pregnant woman, especially those pregnant for the first time, were in their care. People even believed that they were able not only to predict the child's gender, but that they possessed methods to influence whether the child would be a boy or girl. The old women knew a variety of incantations, charms, and remedies "tested out" for any emergency. They could ward off: a "good eye"; a toothache; a sprained foot; an abscess, a "rose" [a severe skin disease known as erysipelas]; a dog bite; epilepsy and other afflictions; they performed "magic" with knifes, socks, and hair combs; they spilt wax [and] lead; they "rolled eggs" on [the body of] a frightened person; tore the hem of undershirts and performed hundreds of other cures and remedies.[120]

Rather than dismissing such practices and beliefs as *narishkayt* (foolishness) or *bobe mayses* (fairy tales), Rechtman identified them as an important part of the Oral Torah that the common Jewish folk had created and transmitted over the generations or, as he put it, "all sorts of remedies and cures [were] passed down from previous generations as a kind of *yerushe* [inheritance]."[121] Indeed, Rechtman went to great pains to demonstrate that these very beliefs and practices were among the most ancient in the Jewish tradition and were widely attested in the Talmud itself, the core text of the rabbinic Oral Torah. Nor did Jewish women healers in the Pale of Settlement operate in the shadow of their male competitors. On the contrary, Rechtman asserted, despite the existence of "old men who were no less expert in the profession.... Fewer people placed their trust in the 'old men,' however, than in the 'old women,' and turned to them less frequently."[122]

Because of the sensitive nature of their work, women healers were especially wary of the Jewish Ethnographic Expedition, and, therefore, its members had to devise intricate stratagems for documenting their activities in the field:

> The female exorcists were deadset against teaching anyone, even close relatives, their incantations, remedies, or charms because there was a belief that as soon as one taught an incantation or gave a charm to someone who did not believe in its efficacy, it would immediately lose its power. There even existed the danger that one who had recited the incantation would be hurt the next time they attempted to use it. We employed various means to extract these incantations from female exorcists. Often, one of us would pretend to be sick, lie in bed, and have someone send for a female exorcist.[123]

In other cases, Rechtman was able to record incantations from women he knew personally, such as "Hilde the bath-attendant" in his hometown of Proskurov, or after the Jewish Ethnographic Expedition was long over, Khaykele Twersky, who was his neighbor in the Sholem Aleichem Houses in the late 1940s.[124]

Khaykele Twersky was only one of several figures whom Rechtman consulted in New York City while composing his account, thereby blurring the boundary between memoir and oral history. Twersky's recollections, in particular, provided a different perspective from Rechtman's since she was both a woman and had grown up in an elite Hasidic home in Shpikov (now Shpykiv, Ukraine) in Podolia. On the one hand, Twersky was closely related by blood or marriage to three of the most important Hasidic dynasties in Eastern Europe—Chernobyl, Ruzhin, and Stolin—yet, on the other hand, she and her siblings all distinguished themselves as rebels to one degree or another. Indeed, from childhood on, Khaykele was exposed both to Hasidic traditions and to modern intellectual and cultural currents. Her son, the author Yohanan Twersky, recalled that the women and girls in Khaykele's family were exposed to literature by a traveling bookseller.[125] David Assaf, who wrote about her brother, Rabbi Yitzhak Nahum Twersky of Shpikov, noted of Khaykele, "She was famous for her erudition, and from a young age she was attracted to Haskalah [Jewish Enlightenment] literature and to a life of emotion and imagination." After marrying and divorcing Rabbi Menachem Nahum Twersky, a scion of the Trisker branch of the Chernobyl family, Khaykele lived with their two sons, Yohanan and Abraham, in Warsaw—where she interacted with members of the local Jewish literati—Shpikov, and Berlin, before immigrating to New York City in the 1920s. Menachem Nahum Twersky returned to Trisk, where he was murdered in 1942. Khaykele became a part of the transplanted Eastern European Jewish cultural and literary scene in the Sholem Aleichem

Houses in the Bronx that included Abraham Rechtman. Indeed, so close did Twersky and Rechtman become that she asked him to record her *tsava'ah* (last will and testament) in December 1950, a copy of which he preserved for posterity.[126]

In his book *Zakhor*, Yosef Hayim Yerushalmi strove to "understand the survival of a people that has spent most of its life in global dispersion," by writing "the history of its memory."[127] In *Jewish Ethnography and Folklore*, Abraham Rechtman sought to produce what might be termed an *ethnography of memory* in one corner of this same diaspora. For the Jews of the Pale, memory could serve as a talisman, as in the Hebrew invocation for the deceased, *zikhrono livrakhah* (may his memory be for a blessing); a curse, as in the phrase *yemakh shemo* (may his name be blotted out); and a commandment, as in the imperative to *zakhor* (remember) the Exodus from Egypt and other paradigmatic events in Israel's past. These and many other ritual uses of memory appear throughout Rechtman's book, as they would in any text that sought to reproduce the pervasive culture of memory that characterized the Pale. So, too, do numerous instances of Jewish communities visited by the expedition whose residents marked the passage of time and, just as importantly, gave meaning to the present, by memorializing their experiences of catastrophe, tragedy, and martyrdom in the form of special prayers, scrolls (*megillahs*), tombstone inscriptions, and so on. Thus, the power and vicissitudes of memory, as well as the specter of forgetting, are recurring themes in the book.

Even the very origins of Jewish ethnography itself could be traced to the fear that the common folk's Oral Torah, created and passed down by generations of Jews in the Pale, was in imminent danger of being forgotten, or, as Rechtman put it, "Only at the beginning of this century, when Jewish life started to undergo a dramatic transformation, casting off the old and taking up the entirely new; when people ceased to be observant and adhere to the old, received customs; when they only seldom told the old, beautiful folk tales, and the entire past started to be forgotten and little by little vanished—at that moment, some of our finest men of letters took up the work of Jewish ethnography."[128] By the time the Jewish Ethnographic Expedition set out, many traditional beliefs and practices had already become memories, a process that was itself a step toward forgetting, as Rechtman realized: "The greater part of our customs and traditions, which for our grandfathers and parents was the essential substance of their lives, had for us become merely memories of former times, which were becoming weaker and dimmer in our memory from generation to generation. They understood that if we did not act quickly to salvage what remained while there was still time; if we did not hasten to gather all of these traces—the memory of our past might, God forbid, be lost forever."[129]

Throughout the book, Rechtman acknowledged, sometimes painfully, the failings of his own memory. For instance, after transcribing two stanzas from a song associated with the Chabad Lubavitch branch of the Hasidic movement, he concluded, "There is a third stanza that I cannot remember."[130] Elsewhere, Rechtman expressed frustration at his inability to reproduce a Hasidic tale precisely as he had heard it during the expedition; frustration that was exacerbated by the fact that he had recorded it carefully at the time but no longer had access to his notes: "I recorded the story word by word exactly as it was being narrated, including the heckles from the several old men. . . . It is simply a shame that I am unable to convey his language, his idioms, his intonations and, most importantly, his detailed, wonderful depiction of this incident. . . . At any rate, this is the gist of what the old man told us."[131] In another case, Rechtman was not even able to recall the "gist" of a tale and he implored readers to fill in the blanks of his memory if they could: "Regarding the doctor's son, we recorded a wonderful story. However, I cannot recall the tale. Who among the former residents of Khmelnik remembers it?"[132]

Literally inviting his readers to add a missing tale to those already in his book was only one of the ways that Rechtman drew attention to the enduring power of storytelling in Eastern European Jewish culture. Storytelling not only connected the different stages of Rechtman's own life—his childhood in Proskurov and Mikolayev, the two seasons he spent with the Jewish Ethnographic Expedition, and the years he lived in the Bronx; it was also the thread that ran through *Jewish Ethnography and Folklore*. Stories make up the lion's share of the book's content and are also the primary way that other important aspects of Jewish folk culture, including synagogue architecture and music, are communicated to the reader. Nor were all of the stories collected by the Jewish Ethnographic Expedition about long ago events and people. Instead, up until the very end of the Pale, new tales were constantly being created by its residents, including, as Rechtman discovered, concerning the latest recording technology and its inventor, Thomas Alva Edison: "In the eyes of these simple Jews, the phonograph seemed like one of the seven wonders of the world and Edison, its inventor, a great genius. It is truly astonishing just how popular the name Edison was amongst these Jews. Wherever one went, people knew of him and told remarkable tales and legends about him."[133]

Yet, Abraham Rechtman did not merely succeed in producing a collection of Jewish folk tales, however valuable that might have been in its own right. More than any other study before or since, *Jewish Ethnography and Folklore* depicted the who, where, and how of storytelling in the shtetls of the Pale at the beginning of the twentieth century. This contextual approach to storytelling contrasted with the dominant mode of representing Hasidic tales, in particular, in this period, exemplified by Martin Buber, whose popular collections of tales provided few details regarding the lived environment in which they were still being transmitted. Rather than seeking to universalize Hasidic tales like Buber and those who followed in his footsteps, Rechtman stressed their rootedness in local contexts and histories. Among the storytellers Rechtman recorded were individuals who claimed they had either known major figures from the early years of the Hasidic movement personally or were only one generation removed from those who did. Esterke, for example, told Rechtman and his fellow cheder students in Mikolayev a story from her own childhood, when the Apter Rov, Abraham Joshua Heschel (1748–1825), gave her a blessing for long life while staying at her parents' home. In Medzhibozh, Rechtman recorded a story from "an elderly peasant [who] told us a tale about the Besht. His father, who knew the Besht personally, told him the tale when he was a small child."[134] In addition to documenting these and many other individual storytellers in situ, Rechtman also revealed how entire communities were defined, in part, by their collective knowledge of certain tales. Thus, for example, Rechtman observed, "The Jews of Piliave told many tales about their Reb Leyb," and "Nearly every Jew in town [Tshitshelnik] could tell the following exquisite tale about Reb Hershenyu," and so on.[135]

As important as storytelling was for the Jews of the Pale, theirs was also a culture of writing. Documenting the extraordinary range of writing in traditional shtetl society was among the signature achievements of the Jewish Ethnographic Expedition. In his "Introduction" to the *Jewish Ethnographic Program*, An-sky had reiterated the commonplace description of Jews as the "People of the Book." Yet, the expedition also revealed that alongside the Book, the Torah itself, there existed many other forms of writing in the Jewish communities of the Pale, each with its own significance, including the tombstone inscription, the *kvitl* or written request to a Hasidic rebbe, the megillah, the pinkes or communal record book, the so-called love brick (employed for magical purposes), and so on.

For residents of the shtetl, there was a powerful, even sacred, aura surrounding writing, especially in Hebrew and Aramaic. Indeed, the very act of writing Jewish religious texts was considered holy in its own right and the professional scribes who engaged in this activity were typically treated with great respect. For this reason, according to Rechtman, "The expedition made it a point to visit the local scribe of every city it visited. As a result, we accumulated an impressive collection of material related to the scribal craft, including samples of calligraphy."[136] These efforts enabled Rechtman to produce the single most important ethnographic account of the Jewish scribal craft in Eastern Europe, including detailed descriptions of scribal materials and tools, profiles of legendary scribes, and the "wonderful legends about them, depicting their extraordinary holiness and righteous ways and the extreme care that they took when writing every letter, as well as the special kabbalistic techniques they employed when writing God's name."[137]

Similarly, texts themselves—and not only those considered a form of Torah—were treated with great reverence by inhabitants of the shtetls. Just as Jewish women healers in the Pale jealously guarded their incantations, including from members of the Jewish Ethnographic Expedition, so, too, did the keepers of certain written texts:

> The tale, which I present here, we copied from an old manuscript, which belonged to the rabbi, Reb Daniel Slabodiansky, of Khmelnik. He initially refused to let us copy the manuscript, because he held to the tradition that if a skeptic examined it, that person could, God forbid, be harmed. Therefore, he did not want any of us to look at the manuscript, because he did not want to feel personally responsible for anything bad that might happen to us, because he had violated the commandment, "Do not place a stumbling block before the blind" (Leviticus 49:14). An-sky, however, twisted his arm until he relented and he let me copy the manuscript in its entirety at his house.[138]

Most strikingly, the pinkesim, or record books kept by Jewish communities in the Pale and by communal organizations such as the *Hevra Kadisha* (burial society) were treated as important objects of veneration despite their typically mundane content, as Rechtman noted: "The *pinkes* was always considered to be a holy object. There was even a belief that fire could not damage a house in which a *pinkes* was present and that a woman in labor would never experience any difficulty giving birth there. Until very recently, there was a custom in many Ukrainian towns, that when a woman experienced difficulty in giving birth, the town *pinkes* was brought there as a charm and placed at her bedside."[139] Reflecting this special status, such texts were also transformed into works of folk art in their own right:

> Nearly all very old *pinkesim* were made from *klaf-tsvi* (deer-skin parchment) and only a small number from thick, bluish paper. They were bound in beautiful leather binding, gilded with gold, in the same format as large *gemoras* [copies of the Talmud], often, even longer and wider.... The title page of a record book, as well as the first letters of every new paragraph, containing the rules, were decorated with extraordinarily beautiful ornamentation and illustrations. Often, each individual page of text was adorned with a hand-drawn frame, painted with exquisite artistic images, in various color schemes. And it is truly astounding how much understanding of color and how much creative ingenuity our great-grandfathers possessed—those prayer house-goers of old, the "Bench squeezers."[140]

Among its other functions, the pinkes also served as a place where the spoken word could take on written form. During the expedition, storytellers sometimes attempted to bolster the authenticity of their tales by stressing that they had once been written down in the town pinkes. However, whatever sense of authority writing may have conferred in these cases, it did not necessarily assure a tale's survival more effectively than oral transmission. Indeed, Rechtman documented several instances in which an originally oral tale was written down in a pinkes for posterity's sake only to have the pinkes itself be consumed by fire. Thus, in Brailov, Rechtman encountered a "Reb Yekusiel [who] assured me that his father had watched the tale being recorded in the local *pinkes*, which was lost in a fire a few decades back," while in Ostroh, "an old man... told us that he personally saw the following tale ... recorded in the old community *pinkes* which was destroyed in a fire years later."[141] In these instances, the very act of recording tales in pinkesim, as well as their subsequent destruction, had become oral traditions. Later, during the Jewish Ethnographic Expedition, Rechtman recorded these oral traditions only to have his written notes destroyed in the pogrom in Proskurov. This, in turn, forced him to remember what he had recorded in order to write it down yet again in *Jewish Ethnography and Folklore*. The spoken and written words were thus intertwined and inseparable, neither one completely displacing the other, linked together in a *shalshelet* or chain of transmission.

Despite this complex and interdependent relationship between orality and writing, Rechtman nevertheless argued that in its original, premodern condition, Jewish folk culture in the Pale of Settlement had not required writing in order to be transmitted from one generation to the next or, as he put it, "They did not find it necessary to record on paper all of these creations, all of their lifeways and mores, their entire Oral Torah so that it would be preserved in memory for subsequent generations."[142] Instead, Rechtman argued that oral transmission and mimetic repetition had once been sufficient to ensure that the *goldene keyt* or "golden chain" of tradition would continue unbroken, as in the case of Jewish folk music: "The melodies and wording of the prayers of our grandfathers and great grandfathers that were transmitted to us, are in the category of Oral Torah. Since no one could read musical notation, naturally no one recorded any of the complicated tunes or lyrics. Thus they were kept from being forgotten only because they were always sung."[143] The dramatic changes brought about by modernization, including the crises that buffeted the Jewish communities of the Pale of Settlement at the turn of the twentieth century, created an irreparable rupture in this fabric. It was into this breach that the members of the Jewish Ethnographic Expedition, Abraham Rechtman among them, stepped more than a century ago, hoping to stem the tide of forgetting.

NOTES

1. While there are a number of ways that Rechtman's name could be spelled, we have chosen to use the form that he preferred according to members of his family, that is, "Abraham Rechtman," rather than, for example, "Avrom Rekhtman."

2. On Solomon Yudovin (also, Iudovin), see Apter-Gabriel, "Solomon Borisovich Iudovin."

3. Rechtman, *Yidishe etnografye un folklor*, 15. Gabriella Safran has uncovered a letter from Moisei Solomonovich Libernson to An-sky dated May 3, 1914, which places the arrest of Rechtman and Yudovin in Zhitomir at the beginning of March 1914, which is before World War I started, rather than at the end of the year, as Rechtman stated in his account. On the letter, see Sergeeva, *Arkhivna spadshchina Semena An-s'kogo*, 320, letter 492. My thanks to Gabriella Safran for pointing this out to me in a personal communication, August 3, 2017. In *Yidishe etnografye un folklor*, Rechtman himself apologized in advance if he had made any errors due to his reliance on memory to reconstruct the events of the expedition, or, as he put it, "I therefore had to rely to a considerable degree on my memory. For this reason, I ask you to forgive me if I have blundered somewhere." Rechtman, *Yidishe etnografye un folklor*, 25.

4. On the expedition, see Deutsch, *Jewish Dark Continent*, 6–15; Lukin, "An-ski Ethnographic Expedition and Museum"; Safran, *Wandering Soul*, 186–205, and other sources in a variety of languages.

5. Dubnow, *Ob izuchenii istorii russkikh evreev*, 36–37; Deutsch, *Jewish Dark Continent*, 7–8. See also Nathans, *Beyond the Pale*, 378.

6. For these figures, see Lukin "An-ski Ethnographic Expedition and Museum."

7. For an annotated translation of *The Jewish Ethnographic Program*, see Deutsch, *Jewish Dark Continent*, 103–313.

8. Shmuel Shrayer (a.k.a. Sherira), unpublished diary. For published excerpts of the diary, see Sherira, "With An-sky on His Travels." Shrayer's granddaughter, Eilat Gurfinkel, generously provided access to his diary and other documents.

9. Rechtman, *Yidishe etnografye un folklor*, 15.

10. The Russian imperial police frequently harassed and arrested ethnographers working in various parts of the empire (my thanks to Gabriella Safran for reminding me of this phenomenon). See, for example, the treatment of Boris and Yuri Sokolov, brothers who engaged in ethnographic fieldwork in the Belozersky and Kirillovsky Districts of the Novgorod Region a few years before the Jewish Ethnographic Expedition.

11. Rechtman's Russian passport lists his birth date as August 13, 1888. In *Yidishe etnografye un folklor*, 22, he describes himself as "already a man of seventy," which, given that the book was published in 1958, would also place his birth in 1888. Nevertheless, other sources list Rechtman as being born in 1890. See, for example, the US Census from 1940 that lists him as "49" and a Yiddish autobiographical sketch that Rechtman himself wrote by hand on April 8, 1927, in which he states "I was born in the year 1890 in Proskurov." See YIVO RG 3, folder 2934. The population of Proskurov is from the All Russia Census of 1897.

12. Rechtman, *Yidishe etnografye un folklor*, 283–284.

13. Rechtman, "Bazilier Rebbe," 51.

14. See YIVO RG 3, folder 2934.

15. Interview with Hannah Storch, Abraham Rechtman's granddaughter, July 29, 2015.

16. Interview with Renée Gladstone, Abraham Rechtman's daughter, July 31, 2015.

17. See B. Horowitz, *Jewish Philanthropy and Enlightenment*, 198–201; Beizer, *Jews of St. Petersburg*, 111.
18. Beizer, *Jews of St. Petersburg*, 113.
19. It appears that Rechtman did not travel with either Pikangur or Shrayer and must have visited different sites during his time with the expedition. See Gur Aryeh (Pikangur), "An-sky, Ha-Ish Umafal Hayav," 115–119.
20. Rechtman, *Yidishe etnografye un folklor*, 22.
21. On Jewish casualties in the pogroms that accompanied the Russian Civil War, see Abramson, "Russian Civil War."
22. Abramson, "Russian Civil War."
23. For an English-language description and discussion of the pogrom in Proskurov, see Yosef Nedava, "Some Aspects of Individual Terrorism," in Alexander and Myers, *Terrorism in Europe*, 31–39. For Yiddish accounts, see Tcherikower, *Di ukrayner pogromen in yor 1919*.
24. "Jews Slain in Ukraine," *New York Times*, September 14, 1919. In his study of the pogroms that erupted in Ukraine in 1919, Tcherikower (*Di ukrayner pogromen in yor 1919*, 157) described the slaughter in Proskurov as "a symbol of those horrible years." Veidlinger (*In the Shadow of the Shtetl*, 34–35) includes an interview with Naum Gaiviker, a child survivor of the pogrom in Proskurov.
25. Milamed, "Proskurover Landsmanshaftn," 40–55.
26. On the significance of *Khurbn Proskurov* for the memorial book genre, see Kugelmass and Boyarin, *From a Ruined Garden*, 18–19.
27. Rechtman, "Foreword," *Khurbn Proskurov*, 10.
28. See Deutsch, *Jewish Dark Continent*, 104.
29. Interview with Renée Gladstone, July 31, 2015.
30. Rechtman, "Bazilier Rebbe," *Khurbn Proskurov*, 51.
31. Rechtman, *Yidishe etnografye un folklor*, 24–25.
32. Interview with Hannah Storch, July 29, 2015.
33. Interview with Renée Gladstone, July 31, 2015.
34. Plunz, *History of Housing*, 162.
35. Plunz, *History of Housing*, 151, 156.
36. Plunz, *History of Housing*, 152.
37. Plunz, *History of Housing*, 152.
38. Interview with Renée Gladstone, July 31, 2015.
39. Plunz, *History of Housing*, 157.
40. Plunz, *History of Housing*, 157–158.
41. See Chaban, "At Bess Myerson's Former Home"; Plunz, *History of Housing*, 152.
42. Interview with Esther Nelson Sokolsky, July 29, 2015; Chaban, "At Bess Myerson's Former Home."
43. Interview with Renée Gladstone, July 31, 2015.
44. Interview with Renée Gladstone, July 31, 2015.
45. Renée's own marriage to Herman Gladstone, a cousin of Yankev Glatshteyn, established a connection between Rechtman and the celebrated Yiddish poet.
46. Letter from Yankev Glatshteyn to Abraham Rechtman, September 24, 1945. YIVO RG 677, folder 14. Jan Schwarz, *Survivors and Exiles*, 171.
47. J. Goldberg, "David Twersky."
48. Letter from Abraham Twersky to Abraham Rechtman, January 7, 1953. YIVO RG 677, folder 25.

49. Brisman, *History and Guide to Judaic Dictionaries*, 146, 252.

50. Letter from Yisroel Shtenboym to Abraham Rechtman, May 13, 1955. YIVO RG 677, folder 16.

51. Letter from Yisroel Shtenboym to Abraham Rechtman, July 9, 1957. YIVO RG 677, folder 16.

52. See Mark and Yoffe, *Groyser verterbukh fun der yidisher shprakh*, vol. 1, 24.

53. Rechtman, "A tsol minhogim un zeyre folkstimlekhe," 249–265.

54. Interview with Hannah Storch, July 29, 2015.

55. Rechtman, "Mi-dor holekh," 329. Unfortunately, this pinkes may no longer be extant. On women's role in the production and use of *tekhinot*, see Weissler, *Voices of the Matriarchs*.

56. Rechtman, "Mi-dor holekh," 335. See Veidlinger, *In the Shadow of the Shtetl*, 319n7, for a comparative discussion of various sources regarding the number of pogroms and victims during the Russian Civil War.

57. Abraham Rechtman, autobiographical sketch, April 8, 1927. YIVO RG 3, folder 2934. This sketch served as the basis for the entry on Rechtman in Rejzen's *Leksikon fun der literatur, prese, un filologye*, 418–419. Unfortunately, I have not yet been able to locate any of the articles Rechtman published under these pseudonyms. *Doktor Zamler* means "Doctor Collector," and referred to Rechtman's participation in the Jewish Ethnographic Expedition; *Ish Yemini* means "man on my right" (it appears in Esther 2:5) and is an approximate Hebrew translation of "Rechtman."

58. Interview with Renée Gladstone, July 31, 2015.

59. Heschel, "Di mizrekh-eyropeishe tkufe in der yidisher geshikte," 163–183.

60. Congress for Jewish Culture, New York, NY, radio broadcast manuscript, December 10, 1950. YIVO RG 677, folder 4.

61. Rechtman, "Sh. An-sky and the Ethnographic Expedition"; Gur Aryeh, "An-sky, Ha-Ish Umafal Hayav," 115–119. Also, see a letter from Yitzhak Gur Aryeh to Abraham Rechtman, November 11, 1953, in which he discusses their common participation in the expedition and the role of Yohanan Twersky in connecting them. YIVO RG 677, folder 13.

62. Abraham Rechtman to L. M. Shteyn, June 22, 1954. YIVO RG 677, folder 65.

63. N. L. Horeker, "Liova Fradkin—L. M. Shteyn," 9; as cited in Stein, "Illustrating Chicago's Jewish Left," 74. See also Michels, *Fire in Their Heart*, 150.

64. Stein, "Illustrating Chicago's Jewish Left," 88.

65. As cited in Stein, "Illustrating Chicago's Jewish Left," 89.

66. Stein, "Illustrating Chicago's Jewish Left," 90.

67. L. M. Shteyn to Abraham Rechtman, June 26, 1954. YIVO RG 677, folder 65. On Shteyn's character, see Stein, "Illustrating Chicago's Jewish Left," 75.

68. See https://web.stanford.edu/class/polisci120a/immigration/Median%20Household%20Income.pdf; https://www.infoplease.com/business-finance/us-economy-and-federal-budget/average-monthly-social-security-benefits-1940-2015, source: Social Security Administration, Social Security Bulletin: Annual Statistical Supplement.

69. See Dujovne, *Una historia del libro judío*.

70. Interview with Renée Gladstone, July 31, 2015.

71. See Schwarz, *Survivors and Exiles*, appendix 1, 264 (part of a complete list of all the books published in *Dos poylishe yidntum*).

72. Schwarz, *Survivors and Exiles*, 94.

73. Schwarz, *Survivors and Exiles*, 95.

74. Schwarz, *Survivors and Exiles*, 98, 100.

75. Schwarz, *Survivors and Exiles*, 94. Abraham Lichtenbaum, who was educated in the Yiddish classics via the *Musterverk* series during his youth and later went on to direct IWO in Buenos Aires, recalled that "the books that [Shmuel] Rozhanski edited were designed for high school students. They aren't academic editions." Abraham Lichtenstein, "Reading Rozhansky's *Musterverk Yiddish Textbooks in Buenos Aires High School*," interview with the Yiddish Book Center's Wexler Oral History Project, see https://www.yiddishbookcenter.org/collections/oral-histories/excerpts/woh-ex-0002338/reading-rozhansky-s-musterverk-yiddish-textbooks-buenos-aires-high-school.

76. Schwarz, *Survivors and Exiles*, 93.
77. Publishing contract between IWO and Abraham Rechtman. YIVO RG 677, folder 28. Shmuel Rozhanski, the director of IWO at the time, had an interest in An-sky. See S. Goldberg, "Paradigmatic Times," 45.
78. On Abraham Zak, see http://yleksikon.blogspot.com/2016/08/avrom-avraham-zak.html.
79. Abraham Zak to Abraham Rechtman, November 7, 1957. YIVO RG 677, folder 24.
80. IWO in Buenos Aires to Abraham Rechtman, June 5, 1958. YIVO RG 677, folder 28.
81. "Der kultur ovent in yivo lekoved siem hasefer fun a vertful historish verk," *Di Presse*, July 12, 1958.
82. Letter from IWO to Abraham Rechtman, August 19, 1958. YIVO RG 677, folder 28.
83. Zipperstein, "Underground Man."
84. Nevertheless, many viewers praised the musical precisely for its presumed authenticity, as Howard Taubman wrote in a review of the premiere: "It touches honestly on the Jewish customs of the Jewish community in such a Russian village." Taubman, "Theater."
85. Shenderay, "A bukh vos iz a sefer."
86. It is possible that one or more publications published a review, but I was unable to uncover any in my research.
87. See https://wpt.org/University-Place/science-people-visnshaft-yiddish.
88. Aleph Katz to Abraham Rechtman, June 6, 1963. YIVO RG 677, folder 31.
89. On Chaim Bick, see "Rabbi Chaim M. Bick," *New York Times*, May 26, 1964.
90. Chaim Bick to Abraham Rechtman, October 20, 1958, YIVO RG 677, folder 9.
91. Ben Dvorkin to Abraham Rechtman, August 24, 1958, YIVO RG 677, folder 18.
92. Chaim Grade to Abraham Rechtman, February 16, 1961. YIVO RG 677, folder 15.
93. Grade, *Tsemakh Atlas*. Published in English as *The Yeshiva*, trans. Curt Leviant (New York: Macmillan, 1977). My thanks to Noah Barrera for pointing out the parallel passages in *Yidishe etnografye un folklor* and *Tsemakh Atlas*.
94. Rechtman, *Yidishe etnografye un folklor*, 68.
95. Grade, *Tsemakh Atlas*, vol. 1, 376.
96. Grade (*Tsemakh Atlas*, vol. 1, vi) writes, "The author owes a debt of gratitude to his colleague, the poet Aleph Katz, for his assistance in editing this book."
97. Kugelmass, *Between Two Worlds*, 19, 43.
98. Weinreich, *Yiddish Folktales*; Beukers and Waale, *Tracing An-sky*; Neugroschel, *Dybbuk and the Yiddish Imagination*.
99. Cashman, "Not Just for Old Times' Sake."
100. See Rabinovitch, "Positivism, Populism, and Politics," 227–256.
101. Roskies, "S. Ansky and the Paradigm of Return," 258.
102. Kirshenblatt-Gimblett, "Theorizing Heritage," 367–380.
103. Heschel, *The Sabbath*. My thanks to Noah Barrera for noting this contrast.
104. Rechtman, *Yidishe etnografye un folklor*, 344.

105. See, for example, Rechtman, *Yidishe etnografye un folklor*, 308–309, 333, 341.
106. See, for example, Rechtman, *Yidishe etnografye un folklor*, 133, 140.
107. See, for example, Rechtman, *Yidishe etnografye un folklor*, 218–219.
108. See, for example, Rechtman, *Yidishe etnografye un folklor*, 247–248.
109. See, for example, Rechtman, *Yidishe etnografye un folklor*, 293, 301.
110. Rechtman, *Yidishe etnografye un folklor*, 254.
111. Rechtman, *Yidishe etnografye un folklor*, 218.
112. Rechtman, *Yidishe etnografye un folklor*, 294.
113. Rechtman, *Yidishe etnografye un folklor*, 224.
114. Deutsch, *Maiden of Ludmir*, 29.
115. Interview with Hannah Storch, July 29, 2015.
116. Rechtman, *Yidishe etnografye un folklor*, 39.
117. Rechtman, *Yidishe etnografye un folklor*, 79.
118. Rechtman, *Yidishe etnografye un folklor*, 307.
119. Rechtman, *Yidishe etnografye un folklor*, 306–307.
120. Rechtman, *Yidishe etnografye un folklor*, 290.
121. Rechtman, *Yidishe etnografye un folklor*, 290.
122. Rechtman, *Yidishe etnografye un folklor*, 300.
123. Rechtman, *Yidishe etnografye un folklor*, 291.
124. Rechtman, *Yidishe etnografye un folklor*, 295.
125. On Khaykele Twersky's household growing up, see Twersky, *He-Hatzer ha-Pnimit*. On Haykele and her siblings, especially her brother, Yitzhak Nahum, see Assaf, "'My Tiny, Ugly World,'" 1–34; Assaf, "Viduyo shel Reb Yitzhak Nahum Tversky mi-Shpikov," 49–79. Also published in Assaf, *Untold Tales of the Hasidim*.
126. For a copy of Khaykele Twersky's last will and testament, see YIVO RG 677, folder 77.
127. Yerushalmi, *Zakhor*, 5.
128. Rechtman, *Yidishe etnografye un folklor*, 13.
129. Rechtman, *Yidishe etnografye un folklor*, 14.
130. Rechtman, *Yidishe etnografye un folklor*, 259.
131. Rechtman, *Yidishe etnografye un folklor*, 345.
132. Rechtman, *Yidishe etnografye un folklor*, 325.
133. Rechtman, *Yidishe etnografye un folklor*, 247.
134. Rechtman, *Yidishe etnografye un folklor*, 218.
135. Rechtman, *Yidishe etnografye un folklor*, 145, 267.
136. Rechtman, *Yidishe etnografye un folklor*, 340.
137. Rechtman, *Yidishe etnografye un folklor*, 334.
138. Rechtman, *Yidishe etnografye un folklor*, 309.
139. Rechtman, *Yidishe etnografye un folklor*, 195.
140. Rechtman, *Yidishe etnografye un folklor*, 195.
141. Rechtman, *Yidishe etnografye un folklor*, 136, 234.
142. Rechtman, *Yidishe etnografye un folklor*, 13.
143. Rechtman, *Yidishe etnografye un folklor*, 244–245.

ONE

SH. AN-SKY AND THE JEWISH ETHNOGRAPHIC EXPEDITION

The Participants in the Expedition

At the beginning of the present century, Jewish ethnography with all of its branches was an almost entirely new phenomenon in our literature. Until then, very little attention was paid to Jewish folk creativity, and a dearth of researchers devoted themselves to it.

And it is entirely understandable why this was so: as our grandfathers and great-grandfathers lived out their characteristically patriarchal lives and even produced, unconsciously, genuine pearls of pure folk creativity, whose worth and splendor are inestimable, they received and transmitted from mouth to mouth, from generation to generation, legends and tales, full of spiritual content, poetic beauty, and rich imagination. However, they did not find it necessary to record on paper all of these creations, all of their lifeways and mores, their entire Oral Torah [Yiddish/Hebrew, *Toyre shebalpe*], so that it would be preserved in memory for subsequent generations.[1] For the essence of their life was rock solid, the forms, clear and fixed: a generation passed, a new one arrived, yet their ways of life stayed unchanged. The synagogues and study houses remained the sole centers from which they drew their spiritual sustenance, the customs received from previous generations were protected and preserved, and the tales and legends were transmitted with great respect and love from person to person, from grandfathers to fathers, and from fathers to children.[2]

At the beginning of this century, when Jewish life started to undergo a dramatic transformation, casting off the old and taking up the entirely new; when people ceased to be observant and adhere to the received old customs; when they only seldom told the beautiful old folktales, and the entire past started to be forgotten and little by little vanish—only then did some of our finest men of letters take up the work of Jewish ethnography.[3] They comprehended that the greater part of our customs and traditions, which for our grandfathers and parents were the essential substance of their lives, had for us become merely memories of former times, which were becoming weaker and dimmer in our memory from generation to generation. They understood that if we did not act quickly to salvage what remained while there was still time, if we did not hasten to gather all of these traces, the memory of our past might, God forbid, be lost forever.

This, then, is what a few of our men of letters comprehended fifty years ago, and they devoted themselves to Jewish ethnography. They began collecting the surviving remnants of folktales, expressions, and customs, gathering all the "sparks" of the folk-soul and recording [the people's] Oral Torah and adapting it. It was then that the first Jewish Historical-Ethnographic Society was founded in Petersburg in honor of Baron Naftali Hertz Gintsburg and issues of the journal *Perezhitoe* [Experience] began to appear in print.

And one of the very first individuals to devote himself body and soul to the work of collecting the inheritance of the preceding generations was the beloved writer, poet, and collector Shloyme Zanvil Rapoport (Sh. An-sky), may his memory be a blessing.

With great love and dedication, he committed himself to this work. In 1912, with the Jewish Historical-Ethnographic Society, he organized, together with the support of Baron Vladimir Horacevich Gintsburg (a son of Naftali Hertz Gintsburg), the self-standing Jewish Ethnographic Expedition.

It did not take long for the personnel of the expedition to be assembled. Baron Vladimir Gintsburg from Kiev provided the necessary funds and the expedition set off on its journey.[4] Besides An-sky, the following people participated in the expedition: Yoel Engel from Moscow, a well-known composer, and Y. [sic] Kiselgof from Petersburg, a researcher of Jewish folk music—both for only a short time; Shloyme Yudovin, a painter and an exceptional photographer [who was], by the way, a son of An-sky's uncle; Y. Fikangur and Sh. Shrayer, students of the Jewish Academy in Petersburg, as well as my humble self.[5]

Over the course of three years, the expedition, under An-sky's direction, traveled throughout the remotest corners of Ukraine, collecting the surviving treasures of our past everywhere it went: from both men and women we recorded stories, legends, historical events, exorcisms, *sgules* [protective charms, spells, or rituals], and *trufes* [traditional remedies], including stories about *dibukkim* [malevolent spirits that possess human beings] and demons and evil beings as well as songs, parables, aphorisms, and sayings. On phonograph discs, we recorded old nigunim [traditional melodies], *tfiles* [prayers], and folk songs; we photographed old synagogues, historical places, tombstones, shtiblekh [tombs] of zaddikim, typical characters, and ritual scenes; we collected and purchased with money: Jewish antiques, documents, pinkesim [communal record books], ritual objects, ornaments, clothing, and all kinds of Jewish antiquities for a Jewish museum.

At the end of 1914, while World War I raged, the artist S. Yudovin and I were arrested in Zhitomir, under the suspicion that we were spies. This was a reasonable assumption since, on account of our work, we were carrying around a camera and taking photos out in the open. We were both put under arrest, and the police confiscated the materials we had collected, including all the photographic plates that we had in our possession.

An-sky was then in Petrograd (during the war, the name Petersburg was changed to Petrograd).[6] We informed him about our arrest via telegram. An-sky immediately got in touch with L. I. Shternberg, the manager and senior ethnographer of the Russian Peter the Great Museum of Anthropology and Ethnography, and through him An-sky successfully acquired a document [stating] that we were sent on behalf of the Imperial Anthropological-Ethnographic Museum. As soon as the Zhitomir police received this document, we were freed, and the confiscated materials and objects were returned to us. We then packed everything that we were taking along with us and returned to Petrograd.[7]

The work of the expedition was now officially put on hiatus. An-sky, however, tirelessly forged ahead alone, in spite of everything, with the task of collecting. Even later, at the height of the war, when he was traveling around Galicia as a representative of the Relief Committee for the War-Victims—organized by the Gosudarstvennaya Duma (the Russian Parliament)—dressed in a military uniform, with a sword by his side, even then, An-sky did not neglect his folkloristic and ethnographic work. Literally crawling through fire, visiting destroyed synagogues and other holy places, speaking with rabbis and communal leaders, and, when he used to return from time to time, a weary soul, to Saint Petersburg for a brief reprieve, always bringing with him chests full of treasures, priceless historic-ethnographic materials, including printed ordinances regarding Jews, secret decrees, documents concerning terrifying defamations, torn *seyfer toyres* [Torah scrolls], bloodied *yeries* [parchment sheets sewn together to make a Torah scroll], *poroykhes* [curtains for the Torah Ark] and *mentelekh* [embroidered Torah covers] drenched in Jewish blood, *mizrokhim* [wall fixtures, usually a picture of the Land of Israel, indicating East for prayer], seals, and so forth.

Once, I recall, he also brought along with him, among the other objects, a *kol-bo* [Hebrew, All is in it] prayer book written on parchment, which he found while roaming through a half-ruined and abandoned study house, in a small shtetl on the front with Galicia, as well as a torn page from a Torah scroll from another shtetl located in the same territory.[8] An-sky said that he had found the page from the Torah in a destroyed study house. The shtetl was utterly desolate and in ruins, with no trace of Jews. And when An-sky went inside the devastated study house, he encountered everything broken and ravaged, utterly ruined; on the earth, empty bottles and torn bits of women's clothing lay sprawling—silent witnesses of all that had taken place there—and from under a heap of wood, glass, and rags, he noticed pieces of parchment sticking out from a torn Torah scroll. When he pulled out one page, he became petrified. This was the page containing the Ten Commandments, torn in two. On one half was "Murder," "Adultery," "Steal," and, on the other half, the "Thou Shalt Nots."

In his private life, An-sky was a good-natured person, very rarely refusing someone a request, but, when it came to matters concerning the honor of *klal yisroel* [the Jewish people], he was an implacable zealot and knew no compromises. The following incident will illustrate this [point] best: one time in Saint Petersburg, at a gathering of journalists, an acquaintance of his, also a famous journalist, approached him, announcing, "You know, Semyon Akimovich (An-sky's Russian name), I already have the right of residence in Petersburg!" (because he had converted to Christianity) and reached out his hand to An-sky. Looking at him from head to toe with a withering stare, An-sky replied, contemptuously: "I have never in my whole life shaken hands with a traitor!"

An-sky worried little about himself. For all the years he spent in Petersburg, he was there illegally. He had no right of residence.[9] He did not have a corner to call his own, he would do his literary work in restaurants or hotels, he used to sleep at the home of an acquaintance, and, beyond his suit and coat, he owned nothing. If, however, one saw him traveling around with trunks and baggage, they were always packed with ethnographic materials.

After the expedition came to a halt in the year 1914, An-sky devoted himself mostly to the redaction of the *Jewish Ethnographic Program*, which he prepared together with a group of students of the Jewish Academy in Saint Petersburg: Sh. Vaynshteyn, A. Yuditski, Sh. Lokshin, Y. Luria, Y. Neusikhin, Y. Fikangur, Y. Kimelman, Y. Ravrebbe, A. Rechtman, and Sh. Shrayer.[10]

This was an immensely rich resource, consisting of thousands of different questions regarding all matters physical and spiritual that had a connection to the life of a Jew, from his coming into the world to his passing away, his beliefs and superstitions, his joy and sorrow, his workweek and holidays.

This material was divided into two volumes: the first, *Der Mentsh* [The person]; the second, *Shabbes un Yontif* [Sabbath and holiday]. By the end of 1914, *Der Mentsh* had appeared in print under the redaction of L. Y. Shternberg, the senior ethnographer at the Russian Anthropological-Ethnographic Museum of the Imperial Scientific Academy. The volume consisted of 238 pages in a large format and was divided into five sections, namely: (1) The Child, from Conception until the *Kheyder* [traditional elementary school], 54 pages—304 questions; (2) From *Kheyder* until Marriage, 64 pages—633 questions; (3) Marriage,

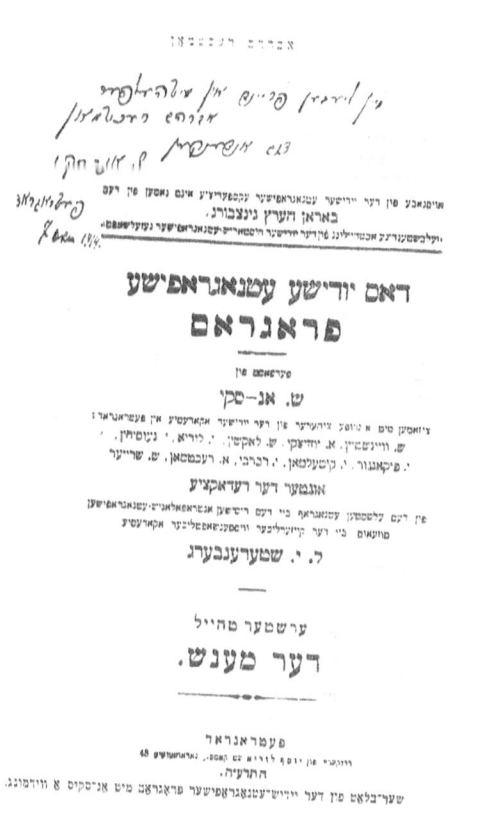

Figure 1.1. Title page of the *Jewish Ethnographic Program* with an inscription from An-sky.

26 pages—231 questions; (4) Family Life, 56 pages—518 questions; and (5) Death, 38 pages—401 questions. In total, 2087 questions.[11]

Shabbes un Yontif, which had already begun to be typeset (I myself saw several page proofs), did not have the honor of being published. So, if the material did not get lost in the course of An-sky's peregrinations, or disappear at the printer's, it is probably lying around somewhere with the other collected treasures awaiting their redeemer.[12]

In the beginning of 1916, An-sky traveled throughout the great Jewish centers of Russia, lecturing on Jewish ethnography and folklore. During the journey, he became seriously ill (diabetes), and, on the advice of doctors, he traveled in the beginning of the summer to the Caucasus.

Regarding his health and work plans, An-sky wrote to me in a Russian postcard from June 1916. This is the Yiddish translation:

> 14–27th of June 1916, Petrograd
>
> My Dearest!
>
> I cannot express the joy that your letter gave me. I send you my best regards and greetings. Write often and with more detail. Regarding Solomon (Shloyme Yudovin, the artist and photographer of the expedition—A. R.), I do not have any information. In the beginning of the year I was in Kiev, Odessa, Kishinev, and Moscow. Gave lectures in Kiev and Kishinev on ethnography. Became quite seriously ill (diabetes). Now the doctors are sending me to the Caucasus. Nevertheless, I feel cheerful and strong. I've been here in Petrograd for two weeks. I work a lot. I have immersed myself in going through the material. I'm putting [it] back in the museum. We ordered a special exhibit case, which cost a thousand rubles. I lack only the energetic Avraham!* with whom the work would be enlivened. Perhaps when you'll be in New York, seek out Zhitlovsky and let me know his address. Write, my dearest. I give you a warm embrace.
>
> Your Semyon (Shloyme—A. R.)

At the end of the summer of 1916, An-sky returned from the Caucasus to Petrograd. Now a rejuvenated man, with renewed energy, he proceeded with the adaptation of the collected ethnographic materials, preparing them for publication. He also began to prepare for the opening of the renovated Ethnographic Museum.[13]

Regarding these plans, An-sky wrote to me in Russian, dated October 1916. Here is the Yiddish translation:

> (?) October 1916, Vasilevski Ostrov, 5th line 50 (Petrograd)
>
> Beloved and Dearest Avrom!
>
> Was in the Caucasus the whole summer. Recovered from diabetes, with which I was stricken. When I returned, I encountered your letter, which pleased me very much. Alas, it annoys me that you write so little about yourself. I don't feel all that bad. It appears that I will be settling in Petrograd and will occupy myself with the adaptation of the materials in order to have them completed for publication. I've already undertaken [the task]. We are arranging the opening of the museum. We've already prepared the special exhibit case, which cost a thousand rubles. Many new items have been added. Very often I am reminded of you. There isn't another worker like you. I am writing stories based on Hasidic life. My play "The Dybbuk" was accepted by the "Studio of the [Moscow] Art Theater" ("Habima," Moscow—A. R.).[14] For God's sake,

---

*Referring to my humble self.

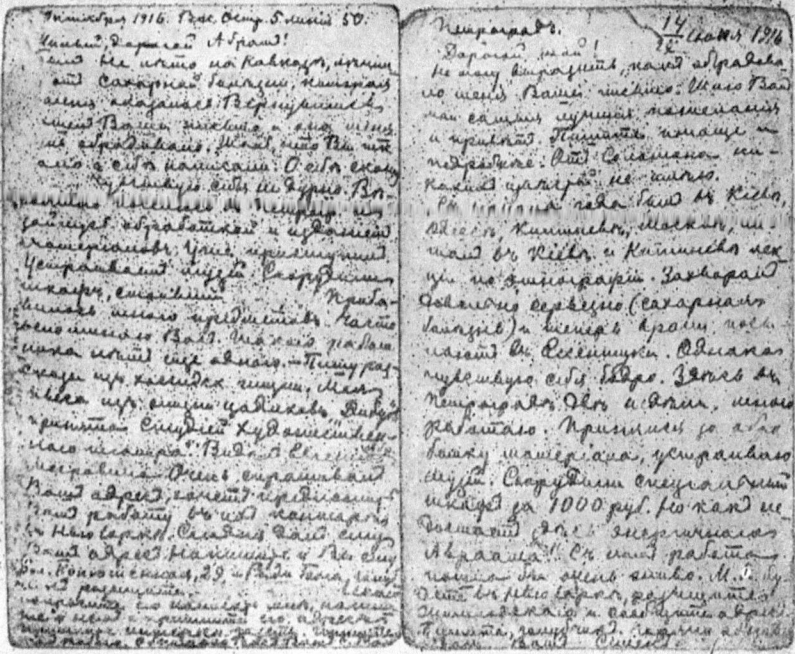

Figure 1.2. An-sky's letter.

dearest! Seek out [Chaim] Zhitlovsky for me and ask him to write me.[15] Write to me about him and also send me his address. Send interesting periodicals. I give you a hug.

S. Rapoport.

After the Bolshevik Revolution, An-sky once more returned with great zeal to his literary and scholarly work. He guarded the material collected during the expedition and all the objects from the Ethnographic Museum like the apple of his eye.

Once, when he was in Moscow, someone informed him that the Bolsheviks had sealed shut his museum. He rushed back to Petrograd, broke off all the locks bearing wax seals, and then called on the commissariat in person and explained that he understood the gravity of the act he had committed—however, he was compelled to do so out of the deep conviction that sealing off the Jewish museum was an insult to the entire Jewish people and to him personally, since he was responsible for the institution.

In September 1918, An-sky fled Russia disguised as a priest and arrived in Vilna, a sick and broken man.[16] He was very productive in Vilna, where he established a historic-ethnographic museum, the Culture League [*Di Kultur Lige*]. In 1919, when a bloody pogrom broke out in Vilna, and among the large number of casualties was his close friend, the author A. Vayter [Ayzik Meyer Devenishski], An-sky, due to his great grief, developed a serious heart condition. He traveled at the time to Warsaw, and on the counsel of the Warsaw doctors settled in Otvosk, which was surrounded by the Sosnove woods. His condition, however, did not significantly improve.

In a letter to me, dated March 6, 1920, An-sky wrote among other things:

> Survived quite a lot, two years traveling around Galicia, then the first revolution! The political activities as a member of the Petrograd Duma; of the constituent assembly in a temporary government counsel; then the second revolution in the position of a "counterrevolutionary"; September 1918, escaped from Russia; all the ethnographic materials packed and left with the Moscow Jewish community; the Ethnographic Museum abandoned. Who knows whether anything remains. Off to Vilna. Survived the local upheavals. Last year fell ill with a heart condition, thought that my time was up. Had to decline all political and social activities.

In another letter from Warsaw, dated October 11, 1920, An-sky wrote: "In regards to myself, I cannot write any happy news. Even sicker. My feet have swollen. Am almost immobile. Getting ready to go to Berlin in a few months—perhaps . . . in spite of everything!"

An-sky never traveled to Berlin. Death denied him this journey. Less than a month later, on the twenty-second of Marcheshvan [in the Jewish year] 5681 (November 9, 1920), An-sky's light was extinguished.

And almost four decades after An-sky's death and more than forty years since the peregrinations of the expedition through Ukraine, now—when nothing remains of the homey Ukrainian shtetls, when only sacred memories survive from the loving generations of Jews and their way of life, and when I myself reflect that I am a man of seventy and my sun is already setting in the West—I feel that as long as my soul is within me, I must recall the little that I still remember from what was told to me then, in the few fortunate years when I had the honor of traveling with the expedition, together with the son of R. Aaron HaCohen Rapoport, the beloved Shloyme Zanvil, known as Sh. An-sky, may his memory be a blessing.

A small apology: what I am narrating is based on the meager notes and the few photographs that miraculously remained in my possession from that time. For, when I fled to China via Siberia, in 1915, and from China to America by way of Japan, in 1916—I did not manage to take along with me the great collection of ethnographic pictures (approximately 1,500) and the few hundred journals containing notes on the expedition.

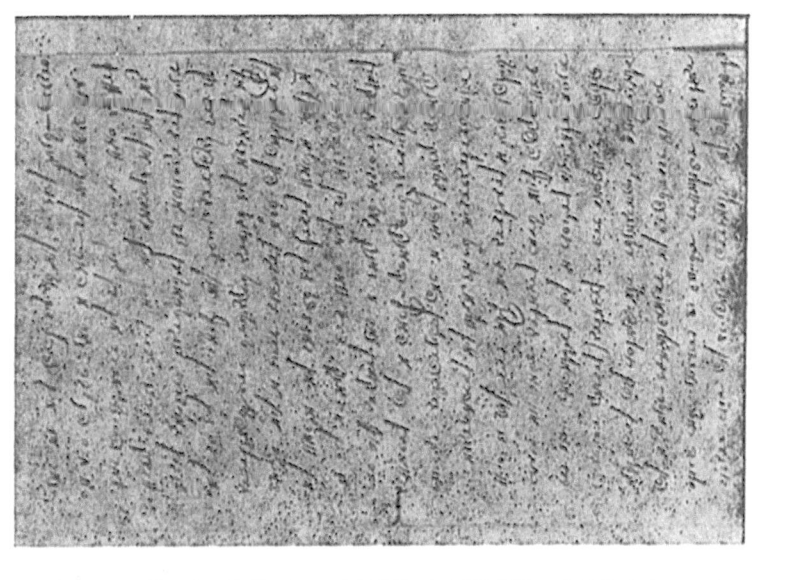

Figure 1.3. An-sky's letter.

אברהם רעכטמאן

א קלײנע התנצלות: דאָס, װאָס איך דערצײל, איז אױפֿן סמך פֿון אַ ביסל מאַגערע נאָטיצן און עטלעכע געצײלטע פֿאָטאָגראַפֿיעס, װאָס זײנען בײ מיר על־פּי־נס פֿאַרבליבן פֿון יענער צײט. װײַל אין 1915, װען כ'בין אַנטלאָפֿן דורך סיביר קײן כינע, און אין 1916 פֿון כינע דורך יאַפּאַניע קײן אַמעריקע — האָב איך נישט באַװיזן מיטצונעמען מיט זיך די גרױסע קאָלעקציע (בערך 1500) עטנאָגראַפֿישע בילדער, װי אױך די פּאָר הונדערט העפֿטן נאָטיצן װעגן דער

13-го Іюля 1914 года.

КОМИТЕТЪ
ЕВРЕЙСКАГО
ИСТОРИКО ЭТНОГРАФИЧЕСКАГО
ОБЩЕСТВА

Г-ну
А. В. Рехтману.

ПЕТЕРБУРГЪ
7 ая Рождественская д. 6 кв. 24
Телеф 513 20

Милостивый Государь
Аврумъ Вигдоровичъ.

На основаніи §§ 1 и 3 устава Общества, Комитетъ Еврейскаго Историко-Этнографическаго Общества симъ уполномочиваетъ Васъ въ теченіе сего 1914 года заняться изслѣдованіемъ еврейской исторіи и этнографіи въ разныхъ городахъ Россійской Имперіи, для чего комитетъ предоставляетъ Вамъ право собрать для научныхъ цѣлей Общества рукописи, памятники старины или снимки съ нихъ, народныя пѣсни и сказанія и другіе историческіе документы и этнографическіе предметы. Все собранное Вами надлежитъ затѣмъ переслать въ Комитетъ Общества въ С.-Петербургъ для музея-архива Общества.

За Предсѣдателя М. Кулишеръ
Секретарь Стольц

מײן פֿולמאַכט־דאָקומענט (כוח הרשאה) פֿון דער „היסטאָריש־עטנאָגראַפֿישער געזעלשאַפֿט".

Figure 1.4. My authorization document (proxy) from the "Historic-Ethnographic Society."

TO SECTION 1

Figure 1.6. Sh. An-sky (1863–1920).

Everything remained in my hometown of Proskurov and there, during Petlyura's pogroms, vanished. I therefore had to rely to a considerable degree on my memory. For this reason, I ask you to forgive me if I have blundered somewhere.

Furthermore, in my narrative, I have related things according to how I remember them from those days—as simple, naive, and exaggerated—as was the mode of those loving, warm-hearted Jews who were given to speaking, and at great length.

My notes date back, as I previously stated, from over forty years ago (some chapters were published in Hebrew and Yiddish journals). Over the years, a great number of folkloristic and ethnographic anthologies and journals, containing ethnographic materials from the same Ukrainian shtetls, have appeared in print. I have been careful not to include previously published materials and stories, except in a few cases where the versions were different. If, nevertheless, I was unable to preserve everything, this was done unintentionally—*"ve-ayn danin le-shogeg ke-mezid"* (And we do not judge one who has committed a transgression unintentionally like one who has done so intentionally).¹⁷

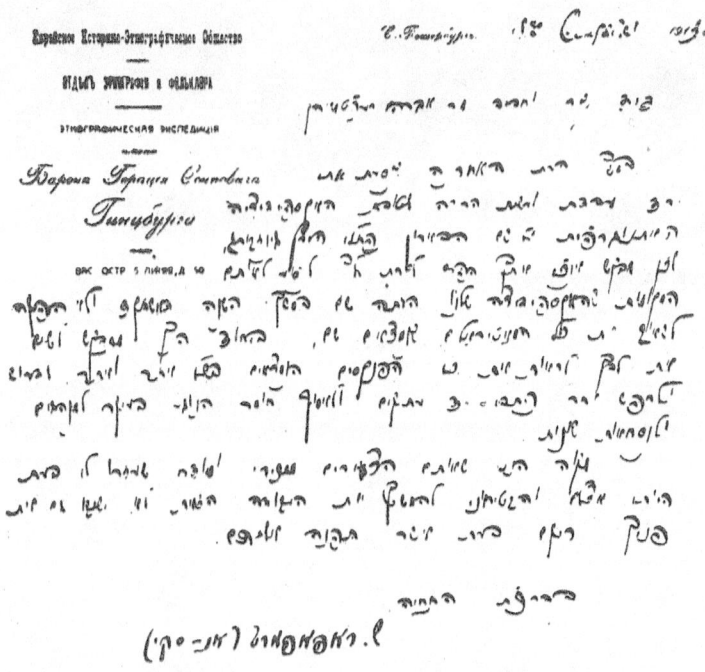

Figure 1.5. My authorization document (proxy) from the Ethnographic Expedition.

Figure 1.7. In the Ethnographic Museum. *Right to left:* A. Rechtman, Sh. An-sky, S. Vaynshteyn, Shlomo Yudovin.

Figure 1.8. Sh. An-sky in the year 1915, while he was traveling throughout Galicia as a representative of the Relief Committee for the War-Victims, organized by the Russian Parliament (Gosudarstvennaya Duma).

Figure 1.9. Baron Vladimir, son of Naftali Herts (Goratsii) Gintsburg, the son-in-law of the Brodsky family of Kiev, who subsidized the Ethnographic Expedition.

NOTES

1. In *Dos yidishe etnografishe program* (*The Jewish Ethnographic Program*), An-sky had argued that Eastern European Jewish folk traditions should be viewed as a form of Oral Torah. See Deutsch, *Jewish Dark Continent*, 103.

2. Here, Rechtman stresses the patriarchal character of shtetl society and the transmission of Jewish folk culture from one generation of men to another. Yet, several chapters of his book, in particular, and An-sky's ethnographic project, more generally, demonstrate the crucial role of women in creating and transmitting various aspects of Jewish folk culture in the Pale of Settlement.

3. Rechtman had in mind An-sky and Simon Dubnow but also figures such as Shaul Ginsburg and Peysekh Marek, who produced a major anthology of Yiddish folk songs in 1901. Earlier in the nineteenth century, Moisei Berlin had published perhaps the first ethnographic work on Jews in the Russian Empire, *Ocherk etnografii evreiskogo narodonasileniia v Rossii*. While men certainly dominated the nascent field of Jewish ethnography in Eastern Europe, Regina Lilientalowa, a native of Poland, published a number of pioneering ethnographic studies beginning in 1898 and left behind some important unpublished manuscripts on Jewish folk culture when she passed away. See Opalski, "Regina Lilientalowa." Lilientalowa's work, which is largely in Polish, remains to be translated and made accessible to a much wider audience.

4. On Vladimir Gintsburg and his family, see Safran, *Wandering Soul*, 189; Klier, "Gintsburg Family."

5. Zusman (Zinovii) Kiselgof (1878–1939) was a specialist in Jewish folk music who accompanied the Jewish Ethnographic Expedition. On the other figures who accompanied the expedition and helped compile *Dos yidishe etnografishe program*, see Deutsch, *Jewish Dark Continent*, 67.

6. As already mentioned in note 3 of the introduction to this volume, it is likely that the events described here actually took place in March 1914, that is, before World War I started. My thanks to Gabriella Safran for pointing this out to me in a personal communication, August 3, 2017.

7. See Kan, *Lev Shternberg*. Shternberg (1861–1927) grew up in the Pale of Settlement and became an ethnographer while living in forced exile on Sakhalin Island as a result of his political activities. He served as a consultant to both the Jewish Ethnographic Expedition and the *Dos yidishe etnografishe program*.

8. See An-sky, *Yudisher Khurbn* [a.k.a. *Khurbn Galitsye*], vols. 4–6. See also Neugroschel, *Enemy at His Pleasure*, 249–250; Roskies, "Master Narrative of Russian Jewry," 42. My thanks to Polly Zavadivker for pointing out the parallels between Rechtman's account and *Khurbn Galitsye*. Although Rechtman states that he "recalls" the events he is describing, they appear to have taken place when he was already in the United States. For an English translation of An-sky's Russian language diary from part of the period that he described in *Khurbn Galitsye*, see Zavadivker, *1915 Diary of S. An-sky*.

9. On the "right of residence," which Jews required in order to live in Russian cities such as Saint Petersburg and Moscow that were outside the Pale of Settlement (as well as Kiev, which lay within its borders), see Nathans, *Beyond the Pale*, 106.

10. On the team of researchers who compiled the *Jewish Ethnographic Program*, see Deutsch, *Jewish Dark Continent*, 54–71.

11. On the structure and content of the *Jewish Ethnographic Program*, see Deutsch, *Jewish Dark Continent*, 72–92.

12. Unfortunately, this manuscript remains lost.

13. On the museum, see Lukin, "Ansky and the Jewish Museum," 281–306.

14. Much has been written on An-sky's play *The Dybbuk*, one of the most widely performed dramas in the history of the Jewish theater. See, for example, Roskies, *Dybbuk and Other Writings*.

15. Chaim Zhitlovsky (1865–1943) became An-sky's closest friend when both were boys in Vitebsk. He later went on to become a socialist revolutionary and one of the most important advocates for a secular Jewish culture. He settled in New York City in 1908. On Zhitlovsky's life and work, see Michels, *Fire in Their Hearts*, 125–178.

16. On An-sky's final years, see Safran, *Wandering Soul*, 258–291.

17. Here, Rechtman employs the Halakhic distinction between one who has committed a transgression by accident—a *shogeg*—and one who has done so intentionally—a *mezid*.

TWO

SYNAGOGUES AND PRAYERHOUSES

1. HOW PEOPLE IN SYNAGOGUES AND STUDY HOUSES REACTED TO THE EXPEDITION

For approximately three years, the expedition traveled throughout the cities and shtetls of Ukraine, principally in Podolia and Volhynia. Wherever we went, the Jews from the small shtetls received us with great *derekh erets* [respect or politeness]. In their answers to our questions, it was even frequently possible to detect a sense of pride and self-importance. It seemed as though they were greatly taken by the fact that we, Jews from Petersburg, from the capital itself, from the *stolitsa* [Russian, capital city], who most certainly had a *pravozhitel'stvo* [Russian, residence permit], who had surely seen the czar himself—such important Jews were coming to them, to the Jews in small remote shtetls, going into their synagogues, taking interest in their way of life and customs and habits, searching through all their pinkesim, and even paying a good price for every trifle that carried a stamp of Jewishness.

The first places that the expedition always visited were the synagogues and study houses.[1] Each day, we would pray in a different place of worship and acquaint ourselves with the congregants. After the prayer services, the congregants would surround us and pepper us with questions. An-sky used to answer them and tell stories from the big city, engage in conversation, and conclude by inviting the older gentlemen to the inn where he was staying; then over a glass of tea or, more often than not, a shot of liquor and a bagel for a snack, An-sky would at last ask questions. The old men gladly responded and told stories, and we jotted down notes on paper.

And oh, how the Jews of the small shtetls loved An-sky! What a wonderful capacity An-sky, with his artistic and warm Jewish soul, displayed, for speaking to their hearts and souls, winning their friendship, and inspiring them to talk. Young and old filled his room all day long and into the evenings. And only thanks to his sincere love did we successfully collect the great wealth [of traditions] that were gathered [during the expedition].

In every city and shtetl in Ukraine, the synagogue was by far the most beautiful building. And, even though most settlements were located in a valley, the synagogue was still the tallest building, standing out among the rest of the town's houses. Even in the most remote, poorest shtetls, whose houses were mostly low lying, made of lime, covered with straw, and half sunken in the ground, even there the synagogue was fortified with brick and mortar; standing firmly, tall and majestic. This contrast made the synagogue even more splendid and beautiful, even more holy and sublime, and the inhabitants, the sincere-hearted Jews, took pride in [their synagogue] and boasted about it.

It is interesting to note that in many shtetls where very old synagogues were located, when we posed the question—"When was your synagogue built?"—we almost always received the same answer, that no one knew when or who built the synagogue; and, then, someone would tell a wondrous legend about its origins. According to the majority of these legends, the oldest of the synagogues were not built but discovered: children played on a hill, dug and picked at the earth with sticks, and eventually struck upon a roof. The news quickly spread throughout town, and people came, excavated the roof, and found an entire synagogue with all of its magnificent ornaments, wall and ceiling paintings intact.

Regarding other ancient synagogues, people said that they were built by dukes and noblemen of old who had indeed existed. And although the tales and their details differed, all of these heartfelt legends were infused by the same pure faith, poetic beauty, and aesthetic loftiness.

And, to give you an idea of the content of such legends, hundreds in number, that the expedition succeeded in recording about the Ukrainian synagogues, I relate some that are particularly characteristic.

2. THE RADZIVILOVER SYNAGOGUE AND THE TORAH ARK THAT WAS STRUCK BY A THUNDERBOLT

The great synagogue of Radzivilov was known throughout all of Ukraine for its extraordinary architecture and one-of-a-kind originality.[2] Although built of wood, it was a very tall structure, featuring magnificent handcrafted cornices and elaborate balconies, and it was decked with spiral stairs that led to the women's section and higher up to the little windows of the small quadrangular-carved tower that was situated at the very center of the roof. There was a round cupola [lit., kolpak, a type of cap] over the tower, which looked like a large, velvet *yarmulke* [skull cap]. On the ceiling inside were painted the twelve signs of the zodiac.[3] The walls were decorated with rare paintings based on verses from the Tanakh, among them: "The mountains skipped like rams, the hills like young sheep" [Psalms 114:4]; "Our hands spread like the eagles of the sky, and our feet as swift as the deer" [the Nishmat Kol Hai prayer]; "The horse and its rider He has thrown into the sea" [Exodus 15:1], and others.

And just like the paintings, the verses themselves were also painted in marvelous color combinations. The letters large [and] beautifully illuminated. It is obvious that the anonymous artist had great love for graphic art, as one could see from the other verses and prayers written in calligraphy with which he had decorated all four walls of the original synagogue.

In the communal *pinkes* [record book] of Radzivilov, it was recorded that, in the time of the zaddik, Rabbi Itsikl Radziviler and Rabbi Velvele Zborzsher, the sons of Rabbi Yekhiel Mikhel Ztlotshever, came to Radzivilov for a Sabbath and prayed in the great synagogue.[4] The synagogue made a powerful impression on him and he showered it with praise. After the Sabbath, as he was leaving and bidding farewell, as was his custom, he blessed the city; he gave the synagogue a blessing as well, that it should never be destroyed and that no fire should harm it.

As would later be demonstrated, his blessing would be fulfilled to the letter. This occurred in the year 5643 (1883). On the Sunday of the Torah portion, *Ve-etkhanan* [Deuteronomy 3:23–7:11], at 10:00 a.m., a hellish fire broke out. The fire began in a butcher's house where *shmaltz* was frying. The day was hot and sunny and the flames consumed almost the entire town. Most homes in Radzivilov were made of wood and some were covered in straw, and these small houses were the first to burn. They immediately went up in flames and burned to the ground. The taller fortified houses took longer till they too were consumed by the fire. For two days straight, the fire raged. The inhabitants of Radzivilov, kith and kin, along with the few possessions they could rescue, gathered in the cemetery located a good distance [away] from the city. The entire town was wiped out. The fire spared nothing, save the old wooden synagogue. It was not even touched by the fire.

All the other holy places, including the Husatiner prayerhouse, the Trisker prayerhouse, the Rebbe's study house, the Braner study house, all of the prayerhouses that were actually connected to the great synagogue, perished in the fire. But the great old wooden synagogue miraculously remained fully intact, without a scratch.

Eyewitnesses would later tell of how they saw with their own eyes that as the fire began to flare up, flocks of white doves flew in from all four sides. The doves perched themselves across the entire roof of the synagogue, flapping their wings and preventing the fire from approaching.

* * *

The elders of Radzivilov also told of a second remarkable event that occurred later with the same blessed synagogue.

This happened ten years after the great fire.*

Radzivilov had already been rebuilt by then with the help of our merciful Jewish brothers. Jews went back to business, and the profits were great. The community decided that in order to commemorate the great miracle of the synagogue's survival during the fire—and also because rescued Torah scrolls from other holy places that were not spared by the fire were being sheltered there—they should commission the construction of a new Torah Ark, which would achieve great fame and glory.

The community leaders traveled to Kremenets and returned with a famous wood-carver who was renowned throughout all of the Jewish communities in Ukraine as a master craftsman.

The master wood-carver worked for an entire year on the Torah Ark. And it turned out to be a resplendent vessel, a rare and beautiful work of art: carved lions and leopards, deer and turkeys, eagles, doves, and large and small animals as well as all kinds of flowers.

Connoisseurs would come from far away towns to admire the Torah Ark, its structure and precious wood carvings.

And when the wood-carver finished his work, he carved his name under the Torah Ark: Ozer son of Yekhiel, "the work of my hands that I may glorify" [Isaiah 60:21].

Five months later, after completing the Torah Ark, on the first day of Shvues [Shavuot], at two in the afternoon, a great rainstorm suddenly broke out with thunder and lightning. A thunderbolt struck the synagogue, splitting the cupola over the roof, entering the synagogue, and burning the Torah Ark from below, along with the name of the wood-carver and the quote, "The work of my hands that I may glorify." Nothing else was damaged. Only the cover of the Holy Ark was singed. Everyone was astonished and asked themselves: How could this be? Why should the wood-carver's right to have his name engraved be undermined, especially on a work that he had invested so much effort to make with his own hands? The Torah Ark is after all "the work of his hands that he may glorify."

---

*Due to the frequency of fires, it was typical in the shtetls to calculate the years according to the number of fires: so-and-so many years after the first fire and so-and-so many years after the second, and so forth.

Shortly after, they learned that this same wood-carver had made several similar carvings in a Catholic church. People saw in this a kind of sacrilege. And it became clear why his name and the phrase, "The work of my hands that I may glorify," were consumed by fire from the Heavens.

※ ※ ※

When the expedition visited Radzivilov, nothing still remained of the old synagogue.[5] The millionaire Reb Moshe Ginzburg, famously known as the Baron of Port Arthur, a native of Radzivilov, who became a millionaire many times over as a result of the Russian-Japanese War, generously supported his birthplace, Radzivilov, by putting up a row of buildings there to house charitable institutions—at the time, he also renovated the old synagogue and modernized it from the inside out.[6] He discarded the old metal lanterns and menorahs and, in their place, installed electric lamps. On the walls were left no traces of the former paintings. And, just like that, all the ancient luster and marvel of the old blessed synagogue of Radzivilov was gone.

Figure 2.1. Agile like the deer (wood carving).

3. THE SYNAGOGUE OF MIKOLAYEV AND THE RARE DRAWING ON THE LECTERN

The small shtetl of Mikolayev was put on the map of the Hasidic world by the great zaddik, Rebbe Dovid of Mikolayev, a longtime disciple of the Baal Shem Tov.[7] Before Reb Dovid was revealed as a zaddik, he wandered in exile for years, until, gaining this recognition, he eventually settled down in Mikolayev, where he spent the rest of his life.

During Rebbe Dovid's time, Mikolayev fell under the rule of the Polish nobleman, Count Tipinitsky. His domain included scores of villages around Mikolayev and stretched over hundreds of miles of fertile fields, ancient forests, gardens and orchards, rivers, and mills. The village peasants toiled under "pańszczyzna" [Polish, serfdom] and were considered the nobleman's personal slaves who had to do his will. For not following his orders, they were given the harshest punishments—often even death. His rule knew no limits. The Jews also paid him taxes and fell subject to his caprices and evil decrees.

The count spent most of his time living in distant lands: either in the large cities of Poland or abroad. Only a few times each year would he come for the "polowanie" (Polish, hunt). His magnificent palace was located several *verst* from Mikolayev.[8] During his visits, he made the rounds of his "parafia" [Polish, parish or territory], checked on his feudal estates and the peasants in their villages, and also paid a visit to his Jews in Mikolayev. During such trips, the Jews would make requests related to their communal needs, such as for wood to heat the *talmud-toyre* [tuition-free elementary school maintained by the community for poor children], a new roof for the bathhouse, or a fence for the cemetery—and he rarely denied them a request.

Old folks say that once, when the count, after inspecting his "parafia," was returning on the road to his palace, he passed through Mikolayev. It was the evening of Yom Kippur before Kol Nidre. The sun had already set and the night had fallen. As the count was traveling into town, he noticed how all the houses were dark, except for one brightly lit building.

That building was the old synagogue.

The count commanded that they stop beside the synagogue. He dismounted his carriage and puzzled over the small, brightly lit wooden synagogue with a straw roof, and he slowly made his way inside. His eyes began to blink from the yellow light emanating from the ten thick wax candles, which were dripping yellow drops, as if boiling hot tears were rolling out of them. He saw the men dressed in white *kitlen* and wrapped in striped prayer shawls.[9] His ears were filled with the sweet, sad voice of Reb Dovid of Mikolayev, who was standing before the lectern chanting the traditional, soulful tune of *Kol Nidre*. The nobleman was entranced by this extraordinary scene and by the beautiful singing and he remained standing as if bewitched.

As soon as the community leaders noticed what an important guest they had in their midst, they led him with great veneration to the front and sat him near the eastern wall.[10] The count was riveted by the mournful, heartfelt tunes of *Kol Nidre*, the *Yayles*, and other prayers, and remained seated until the very end.[11]

After the prayer service, the congregants surrounded the nobleman with great respect and accompanied him outside. Before settling into his carriage, he contemplated the holiday gathering, threw one last glance at the pitiable building of the synagogue, called to the rabbi, Rebbe Dovid of Mikolayev, and said the following to him: "Rabbi! Being that your 'molelnye' [Russian] (prayerhouse) is small and wooden, with a low-lying roof made of straw, all those lit candles could cause a fire. I, therefore, will take it upon myself, rabbi, to build you Jews a new 'sinagoga' [Slavic, synagogue] that is large with a roof covered in 'cherepytsya'" [Russian/Ukrainian, terra-cotta tiles].[12]

In the middle of his speech, he turned to face everyone, to the entire community, and said: "Right after the holidays, send your messengers to me into the forest, so they can chop down the tallest, sturdiest trees; my wagons will transport them here, and begin building a beautiful 'sinagoga' at my expense. I will cover all the costs!"

And immediately following the Days of Awe, several Jewish householders, lumber merchants who were experts in timber, went into the "Chepelevka" forest, chopped down large, sturdy oaks, and hewed the timber there. And before the arrival of winter, the nobleman had the wood transported to the synagogue courtyard and the work began.

At the laying of the cornerstone, Rebbe Dovid of Mikolayev penned a new prayer in honor of Count Tipinitsky. He also issued several special *takanos* [Hebrew, ordinances]. This was all recorded at the time in the communal pinkes for the sake of future generations, in eternal remembrance.

And it was not long before the *ryshtuvannye* [Ukrainian, scaffolding] was set up and the walls were underway. Jews dug several pits in which they kneaded, with their bare feet, lime mixed with straw, and they roughcasted the walls. Almost all the Jews of Mikolayev were involved in the work with great diligence and passion.

And, then, one day, while the Jews were hard at their holy work, the count appeared. He came to check up on the progress of the building. He was not happy to find that the walls were being made with lime and straw. It was not to his liking and beneath his dignity. He ordered them to stop making the walls from

The old folk of Mikolayev relate that their grandfathers told them that the Baal Shem Tov himself came to the dedication of the new building, along with scores of famous rabbis, zaddikim, and mystics and hundreds of Hasidim from both near and far. They were also told that the celebration of the dedication of the synagogue of Mikolayev lasted for seven days straight.

※ ※ ※

It is worth telling that, in 1913, when we were in the Mikolayever synagogue, we saw on the ceiling a large number of traditional paintings, such as the twelve signs of the zodiac, and, on the walls, the *Exodus from Egypt, Hannah and Her Seven Sons* [2 Maccabees 7], and so forth. It was all the work of an anonymous artist. But, more than anything, our eyes were drawn to the depiction of the *Hands of Aaron* (two hands raised in the traditional priestly blessing), in which the right hand of the *Hands of Aaron* was missing the thumb and, in the spot where the digit used to be, blood dripped.

We asked [about the drawing] and learned that it was made during the times of the *khapunes* [Yiddish, kidnappers], when small Jewish boys were kidnapped and pressed into service as "Nikolayevski" soldiers.[15] To prevent their children from falling into Fonye's hands, parents would have their children's thumbs cut off, for the law prohibited the handicapped from becoming soldiers.[16] The anonymous painter, a *kohen* [member of Jewish priestly caste], had his only son's thumb cut off from his right hand.* The boy subsequently contracted blood poisoning from the operation and died. To commemorate his child, the unfortunate father immortalized this event in the painting of the *Hands of Aaron* on the lectern over [the verse], "I have placed the Lord before me always." [Psalms 16:8]

4. THE LAWSUIT WITH THE DUKE OVER THE SYNAGOGUE OF MEZERITCH

When the duke of Mezeritch married off his only son and gave gifts to everyone with great generosity, he also granted the Jewish community their long-standing request to build a prayerhouse.[17] And, being the pious Catholic that he was, he even decided that the location of the synagogue should be across from his palace, so that he himself could see whether all the Jews of the city were being pious and going to pray.

---

* The amputated finger was preserved until the death of the individual and then was buried along with the body [as required by Jewish law so that the entire body could be resurrected intact at the End of Days]. The expedition purchased one such amputated finger from an old man in Proskurov for the Ethnographic Museum.

lime and promised to send bricks. And, indeed, a couple of days later, dozens of wagons arrived with burnt red bricks for the walls of the synagogue.

The bricks were placed in the synagogue courtyard and the entire city rejoiced in the fact that they would actually have a fortified synagogue with walls made of burnt red bricks. When Rebbe Dovid of Mikolayev noticed the bricks, he immediately called a meeting and warned the community against using the brick for the building of the synagogue. Early the next morning, he ordered his horse and wagon drawn and, along with the rabbi and several important town leaders, traveled to the count.

When they arrived at the palace, the count, from his window, caught sight of the zaddik Rebbe Dovid, as he was dismounting his wagon, and went over to him. He asked, in wonderment, why he had come and what it was he wanted. With great humility, Rebbe Dovid bowed before the count and, in a clear resounding voice, said the following:[13]

> Merciful lord! Out of your great kindness and benevolence, you deigned to gift us with bricks so we could fortify the house of prayer for our Jewish God. We are sure that your goodness towards us came from the depths of your pure heart. However, we regretfully cannot make use of your worthy gift. We cannot because we must not, and we must not precisely because the bricks which you gifted us were made by means of coerced labor, by the hands of slaves under your reign, and our faith is against slavery. Our God instructed us to always remember: "That we were slaves in the land of Egypt and I brought you out of there" [Deuteronomy 5:15]. Therefore, you will, brilliant lord, with your wisdom, understand, that we cannot use brick made by slave labor to build a prayer house for our God, in which we will pray to him everyday and praise him for freeing us from slavery. We beg you, our lord! Our friend! Take back your generous gift and allow us, Jews, your loyal and faithful servants, to knead and burn all the bricks ourselves that are necessary for building our holy temple, and the blessing of our Jewish God will rest upon your head for many long years.

With great astonishment and consideration, the count heeded Rebbe Dovid's request. He immediately summoned the person responsible for the bricks and ordered him to let the Jews of Mikolayev knead, form, and burn as many bricks as they would need. Tens of Mikolayever Jews traveled to "Chepelevka" to the brickyard and did indeed knead, form, and burn bricks for the building of their synagogue. They considered it a great privilege to take part in the building of the *mikdash me'at* [Hebrew, small temple or sanctuary] in their city of Mikolayev.[14] It took a total of two years to build, put on the finishing touches, and furnish the great synagogue of Mikolayev, which was thereafter known for its original style throughout all of Jewish Ukraine.

However, before he could embark on building the synagogue, he grew sick and soon enough died from the illness.

When his only son and heir came to take over the shtetl, after his father's death, the Jews informed him of his father's promise and asked him to keep it. The young duke refused to fulfill his father's promise. He rejected the request of the Jews on the pretext that, first, his father never told him anything about it and, second, he could not believe that his father, pious Catholic that he was, would ever make such a promise to Jews, those "Antichrists."

The Jews of Mezeritch relate that the late duke came to his son that night in a dream and ordered him to keep his promise to the Jews of Mezeritch to build them a synagogue.

But the young duke, who fancied himself a learned and modern person, scoffed at the dream and had even begun preparations to return to his home in distant parts.

The Jews of Mezeritch deliberated among themselves and summoned the young duke to appear before a rabbinical court. This made him livid: "What is the meaning of this! Such insolence! I ... should have to appear before their rabbi in a 'sprawa' [Polish, lawsuit or legal case]? His anger, however, soon abated. He was, in fact, tickled by the Jewish chutzpah and, at the appointed time, went to their courthouse, where, along with the rabbi, were seated at a table two judges, the *shiva tovei ha-ir* [Hebrew, seven good citizens of the city] and the *parneysim* [communal leaders]."[18]

Immediately upon entering, the duke, who bore a mocking smile on his lips beneath his pointed whiskers, directed an impudent question to the rabbinical court: "*Proszę bardzo* [Polish] (If you please), give me an explanation for why you are demanding that *I*, a non-Jew, should build a 'sinagoga' for *your* God. Why can't you, with your own *Jewish* means, build a prayerhouse for your *Jewish* God?"

The head of the *tovim* [lit., good ones, i.e., communal leaders] answered: "We Jews are poor. We do not own our own fields, nor our own forests, horses or wagons; nor brickeries. The *poretz* [lord, referring to the duke] is our master and we are his subjects, so to whom else should we turn if not to you, merciful lord! Especially being that your noble father promised to build us a synagogue!"

The young duke sat comfortably with the same sneer on his lips.

At this point, the aged rabbi raised his glowing eyes, fixed them on the duke, and said: "Great lord! The Ten Commandments are not only sacred to us, Jews, but to you, Catholics, as well. Do not forget that the fifth commandment is, 'Honor your father and mother.' So I ask you then: why are you violating this commandment by not carrying out the promises, which your honorable father, the noble duke, made to us?"

The rabbi's reproach and his piercing glance brought the baffled young duke to his feet. He remembered how his father, the duke, commanded him in a dream to fulfill his promise to build the Jewish synagogue. The mocking smirk disappeared from his lips. He stood glued to one spot like someone lost. Quickly, he regained his composure, raised his bent head, looked at the aged rabbi with great respect, and sat back down.

A gentle smile stretched over his tense face, and, in a peaceful tone, he addressed the rabbinical court: "I am ready to fulfill my father's promise to you. I would only ask that you specify how far my obligations must go to meet my father's promise, for I do not think it fair for you to place the entire burden on me alone. All of you, your entire community, need to take part [in the work] and lend a hand. I am relying entirely on the 'rabin' [Polish, rabbi]. Whatever he judges, I will agree to do and fulfill in its entirety."

After saying this, the duke stood up, took a deep bow, and left the courthouse.

And this was the decision of the court: that the duke should only supply the raw materials, such as lumber, brick, and lime, and all the construction implements, such as wagons, horses, shovels, wheelbarrows, trowels. All the actual work—kneading, laying brick, roughcasting the walls, putting on the roof, and painting—the Jews would do themselves.[19]

And the duke followed the rabbinical decision to the letter. He supplied everything and even sent them their very own architect. The Jews worked hard for many long months until the great synagogue of Mezeritch was completed.

Figure 2.2. Agile like the deer (wood carving by Shloyme Yudovin).

5. RABBI YEHUDAH'S BES MEDRESH [STUDY HOUSE] IN LUTSK

In Lutsk, there is a study house that bears the name of "Rebbe Yehudah the Martyr."[20] When we started asking who exactly this Rebbe Yehudah was that he should merit the title of "martyr" and why a study house was named after him, we were taken to the old cemetery where the caretaker pointed out a gravestone on which we barely deciphered this epitaph:

> This is the grave of a holy martyr who died a cruel death and suffered cruel punishments in sanctifying the Divine Name. The Torah scholar Yehudah the son of our master and rabbi Tuviah ascended on high on the Sabbath and he accepted his sentence with bitterness on the 25th of Tammuz, 1772, may his soul be bound in the bundle of life.[21]

Regarding this Rebbe Yehudah, we heard two different legends that varied in content but both versions concluded with the same motif of martyrdom.

According to the first legend, Rebbe Yehudah was a pious scholar as well as an authority on Jewish apocryphal literature. He also knew several languages. Lutsker priests would often publicly debate issues of faith with him. However, he would defeat them with his great learning and intelligence and the priests would always go away humiliated and disgraced. His constant victories irritated them so much that they looked for a ripe opportunity to take revenge on him.

A new church was built in Lutsk. Famous priests and high-ranking clergyman gathered to celebrate the dedication of the church. The Lutsker priests complained to the visiting ones about the invincible Rebbe Yehudah and asked them for advice about how to defeat him. Everyone agreed that Rebbe Yehudah should be challenged once more to a public debate. This time, however, the foreign priests, with their great wisdom, would prepare a long list of difficult questions and baffling problems. Moreover, they themselves would participate in the debate, bombarding Rebbe Yehudah with so many hard and confusing questions that it would make him so discombobulated and disoriented that he would not know how to answer them.

And that is, indeed, what they did. Rebbe Yehudah was once again invited to a public debate, and, as usual, Rebbe Yehudah agreed to come. In the middle of the marketplace a tall raised wooden platform was erected. And, on a designated Sunday afternoon, a large crowd of peasants, men and women, who learned of the rare debate from their priests, traveled en masse from the surrounding towns and villages. At the set time, the famous visiting priests, dressed in full religious garb, mounted the platform and sat in a half circle. Rebbe Yehudah arrived, too, and they placed him right in the middle—and the debate began.

The bitter battle of words went on for hours and yet again Rebbe Yehudah came out the victor.

The distinguished visiting priests were left ashamed and humiliated before the public.

In their burning rage, these wrathful lords, along with the priests of Lutsk, began to search for a way not only to take revenge on Rebbe Yehudah but to get rid of him altogether, so that they would no longer have to suffer any more humiliation at his hands.

So, they thought and thought, until, at last, they came up with something!

In Poland at the time, there was a strange law that if a dead pig were found in someone's house, and the pig did not belong to him, said person in whose house the pig was found was required to give its owner as much millet as it took to cover the pig's carcass while set on its hind legs.

If the guilty party did not have enough millet, he would be put in jail and the judge would render a sentence against him. The judge even possessed the right to sentence him to death.

So the priests decided to use this law against Rebbe Yehudah. For the evildoers knew perfectly well that Rebbe Yehudah was poor and could not satisfy the requirements of the law to provide enough millet. He would be put in jail, and, once in their hands, they would convince the judges to do away with him.

And so, a large pig was slaughtered and tossed at night into his home. When Rebbe Yehudah woke up, he found the pig's carcass lying there in his house. But, before he could do as much as look around, the police arrived and put him in jail.

They demanded the full amount of millet from him, just as the law required, which he could not provide, and the judges, who had been bribed by the priests, sentenced him to hanging.

Before being hanged, he was given the option to renounce his faith in exchange for his life. Rebbe Yehudah died a martyr and his soul left the gallows as he recited the word *ekhad*. [Hebrew, "one," the final word in the Shema prayer].[22]

And that was the first version of the legend.

* * *

The second version of the legend tells of how someone brought a blood libel against the Jews of Lutsk. A dead Christian child was left in the great synagogue, and the Jews were granted one month to give up the guilty party.

If they failed to do so, they would all be killed.

Jews prayed in all of their holy places, declared a communal fast, prostrated themselves in prayer over graves of zaddikim and martyrs, collected money, and lobbied the authorities—but to no avail; for, in their great cruelty, the judges and the priests above all would not give up their stubborn demand to hand over the "guilty."

Once the deadline was up, on a Sabbath evening, when the rabbi and his entire congregation were in the public bath, police surrounded the bath, broke inside, and declared that, if they did not immediately surrender the guilty party right then and there, they would set fire to the entire bathhouse.

Rebbe Yehudah broke from the crowd, approached the police, and announced that he was the one they were seeking; he had murdered the Christian boy. With no other choice, the police arrested him and the Jews of Lutsk were rescued from certain death.

Rebbe Yehudah was quickly sentenced to the gallows and hanged in the middle of the city.

Both versions conclude that the Jews of Lutsk gave Rebbe Yehudah a proper Jewish burial in the old cemetery, crowned him a martyr, and erected the previously mentioned gravestone. And, at the site of the gallows (or where the public dispute occurred), people later built a study house and named it after him to honor his memory.

※ ※ ※

The same cemetery caretaker who led us to the gravestone of the martyr Rebbe Yehudah, also pointed out other very old gravestones.[23] On several of them, it was still possible to make out the years 5422 (1662), 5428 (1668), and 5472 (1672). He also led us to the tomb of two brothers who were zaddikim: Reb Yitskhak-Ayzik, son of the zaddik Reb Barukh, died in the year 5486 (1726), and Reb Yehoshua Heshel, son of the zaddik Reb Barukh, died in the year 5611 (1851). Inside the tomb was the stand at which Reb Yitskhak-Ayzik learned. The cemetery caretaker told us a few stories about the two zaddikim, which we recorded at the time.

An-sky found such favor among the leaders of the Lutsk community that the burial society gave him, as a gift for our Ethnographic Museum, an old pinkes that the community had in its possession.

Figure 2.3. Wood carving by Shloyme Yudovin.

6. THE SYNAGOGUE OF OLYKA THAT RESEMBLES A CHURCH

The duke, to whom the town of Olyka belonged, was very wicked.[24] He tormented his peasants and did not let the Jews out of his sight.

The Jews came to him on many occasions for permission to build a synagogue, but he denied their request each time.

He also rejected the peasants' request to build a church.

And then one day the duke became very ill. The best doctors came but were unable to cure him—on the contrary, from day to day his condition worsened, and he became dangerously sick.

The duke sent for a priest and begged him to ask God for a cure, promising him that, if God answered his prayer and he recovered, he would build a new church.

The duke, however, did not improve.

He could feel his strength dissipating and was nearing the end, so he sent for the rabbi of Olyka and asked that he, too, pray for his health. The duke also promised the rabbi that, if his prayer worked, he would build the Jews a synagogue.

And it happened that, as soon as he made the promise to the rabbi, he felt relief. He began to improve and within a few days the sickness had completely receded.

When he got down from his sickbed, he did not forget the promises he had made to both the Christians and the Jews, and he made up his mind to follow through with them. However, he could not decide which of the two vows to fulfill first: If he started to build the church first, the Jews would protest. If, on the other hand, he built the synagogue first, the Christians would take offense. Then he found a solution: he would build both buildings at the same time.

And that is what his architect did. Two identical pits, not far from one another, were dug for the foundations, and they were laid at the same time. A brick for the church was laid as one was laid for the synagogue. And, in a short time, both buildings were completed, alongside each other, and they both looked exactly the same.

It is said that once the synagogue and church were completed, the duke made a visit to examine both buildings and could not take his eyes away from the beauty of the extraordinary and original architecture.

He left inspired. The following day, he sent for his architect and murdered him. For the duke could not bear the idea of him possibly replicating other such buildings somewhere else for another duke.

7. THE GREAT REB LIBER'S SYNAGOGUE IN BERDICHEV

The old folk of Berdichev tell a very beautiful and touching legend about the old synagogue known as "The Great Reb Liber's Synagogue." The zaddik Rebbe

Liber* was a contemporary of the Baal Shem Tov,[25] though he was actually several years older and outlived the Besht by many years. The Besht considered Reb Liber to be a great zaddik and showed him much respect, saying of him, "There are *zaddikim* who are worthy of seeing Elijah the Prophet. However, in Reb Liber's case, it is the opposite: Elijah is worthy of seeing Reb Liber." The Besht would travel a few times a year to Berdichev to meet with Reb Liber and, most of all, to bath in his *mikveh* [ritual bath].† It was believed that the water in Rebbe Liber's mikveh was a sgule [remedy] for illnesses of the eye. And people with such illnesses would travel long distances to immerse themselves in the mikveh.

According to legend, Reb Liber grew to a great height, truly head and shoulders above everyone around him. He had thick brows that hung over his eyes. If he needed to look at someone, he would lift up his eyebrows with his fingers, take a glance at the person, and let them drop down again. His beard was long and thick, reaching past his *gartel* [belt], and he never combed it for fear of losing a single hair.[26]

It is said that when the Besht was once with Reb Liber, the Besht asked him to let him comb his beard with his fingers, while at the same time guaranteeing, with his portion of the World to Come, that the beard would not be diminished by a single hair. Reb Liber, however, did not agree. And, a certain old synagogue, in the heart of Berdichev, bears his name as a result of the following true event.

Reb Liber was accustomed throughout his life to pray *mincha* [the late afternoon prayers] during the week in an open field. One time, when he was standing, as usual, under a tree in an open field, deeply absorbed in prayer, the duke happened to pass by and take notice of this Jew as he stood under the tree, swayed rhythmically, and did not even notice him. Then, the duke began to crack his whip and scream like one possessed: "*Zhidzye, zhidzye!*" [pejorative, Jew]. However, Rebbe Liber was deep in prayer and heard nothing: neither the cracking of the whip nor the duke's screaming. He stood as before and continued the late afternoon prayers. The duke grew livid: "What chutzpah!" He sent his two servants, the driver and the lackey (manservant), to call the Jew over to his coach. The servants spoke, then called, but Rebbe Liber heard nothing. This angered the duke, and he ordered them to bring him the stubborn Jew by force.

---

*Rebbe Liber the Great: his father was Avraham Ashkenazi, maggid [preacher] in Kraków; his mother was a grandchild of the zaddik Reb Yekhiel Mikhel, who was martyred, along with his mother, in Nemirov on the twentieth day of the Jewish month of Sivan, 5408 [1648] (see p. 231). In the year 5430 [1670], when the Poles exiled the Jews of Kraków, Rabbi Avraham Ashkenazi settled in the then-small town of Berdichev, where he became a preacher. After his death (5451 [1691]), Reb Liber assumed the position of preacher.

† The mikveh was still there in 1913 when the expedition was in Berdichev.

The two servants seized him, brought him over, and placed him in front of the duke. The duke spoke harsh words to him, grew more livid, cursed him out, and, when there was still no answer from Reb Liber, the duke grabbed his whip and beat him with murderous blows. Reb Liber did not even flinch or break from prayer. The duke was astonished by the strength of this strange Jew. How is it possible to suffer so much physical pain without even letting out as much as a groan? He dropped his whip. His anger began to subside, and his curiosity was piqued. He ordered the Jew to be brought back to his original position under the tree. He went back into the carriage by himself and waited patiently to see what would happen next.

Once Reb Liber had finished his prayers, he quickly walked over to the duke, bowed, and said: "My brother! What did you want to ask me earlier? I am now ready to answer your questions!"

Agape, the duke contemplated Rebbe Liber and asked him: "Tell me, why did you not come over when I called to you earlier?"

"How could I come to you, merciful lord, when I was standing before the Lord of Lords, confessing my sins? Nu, could I then interrupt it?"

"Why do you still call me brother after I caused you so much suffering?"

"I call you brother for all people are children of God. He is the Father of us all and children from the same father are brothers!"

"Are you not at all mad at me for having beaten you so badly?"

"No! You did not beat me. I had certainly sinned, which is why God punished me with blows. And you were merely his messenger. So, no, I am not mad at you, but I do pity you."

"Pity!" the duke wondered in amazement. "Pity! Why?"

"For God chose you out of all people to be his messenger to beat someone and, in so doing, cause him great suffering."

The duke was astonished by his answers. He had disturbed a godly man and for this he was greatly afraid. He begged Reb Liber to forgive him for the suffering he inflicted on him and asked how he could atone for his sin. Reb Liber answered: "If you are truly sorry for your wrongdoings and you seriously want to repent, with your entire heart, then promise me one thing, that you will never raise your hand against anyone. No one! You cannot beat anyone."

"Nu, and my peasants, I shouldn't beat them either? They are after all mine, my serfs, my property!"

"No! Even against your peasants, you may not lift a hand! For they too are God's children. They too, like you and I, are slaves of God, and not slaves of a slave!"

The duke humbly bowed his head and said: "Rabbi, I swear to you! I promise from this moment forward to control my anger! I promise never to raise my hand against anyone again! And for causing you so much pain when you were standing and praying to your Jewish God, I will build in that same spot, over there where the tree is, a large, beautiful synagogue, where you can freely pray to your Jewish God in an unimpeded manner."

The duke kept his word, and, in the spot where Rebbe Liber had prayed *mincha* [the afternoon prayer], he built a large synagogue made of stone. To this day, the synagogue is referred to as "The Great Reb Liber's Synagogue," in memory of the great miracle that happened to Reb Liber there.

The synagogue was originally built outside of the city. However, Berdichev grew, and, by 1913, when we were in Berdichev, the synagogue was already within the city limits.

8. THE SYNAGOGUE OF LUDMIR

The nobleman, Count Lubomirski deigned to build a synagogue for the Jews of Ludmir (Vladimir-Volynsk).[27] He supplied them with sufficient construction material and one of his own architects.

And, when the architect asked the nobleman how thick to make the walls, he replied: "Make the foundation so wide, that I will be able to drive over it with my carriage drawn by three horses abreast. That is also how thick the walls should be all the way to the top."

It is said that after the foundation had been laid, before starting work on the walls, the nobleman came to ride over it in his golden carriage. The Jews of Ludmir, led by their rabbi, met him at the foundation, Torah scrolls in hand. The cantor led his choir in a special *[ha]noten-teshua* [traditional prayer for the government], which the rabbi had prepared in honor of Count Lubomirski.[28] And, when the cantor and the entire community began singing Psalm 118, "Give thanks to the Lord, for He is good and His kindness endures forever!" the nobleman invited the rabbi to sit with him in his carriage, and they rode over the foundation together until the chapter of Psalms was sung to its end.

9. OSTROH, THE MAHARSHA, THE GREAT SYNAGOGUE, THE TAZ, THE BACH, AND RABBI YEVI'S STUDY HOUSE

A

The Maharsha (an acronym for Our Teacher Rabbi Reb Shmuel [Eliezer] Eydels) arrived in Ostroh after having served as the rabbi and head of the yeshiva in several other large and important Jewish communities.

He was born in Kraków in 5325 (1565) and married in Posen where he headed a yeshiva with several hundred students.[29] The yeshiva was [financially] supported by his mother-in-law, Eydel, who ran large businesses. He showed his mother-in-law great respect and, in recognition of her kindness, would often sign with her name Eydel (Shmuel Eydels). As a result, he became known across the Jewish world as Reb Shmuel Eydels (Maharsha).[30]

After the death of his rich mother-in-law, the Maharsha was forced to search for a rabbinic position to earn a living. So he became a rabbi: first in Khelm, then in Lublin, until he was appointed by the community of Ostroh—which was at the time the capital of Volhynia—as the chief rabbi of Ostroh and the surrounding region, including several scores of small towns.

As soon as he arrived in Ostroh, the Maharsha established and ran a yeshiva of about two hundred students, who subsequently developed into famous rabbis, leaders, and spiritual giants. In Ostroh, he wrote his many books and, in particular, his novel interpretations of the Gemara [section of the Talmud], which every student of the Gemara devotes himself to investigating. The commentary of the Maharsha was considered to be the third most important Talmudic commentary after Rashi and Tosfos.

Over the door of his house, the Maharsha had fixed two large quadrangular-shaped stones, on which he had engraved the following verse: "No sojourner spent the night outside, I opened my doors to the road" (Job 31: 32). It is said that, once, during a crisis, which Ostroh had survived many times before, when a band of robbers attacked the community, the two stones with the verse from Job were torn off from the front of his house and vanished into thin air. People searched for them everywhere, but to no avail.

An old woman, a relative of the Maharsha, took the disappearance of the stones very strongly to heart. She ceaselessly prayed and fasted, pleading with God for the sacred stones to be found.

It was the custom of this relative to go from house to house before the Sabbath to collect alms for the poor. One Sabbath eve, this woman was walking not far from the Maharsha's house, and she tripped on something along the way, fell, and banged up her feet. She picked herself up and paid it no more attention. The following Sabbath eve, when she passed the Maharsha's house again, she fell a second time at the very same spot and once again banged herself up. This happened three Fridays in a row. It occurred to her that something was clearly trying to give her a hint. She went to the community heads, told them what had happened to her, and requested that they dig up the spot where she had fallen three times. The heads of the community agreed and in that very spot unearthed the two lost stones. They were once again mortared into their original spot over the door of the Maharsha's house. By the time the expedition was in Ostroh, the two stones were housed in the great synagogue, which was named after the Maharsha. An-sky enthusiastically lobbied to have the stones donated to his Historic-Ethnographic Museum but without success. The rich Zusmans would not allow it.[31]

B

I relay here only two short stories out of the hundreds of stories that were told in Ostroh of the Maharsha, so as to illustrate how holy and distinguished the Jews of Ostroh considered him.[32]

The Maharsha strongly insisted on deducting tithes for charity from all of his sources of income. He would painstakingly record everything in a special pinkes and make the final accounting on the night of *nitl* (Christmas Eve), when, as was customary for Jews from time immemorial, they did not learn [Torah] or even glance inside a holy book.[33]

In the following paragraphs, the Maharsha explained to his students the reason for the custom not to learn on Christmas, or as much as open a holy book.

It is well known that *Yoyzl* (Jesus) was a Jew and studied Torah. We also know that on Christmas Eve the Heavenly Court judges him each and every year. Therefore, if Jews occupy themselves with learning Torah on this particular night, it could serve as a reminder that he, too, "that man" [euphemism for Jesus] learned and the learning could be used to defend him. For this reason, Jews should be very careful not to study on that night so as not to give the Nazirite any merit.

There was a powerful Jew, a butcher, in Ostroh, whom the Maharsha excommunicated after he was caught selling nonkosher meat to Jews. This powerful man waited for a good opportunity to pay him back. After he heard the Maharsha's take on *nitl* night, he went to the police and informed on him for defaming the name of Jesus on the Sabbath in front of his entire congregation by saying that the night of Jesus's birth was abominable. The air itself was defiled, and, on account of Jesus's impurity, the rabbi said that one was not allowed to open any Jewish book. And to prove that he was telling the truth, the informant advised them to charge inside the Maharsha's house without warning and the police would see for themselves that the Maharsha, who constantly sat there learning, would, on this night, not even have an open book in his hand.

That *nitl* night, the Maharsha, as was his custom each and every year, was leaning over his accounts, making the yearly calculation of his income, in order to determine whether he had accurately set aside the entire tithe for charity. Suddenly, he heard something fall on the floor. He looked around and noticed that a Gemara had fallen from the bookcase. He bent over, picked up the Gemara, gave it a kiss, and put it back on the shelf. A few minutes later, the same Gemara fell again. He returned it to its place. But when the Gemara fell a third time, the Maharsha picked it up with trembling hands, opened it, and it landed on the Talmudic tractate "Avoda Zara" [Idolatry]. He sat at the table and immediately became engrossed in learning.

Exactly at that moment, the door flew open and several policemen, with their leader at the head, charged inside and found the Maharsha over a Gemara engrossed in learning. They apologized and left the room embarrassed. It is said that this *takef* [powerful man], the informant, was arrested and sent far away, and Ostroh was free of him for good.

The Maharsha's yeshiva in Ostroh grew considerably in size and reputation. Students would arrive almost every day from both near and far. As a result, the building became too small to house the yeshiva. So, the leaders of the community took it on themselves to build a large new building for the yeshiva. Once it was time to lay the foundation, the affluent property owners, the rich men of Ostroh and the surrounding area, began auctioning off the mitzvah [commandment or good deed] of laying the cornerstone. The head of the community stood on a stool in the center of the crowd and called out how much was being bid. In the midst of the proceedings, a poorly dressed Jew approached the Maharsha's sexton and, without as much as a word, dropped a small sack of golden coins into his hands, five hundred in total, and asked the beadle to purchase the mitzvah on his behalf; he should raise the price a coin at a time, until he reached five hundred gold coins. And the beadle did just that. The wealthy men drove the price up and the beadle kept adding a golden coin. When it reached five hundred, the rich men yielded and the honor of laying the cornerstone went to the anonymous Jew. And, because he did not want people to know his identity, he had the beadle honor the Maharsha with the mitzvah. The Maharsha accepted the honor. He only asked that the Jew come to him. The following day, the Jew secretly came to the Maharsha, and he turned out to be far from a rich man but rather a simple craftsman, who, along with his wife, had saved up the five hundred golden coins through their own manual labor over the course of several years.

"We did not have the privilege of having our own children who could learn God's Torah," the Jew explained to the Maharsha. "So we both agreed to give our entire savings for the new building of the yeshiva, where the children of other mothers and fathers will learn Torah."

Old people related that the Maharsha then blessed him, that he too should merit having his own child, a son, and raise him in the study of Torah—and his blessing was fulfilled.

C

The great synagogue in Ostroh is named after the Maharsha: "The Maharsha's Synagogue."[34] It was built as a fort with a tall tower at the very center of the roof. The following biblical verse was spelled out with small quadrangular stones in a mosaic and mounted over the door: "How awesome is this place. It is none other than the house of God, and this is the gate of Heaven." (Genesis 28.17). According to tradition it was estimated that the synagogue was already over eight hundred years old. Ostroh survived many catastrophes. During each catastrophe, the synagogue was damaged and then afterward repaired and newly renovated.

In the Jewish year 5542 (1792), when the Russian soldiers laid siege to the city of Ostroh, because there were a large number of soldiers from the Polish army at the time, the Russians saw the synagogue from afar, which was the tallest building in the city, mistook it for a fort and shot at it with cannons for several days straight, day and night.[35] The cannonballs flew in the vicinity of the synagogue and caused great destruction. However, the synagogue itself went undamaged. Only two cannonballs ripped through the southern wall; one got stuck in the wall and a second burst through and, according to legend, remained suspended in the air, completely intact. To commemorate this miracle, the bomb was hung on chains in the middle of the vaulted ceiling of the synagogue and a year later the entire event was recorded in a special megillah, known as: "Megilas Nes Ostroh" [The Scroll of the Miracle of Ostroh].

Ever since, the seventh of Tammuz has been designated as a day of celebration and festivities: the Purim of Ostroh.[36] A day earlier, a fast with all the traditional details was observed. "VaYekhal"[37] was also read, as is done during a typical fast, and, the next day, the seventh of Tammuz, people dressed in their Sabbath clothes and went to the great synagogue to hear the recitation of the "Megilas Nes Ostroh." Afterward, people celebrated with great feasts, as on Purim, and gave alms to the poor.

The following copy that we present here,* we wrote down from a text that was hanging on the western wall of the Maharsha's synagogue, where the miracle took place.[38] It was written [in a combination of Hebrew and Yiddish] on parchment in a scribal hand and mounted, under glass, in a large, wooden frame, followed by the letter below:

> An open letter, signed.[39] What occurred on the sixth and seventh days of the month of Tammuz in the year 1792 was like one of the ten miracles that took place in the Temple [in Jerusalem].[40] Placed in order to make these things

---

*In its original orthography.

known to the public so that the blessed name of God shall be exalted and magnified.

Our brothers, the children of Israel! Pay heed to all the things that your eyes have seen. Great and famous miracles were revealed and performed by God in his great mercy and kindness for us in this city, the holy community of Ostroh. From the fifth day of the month of Tammuz several hours before nightfall until the seventh day of the month in the year [5]552 a revealed miracle took place that was truly outside of the natural course of events. Hundreds upon hundreds of cannonballs filled with gunpowder fired by large cannons specially designed to bring down walls and buildings rained down upon the city, along with small bullets. And, as was heard from the Muscovite military officers, they also hurled bombs and, yet, no synagogue in the community was damaged and only one man was killed—on account of our many sins—who was standing next to the wall of the synagogue of our late famous teacher Shmuel, may his memory be for a blessing. And his head flew to the door of the women's section of the synagogue of the famous *nagid* [lit., prince], our teacher Yuzpa, may his memory be for a blessing.[41] And men, women, and children filled the holy great synagogue in town, including the women's section, the courtyard, and all of its attic spaces. The Muscovite soldiers fixed their cannons on the synagogue because rumor had it that the building was being used as a fortress by the Polish troops. Yet the cannonballs that they shot at the walls did no damage. Cannonball upon cannonball fell from different angles but none of them exploded. And additional miracles occurred in those days but were not revealed to all. It is known that all that God did for us in those days cannot be described in writing. In particular, on the seventh day of the month of Tammuz, God saved us from the gentiles, for, according to their prevailing custom, the residents of a city would plunder and loot when war broke out in a place. Moreover, on the seventh day, the Muscovite soldiers postponed their plan to attack the city and turn it into a heap of rubble. This is known to all. In addition, twenty big and terrible bombs were set to fall on the city at day break and God in his great mercy and kindness saved us and we did not lose a man, only a single woman who was killed on the bridge. And in His holy writ, it is said [Psalm 111:4] "He has made a memorial to his wonders." This indicates wonders of the Holy One Blessed Be He that concern oneself. For when he performs miracles and wonders on behalf of Israel it is certainly for an eternal memorial because we, the children of Israel, do not forget to recall his everlasting miracles. Consequently, there is an obligation on every man of Israel to stir his heart to recognize the great and awesome miracles and wonders that God, in his great kindness and mercy, performed for us in this city. And we must make a great memorial to the tremendous miracles, wonders, kindnesses, and mercy of God through which he has redeemed us.

A revealed miracle such as this has not been heard or seen for hundreds and hundreds of years and it is known that the name of the Holy One Blessed Be He will be made great and holy in all the worlds when we, Israel, make a memorial to the miracles which He performed for us and we are thankful to Him.

Therefore, we must thank, praise, and memorialize unto the last generation of all who will come after us and our seed and the seed of our seed and all who live in this city, that these days should be commemorated every year. And this tradition has been established by the secret of the upright and by the assembly, the honorable leaders of all the communities, the heads of the *kahal* [community leadership] of Krasny Gora and Mezeritch Katan [lit., Small Mezeritch; also known as Mezherichi] and the leading rabbis and members of the *kloyz* [study house or prayerhouse][42] and the leading scholars of Torah and at their head the glorious rabbi, light of the exile, the famous teacher and rabbi, Asher Tsvi,[43] the preacher of justice and teacher of righteousness, who is here in our community, that a law should be established permanently that the two days, the sixth and seventh days of the month of Tammuz, should be an eternal memorial and "shall not depart" [Isaiah 59:21] from our mouths and from the mouths of our seed and from all who dwell in this city. We should recite in the ears of our children and the children of our children and recall forever the miracles on these days, each and every year, and also take upon ourselves the words that the children of Israel screamed and the supplications and the great cries of the men, women, and children, from the fifth of the month before nightfall until the morning of the seventh. On the sixth day of the month of Tammuz all the stores should be closed from dawn and not opened until all the five sections of the Psalms are completed in all the synagogues and no minyan [quorum of ten men] should gather, even those who rise early to pray, save for those in actual synagogues. People should fast on the sixth of the month until after they pray *mincha gedola* [lit., big mincha, the afternoon prayers that can be recited starting at 12:30 p.m.]. And no one is permitted to eat except for pregnant women or those who are nursing or a sick person—they may eat a little—or one who is younger than eighteen years old may exempt himself from the fast and give charity with a generous heart. And after the *shir shel yom* [daily Psalm read at the end of the morning prayers], they should recite the chapter "I love that the Lord should hear, etc." [Psalm 116:1] The next day on the seventh day of the month of Tammuz, a day of rejoicing and happiness should be established and people should make feasts like the feast of Purim and should dress in their Sabbath finery and not recite *takhanun* [lit., supplication, daily prayer following the *Amidah* that is not recited on Sabbath or holidays]. And it is forbidden to fast even for a yahrzeit [anniversary of a death] and people should give gifts to the poor [as on Purim]. All of this we have taken upon ourselves and upon our seed and all who are known to us in this city and no one may transgress the order on these days, each and every year, neither one who is here nor even one who establishes residency in another city. God, in his great and expansive mercy that is without limit or measure, should continue to be with us and with the people of Israel, performing miracles and wonders to save us from all evil decrees even when we transgress. May our needs be revealed before Him so that all the nations of the earth shall know that we are called by the name of the Lord and all shall declare that the Lord is God of Israel, a king who helps us in the day that we call.[44] Such are the words of those who come to sign to honor His Blessed Name. The day is Tuesday, Rosh Khodesh, Tammuz, 5553 [1793].

Beneath the megillah, there are fifty-eight signatures from the rabbis, *parneysim* [elected Jewish community council members], and leaders of the community of Ostroh at that time.

D

The Maharsha's synagogue possessed rare antiques, including gold and silver ritual objects: Torah crowns, *yadayim* [lit., hands, i.e., Torah pointers], ornaments, chandeliers, Hanukkah menorahs, and other such things. In the years of *Takh veTat*, 5408–5409 (1648–1649), Khmelnytsky's Cossacks pillaged the synagogue and stole the majority of the valuable objects there. Much of what remained melted in the great fire of 5559 (1809).

It is also worth noting that there was a *kune* in the *polish* [anteroom] of the synagogue, a kune being a small, tall cell in which the rabbinical court would sentence a sinner to be "placed in kune." Only one person could fit in the kune at a time, but only by standing with their hands hanging at the sides. In the top part of the little door of the kune, there was an opening through which one could see the face of the condemned. Usually, when the guilty party stood in the kune for an egregious sin, such as theft, informing on a fellow Jew, being caught with a married women, and the like, the rabbinical court ruled that, after the congregants were done praying and as they were leaving the synagogue, they should pass the kune and, through the opening, spit in the face of the sinner, so that the humiliation should be even greater.

On the floor of the *polish*, there was a massive iron door, secured with a large metal lock. Beneath the door, stone stairs led to several deep underground tunnels. We heard many wonderful stories about the tunnels underneath the synagogue, which lead in several directions and stretched on for miles and miles! A number of Jews even assured us that they themselves had traveled for hours through the tunnels without reaching the end.

A legend even circulated there that one of the tunnels stretched all the way to Jerusalem.

E

The Maharsha passed away in 5392 (1632) and was buried in the old cemetery. The Jews of Ostroh took pride in the grave and considered it to be holy. This is the text on his gravestone:

> Here is gathered and hidden away a holy man, the crown of a king. He was a master, the son of a master, a paragon of the generation, the "pure turban" [Zachariah 3:5], a rabbi distinguished in wisdom, humility, and fear of the Lord. And hear that he went out from the "rising of the sun until its setting" [Psalm 113:3]. He illuminated all the sages of Israel with his works. The great one who innovated with his *pilpul* [method of learning Talmud] and with his sharpness in Gemara [Talmud], Rashi's commentary, and *Tosfos* [medieval commentaries of Talmud]. The genius, his candle will illuminate the glory of the generation, our teacher and rabbi, Shmuel Eliezer son of our teacher and rabbi Yehuda ha-Levi, may the memory of the righteous be a blessing for the life of the World to Come. He was summoned to the yeshiva on high and died by means of a kiss and ascended to heaven.[45] And his "resting place shall be glorious" [Isaiah 10:11] on the evening of rest. And he was gathered on Sunday, the fifth day of the month of Kislev in the year 5392 [1631]. May his soul be bound up in the bond of life. [1 Samuel 25:29][46]

Over the years, the gravestone began to wear away. It cracked and risked collapsing altogether, so the heads of the community, in the year 5611 (1851), replaced it with a large new gravestone from granite, carved on one side with the old text (just as before) and, on the other side, with the following addition:

> A cornerstone prepared and erected anew by the burial society here in our community, the holy community, on Sunday, the sixth day of Tammuz in the year 5611 [1851]. A letter of Torah for the glory and splendor of our leader, teacher, and rabbi, the rabbi of rabbis, genius of geniuses, light of Israel. And his holiness, his holy and pure name, went from one end of the world to another. "A righteous one is the foundation of the world." [Proverbs 10:25] Our rabbi, the Maharsha, may the memory of the righteous and holy be a blessing for the life of the World to Come.

F

Not far from the Maharsha's grave, there were three graves with exquisitely beautiful gravestones. Two of them were from the year 5501 (1741) and one was from 5502 (1742). Tradition has it that the graves belonged to the Maharsha's grandchildren who were buried not far from their great-grandfather.

G

For a brief time, Rebbe Yoel Sirkis, the great genius and legal decisor, was also the rabbi and head of the yeshiva.[47] He authored "Bayit Hadash" (Bach), on the "Arba Turim"; "Hagahot HaBach," on the Talmud; as well as a large number of responsa.[48] A saying is attributed to him, which he supposedly said of his students, who, after their weddings, devoted less of their time to learning. The Bach said the following of them: "As soon as my students give a *ketubah* [marriage contract] to their wives, they give a *get* [writ of divorce] to the Torah!"

After the Bach's passing in 5401 (1640), the Ostroh rabbinate went to his son-in-law, the world-renowned genius, the greatest commentator of the Akhronim [later rabbinic authorities], Rabbi David ben Shmuel HaLevi Segal, who was famous in the scholarly world for his work "Turei Zahav" on all the laws of the "Shulhan Arukh" and "Arba'a Turim."[49]

In the year 5408 (1648), when Khmelnytsky's Cossacks slaughtered thousands of Jews in Ostroh, the TaZ succeeded in escaping with his household to Olyka, a small shtetl surrounded by strong fortifications with old-fashioned cannons. Initially, Khmelnytsky's soldiers were afraid to approach the fort of Olyka; later, however, in the year 5409 (1649), the Cossacks attempted to storm the fort. They approached Olyka and started to shoot at the city. The Jews of Olyka sought refuge in their synagogue, which was also built as a fortress, and prayed and fasted there. The TaZ, who was a sickly man, stayed in the synagogue with the Jews of Olyka. During the prayers, lamentations, and fasts, he could not stand on his feet. It is said that, faint from exhaustion, he leaned his head against the lectern and immediately fell fast asleep. In a dream, he heard someone recite with great sweetness the verse from 2 Kings 19:34, "And I will protect this city, helping her for my sake and the sake of my servant David." Then, he woke up and ordered everyone to pray with more cries and lamentations. "For," he said, "salvation is nigh." And a miracle did indeed take place. The old, rusty cannons suddenly began to fire; the band of murderers retreated, and the city of Olyka was saved.

To commemorate the miracle, the TaZ wrote special *slikhes* [traditional penitential prayers], which the Jews of Olyka said every year on the day of the miracle, the twenty-sixth day of Sivan (see p. 184).

H

Many other great geniuses, famous rabbis, and authors of Jewish legal works served at one time or another in the rabbinate of Ostroh.* Much was written

---

* The Jews did not call the city, "Os Torah" [Letter of the Torah, pronounced in the Ashkenazi manner] for nothing. Maskilim paraphrased and said, "Oys Torah" [Out of Torah, i.e., no more Torah].

and said about them and their works: I would be remiss not to mention this native son of Ostroh, the wonderful zaddik, the man of great humility, the pious and God-fearing, the star pupil of the Maggid of Mezeritch: Rabbi Yaakov Yosef [ben Yehuda], who was for many years the rabbi and preacher in Ostroh, his birthplace.[50] He wrote the famous book *Rav Yevi*, on the Psalms, in addition to other important commentaries. Incidentally, in his commentary on the Psalms, he produced fifty-three short chapters and he passed away at the age of fifty-three. Until recently, his study house, called Reb Yevi's Study House, could be found in Ostroh. His father, Rabbi Yehuda Leyb, who was the rabbi and preacher in Ostroh many years before his son, was famous for his learning, righteousness, and piety. Reb Yevi used to say that his father descended from thirteen generations of rabbis, masters of the holy spirit.

Wonderful stories are told about Reb Yevi that depict his conduct as a rabbi and his mode of spreading Hasidism. I note only two small episodes here, both of which underscore his utter devotion to fulfilling a commandment, his humility on the one hand and his self-confidence on the other.

One time, on the day before the eve of Passover, not long before sunset, Reb Yevi was walking with a large jug in his hand. He himself was going to draw and prepare *mayim-shelanu* [water that has been left overnight to cool, considered a requirement] for baking matzah the next day on the eve of Passover. The well was located outside of the city. The snow had already melted away, and the mud was knee deep. Rebbe Yaakov Yosef strode to the well through the thick mud, carefully carrying the jug on his shoulder. Halfway into the journey, the rich man of the city drove by in his carriage drawn by three horses. He was also headed to get *mayim-shelanu*. When he saw the rabbi, Reb Yevi, striding by, he came to a halt and invited him into the carriage to join him in traveling to the well. The rabbi thanked him and sincerely apologized for having to refuse this honor, and, with a bright smile on his sweaty face, he gave this excuse: "I only get to fulfill the great commandment to prepare '*mayim-shelanu*' once a year, so I want to do it with all my body and might."

One of the most affluent men in Ostroh was Reb Abele Zusman. He was a pious, God-fearing Jew, a Talmudic scholar who faithfully worked on behalf of the community and was an important philanthropist who financially supported Talmudic scholars and shouldered all the financial costs of a Yeshiva. Reb Abele prayed in Reb Yevi's study house. The seat he rented in the synagogue was at the *mizrekh* [eastern] wall near the town rabbi, Reb Yevi. It happened once that his gentile servant, who was in charge of the horse stalls, had arisen at dawn on the Sabbath, when everybody was fast asleep, proceeded to clean out the stalls, and carried the manure outside of the city. Reb Yevi was made aware of this.

On Sunday, the following day, he fetched his servant and the two of them went together to Reb Abele.

Reb Yevi approached the large table, snatched the large silver candelabrum, and said nonchalantly: "You caused your servant to desecrate the Sabbath, so I am taking these candlesticks as collateral for the fine of desecrating the Sabbath, which the court will impose upon you later today." And, with the candelabrum in hand, he took his leave.

Reb Abele followed after him, begging him not to take the candelabrum. "Rabbi," he implored, "My servant acted on his own initiative, without my knowledge. If I should have to pay a fine, I am ready to give to you as much as you so demand, just as long as you do not humiliate me."

However, Rabbi Yaakov Yosef would not relent and stubbornly replied: "On the contrary! I will carry this candelabrum in public before everyone, so that all may see and know that no one is treated with partiality when it comes to desecrating the Sabbath, not even the rich Reb Abele."

Rabbi Yaakov Yosef (Yevi) died in Ostroh, during *Khol Hamoed Sukkos* [the intermediary days of Sukkot], in the year 5551 (1791), and this is the text of his epitaph in the old cemetery:

> Here lies the rabbi and preacher, our teacher and rabbi Yaakov Yosef son of the rabbi and preacher, the great teacher and rabbi Yehuda Leyb, preacher of righteousness and teacher of justice, here in Ostroh. He passed away on Wednesday, *Khol Hamoed Sukkos*, in the year 5551. May his soul be bound up in the bond of life.

In Reb Yevi's times, there was a priest in Ostroh who was an enemy of the Jews. The path to the Jewish cemetery was located not far from his church. During Reb Yevi's funeral procession, the priest ordered all the church bells to be rung. He knew that it would infuriate the Jews. It is said that when the pallbearers approached the church, Reb Yevi suddenly sat up, and recited the biblical verse: "But you shall utterly detest it, and you shall utterly abhor it; for it is to be destroyed" (Deuteronomy 7:26). The church began to sink slowly, until it had completely sunk into the earth. Then Rabbi Yevi laid back down onto the bier and was brought to his eternal rest.

Until Rabbi Yevi, Ostroh, a city of Torah scholars, was far from Hasidism. On account of the great influence of the impressive, luminous personality of Rabbi Yevi, Hasidism also began to take root and spread in Ostroh. Rabbi Pinkhes Koretser, a friend and disciple of the Baal Shem Tov, played a large part in this, as well.[51] Rabbi Pinkhes settled in Ostroh in Reb Yevi's time, built his own kloyz, and soon enough attracted a large following of Hasidim and disciples. The influence of these two men was immense, and it was not long before Ostroh became a distinguished center of Hasidism.

I

According to Hasidic sources, it seems that the Besht planned several times to travel to Ostroh but never did so. However, in Ostroh itself a tale circulated that made it clear that the Baal Shem Tov had, in fact, been in Ostroh. And he came because of Reb Itzikl Drohobitsher.

The legend goes that in his younger years before he married, Reb Itzikl was a *misnaged*, and as a *misnaged* he was strongly opposed to Hasidism. Reb Itzikl was a distinguished scholar and a faithful servant of the Lord. The Besht heard a lot about his greatness in Torah and in character. So, he went to Ostroh in secret and managed under various guises to enter Reb Itzikl's house and listen to his teaching. It was not long before the Besht became part of the household, a real family member, and would even serve Reb Itzikl from time to time.

The Besht once served Reb Itzikl a glass of tea, silently slinking away into a corner, where he waited with great respect for him to finish his tea. He then returned, took the empty glass, and was wanting to bring it back to the kitchen. Reb Itzikl, however, stopped the Besht, smiled, and said to him: "So, I see you brought me a glass of tea because you thought, he is a Torah scholar and you want to fulfill the commandment of serving Torah scholars! But which commandment will you fulfill by carrying this empty glass back into the kitchen?" The Besht replied without missing a beat: "Part of the 'service' of the High Priest on Yom Kippur was to return the fire-pan and the incense spoon to the chamber of utensils [in the Temple in Jerusalem]."[52]

From this answer, Reb Itzikl suddenly saw a great light of divine holiness radiating from the Besht's eyes. He jumped to his feet and at that moment the Besht revealed himself to him. And Reb Itzikl devoted himself heart and soul to the Besht's ways and became one of his closest disciples and their souls joined one with the other.

The Besht once remarked that God gave Reb Itzikl an itty-bitty soul, the smallest of all souls. Yet, he [the Besht], with his great righteousness, made his itty-bitty soul bigger and elevated it to the highest levels of the supernal realms.

It is also said that Rebbe Itzikl would fast throughout the week and on the Sabbath he feasted. He used to say regarding this: "I fast the whole week, so that I may in turn enjoy eating on the Sabbath. I feast on the Sabbath, so that I may in turn fast the whole week." Legend has it that none of Reb Itzikl's children survived, even though his wife would give birth to a child every year; before the circumcision, Rebbe Itzikl would go to the *kimpeturn* [woman who has given birth], glance at the child, and the next day it would die. And this is what happened for five straight years to five newborns.

When his wife became pregnant with their sixth child, she went to the Besht and asked him to pray that the child should survive.

The Besht blessed her and instructed her not to show her husband the child until after the circumcision.

On the evening of the circumcision, Reb Itzikl came, as was his custom, to his wife and ordered her as always to show the child to him, but she refused. No matter how many times he asked her, she would not let him lay his eyes on the child. He returned the day after the circumcision. She passed the child to him at once. He took the child, peered into his little face, gave him back to her, and commented: "You should know that I rejected much more beautiful souls, which I sent back underneath the divine throne.[53] Now I promise you that this one will have a long life."

And this child grew up to be the great zaddik Rebbe Yekhiel Mikhel Zlotshev, who was one of the most steadfast pillars of Hasidism.

10. THE SYNAGOGUE OF NEMIROV, WHICH WAS BUILT ON THE RUINS OF AN OLDER, DISCOVERED SYNAGOGUE

The great synagogue of Nemirov was famous for its extraordinary architecture and original style.[54] The Jews of Nemirov had a tradition that the synagogue was built with the help of Count Potoski, a friend of the Jews, to whom Nemirov belonged.[55] They told the following remarkable tale.

There was a fire in Nemirov that burned down the church and the good-hearted count promised the Christian population that he would build a new one.

He was fond of a hill in the center of the city, so he decided to build a new church on that very spot. The entire winter was devoted to making the necessary preparations: sleds brought wood to the site, bricks were piled, hundreds of peasants hewed timber and sawed planks. After Passover, when the snow had melted, the frost subsided, and the soil softened, the count sent workers to dig the foundation.

And then, just as they started digging, the workers began to sink. They were barely dragged out alive. The following day, they started digging from a different side, and the same thing happened as had the day before. Likewise, on the third and fourth days, too, when they tried to dig from the remaining two sides. When the count was told of what had happened, he ordered them to stop working.

The count, in his wisdom, understood that the situation was not so simple, that it had not happened by chance; rather there must be a deeper reason at work. He began questioning the elders in Nemirov, both Jews and non-Jews alike; examining and rummaging through chronicles of yore; investigating and studying old maps of Nemirov, until he determined that the hill, on which he planned to build the church, was once the site of a Jewish synagogue, which was destroyed in 1648 by [Bogdan] Khmelnytsky's Cossacks.[56]

The count realized that this was a holy place and that he had committed an injustice in attempting to erect a church over a Jewish synagogue. This began to plague his conscience and left him uneasy. He became terribly afraid, lest he enrage the Jewish God and provoke him to take revenge.

It is said that on the second day of Shavuot, while the Jews of Nemirov were in the middle of reading the Book of Ruth in the large *bes medresh*, Count Potoski suddenly appeared. He approached the rabbi near the Torah ark, and, with a trembling voice, told the congregants what he had discovered about the hill and, at the same time, lifted his hands and swore that, when he had contemplated building the church, he had no idea that there had once been a Jewish synagogue there.

The count immediately turned to face the rabbi and, with tears in his eyes, begged him to pray to the Jewish God not to punish him for his unforeseeable error, and, as proof of his sincere remorse, the count added that he would help the Jews build on that very same hill where the old synagogue had once stood, a new, fortified synagogue, and he would give all of the construction materials around the hill to the Jews as a gift to be used in the building.

The rabbi calmed the count, looked at him with his clear eyes, and assured him that according to Jewish law he had committed no wrong and added that he and the entire community will pray to God for his health and well-being.

Reassured, the count left the study house.

And indeed, right after Shavuot, the Jews of Nemirov took up the holy work. The old gray-haired rabbi dug up the first shovel of earth and made the "Shehecheyanu" blessing![57] Right afterward, everyone dug with great ardor around the hill. Soon, they had revealed the roof and the broken-down walls of the destroyed old synagogue. All the ruins were removed with ease down to the foundation. And, on the old foundation, the new walls of the synagogue were erected.

Count Potoski would regularly check up on the work. If there was something lacking, he promptly sent for it without a second thought.

People traveled from far and wide to attend the dedication of the building. The count and his family members were among the chief sponsors, and they greatly rejoiced.

Figure 2.4. Agile like the deer (wood carving by Shloyme Yudovin).

11. MIRELE'S SYNAGOGUE IN BRAILOV

In many Ukrainian shtetls, there were synagogues named after pious women who were the subject of many wonderful tales and events.

I now relate one such tale from Brailov, "Mirele's Synagogue."[58] The tale was told to me by the elderly Reb Yekusiel Segal of Brailov, a grandchild of the *gaon* and zaddik, Rebbe Avrom Moshe Segal, the Brailov rabbi, author of the book *Mayim Kedoshim* [Holy Waters] on [the tractate of the Talmud] Kedoshim.[59] For years, the Jews of Brailov rationed the bread from their own mouths and collected groschen upon groschen until enough money was saved up in the communal treasury to build a synagogue.

The whole shtetl participated in the holy work. For months on end, everyone worked like busy bees: they lugged beams, kneaded lime, sawed boards, and with each passing day the building of the synagogue progressed. And, along with the building, the joy in the hearts of the Jews of Brailov also grew. All rejoiced and everyone did whatever they could to help.

When the synagogue was almost completed and the Jews of Brailov were admiring its magnificence, its decorative cornices, and its mesmerizing lustrous roof, which towered above the city buildings, even above the tall mountain outside of the city—just then, the duke blew in with the wind, arriving from his faraway lands, perhaps from across the sea. He came to relax in his beautiful castle, which was in Brailov, tucked away in the thick forest nearby.

The duke was a wretched man and a stubborn Jew-hater who could not even stand to have Jews in his sight. On that evening, as the sun was setting in the west, her last golden rays sparkling in the synagogue's large new windows, the evil duke arrived in Brailov. And, when he noticed the new synagogue, he was so captivated by the beautiful building, he made up his mind right then and there to take the synagogue away from the Jews and turn the large, towering building into a church for the gentiles.

And, indeed, immediately the next day, the duke sent for the city leaders with the rabbi at their head and ordered them, without any introduction, to kindly hand over the keys to the new synagogue. That is what he wants, and that is how it must be! If not, all the Jews of Brailov will be doomed. Saying what he had to say, he turned around and disappeared.

The city leaders and the rabbi returned to the city like mourners at a funeral. The bitter decree broke their spirit. They wept and lamented for several days straight. The most upstanding householders, the most distinguished and affluent men lobbied the duke to annul the evil decree and to have mercy on his loyal Jews by not taking the holy prayerhouse from them, their *mikdash me'at*, which they took so many pains to build. The duke, however, did not budge. A couple of days later, he sent his servants to hang a lock over the synagogue.

There was an important woman in Brailov. She was wealthy, truly pious, and very beautiful. Her name was Mirele. She took her entire fortune and went to the duke in his castle, laid her gold before him, her silver and jewelry, and with tears in her eyes, begged him to have mercy on her and on her Jewish community and annul his harsh decree.

As soon as the duke laid eyes on her beauty, he was very taken by her and his lust was kindled within him. He told her that he was ready to fulfill her request and rescind the decree at once, on one condition—she sleep with him tonight. Just for one night only.

Mirele cried, wept, fell at his feet, and begged him to take her entire fortune—anything but touch her. The duke, however, would not change his mind: only in exchange for her body would he change his decision.

When Mirele realized that there was no other alternative, she told the duke that she would fulfill his request on one condition: namely, that he come to her right after midnight. However, the key to the locked synagogue, as well as permission to complete the synagogue, he must give immediately, right then and there.

The duke agreed and quickly wrote the permit, on which he placed his seal, and handed it to her along with the key to the synagogue. Mirele had a special messenger bring it to the Jewish householders and the city of Brailov celebrated. The entire city rejoiced over their salvation.

As for Mirele, the duke locked her in a special room and stationed a guard by the door.

When Mirele was alone, she raised her eyes to Heaven and prayed with all her heart to the Lord: "Master of the Universe! You led me to this temptation, so I ask you, *Gotenyu* [God, term of endearment], to return my soul to the treasury of all your pure souls. Return me to you, that my body should not be defiled by this repulsive villain. Help me, *Gotenyu*, to stay as pure as I am now!"

And she wept from the depths of her soul, until her chaste, unadulterated soul departed her body, in holiness and purity.

After midnight, when the duke came to her, he found her dead.

The Jews of Brailov finished their synagogue right away and, in honor of Mirele's holy soul, they named the synagogue after her: "Mirele's Synagogue."

12. "THE BRESLAUER'S KLOYZ" IN DUBNO

The city of Dubno was surrounded by ancient oak forests,* large fruit orchards, rivers and mills, wheat fields, and gardens. Everything belonged to the nobleman, Count Lubomirski.

A Jewish businessman from Breslau, Germany [now Wrocław, Poland] did business with the nobleman. The businessman harvested the forest for him, leased the orchards, and held the lease to the mills and the rivers. Because of the large scale of the operations, he spent most of the year in Dubno.

The businessman asked himself: why should he continue to wander about when he could settle down in Dubno. So, he built a beautiful home in the heart of the city, brought over his wife (he had no children), and became a resident of Dubno. He carried himself with great importance, gave alms to the poor, generously supporting every communal need. Himself a learned man, he would often sit in the study house and learn, so, above all, he treated Torah scholars with great esteem and supported them financially.

There was an old study house in Dubno, which was at the point of collapsing. Even though the roof was being supported by small planks and the walls were full of holes, the regulars there, Torah scholars and students, sat inside and learned. The sound of Torah never ceased there, day or night.

---

*By the way, this is from where the name *Dubno* is supposed to stem: *Dub* in Russian means *Demb* [oak tree] in Yiddish.

The rich man talked it over with his wife: since they had no children, they would build a new study house for the Torah scholars. A study house for the sake of God's glory, which would remain as a memorial to them after one hundred and twenty years [a traditional Jewish way of expressing long life].[60]

They did not wait too long to execute this plan but rather went to work immediately. The best lumber was brought out of their own forests, beautiful quadrangular bricks were made, Jewish workers were hired, and the holy work was set into motion. They did not spare any expenses, paying workers generously. Soon enough, in the neighborhood of the half derelict study house, a marvelous edifice took shape—the new study house.

At the dedication of the building, the rich man prepared a large feast, gave charity, and greatly rejoiced. He imported a carver, a great artisan, who crafted an exquisitely beautiful Torah ark and they installed large wide bookshelves for religious books. Extra-bright lamps were brought in from Germany, massive metal menorahs were hung up, and everything was of the best quality and finest material.

The rich man and his wife reveled with delight.

Once everything was done, the rich man, who was beaming, went to the regulars [of the study house], the Torah scholars in the run-down study house, handed them the key, and said: "Here is the key to the new study house. It is yours. Come and learn Torah in comfort. And as for me, I will merely have the privilege of serving you."

The scholars turned around, dropped their eyes, and replied with these words: "It does not feel right to accept your gift! We cannot just abandon our study house for no reason. The old walls and the ceiling are saturated with the sound of our learning and they will long for us. As long as they are standing, we will remain here with them!"

The rich man left broken, humiliated, and devastated. He and his wife were unable to find any solace. They both wept bitter tears, crestfallen that their new study house stood empty by day and dark by night.

Several weeks went by like this. The rich man grew gaunt from grief and heartache, his cheeks sagging, his eyes lifeless. He wandered about the entire time in a daze, absentminded and helpless.

While in this condition, the nobleman summoned him on account of his businesses. As soon as the nobleman saw him and asked him what had happened, the rich man was unable to contain his sorrow. He broke out sobbing and told the nobleman the entire story from *alef* [first letter of Hebrew alphabet] to *tav* [the last letter], how the scholars refused to move out of their run-down study house and how his beautiful brand-new study house stood vacant and unused.

The nobleman listened to everything and remained silent. The following afternoon, before the Sabbath, while the Jews of Dubno were in the bathhouse, scores of peasants, sent by the nobleman, appeared with axes and iron bars, and in a matter of a few hours dismantled the old study house, without a stone intact, and moved the Torah ark with the Torah scrolls as well as the bookcases with the holy books into the new study house of the rich man.

When the Torah scholars, the regulars [of the study house], left the bath and saw what had happened, they had no doubt that the rich man intended to force them to move into his study house against their will. They turned away from him completely and scattered themselves throughout the numerous other study houses of Dubno.

Once the rich man saw the unintentional wrong that the nobleman had done him, he ran with great desperation to the town rabbi and with tears in his eyes assured him that the nobleman's disgraceful act was performed without his knowledge, and he begged the rabbi to take pity on him and his wife and remove this unfounded suspicion from them.

Saturday night following the Sabbath, the rabbi convened a large gathering and ordered the scholars from the destroyed study house to attend. The rich man announced before everyone and made a vow while holding on to an object used to perform a commandment[61] [typically a Sefer Torah; less commonly tefillin] that he was not involved in what had happened, that the nobleman had committed this act on his own accord, and he begged the scholars to relent and come learn in his new study house. Upon the rabbi's behest, the Torah scholars agreed. They sat and learned in the new study house and the joy of the rich man and his wife knew no limit.

For himself, the rich man claimed a permanent seat beside the door among the poor people.[62] For the rest of his days, he alone served the Torah scholars. Ever since, the study house has been referred to by his name—"The Breslauer's Kloyz."[63]

13. SYNAGOGUES AS A REWARD FOR TRIUMPHANT DEBATES WITH PRIESTS

The Ukrainian Jews also knew how to tell many beautiful legends regarding synagogues, which noblemen supposedly built as a reward to Jews for triumphant debates with priests.

The usual version of such legends went something like this: the nobleman summons his Jews to a debate with a Catholic priest, who is known to all as a Jew hater. The nobleman warns his Jews that if they do not get someone by the deadline to debate the priest, he will bring down heavy punishments upon them and issue harsh decrees. The Jews fall back on their tested measures, for instance, they decree fasts, pray specially prepared prayers in all of their holy places, lament at graves—the entire community despairs since no one will agree to take up such responsibility. And then, at the last minute, someone appears, usually from among the common folk, or a stranger, a guest, shows up—they inform the nobleman, hold the debate, and triumph. The city rejoices and the nobleman recognizes the Jewish victory by building them a beautiful synagogue as a reward.

By the way, in the old Jewish cemetery of Kiev, there was a small antiquated study house. According to what the caretaker related to me, Christian priests and Jewish rabbis and scholars frequently conducted debates regarding matters of faith in this small study house.

14. THE INTERIOR DESIGN OF OLD SYNAGOGUES

And, as much as the exceptional beauty of these old synagogues, with their wonderful, original architecture, intricate cornices, and small porches, was interesting, even more interesting and more original were the patriarchal beauty and the rich colors and paints that met your eyes when you walked inside one of these old synagogues.

Right away, you were captivated by the paintings on the ceiling* and on the walls, which an anonymous artist had painted with such insight and mastery; there was a special grace emanating from the massive standing metal menorahs, from their branches and candelabras, which were hanging from the ceiling and from the huge Hanukkah lamps, molded by ancient coppersmiths. The spreading branches of the menorahs were decorated with hammered ornaments of birds, beasts, flowers, and grapes. You could not tear your eyes away from the polished Torah arks and prayer stands, from the carved lions and deer, leopards and eagles, which reminded you instantly of the quotation from Yehudah ben Tema: "Be courageous like the leopard, light like the eagle, agile like the deer, and mighty like the lion" [to do the will of your Father who is in heaven] (Pirkei Avot 5:20). You marveled at the velvet and silk curtains covering the Torah ark on which the tablets of the Decalogue were embroidered; "The Hands of Aaron," with the names of donors stitched on them with silver and gold thread; the Torah crowns, pointers, ornaments, and other ritual objects from silver

---

*The ceiling of a synagogue was traditionally called a *raqia*—the firmament, the heavens, from the biblical verse: "And God called the firmament sky" (Genesis 1:8). For this reason, the ceiling (*raqia*) in the old synagogues was painted in a sky blue color, decked with stars, some gold and some silver, some larger and some smaller.

and gold, made by artistic goldsmiths; the metal *tzedakah* boxes, where charity could be given in secret, on which fitting biblical verses were engraved; the big-bellied copper washstands; the copper mezuzah cases. A modest, innocent grace emanated from all of these objects and a rare, true, patriarchal beauty rested on them.

The Ethnographic Expedition collected a rich collection of these traditional ritual objects and took hundreds of photographs of synagogues and objects for the Jewish Historical Ethnographic Museum.

Figure 2.5. Wood carving by Shloyme Yudovin.

TO SECTION 2

Figure 2.6. The newly built Radzivilover Synagogue.

Figure 2.7. Synagogue of Lutsk.

Figure 2.8. Torah ark and lectern in the synagogue of Mikolayev.

Figure 2.9. Bimah [platform where Torah is read] in the synagogue of Lutsk.

Figure 2.10. *Top*, the "Breslauer's Kloyz" in Dubno. *Bottom*, Maharsha's synagogue in Ostroh.

Figure 2.11. The synagogue of Nemirov, renovated in 5665 (1905).

Figure 2.12. An interior view of the synagogue of Nemirov, the Torah ark, and lectern.

Figure 2.13. The courtyard of the synagogue of Korostishev.

Figure 2.14. Lectern in the synagogue of Korostishev.

Figure 2.15. *Top*, the wooden synagogue of Mekhilpoli. *Bottom*, the wooden synagogue of Snitkov.

Figure 2.16. Torah ark in the synagogue of Starokonstantinov.

Figure 2.17. *Top*, the synagogue of Yanov. *Bottom*, the synagogue of Shargorod.

Figure 2.18. Elijah's seat, with a *baldakhin* [ceremonial canopy], in the synagogue of Kremenets.

NOTES

1. Rechtman employs the term *shul* for synagogue and a variety of other terms—kloyz, *klayzl*, bes medresh—that mean study house or prayerhouse.
2. Located in Volhynia, Radzivilov (now Radyvyliv, Ukraine) had 4,322 Jewish residents out of a total population of 7,313 in 1897. See *Sefer Zikaron Radzivilov*, 16. A Hebrew translation of Rechtman's "The Radzivilover Synagogue and the Torah Ark That Was Struck by a Thunderbolt," appears in *Sefer Zikaron Radzivilov*, 55–58; directly following, on pp. 58–59, Rachel Gorman notes that the Austrians "blew up" the old synagogue in Radzivilov during World War I and claims that Rechtman made several errors in his account, "though it is not his fault—he received incorrect information."
3. The zodiac has been an element of synagogue art since Antiquity, most famously in the zodiac-themed mosaics in the Beit Alpha synagogue from the sixth century CE.
4. Rabbi Yekhiel Mikhel Zlotshever (d. 1786) was one of the disciples of the Baal Shem Tov. His five sons, known as the "Five Books of the Pentateuch," became Hasidic leaders in their own right, including Rabbi Itsikl [Yitshak] Radzivilov (d. 1824) and Rabbi Velvele [Ze'ev Wolf] Zborzsher (d. 1822). See Altshuler, "The First Tzaddik of Hasidism," 127–193. On Rabbi Itsikl Radziviler, specifically, see *Sefer Zikaron Radzivilov*, 31–32.
5. For an image of the old synagogue in Radzivilov, see *Sefer Zikaron Radzivilov*, 56.
6. Moshe Ginzburg (1851–1936), was born to a poor family in Radzivilov and became one of the most important Jewish industrialists and philanthropists in the Russian Empire. Even after he moved away from the town, Ginzburg continued to visit his relatives in Radzivilov and support Jewish institutions in the community financially. On Ginzburg, see *Moshe Ginzburg zayn lebn un tetigkayt*. On Ginzburg's connection to Radzivilov, see also An-sky's remarks in Zavadivker, *1915 Diary of S. An-sky*, 48.
7. The small town of Mikolayev (also called Nikolayev) that Rechtman is describing was located in Podolia and should not be confused with the better-known city of the same name located near the Black Sea. On Rabbi Dovid of Mikolayev, see Zevin, *Sipure Hasidim al ha-Torah*, 109–111.
8. A *verst* was a measure of distance in Imperial Russia equivalent to 0.66 mile or 1.06 km.
9. A *kitl* (pl. *kitlen*) is a long white garment traditionally worn by Jewish men during the wedding ceremony and by married men on certain holidays (Yom Kippur, the Passover Seder) as well as for burial.
10. The *mizrekh-vant* or eastern wall of the synagogue, where the Torah ark was located, was considered a place of honor.
11. *Kol Nidre* (All Vows) and *Yayles* are part of the Yom Kippur evening service.
12. Throughout this section and the next, Rechtman attempts to portray the Polish nobleman's speech in a realistic manner by employing a number of Slavic terms.
13. Although Rechtman describes Reb Dovid as showing the Polish count great respect, he nevertheless depicts him as using the informal "Du" (you) form in Yiddish when speaking to him.
14. The idea that the synagogue is a small temple draws on a Talmudic tradition, see BT Megillah 29a.
15. On the phenomenon of Jewish children being drafted—and, sometimes, kidnapped—to serve in the cantonist battalions of the Russian military, see Petrovsky-Shtern, *Jews in the Russian Army, 1827–1917*; Litvak, *Conscription and Modern Russian*; Stanislawski, *Tsar*

Nicholas I and the Jews. Such soldiers were known colloquially as "Nikolayevski soldiers" because the policy was instituted by Czar Nicholas I.

16. *Fonye,* the Yiddish version of the Russian name *Vanya* (the diminutive of *Ivan*), was commonly employed as shorthand for a Russian man or, in this case, the Russian *man* (i.e., the authorities).

17. The town of Mezeritch was located in Volhynia. Rabbi Dov Ber, the Maggid (preacher) of Mezeritch (d. 1772), who succeeded the Baal Shem Tov as leader of the Hasidic movement, put the town on the Jewish map.

18. The rabbinic expression *shiva tovei ha-ir* or "seven good citizens of the city" (see BT Megillah 26b) and the term *parneysim* (sing., *parnes*) both refer to the leaders of a Jewish community.

19. In the list of construction equipment, Rechtman includes the word "matshke," which appears to be a mistake. Rather than the letter "mem" the word should probably start with the letter "tes," resulting in "tatshke," meaning "wheelbarrow."

20. The town of Lutsk in Volhynia had a large Jewish community with many Hasidic prayerhouses and was also home to a small but historically significant community of Karaites. Gashuri, "Bet ha-midrash," 305–306, mentions the visit of the Jewish Ethnographic Expedition to the town. Instead of "Rabbi Yehudah's Bes Medresh," however, Gashuri refers to it as "Rabbi Wolf the Martyr's Bes Medresh." Gashuri, "Bet ha-midrash," 97–99, reproduces Rechtman's Yiddish account—and attributes it to him—except that instead of referring to "Rabbi Yehudah," the text refers to "Rabbi Wolf," without explaining the discrepancy. The memorial book, on p. 97, also includes a photograph of "Rabbi Wolf the Martyr's grave," which does not appear in Rechtman's account.

21. Gashuri, "Bet ha-midrash," 305, reproduces the same tombstone inscription as does Rechtman but substitutes "Yehudah Zeev Wolf," for "Yehudah." Gashuri then provides a Hebrew translation of Rechtman's account followed by some other local legends that Rechtman did not include. Gashuri mentions that that the martyr's grave became a site of pilgrimage for the town's Jewish women, in particular. After the original tombstone sunk into the ground, a new one was erected in its place. At the beginning of the twentieth century, a woman named Haya-Sarah Loyfer dedicated herself to maintaining the gravestone and she ensured that it survived World War I until it was finally destroyed along with the other old gravestones in the Jewish cemetery during the Holocaust.

22. Yehuda's soul departed his body as he was reciting *ekhad* (one), the last word of the Shema, which is the prayer that is supposed to be on a Jew's lips when he is martyred or about to die, in general.

23. On the "old" and "new" Jewish cemeteries in Lutsk, see Gashuri, "Der lutsker alter un nayer bes-oylem," 329–332, which includes a photograph of the old cemetery. The article mentions the interest of the Jewish Ethnographic Expedition in the town's old Jewish graves.

24. Olyka was located in Volhynia and had a population of roughly 2,000 Jews (50 percent of the total) in 1897.

25. Rabbi Eliezer Liber ha-Gadol ("The Great") of Berdichev was a legendary figure. The town later became associated in Hasidic lore with Rabbi Levi Yitzhak of Berdichev (1740–1809), also known as the "Kedushas Levi," after the title of his book. Known as the "Jerusalem of Volhynia," Berdichev was home to nearly forty-two thousand Jews (80 percent of the total population) in 1897.

26. For emphasis, Rechtman uses both the Hebrew and the Yiddish words for hair. In the Kabbalah, the hair of the beard has mystical, even divine, significance and, therefore,

it became customary for pious Jewish men to avoid any activities that might result in their beard hair falling out. For a discussion of this kabbalistic tradition and its relationship to changing fashions, see E. Horowitz, "Early Eighteenth Century Confronts the Beard," 95–115.

27. Ludmir was home to one of the oldest Jewish communities in Volhynia. Among other things, the town was known for its connection to the Maiden of Ludmir, the only woman in the history of the Hasidic movement to function as a rebbe in her own right. For more on this figure and the town, itself, see Deutsch, *The Maiden of Ludmir*.

28. On this prayer, see Schwartz, "'Hanoten Teshua,'" 113–120.

29. Other sources give the Maharsha's birth year as 1655.

30. The title *Maharsha* is the Hebrew acronym for "Our Teacher, the Rabbi Shmuel Eydels."

31. The Zusmans were a wealthy family in Ostroh for generations, including a timber merchant who hired the Maskil (Jewish Enlightener) Isaac Baer Levinsohn to serve as a tutor in his household. See Zinberg, *History of Jewish Literature*, 28.

32. For local Ostroh traditions regarding the Maharsha, see Biber, *Sefer mizkeret le-gedole Ostroh*, 43–46. This is an invaluable repository of information on the Jewish community of Ostroh from a native son and includes numerous older sources. See also Biber, "Gedolei Ostroh," 114–117.

33. Among many Jews in Eastern Europe, it was customary to play cards and other games on *nitl nakht*, i.e., Christmas Eve, so as not to honor it by learning Torah. See Shapiro, "Torah Study on Christmas Eve," 319–353.

34. On the Maharsha's synagogue in Ostroh, see Ilon, "Ostroh birat Volin ve-ha-galilot"; n.a., "Bate kenesyot u-vate midrashot," *Pinkas Ostroh*, 86–87, 114; Biber, *Sefer mizkeret le-gedole Ostroh*, 25–26.

35. This occurred during what is known as the Second Partition of Poland (out of three) in which the Polish-Lithuanian Commonwealth was divided between Russia, Prussia, and Austria and ceased to exist until after World War I, when independent Polish and Lithuanian states were created.

36. For descriptions of the celebration of the Purim of Ostroh by former residents of the town, see Biber, *Sefer mizkeret le-gedole Ostroh*, 23–25; Ilon, "Ostroh birat Volin ve-ha-galilot," 54. On the widespread Jewish custom of creating a second Purim to commemorate a community's salvation from danger, see Yerushalmi, *Zakhor*, 46–48.

37. The first words in Exodus 32:11, "And Moses besought..."

38. A somewhat different version of the scroll is reproduced in the following two sources: Biber, *Sefer mizkeret le-gedole Ostroh*, 334–335; Ilon, "Ostroh birat Volin ve-ha-galilot," 55–58. It is likely that the latter copied the former. It is also possible that Rechtman employed Menachem Mendel Biber's work as a source for this and other traditions from Ostroh but does not cite the text in his own work.

39. The Hebrew phrase *mikhtav patuah* or open letter, refers to a letter that is intended to be read by the wider public rather than a single recipient.

40. According to Pirke Avot (Ethics of the Fathers), 5:5, "Ten miracles were performed for our ancestors in the Temple [in Jerusalem]."

41. For various local legends regarding Rabbi Yosef Yuzpa of Ostroh, see Biber, *Sefer mizkeret le-gedole Ostroh*, 145–148.

42. On the "great *kloyz*" or study house in Ostroh, see Biber, *Sefer mizkeret le-gedole Ostroh*, 26–27.

43. On Rabbi Asher Tsvi of Ostroh, see Biber, *Sefer mizkeret le-gedole Ostroh*, 260–264.
44. Paraphrasing Deuteronomy 28:10 and Psalm 20:10.
45. According to Jewish tradition, certain exalted individuals (e.g., Moses and Miriam) are said to have died by a kiss from God. See Fishbane, *Kiss of God*.
46. The text of the Maharsha's tombstone is also reproduced in Biber, *Sefer mizkeret le-gedole Ostroh*, 48–49. It is possible that Rechtman copied the text in Biber's work but did not cite it.
47. Rabbi Yoel Sirkis (1561–1640), also known as the "Bach," after his chief work "Bayit Hadash."
48. Responsa (Hebrew, She'elot u-Teshuvot) are published collections of Halakic questions addressed to an important rabbi and his answers.
49. Rabbi David HaLevi Segal (1586–1667), also known as the "Turei Zahav" or the "TaZ," after his most famous work, a commentary on Yosef Karo's legal code, the *Shulhan Arukh*. He moved to Ostroh around 1641 and established an important yeshiva. On local legends regarding the TaZ's time in Ostroh, see Biber, *Sefer mizkeret le-gedole Ostroh*, 53–58.
50. Rabbi Yaakov Yoseph of Ostroh (1738–1791), an early Hasidic figure also known as "Rav Yevi," after the title of his book on the Psalms that contains some traditions attributed to the Baal Shem Tov. See Ilon, "Ostroh birat Volin ve-ha-galilot," 55.
51. On Rabbi Pinkhes of Koretz, see Heschel, "Reb Pinkhes Koritser," 9–48.
52. For another version of this story, see Buxbaum, *Light and Fire of the Baal Shem Tov*, 108.
53. On the kabbalistic belief that souls come from a "treasury beneath the divine throne," see Giller, *Reading the Zohar*, 47.
54. Located in Podolia, Nemirov was home to a number of important rabbis over the centuries, including Yom-Tov Lipmann Heller and Yaakov Yosef of Polonye, one of the earliest disciples of the Baal Shem Tov. In the nineteenth century, the town was associated with Noson (Nathan) of Nemirov, the chief disciple of Rabbi Nachman of Bratslav.
55. The description of Count Potoski as a "friend of the Jews," probably alludes to legends that accrued around the figure of Walentyn Potocki, a Polish count who supposedly converted to Judaism at the end of the eighteenth century and was burned at the stake in Vilna as punishment. On Potocki and the Hebrew, Yiddish, and Polish sources for the legend, see Teter, "Ger Tsedek [Righteous Convert]."
56. Bogdan Khmelnytsky (1595–1657) was the *hetman* or leader of a Ukrainian Cossack uprising against Polish-Lithuania Commonwealth rule between 1647 and 1648, during which thousands of Jews were killed (including in Nemirov) or sold into slavery by the Cossacks or their Tatar allies. Beyond the actual carnage, the events, known as the *gzeyres takh ve-tat* (i.e., "the decrees of 408 and 409," an acronym reflecting the Hebrew letters that signify the numbers 408 and 409, since the uprising took place in 5408 and 5409 according to the Jewish calendar), had a tremendous impact on the collective psyche of Eastern European Jews, who produced written chronicles and numerous oral legends regarding the catastrophe that continued to circulate for centuries thereafter.
57. The *Shehecheyanu* [Who has given us life] blessing is recited when doing something for the first time or when embarking on something new.
58. Bar-Itzhak, *Jewish Poland*, 150–152, provides its own English translation of Rechtman's tale and compares it with other similar tales of Eastern European Jewish provenance.
59. The cover of the book states that its author was living in Brailov when it was published in 1790. See Avrom Moshe Segal, *Mayim Kedoshim* (Mezirov, 1790).
60. The Jewish tradition that one hundred and twenty years signifies a long life—as in the Yiddish saying, *biz hundert un tsvantsig* or "till one hundred and twenty"—originates in

Genesis 6:3, "My spirit shall not abide in man forever... therefore shall his days be a hundred and twenty years." Moreover, Moses lived to be a hundred and twenty years.

61. Rechtman employs the Halakic phrase *nekitat hefetz*, which refers to the practice of physically holding on to an object used to perform a commandment while making a vow.

62. The eastern wall of the synagogue, where the Torah ark was located, was considered the place of honor in a synagogue. By contrast, the western wall and the seats near the door were occupied by the lower strata of shtetl society.

63. On the Breslauer's Kloyz, see Katskah, "Batei-tefilah u-vatei-midrash be-Dubno," 177.

THREE

HEADSTONES, GRAVES, AND TOMBS

1. THE BESHT'S GRAVE AND KLOYZ [PRAYERHOUSE] IN MEDZHIBOZH

A. *The Small Roof over the Besht's Grave*

In the old cemetery of almost every shtetl in Ukraine, one could find the grave of a zaddik. Small tombs were typically built over these holy graves and are referred to as an *ohel*, a *tsiyun*, or simply a *shtibl*. These graves are considered to be very sacred and are frequently visited by people, especially, God forbid, in times of emergency, when the townsmen and -women would prostrate themselves on the grave of their zaddik, pray, and leave *kvitlekh* [written petitions to a rebbe from his followers] in his ohel, tsiyun, or shtibl.

When the expedition arrived in Medzhibozh, the city where the Baal Shem Tov had lived and worked, and located the old cemetery, we were astounded to see that, over the grave of the founder of Hasidism, Rebbe Yisroel Baal Shem Tov—precisely over his grave—no one had built a shtibl.[1] There were only four [wooden] posts placed on the four sides of his grave and, on top, a small roof [made] of boards—and nothing more.

We later learned that there was a reason for this. Old folk informed us that, shortly after the Besht's passing, his pupils declared that his grave must be treated with the utmost care, for, as they warned, the soil around his grave is holy, and the grave itself is the holy of holies [a phrase connected to the Temple] *and anyone who touches it shall be put to death* [a biblical phrase referring to holy objects, e.g., Mount Sinai in Exodus 19:12]; this is to say that anyone who agitates or disturbs the grave unduly is liable [for forfeiture] of his life.[2]

It is even related that on several occasions during different periods, individuals—devoted Hasidim—took it on themselves to build a tsiyun over their rebbe's grave, yet every time they went to work they were injured at the very start and were unable to continue.

The Jews of Medzhibozh loved to tell the following wonderful legend about the four [wooden] posts and the little roof, which were, in spite of everything, placed over the Besht's grave and remain there to this day.

A carpenter, just your average craftsman, a person who lives from the work of his hands, and a devout Hasid to boot, could not look on as his holy rebbe's grave was eroded and damaged by the rain. So, he decided that the least he could do was put up a roof that would provide the grave with some shelter from the rain; and, although he was well aware that people had tried to do so before him and had paid with their lives, he was by no means discouraged. Rather, with fear and trembling, he was willing to martyr himself in order to put up a shtibl to protect his holy rebbe's unprotected grave.

And, in order to not get hurt from the very start like all of his predecessors had been, he came up with the following plan: he would first assemble the entire tsiyun at his home, and then, once it was completed, he would bring it to the cemetery and install it over the Besht's grave.

Also, before the carpenter began his work, he sanctified and purified himself for an entire month: by fasting every Monday and Thursday [a tradition of pious Jews], by going to the ritual bath every morning, by reciting all of the Psalms every day, and by praying with fervor.

As soon as the four weeks had passed, he washed all of his equipment, purifying and ritually cleansing it, and then one fine morning he went into the forest and chopped down four straight trees with his own hands. He cut off the branches and hewed [the timber] on all sides. He cut out four straight, quadrangular [wooden] posts and brought them home, where he prepared a small roof from the boards and completed all the other parts of the shtibl to be assembled the following morning.

That night, the Besht visited him in a dream and told him not to go forward [with his plans], for he would be putting his life in great danger. However, the carpenter was not deterred. He was prepared to sacrifice his own life to honor his holy rebbe, the Besht.

And so, he arose at dawn, put up the four posts by himself, and attached the small preconstructed roof. [He] painted [everything] and left it in the sun to dry. After he finished praying *mit groys kevone* [with great intention], he went to the marketplace and fetched three peasants who helped him carry the shtibl, each holding a post, all the way to the Baal Shem Tov's grave. Once there, they quickly drove the sharp-pointed posts into the soft soil of the grave.

As soon as the carpenter had wiped the sweat from his face, lifted his head, and saw how the freshly painted small roof hung over the grave, covering and protecting it, he was beside himself with joy and a warmth suffused his limbs. Radiating light, he slowly walked backward, step by step, his eyes fixed on the Besht's grave, all the while getting farther and farther away [from the grave], until he was beyond the fence surrounding the cemetery.

As the story goes, as soon as he crossed the threshold of his home, he immediately felt weak in all of his limbs. And he knew what this meant. He washed his hands, put on his burial shrouds, laid down in bed, called for his wife and children, and happily informed them that he would soon die. He instructed them not to cry or mourn his death, and then, with great *hislayves* [passion], he began to recite the *vidui* [confession of sins]; after which, he turned his face to the wall and his soul departed in holiness and purity.

* * *

In the same cemetery, not far from the Besht's grave, there are a number of other shtiblekh [pl. shtibl] and graves belonging to the Besht's students, including his grandson, Rabbi Borukhl, and Hershele Ostropoler, who would entertain Rabbi Borukhl, and the grave of the zaddik, Rabbi Avrom Yehoshua Heshel, the Apter Rov.[3]

Facing the Hasidic graves, from the opposite side, were the graves of *misnagdim* [opponents of Hasidim] in Medzhibozh, rabbis, such as the gaon, Rabbi Simkhe Bick, Rabbi Hirsh Leyb, and a number of others.[4]

Velvel, the Talmud Torah teacher, who was escorting us [during our visit], also pointed out the graves of a married couple, Mordechai and Esther. The local *Megillas Medzhibozh* [Megillah of Medzhibozh] tells of how, in the days of Khmelnytsky, they risked their lives and, in a stroke of inspiration, rescued the city (see p. 229).

B. The Besht's Kloyz

The kloyz in which the Besht prayed remained unchanged even after his passing.[5] It was never renovated, or even whitewashed for that matter. For just as it was believed that his grave is holy and must not be touched, so it was believed that the walls of his study house, which had absorbed, in the course of several decades, the holy Besht's praying and teaching, were also holy, for *they are holy unto the Lord and whoever touches them shall surely be put to death* [a play on Exodus 19:12, where the reference is to Mount Sinai]. The entire prayerhouse falls under the rubric of "do not add and do not diminish" [Deuteronomy 4:2]. This meant that it is forbidden to add to its holiness let alone reduce it in anyway. It is for this reason that no repairs were ever done to the kloyz, and it was not even whitewashed—neither the inside nor the outside.

It is said that the Besht's grandson, Rabbi Borukhl, who prayed in his grandfather's kloyz, noticed how the ceiling was starting to crumble and the walls were peeling. So, under his authority, he ordered that the kloyz be whitewashed from the inside out. The whitewash and necessary tools were prepared, and the masons were squared away and set to work the next day. That night, the Besht appeared to his grandson, Rabbi Borukhl, in a dream, and ordered him not to go forward [with the project]. The next day, Rabbi Borukhl called everything off, and, in all the coming years, the kloyz was never whitewashed.[6]

C. The Grave of the Baal Shem Tov's Mother

There is a tradition that the grave of the Besht's mother, Sore [Sarah], is located in Tlust, a small shtetl not far from Kamenets-Podolsk.[7] She died there during an outbreak of violence and was among many victims to be buried in the local cemetery.

When the Besht was revealed [to be a zaddik], the Jews of Tlust decided, in his honor, to place a beautiful headstone on his mother's grave. A famous headstone engraver made a unique headstone: two peaks on the sides and, in their midst, a menorah. It is said that when the headstone was ready to be installed, they did not know the exact spot where she was buried. They asked the Besht how to proceed. He advised them that a minyan of ten Jewish men should carry the headstone between the rows of graves, and, when it suddenly became heavier, it is then that they would know they were at the site of his mother's grave.

They did just as directed. And when they came to the seventh grave in the seventh row, the headstone grew so heavy that they were unable to move a step further. That is where they placed the headstone.

2. "CONVERSION BRICKS" AND "LOVE BRICKS" ON THE GRAVES OF ZADDIKIM

In almost every zaddik's tomb, there are kvitlekh [petitions for help] that his Hasidim had presented to him during his lifetime and that he was given to take along with him after his passing.

It was customary for Hasidim, in times of both personal and communal crisis (e.g., a false accusation or an evil decree), to visit the tomb of a Hasidic rebbe, leave a *kvitel*, and pray [for help].

The kvitlekh were usually written in *loshn-koydesh* [Hebrew/Aramaic]. However, there were also many kvitlekh written in Yiddish. The paper and format varied. Some were even triangular. The style and contents [were] incredibly interesting and of great ethnographic value.

Here is the [Hebrew] text of a typical *kvitel*: A *kvitel* from Moshe son of Rokhel and his wife Malkah daughter of Esther for deliverance in body and soul, and a complete recovery, and for a healthy child, redemption of the soul, one silver ruble.

The expedition amassed a large collection of all sorts of kvitlekh.

In addition to kvitlekh on the graves of famous zaddikim, the expedition also found "burnt" bricks on which were written, or engraved, prayers and incantations against various calamities.[8]

On the basis of their inscriptions, we were able to put the bricks into two categories, which we dubbed: "conversion bricks" and "love bricks."

The conversion bricks were considered a sgule [charm or remedy] for someone who left Judaism and was about to convert to Christianity.[9] The love bricks were considered a remedy for a romance gone awry. The following [Hebrew] text was either inscribed or engraved in a scribal hand onto the conversion brick:

> Just as this brick is burnt by fire, may his (or her) heart, who has turned away from Judaism, burn, so that his (her) heart may return to God for the good.

According to what we were told, the following is how the conversion bricks were prepared.

The parents, wife, or closest loved ones to whomever had gone astray, kneaded the lime with their own hands, and fashioned a brick on which they had the above text either written or engraved. Then, they burnt the brick in an oven for seven days and seven nights straight, after which they removed the brick from the oven, brought it to a cemetery, and placed it on the grave of a very holy zaddik.

Frequently, people would even travel for miles to place the brick on the grave of a *gadol-be-yisroel* [a revered sage or holy man], a great zaddik, who was well known as a *poel-yeshues* [performer of rescues or salvations, i.e., a miracle worker].

Love bricks were prepared in the same way as conversion bricks and a similar [Hebrew] text was either inscribed or engraved onto them.

> Just as this brick was burnt in fire, may his (or her) heart burn in the same way, and just as this brick is broken and separated, may his heart be broken and separated from her heart (or her heart from his) forever and always.

They would also burn the love bricks in an oven for seven days and seven nights straight. Then, they would break the brick in half and place the two halves on two separate graves of two *gedolei hador* [great ones of the generation, i.e., spiritual leaders or Torah sages].

As mentioned earlier, we also found bricks with other texts. However, it was hard to make out the inscriptions and determine in what circumstances they were used as sgules and *trufes* [cures].

We found the largest number of these bricks on the grave of Rabbi Levi Yitzchak of Berdichev. We only found halves of the love bricks there and were unable to locate the other halves.

I remember that in Medzhiboah we found one half of a love brick on the grave of Rabbi Yisroel Baal Shem Tov. We figured that since the graves of many other great zaddikim were located in this cemetery, we would find the second half of the brick on one of these other graves. For two days straight, we rummaged about the graves of the Besht's disciples, including the grave of the Apter Rov, until we eventually found the second half of this brick on the grave of the Besht's grandson, Reb Borukhl of Medzhibozh.

3. THE GRAVE OF RABBI YISROEL MEYS [THE DEAD ONE OR CORPSE]

Not far from the Baal Shem Tov's *tziyun* in Medzhibozh, there is a gravestone (from the year 5625?) with the following inscription:

> Here lies Rabbi Yisroel Meys who died during his lifetime.

The following is a wonderful tale told about the headstone.

It is well known that the Besht's daughter, Odl [a.k.a. Hodel or Edel], had three children: Reb Moshe Chaim Ephraim Sodilkover, Reb Borukhl Medzhibozher, and a daughter named Feyge, the mother of Reb Nahman of Bratslav.[10]

After Rabbi Yisroel Baal Shem Tov's passing, no one in Medzhibozh would name their newborn child Yisroel, for it was thought to be so holy a name that any child named Yisroel would surely die.

And then one day, Feyge, the Baal Shem Tov's granddaughter became pregnant again and in due time had a son. It is said that the Besht appeared to his daughter, Odl, in a dream and asked that the newly born baby boy be given the name Yisroel.

However, Feyge, the child's mother, did not consent. She did not want to put her child's life at risk. Even so, Odl, his grandmother, wanted to fulfill her holy father's request—so, at the circumcision, when the cantor called out: "And he shall be called in Israel" [Genesis 35:10], Odl rushed out and hollered: "Yisroel." The cantor repeated the name, and, there you have it, his name became Yisroel, against his mother's wishes.

The child died three days after the circumcision. The poor mother, Feyge, took her dead child to her mother, Odl, laid him down in front of her, and, with tears in her eyes, said, "Mama! You are responsible for my child's death! Take the child and do with him what you will!"

Odl carried the child to the cemetery and laid it down on her father's grave, saying, "Father! You ordered me to name the child after you and now he is dead. Take him. He is yours!" She had a good cry and then returned home.

It snowed throughout the entire night. The following morning, when the cemetery caretaker left his house, he heard the sound of a child crying coming from the cemetery. He followed the sound until he approached the Besht's grave and found the crying child there.

The whole town was in an uproar. And, right away, the child's mother, Feyge, came sprinting [to the cemetery] and retrieved her unharmed child.

After this incident, the child was called "Yisroel Meys." He lived a long, fruitful life and, after a hundred years, was buried in the same cemetery as his great-grandfather, the Besht. And the following was carved on his headstone:

Here lies Yisroel Meys who died during his lifetime.

4. THE OHEL OF REBBE LEVI YITZCHAK OF BERDICHEV AND THE GRAVE OF RABBI MOSHE YAKHNES

In the spacious and beautifully built white ohel on the grave of the zaddik Levi Yitzchak of Berdichev continually burnt a *ner tamid* [eternal light]. An elderly Jew, who was proud of the fact that he was a grandchild of the rabbi of Berdichev, spent the entire day there. He prepared small lamps, which he filled with oil and strung wicks into, while also saying Psalms and praying various types of special prayers, which he inherited from his father, who had also done the same holy work.

People traveled great distances for the privilege of lighting a lamp on this great zaddik's grave. It was believed that this helped with all sorts of illnesses and was above all a sgule for having children.

The *rebbetsin* [the rebbe's wife] Kholye, their three sons, and the daughters-in-laws were also buried in the ohel. I do not know for sure whether his mother, Sosye-Sore, is also buried there, but it seems to me that she is. The tsiyun was filled with the kvitlekh that Hasidim had left there.

The grave of Rabbi Moshe Yakhnes is located at the foot of Rabbi Levi Yitzchak's ohel. People say that when it was time for Rabbi Moshe Yakhnes to become bar mitzvah his father took him to the Baal Shem Tov. The Besht examined him and said the following: "If you want to live long, you must not become famous." And, throughout his life, he was careful to live in obscurity. Rabbi Moshe was a great zaddik, and it is said that even Rebbe Levi Yitzchak of Berdichev, who was such a holy man, could not reach the [spiritual] *madreyges* [levels] that he attained.

According to a legend in Berdichev, Reb Moshe was once learning [Torah] late at night when he was struck by a complex matter in "Tosfos Yom Tov."[11] While he was sitting there, absorbed in thought, an elderly man came in, sat down across from him, and explained the entire matter to him. Rabbi Moshe was taken aback and asked the old man his name. But the elderly man pretended not to hear [him] and said: "If you want to channel the *Tosfos Yom Tov* [Rabbi Yom Tov Lipman Heller], then you must concentrate your thoughts [on the prayer] *Melekh Khay Ha-Olamim* [Living King of the Worlds]."

At that very moment, Rabbi Levi Yitzchak had a feeling that the *Tosfos Yom Tov* was with Rabbi Moshe Yakhnes, and he ran quickly to him. However, the elderly man was already gone.

When Rabbi Moshe Yakhnes passed away, Rabbi Levi Yitzchak's son, the Pikever Rebbe, asked the burial society to bury Rabbi Moshe at the foot of his father's grave. He offered no explanation as to why. Reb Zelik, who was Rebbe Levi Yitzchak's sexton, explained later: one time, Rabbi Moshe Yakhnes went into Rebbe Levi Yitzchak's private study and stayed there for a long while. I peered through a crack and saw how they both were standing there bent over, their hands on each other's heads.

Rebbe Levi Yitzchak was saying: "Bless me, Moshe dearest!" And Rabbi Moshe was saying: "Bless me, my brother Levi Yitzchak!" Then, I heard Rebbe Levi Yitzchak, who was much younger than Rabbi Moshe, tell [him]: "My dearest Moshe! After one hundred and twenty years, I want you to lie next to me." Rabbi Moshe replied: "No, Levi Yitzchak, my brother! It will be enough for me to lie at your feet!"

It was now clear why the Pikaver Rebbe had Reb Moshe Yakhnes buried at the foot of his father's grave.

It is also said that, during Rebbe Levi Yitzchak's funeral procession, Rabbi Moshe Yakhnes followed him all the way to his grave. Once there, he approached his stretcher [for the corpse], leaned over the deceased, and whispered this verse into his ear: "You shall count seven weeks for yourself" [from Deuteronomy 16:9]. And, indeed, Rabbi Moshe passed away exactly seven weeks later.

5. THE SHTIBL [TOMB] ON THE GRAVE OF THE *NISTER* [HIDDEN ZADDIK] RABBI VELVELE OF ZHITOMIR

In the shtibl of the *nister* Rabbi Velvele of Zhitomir, the author of the book "Or Ha-Meir," may be found the lectern on which he learned and prayed. The bench on which he slept is near the shtibl wall.

This is the extraordinary story of how Reb Velvele was revealed [to be a zaddik] and came to Zhitomir.

Before he was revealed [to be a zaddik], he lived in Pilyava, which is a little shtetl, a considerable distance from Zhitomir. The town was famous for the large fairs that were held there once a month. Reb Velvele ran a tavern [in town] and made his living off of the peasants, who would drink there during the fairs. He spent the other days of the week studying *nigle* [exoteric Torah] and *nister* [esoteric Torah]. Nobody knew of his hidden ways or deeds.

One day, a fur trader from a faraway town drove a wagon of pelts to a fair in Pilyava, where Reb Velvele was living. It was autumn, very muddy, and freezing cold. For the trader to make it to the fair on time, he had to trudge the whole night through. Drenched in the rain, he arrived in the town half frozen. It was still early, so he stopped at Reb Velvele Vohl's tavern (Vohl was Reb Velvele's family name), unharnessed his horses, gave them food, went into the tavern alone, and ordered Reb Velvele to bring him a glass of strong whiskey to warm himself up. Reb Velvele poured him a full glass of whiskey. The trader grabbed the glass and was about to drink it without making a blessing. Reb Velvele was not having this. He grabbed the trader by the hand and said to him:

> You should know that your father Reb So-and-So, who passed away six years ago, was a lifelong sinner. He did not perform *tshuve* [repentance] even on the day of his death. When he arrived in *Oylem Ha-Emes* [lit., The World of Truth, i.e., the afterlife] as a sinner, the Heavenly Court decreed that he be reincarnated into a kernel of rye.[12] The kernel, which contained your father's soul, was sowed into the earth. When it began to rot, your father also rotted. From the kernel, an ear [of rye] grew forth. And as the wind tossed the ear [of rye] to and fro, your father's limbs were tossed and twisted, and he suffered terrible agonies. When the ear ripened, it was harvested with a sharp cutting knife, and your father's limbs were cut up into little pieces. The ear was then bailed and your father's bones ached in agony; and when the ear was threshed with sticks, your father's bones were threshed and broken into little pieces. And then sure enough the rye kernels were cooked over fire to make whiskey out of them, and your father's body parts were cooked over blazing fire. And the very glass that you hold in your hand, contains your father's soul, which has been searching for its *tikun* [repair] for six years now.[13] Today is your father's yahrzeit [anniversary of death]. Do you, his son, want to drink this cup without making a blessing and pass up the opportunity to redeem your father's sinful soul?

The story became the talk of the town and was soon known throughout the region. People began to consider Reb Velvele a holy man, and they even started turning to him with requests and giving him kvitlekh to intercede with God on their behalf. Reb Velvele was no longer able to conceal his true identity.

Figure 3.1. The pallbearers at a funeral (wood carving by Shloyme Yudovin).

That same year, the hidden zaddik, Reb Leyb Sores, visited him.[14] According to legend, he was in charge of all the *lamed vovnik zaddikim* [Thirty-Six Righteous].[15] He would visit them twice a year, riding on a cloud, bring them their means of support, and instruct them on how to behave. In this case, when Reb Leyb Sores visited Reb Velvele, he ordered him to leave his shtetl and settle in Zhitomir.

Reb Velvele Vohl did as directed. He spent the last years of his life as the sexton in the synagogue of Zhitomir. Reb Velvele of Zhitomir was known to pace about the synagogue courtyard every day while saying: "I am pacing and pacing and he is coming back."

After his death, he was buried in the cemetery of Zhitomir where there is a brick shtibl over his grave.

6. THE GRAVE OF RABBI LEYB "BAAL-PARNOSE"

In the old cemetery of Shargorod, there is a grave of a famous zaddik by the name of Reb Leyb Baal Parnose.* The old folk say that the zaddik Reb Leyb left his

---

*H. A. Krupnik tells a similar story about Reb Leyb in *Reshumot* (new series), 2:106.

children a will in which he instructed them not to pray for their livelihood at his grave until ten generations had passed since his death, for he would be unable to help them, as a result of the incident described below.

When Reb Leyb was still a small child in diapers, a band of robbers—one of many who frequently wrought havoc in Ukraine—attacked Shargorod. They pillaged and murdered, and everyone's life hung in the balance. His parents, along with several other Jews, managed to escape to the surrounding mountains, where they sought refuge in a cave. However, before they could do as much as catch their breath, the bandits had already figured out their hiding spot and were in pursuit. They had no other choice but to leave the cave at once and search for a new hiding place. In all the chaos and the darkness of night, Reb Leyb's parents forgot him in the cave. When it eventually occurred to them that they did not have him, it was too late to turn back. The murderers had already surrounded the cave.

His parents cried, grieved, and could not be consoled. Several days later, when the band of robbers had departed, the embittered, despairing parents returned to the cave to retrieve their child's body so they could at least give him a proper Jewish burial. However, they were totally shocked when they entered the cave and found their child alive. He was lying in his diapers, exactly how they had left him. He was sucking his little thumb and was lively and healthy. Just two deep creases had formed under his eyes and led to his mouth.

Figure 3.2. Agile like the deer (wood carving by Shloyme Yudovin).

Reb Leyb grew up to be a great zaddik and lived his whole life in bitter poverty.

Before he died, he called his children [to gather around him] and related that when he was in the cave, he kept himself nourished by sucking his thumb (which explains why it was thinner than his other fingers) and by drinking his tears, the reason for the two creases that formed on his face and extended from his eyes to his mouth. [He explained] that the miracle that happened for him was so great that he consumed not only his *parnose* [livelihood] but also his children's and grandchildren's [livelihood] for ten generations.

The Jews of Shargorod confirmed that [Reb Leyb's] children and children's children for ten generations, and wherever they were found, remained poor for all of their lives, paupers in seven rags.[16]

7. THE GRAVE OF RABBI LIBER HA-GADOL IN BERDICHEV

In the old cemetery, which already lay almost entirely in ruins—the headstones eroded by the rain and some cracked into several pieces—there is but one headstone, although itself lopsided and half sunken in the earth, on which one can still clearly make out the following inscription:

> [Here lies... the martyr Reb Eliezer Liber... who died in the plague in the year 5531]

It is said that in the year 5531 (1771), a terrible plague broke out in Berdichev. Hundreds of people died every day. The rabbis and communal leaders of Berdichev took all the customary measures: they composed special prayers,* they repaired the fence around the cemetery, and they even put up a black *chuppah* [wedding canopy], but not a single one of these measures did anything to stop the plague.[17]

When the zaddik, Rabbi Liber, realized that *kalu kol ha-kitsin* [all possible means had been exhausted/all hope was lost, Babylonian Talmud Sanhedrin 97:2] and that the whole city would soon meet its doom, he called on the judges, the heads of the yeshivah, and the communal leaders, and, before all of them, he took it on himself to be the *korban edah* [the communal sacrifice] for his city.[18]

---

*The special prayers were written on parchment in scribal writing and were kept in the Torah ark in Rebbe Liber's synagogue for use in times of trouble. On Rebbe Liber's synagogue, see p. 49.

That same night, Rebbe Liber died, and, the very next day, the plague ended.

8. THE GRAVE OF THE "MARTYRS OF PAVOLOCH"

Beside the large synagogue in Zhitomir, there is a headstone connected to the following historical incident.

More than half of the headstone is sunken in the earth and [although] the letters have been worn away by time and washed away by the rain, one can still make out the words: "Martyrs of Pavoloch."[19]

I was told the history of the "Martyrs of Pavoloch" in an old people's home in Zhitomir. One of the old men assured me that he had seen with his own eyes in the community pinkes, which had been destroyed in a great fire, the story he was about to tell. And the old man's story went something like what follows.

"Pavoloch, a small shtetl not far from Zhitomir, belonged at that time to a duke who lived in a village on the other side of the Zhitomir bridge. Someone once informed on the Jews of Pavoloch to the duke, claiming that they were preparing a revolt against him and would no longer pay taxes. As a result, the duke issued a decree, prohibiting the Jews from congregating in groups and, if more than three Jews were found together, *there is one law for them, that they be executed* [see Esther 4:11], they would be sentenced to death. The duke appointed a guard to keep constant watch over the Jews and make sure they were not violating his decree.

"The rabbi of Pavoloch at the time, Rabbi Akiva, would always celebrate the Passover seders with a minyan. At the seder on the first night of Passover, eleven of his closest companions secretly gathered in his home, in disregard of the duke's decree, and under the light of the moon began to celebrate the seder together.

"The duke's evil minions caught wind of [their activities]. They surrounded the rabbi's house and brought Rabbi Akiva and his eleven companions to the duke, who had them locked up on the basis of his decree.

"Several days later, the verdict was issued—they would be executed in the most terrible of ways."

The elderly man removed his glasses, wiped his moist eyes, and continued:

"Several of the imprisoned Jews were put in barrels, whose interiors were lined with long nails, and they were rolled down the nearby mountain and were stabbed to death by the nails; others were tied to the tails of horses and dragged around the city until they died; some had sharp stakes jammed into their anuses and were carried in the air until they breathed their last; others were bound by their feet to two trees that had been bent down. The [trees] were then released and the Jews were torn in two. And, as for Rabbi Akiva, the duke ordered him to be quartered, that is, to be cut into four parts and then to have them hung on all four city gates, leading to Zhitomir, in order to deter the Jews from rebelling."

The elderly man caught his breath and continued:

"The duke had the eleven corpses collected and buried in a single grave in the gentile cemetery. He appointed a special guard to keep watch over the grave, so that the Jews would not steal the bodies and give them a proper Jewish burial.

"Rabbi Akiva appeared a few days later in a dream to the sexton of the great synagogue in Zhitomir and ordered him to dig up the martyrs and bury them in the Jewish cemetery. Moreover, he [Rabbi Akiva] promised him that he would merit being buried with them.

"The sexton was ready to sacrifice his life for the sake of this great mitzvah. So he disguised himself as a whiskey trader and, by various means, successfully intoxicated the guard until he fell asleep. Then, with the help of several other Jews, he dug up the corpses of the eleven martyrs, stuffed them into a sack, collected the four parts of Rabbi Akiva's body, transported them by wagon to Zhitomir in the dead of night, and immediately buried them beside the synagogue in which he was the sexton.

"That same night," concluded the old man, "The sexton died, and, at his request, he was buried with the martyrs of Pavoloch, and the aforementioned headstone was put on their grave."

In the pinkes that is kept in the synagogue of Zhitomir, I saw a list of the (thirteen) names of the martyrs of Pavoloch, including the sexton. The story itself is not in the pinkes. It is also worth noting that after the old man finished telling the story about the martyrs, a second elderly man, who was sitting nearby, chimed in:

"That is not the end of the story. There's more. It goes like this: on Sunday morning several days after Rabbi Akiva's body parts were hung on the city gates, the duke, *yimach shemo* [may his name be blotted out], his witch of a wife, and their only daughter, the '*panienkę*' [Polish for young lady; can be euphemism for prostitute], were headed to Zhitomir to attend church. They were traveling in a carriage that was being pulled by four pairs of *stajenne* [Polish, stable] horses in tandem. When they were crossing over the bridge, the wicked duke caught sight of the part of Rebbe Akiva's body that he had ordered to be hung on the bridge. He snatched the whip from the driver's hand and struck the body part, screaming with chutzpah [arrogantly] in Polish, 'Gadaj, Akiva!' (Speak, Akiva), and breaking into loud laughter: Ha Ha Ha and Ho Ho Ho! And then, all of all sudden, the horses bolted [out of fright], the carriage shot over the bridge, landing straight into the river, and the duke, his wife, his daughter, the driver, and all the horses drowned."

"No! No!" hollered several of the elderly men all at once, "The driver was rescued!"

The Jewish sense of justice and the Jewish sense of compassion would not allow a person to be killed who was not directly implicated in the crime.

9. CHAIM SON OF CHAYA WHO WAS BORN IN HIS MOTHER'S GRAVE

In the old cemetery in Ostroh there is a four-sided gravestone on which these raised letters are inscribed:

Here lies ... Chaim ben Chay[a] who was born in his mother's grave.

Regarding this gravestone, an old man from Ostroh told us that he personally saw the following tale concerning this Chaim ben Chaya recorded in the old community pinkes, which was destroyed in a fire years later.

There was a young couple who once lived in Ostroh. He was named Shmuel, and she, Chaya. She came from a rich family, and he was a successful lumber merchant who sent rafts carrying timber by water to Germany. The couple lived in peace and harmony and were strongly in love. And although several years had passed since their wedding, they were not yet blessed with a child of their own.

On account of his extensive business deals, from time to time Shmuel would have to travel with the lumber rafts in order to settle his accounts with his regular vendors in Germany as well as to make new connections with merchants in other cities and countries. Such trips usually lasted for several months and sometimes for an entire year. Once, after having embarked on such a long voyage, when he was already on the road for several weeks, he suddenly realized that he had left behind at home, simply forgotten to bring with him: the accounts, contracts, receipts, and even the addresses of his customers. It was clear to him that without all of these papers and documents his trip would be for nothing. He thought for only a moment before stopping the raft of lumber midcourse and renting a fast boat home.

As he approached his city, he did not want anyone to find out about his accident and run the chance of being made a laughingstock. So, he traveled in disguise through the city until he arrived safely at home.

His wife was overjoyed. They both celebrated. He stayed the night and the following day, at the break of dawn, he grabbed the necessary papers, said goodbye to his beloved wife, and, in disguise, returned to the long journey ahead of him.

No one in town knew that he had come home. It was known, however, that a strange male visitor had stayed the night with his wife.

And, as a result of that night, his wife became pregnant.

Once she reached the point when it was obvious that she was pregnant, the whole city began talking about the night that the strange man spent with her, and she was suspected of harlotry. People began to look askance at her and distance themselves from her.

She noticed the malicious glances that people were casting in her direction. However, she could not make things better. There were no telephones, or telegraphs, at the time, for her to tell her husband the happy news, that God had blessed her womb and that she had become pregnant.

With an embittered heart, she stayed on the lookout day and night for her husband, her dear Shmuel, who she hoped would finally come home and remove this ugly stain, this terrible suspicion, from her.

And now the baby's due date was fast approaching and the women of the city, even her closest neighbors, kept at a distance and wanted nothing to do with her: "She's an *eyshes ish* [lit., a man's wife; an adulteress]—a whore!" they whispered in secret.

And the larger her stomach grew, the angrier the community became, until the whole matter was brought before the *bes din* [Jewish court]. The rabbi made a thorough investigation, receiving testimony from reliable persons who swore in the name of God that they saw the stranger spend the night at her home. As a result, the rabbi ordered the court sexton to proclaim in all the houses of worship that said woman, Chaya, is banished from the camp for the sin of harlotry and no one may be in her presence [lit., "four cubits," the rabbinic expression for the legally defined space of an individual].

When she went into labor, no midwife would deliver the child. And the outcast woman experienced great suffering before she gave birth.

She was laid to rest, her child still in her stomach, in the spot by the cemetery fence that was designated for sinners. Her funeral took place on a cold winter day. A blizzard whipped up the snow and blinded the eyes. By the time the burial society had returned from the funeral, the sun had already set.

Just then, her husband, Shmuel, the lumber merchant, returned from his distant voyage. And, as expected in such weather, he was wrapped in his warm, winter clothing—his head covered in a tall, fur cap—making it difficult to recognize him.

He came across the pallbearers and asked them:

"Tell me, Jews, who died!"

They answered him:

"We buried a young woman who died in labor. But it's nothing to get bent up over. She was wicked and got what she deserved. Her man went abroad on a business trip, and she fooled around with a stranger whose bastard child she was going to have. She died in pain while having [the child] that's who we just buried."

As soon as he heard this, his countenance darkened. He immediately realized what had happened. And that he was responsible for her death. As swift as an arrow, he dashed to the rabbi, broke out in a loud cry, and told [him] everything, from start to finish [of] how he came home that night in disguise. "I got her pregnant. It's my child. The suspicion is unfounded!" And he sobbed and wringed his hands.

Upon hearing this, the rabbi called his court into session, and then the burial society was quickly dispatched to retrieve her body from the grave, so that the child could be extracted from her, as required by Jewish law.

Everyone was shocked as the grave was being opened and they saw a living child, laying [there], sucking from her lifeless breast.

Only then did everyone realize that she was a holy, kosher soul and that the community had badly wronged her.

Figure 3.3. Wood carving by Shloyme Yudovin.

She was reburied in a place of honor. A communal fast was declared, and the entire community came to her grave to beg for forgiveness. The rabbi himself recited kaddish for her for an entire year.

The child was named Chaim after his mother Chaya. His father enjoyed a lot of *nakhes* [pleasure] from him. And Chaim lived to a ripe old age.

When he passed away, the following [text] was engraved on his headstone:

> Here lies Chaim, the son of Chaya, who was born in his mother's grave.

10. THE GRAVE OF A YOUNG MARTYR WHO WAS BURIED ALIVE

In Ostroh, to this day, may be found the grand palace where, in years past, lived the duke who once controlled the city.

Not far from the palace, there is a headstone on which the following words can still be easily read:

> Here lies the young martyr who was buried alive.

It is said that the young man was very handsome, a *yefe toar* [Hebrew, same phrase used to describe Joseph in Genesis 39:6]. He was tall, had big bright eyes, and [stood] straight as a cedar tree. His parents owned an upscale shop with the finest foods, sweets, and an array of wines and meads. The noblemen of the region would come to make purchases, and the young man would often lend a hand in the shop.

It happened that the duke's only daughter was traveling through Ostroh and stopped by the store to get a few things. The young man, who was there at the time, attended to her.

One look at him and she was captivated by his beauty and could not take her eyes off of him. It was as if his luminous face had bewitched her. She lusted after this beautiful young man and obsessed over him even after returning to her palace.

She could not sleep a wink that night. Her mind was filled with images of his beautiful figure, and her lust for him burned like hellfire.

Early the next morning, she ordered her finest carriage to be harnessed and sent her trusty servant to invite the young man to her palace.

The carriage, however, returned empty; the young man did not go to her.

The scorned, capricious princess concocted a diabolical plan to get what she wanted and have the young man brought to her. She called on several of her strongest servants and ordered them to kidnap him from his home, or snatch him on the street, so long as they brought him to her unharmed.

And that is exactly what happened. The young man was kidnapped, forced into the carriage, and brought to her palace.

She locked him in the palace and came to him several times a day, kissing and groping him and tempting him to sin.

This went on for several days, and, with each day, her kisses grew ever more passionate and her lust all the more fiery. However, the young man remained just as cold to her as before.

Seeing that she would not get through to him with sweet talk, she came to him in the middle of the night completely naked and wrapped him in her arms. She fondled and kissed him with so much fiery passion that her soul departed from her body. She was consumed by her own hellfire.

When the duke found out what happened, he became so enraged that he ordered the young man be buried alive in the palace garden not far from his late daughter's grave.

Years later, the Jews of Ostroh placed the aforementioned headstone on the grave of the young man who had martyred himself in the name of God and was buried alive.

11. THE SHTIBL OF THE "BE'ER HEITEV" AND HIS WIFE

In the old cemetery of Mogilev, there is a shtibl over the grave of a martyr. By the western wall of the shtibl stands a tombstone, on which is inscribed:

> Here lie the holy martyrs who were consumed by a fire, Yeshaya, the son of Avraham, the author of the book "Be'er Heitev," and his God-fearing wife, Rekhil, the daughter of Ribaz.[20] They both died on the 13th of Iyar, 5483 (1773). May their souls be bound up in the bond of life.[21]

Rabbi Yeshaya served as the town rabbi in Mogilev. He was said to have been a great scholar of both *nigle* [exoteric subjects] and *nister* [esoteric subjects] and studied Torah day and night. One day, while learning, he became perplexed by a matter of Jewish law. For weeks on end, he poured over texts and sought out an explanation but was unable to make sense of the complex matter. He wrote to many of the great rabbis and sages of his generation, soliciting responsa and seeking an explanation, but none of the responsa he received helped clarify this difficult and confusing Halakic question.

Rabbi Yeshaya was greatly distressed and decided to adjure the *Sar Ha-Torah* [lit., The Prince of the Torah; the angel in charge of the Torah according to Jewish mysticism], for he alone could clarify this baffling matter. In order to do so, he began to sanctify and purify himself through prayer and ritual immersion, fasted every Monday and Thursday, isolated himself from others, meditated on certain *kavanos* [Hebrew, kabbalistic "intentions"], and sought the secret of *tzerufei-shemos* [Hebrew, kabbalistic method of combining the divine names for theurgic effects]. This went on for days and weeks, until one fine day, when he was standing there, in purity and holiness, and praying with great *kavone* [intention] and making *tserufim* [combinations] of divine names, he suddenly saw a fiery angel descending toward him from above. He immediately realized that it was not the *Sar Ha-Torah* who was descending toward him, but the *Sar Ha-Eysh* [The Prince of Fire]. And, in the blink of an eye, he knew that he had made an error somewhere in the combinations of the divine names, and, instead of summoning the *Sar Ha-Torah*, he had summoned the *Sar Ha-Eysh*. He became terrified, for he knew the great danger that was in store for the city: the merciless *Sar Ha-Eysh* could, God forbid, destroy [the city], for it is common knowledge that an angel must carry out its mission. He hurried to tell his wife of the imminent danger and both of them went to meet the arriving *Sar Ha-Eysh*, fell on their faces before him, and declared that, since they, alone, were responsible for troubling him, they themselves were ready to receive the full punishment connected to his mission. They were ready to commit martyrdom [*kidush hashem*], provided that no one else would, God forbid, be harmed.

Rabbi Yeshaya returned home with his wife, where they locked themselves inside and began to recite the final confession. A fire took hold of all four sides of the house, and they were consumed as a *korban olah* [burnt offering], in holy martyrdom for the sake of God's name, the Torah, and the city. And no one outside of the house was affected by the fire, not even a little.

After the fire subsided, the ashes of Reb Yeshaya and his wife Rekhil were gathered and buried in the old cemetery. The shtibl was built over their grave and the aforementioned headstone was placed there.

Until recently, there were charity boxes hanging in the prayerhouses of Mogilev, which bore the inscription: "Yahrzeit candles for Be'er Heitev." For it is said that soon after the incident, Rabbi Yeshaya, the Be'er Heitev, appeared in a dream to several important men in the town, all in the same night, to rouse them to never forget to light *neshome* [soul] candles [i.e., yahrzeit candles] on the anniversary of their death. Ever since then, special *pushkes* [charity boxes], bearing the above-mentioned inscription, have been installed in all the prayerhouses. The money that was collected went to buy candles and ensure that they were lit on the day of their [the couple's] yahrzeit.

An elderly man, who was sitting nearby as the tale was being related to us, added that he remembers how several decades earlier the community had forgotten to light the *neshome* candles on the anniversary of their death. That same day, a great fire broke out and the entire city would have, God forbid, perished, if they had not acted fast. The rabbi sent the sexton to announce to everyone that they should come to the large synagogue immediately. He lit the yahrzeit candles himself, said an *El-Mole-Rakhamim* [prayer said for a deceased person], recited kaddish, and then the fire subsided.

12. REB HERSHENYU AND THE POLISH CHURCH

A

In the small shtetl of Chechelnik, we were shown a tombstone that was worn away by [years of] stormy weather. The words, however, were still visible enough to read:

> Here lies the martyr Zvi Hirsh, known as Reb Hershenyu

The date is either 5502 (1742) or 5520 (1760).[22]

Nearly every Jew in town could tell the following exquisite tale about Reb Hershenyu:*

During one of his frequent visits to Chechelnik, the duke to whom the town belonged decided to build a Polish church. He brought in a cardinal from Warsaw and put him in charge of building the planned church.

The duke and the cardinal chose a plot of land on which to build that bordered the eastern part of the old Jewish cemetery.

Before they started building [there], they brought in several eminent Catholic priests, who sanctified the site [of the church] with religious ceremonies: they sprinkled "holy water" and burned incense. They also held a huge banquet, which brought a myriad of priests from the surrounding cities and villages. The banquet lasted for several days straight.

As soon as the festivities were over, the work of building began. On the very first day, they dug a deep and wide pit to lay the foundation. The builders laid four massive cornerstones in the four corners [of the pit], and the masons spent the day filling the length and width of the foundation with bricks. The first day of work lasted until sunset.

The following day, when the workers returned to work, they discovered the cornerstones and bricks on the eastern side of the foundation (the side that bordered the old Jewish cemetery) had been cast out [of the pit].

---

*A similar variant appears in *Reshumot*, 1:398, Sh. Vigderman, "Kokho shel Zaddik."

When the cardinal who was in charge of the construction project saw what had happened, he immediately blamed the Jews: the Jews must have come at night and caused the destruction. Livid, the cardinal gathered his workers and they all went to the duke, told him about the incident and demanded that the Jews, who were without a doubt responsible [for the incident], be punished.

The duke was by nature a good person. He had never done anything bad to the Jews before, so he did not accept the bishop's denunciation in this case either. He told him to get a hold of himself and control his anger. They would see what unfolded tomorrow.

The following day, the workers enthusiastically returned to work. They placed the cornerstones back in their original spots, and the masons relaid the foundation with bricks.

The duke deliberated throughout the day and assigned a special guard consisting of several robust peasants. He ordered them to go to the construction site in secret right after the workers had departed and keep watch for the entire night.

And so, as soon as the sun had set and the workers had gone home, the special guards arrived, hid behind the piles of bricks and construction materials, and kept their eyes on the entire length of the east side [of the foundation], which bordered the Jewish cemetery. They kept "watch" in order to apprehend the guilty parties.

In vain they strained their eyes in the darkness of the night . . . alas, no one appeared.

Then, when midnight arrived, the guards suddenly saw the heavy cornerstones rising out of the eastern part of the foundation and the light red bricks flying in the air like fiery birds, one after the other. A great fear, a dark terror, befell the guards. Scared to death, they ran to the duke and told him what they had seen with their own eyes.

After much deliberation, the duke concluded that the only possible explanation was that there were Jews buried underneath the foundation on the eastern border of the Jewish cemetery. The dead could not bear the weight of these stones and bricks, so they threw off the entire foundation and bricks.

The duke told the cardinal his hypothesis, and he accepted it. However, he was not alarmed. On the contrary, he told the duke to send for the rabbi and the important Jewish householders in the shtetl, and to demand with strong language that they convince their dead not to interfere with the construction of the church, or else—he should warn them—there would be terrible consequences.

The duke followed his advice and, early the next day, sent for the rabbi and the prominent townsmen and said to them:

"Jews! You should know that your dead will not let us build our church! If I had known in advance that Jews were buried there, I would have never built the church there in the first place. But I didn't know that and now it's a done deal. The site has been sanctified by our high clergymen, so there can be no talk of not building. Therefore, I kindly command you Jews, for your own sake, to persuade your dead to rest in their graves and stop interfering with the construction [of our church]. I know that you can accomplish this!"

The duke's stern words left the Jews paralyzed. No one could utter a word. The duke shot cold, piercing glances at them and waited for an answer.

The rabbi gathered his strength, mustered up enough courage, and, with great effort and a good measure of humility, declared:

"Merciful prince! We promise you to do everything within our power. We will do all that we can do and that we have the authority to do. We will pray day and night. We will prostrate ourselves on their graves, cry and lament, and beg the dead to have mercy and not interfere with your work. However, we cannot guarantee that they will obey us, for it is outside of our power to force them to heed our requests. The dead live in a different world, one in which we, the living, do not have the slightest power. Therefore, we beg you, noble lord, that if our prayers and supplications are, God forbid, futile and the dead do not relent, may you, great duke, spare us from your wrath!"

The duke suddenly became incensed. His face burned with a hellish fire. He approached the frightened Jews, positioned himself face-to-face with them, and thundered:

"Listen here! If your dead disturb our holy building again, I am warning you that I will have all of your holy buildings destroyed. I will not leave a stone unturned. My laborers will go back to their daily work and I will wait a month's time. Remember what I have said to you! You will pay dearly!"

The duke said what he had to say and then quickly disappeared.

With downturned heads and trembling knees, scared to death, the distinguished Jews with the rabbi at their head left the palace and returned to the city. News of the prince's evil decree quickly spread throughout the shtetl. Jews in Chechelnik, men, women, and children, gathered in the great synagogue to pray and brainstorm ways to mollify and appease the dead. Then they all went to the cemetery and prayed collectively over their graves. They shed rivers of tears, begged for forgiveness, and lit memorial candles. Yet nothing helped. The dead remained as stubbornly unyielding as before: whatever the builders constructed in the daytime was demolished after midnight.

B

At that time in Chechelnik, there lived a simple Jew, almost an *amorets* [ignorant person]. However, he would pray with great fervor and loved to recite Psalms.

People called him Hershenyu. He fraternized with the common folk: with coachmen, craftsmen, and village peddlers. He traded in whatever presented itself at a given moment. He was mostly seen hanging around the marketplace, doing business with male and female peasants, and roaming about with them. He was also quite frequently seen in the taverns having a drink. The tavern keepers, incidentally, considered him a welcome guest, for they believed that whatever barrel of liquor he drank from was blessed with good luck.

The final day of the duke's deadline arrived. All the Jews gathered in the great synagogue where they prayed and sought a last-minute way to appease the dead—but nothing came of it. Everyone's faces were filled with hopelessness. The congregants wailed loudly. Then, suddenly, Hershenyu rose among the crowd. Bent over, he slowly made his way onto the *bime* [synagogue platform] and quietly announced in a few words that he would try to persuade the dead that very night ... at midnight.

Right after the evening prayers, Hershenyu gathered a minyan of ten Jews and led them to the cemetery. They all arrayed themselves by the edge of the freshly laid foundation and recited Psalms until midnight. At midnight, when the stones and bricks began to fly out of the foundation, Hershenyu stood there silently and waited until the dead threw out the last brick and it grew still. At that point, Hershenyu bent over the open pit, his face beaming into the thick darkness of the night, and, with a booming voice that resounded with a thousand echoes, he yelled into the pit:

> Listen, you holy dead. We come to you now as loyal messengers of our community of Chechelnik to ask for forgiveness and mercy from you. We are pleading for forgiveness from you because our hearts are deeply pained by the fact that your rest has been disturbed. We want you to know with all assurance that this disruption will not go on for much longer. The building will soon be completed, and you will no longer be disturbed in your eternal rest. We are also asking for your mercy because if you continue to interfere with the laying of the foundation and prevent [the church] from being built, all of our holy places will, God forbid, be destroyed, on your account, and it is possible that we will be driven out of the city. It is for this reason that we ask you, holy dead ones, to have mercy on us, the living, and do not allow our sanctuaries to be desecrated and our community to be destroyed. And, if the stones and bricks are, indeed, too heavy to bear, and you cannot stand it, we beg of you, in the name of God and in the name of this holy community, abandon your places here and relocate to our new cemetery, where you can find your final resting place. If, however, you choose to remain stubborn and reject our plea, I, Tsvi-Hirsh ben [son of] Chaya-Sore, am warning you that I have the authority to expel you from these parts by force and can even drive you all the way to

the *Mountains of Darkness*.[23] Holy dead ones! We stretch out our hands, once more, in supplication and beg for your mercy: do not make us use force against you. Sanctify and make the name of God great, for both our sakes! *Yehi shem ha mevorakh me-ata ve-ad olam* [May the name of the Lord God be blessed forever and always]!

As soon as Hershenyu finished speaking, a fiery pillar arose from the pit and then formed into a great many glowing, sparkling flames. For several seconds, the flames twisted and turned over the open pit of the foundation. And then, all at once, they took off for the new cemetery and disappeared among the graves.

Following that night, there were no more disruptions to the building of the church. And, to this day, the Polish church can still be found standing next to the old cemetery.

When Hershenyu died, he was buried with great honor in the new cemetery, and the above-mentioned headstone, bearing the inscription:

Here lies the holy man Reb Tsvi-Hirsh, nicknamed Hershenyu

was placed there. Over the years, the grave was treated with great holiness.

We recorded a similar variant [of this story] in Korets. There, too, a monastery was erected near an old Jewish cemetery—and everything that was built there during the day sunk throughout the night. And none of the ceremonies

Figure 3.4. Agile like the deer (wood carving).

and incense burning by the high-ranking priests, archimandrites, and bishops who came there were of any help. An elderly priest, likely a convert [from Judaism], advised them that a Jew should begin to lay the foundation. And so a Jew from Korets, an ironsmith named Moshe Zalyoznik, agreed to lay the first stone of the foundation—and it actually helped. The monastery was built, and the Jews of Korets referred to it as Moshe Zalyoznik's Monastery.

13. THE GRAVE OF RABBI AHARON DOKTOR GORDA IN OSTROH

A

Among the hundreds of graves of zaddikim, geonim, rabbis, and famous authors in the cemetery of Ostroh, there is also a round tombstone with the following inscription:

> Here lies the venerable elder who went and served sages, who served the rabbi and holy lamp, the Maggid of the holy community of Mezeritch. Our teacher Aharon the son of our teacher, the rabbi Shimshon Doktor Gorda, who passed away on the 26th of Adar Sheni, 5570 [April 1, 1810] may his soul be bound up in the bond of everlasting life.

The Jews of Ostroh tell the following wonderful tale about Rabbi Aharon Doktor Gorda.[24]

Two wealthy men came to the Maggid of Mezeritch with a lawsuit. One was a *misnaged* [traditional opponent of the Hasidim], and the other a Hasid of [the Maggid of] Mezeritch.[25] The Maggid settled their [legal] dispute. The day after the proceedings, the *misnaged* went to the Maggid of Mezeritch to bid him farewell, and the Maggid said this to him: "You should keep in mind and not forget that a sick person is not only helped by the remedies prescribed by a doctor but also by the merit of the doctor himself, for every doctor is accompanied by an angel, and the czar's doctor is accompanied by none other than the angel Raphael himself."[26]

The *misnaged* was caught off guard by the suddenness of the Maggid's words. He shrugged his shoulders and thought to himself: "There is no telling what occurs to a Hasidic rebbe!"

Soon after returning home, the wealthy *misnaged* was pulled back into his many business affairs and the Maggid's strange words soon vanished from his memory altogether.

Several years later the rich man grew dangerously ill. The best doctors gave up all hope of recovery and declared him to be a terminal case. And then, when his illness had taken a turn for the worse, and he was stricken with a high temperature, something shot through his mind like a bolt of lightning, and he suddenly remembered the Maggid's words: "The czar's doctor is accompanied by none other than the angel Raphael himself." With great strain, he called his family over and ordered them to send a special messenger to Petersburg right away; money should be of no concern and they should see to it that the czar's personal doctor, Doktor Gorda, who was famous throughout all of Russia, be brought to him.

The messenger departed immediately. And, with much effort, intercession, and great sums of money, he managed to bring the czar's doctor, the great expert, Doktor Gorda.

When the doctor had examined the patient and saw that he would soon die, that his time had come, he called [the man's] wife and children into another room and bluntly explained to them that his efforts were futile: "I am only a healer of the sick, not a reviver of the dead!" Having said what he had to say, he gathered his instruments, said goodbye to the members of [the man's] household, and went to the door.

However, before stepping over the threshold, he took one last, sideways glance at the sick man and was astounded by the sight of [him] looking straight at him with his eyes wide open. Surprised, the doctor turned around and went to the sick man, took his pulse, and was greatly astonished by his sudden improvement. He did not leave after all and quickly wrote down a prescription and sent someone to pick it up. In the meantime, he sat beside the sick man on his bed and could not take his eyes off him, for he noticed how much he was improving with every minute. When they brought the medicine and the sick man took the first teaspoon of it, he begged Doktor Gorda, with a weak voice, to bend closer toward him. And the sick man told him that years ago, the Maggid of Mezeritch had enjoined him to remember "that the czar's doctor is accompanied by the angel Raphael himself."

The aphorism of the Mezeritcher greatly pleased Doktor Gorda, and it made a strong impression on him. He jotted down the name and the city of the Maggid and returned to Petersburg.

The unusual case of the terminally ill patient and the extraordinary prophecy of the Maggid gave Doktor Gorda no rest. His heart began to pull him to Mezeritch... and he grew melancholic and paced around pensively.

It is even related that a short time after this incident, Doktor Gorda left the czar's court, went to Rebbe Dov Ber in Mezeritch, and said:

"Rebbe! I have come for you to heal my soul and I ask you to let me heal your body! Allow me to stay with you permanently!"

The Maggid agreed.

Doktor Gorda took off his military clothing and removed the sword that he wore by his side. He changed into traditional Hasidic garb and became the resident physician in the rebbe's court. Doktor Gorda devoted his free time to *tshuve* [repentance], *tfile* [prayer], the study of *toyre* [Torah], and the giving of *tsedakah* [charity].* He remained in the Maggid of Mezeritch's court for the rest of the Maggid's life.

After the Maggid's passing, the community of Ostroh made him their district doctor. He always sat in the study house and learned [Torah], so when a sick person was in need of [his services], everyone knew exactly where to find him.

The town rabbi of Ostroh at the time was Rabbi Asher Koretser, the author of the book *Ma'ayan Ha-Chokhmah*.[27] Doktor Gorda loved to debate him about all sorts of topics, including medical matters. Curiously, Gorda, the doctor, was not a huge fan of medicine. He always said that Jews do not need doctors at all and that medical treatments are also unnecessary. A sick person need only believe with his whole heart that the Master of the Universe alone heals the sick and that belief alone is sufficient for a sick person to be healed. On the other hand, Reb Asher, the rabbi, was a big believer in doctors and medical treatments. He would argue that it is explicitly written, "And he shall provide for his cure" (Exodus 21:19). The [rabbinic] sages expound regarding this: "The physician has therefore been given the authority to heal" (BT Berachot, 60), and it is thereby inferred that a doctor does God's mission and that remedies are necessary to heal the sick.

And then, one day, during one such debate with the rabbi, the door to the study house opened and a woman collapsed inside, crying. She begged Doktor Gorda to come save her sick husband, the father of her seven children, who was laid out in excruciating pain and whose strength was leaving him completely.

---

*One time, Doktor Gorda came to the Maggid distraught. He showed him [the verse] in the Mishnah: *Tov she-ba-rofim le-gehenom—der bester fun di doktoyrim iz ongebreyt farn gehenem* [The best physicians are headed for Gehenom] (Kiddushin 4:14) and told him that he would no longer be a doctor. The Maggid calmed him down and explained that this Mishnah's aphorism referred only to a physician who did not believe in God, for such a physician would usually tell the sick person: "Take the remedy that I am giving you and you will get better." By saying this, he negates the blessing of *Refaeinu*, "Heal us, God, and we will be healed," and so now, instead of eighteen blessings in the *Shmone Esre* [the "eighteen benedictions" or Amidah prayer service], there are only seventeen, which is the *gematria* [numerical equivalence] of *Tov* [Hebrew, for "good"]. And so, this is what the Mishnah actually meant: "*Tov she-ba-rofim*," a physician who reduces the eighteen blessings of the *Shmone Esre* to seventeen is deserving of Gehenom [Hell]. However, a doctor who says to the sick person, "Take this remedy and God will make you healthy," does not negate the blessing of *Rafaeinu*, and, therefore, all of the blessings of the *Shmone Esre* remain intact. Such a doctor sanctifies the name of heaven and his end is Gan Eden [paradise].

Doktor Gorda, who was not one to let someone beg for too long, especially a poor person, immediately followed the woman as she led him through twisted, impoverished alleyways, until they came to a half-collapsed wooden shack outside of the town.

When Doktor Gorda went inside to examine the sick man, he realized right away that he did not have much longer to live. However, he did not have the heart to break the news to the desperate, unfortunate woman, who was sobbing uncontrollably and tearing the hair from her head. So, for the sake of appearances, he wrote down a prescription and ordered that the sick man be given a tablespoon [of the medicine] every hour.

Doktor Gorda returned to the study house in low spirits. The hopelessness of the dying man's situation and the disturbing images of poverty and destitution that had unfolded before his eyes would not give him a moment's rest. He could not focus his thoughts and learn, and, also at night, in his bed, he was unable to fall asleep.

As soon as dawn began to break, he got out of bed, quickly got dressed, and went shopping for food: milk, bread, sugar, and tea. He then made his way to the dilapidated small house of the sick man, with the sole intention of bringing comfort to the unfortunate lady, who was mostly certainly already a widow, and to feed her children, who were most certainly orphans, for he did not have the slightest doubt that the dying man was no longer among the living.

When he neared the house, he expected to hear the sound of mourning. He was greatly astonished, however, by the silence and calm about the house. He cautiously opened the door, crossed over the threshold, and saw the sick man lying peacefully in bed. He went over to him, checked his pulse, and, wonder of wonders, it was almost back to normal. His condition had taken a turn for the better, and it now looked likely that he was on his way to making a full recovery.

Once the lady noticed the doctor, she kissed his hands and thanked him profusely for the wonderful treatment that had taken a sick person who was almost dead and restored him to life.

Doktor Gorda just stood there, his eyes blinking and mouth agape. He asked for the medicine... the woman carried an earthenware pot to him and said:

"Herr Doktor, here's the remedy! I did just as you instructed. As soon as you left, I lit a fire and boiled water in this pot here. I added the prescription, which you, Herr Doktor, wrote, to the boiling water and gave my husband a tablespoon every hour. And thanks and praise be to God, and then to you, the sickness subsided. My husband opened his eyes and improved by the hour. And now, as you can see, he feels like a new man. May God reward you for the great kindness that you did us!"

Doktor Gorda took the pot from the woman and placed it in a corner. He once again examined and took the pulse of the sick man and confirmed that he

Figure 3.5. Pallbearers at a funeral (wood carving by Shloyme Yudovin).

would soon make a full recovery. He said goodbye and, with the pot in hand, almost sprinted back to the study house. He told Rabbi Asher Korets in detail what had happened, showed him the pot, and triumphantly concluded: "So what do you have to say now, Reb Asher? Are doctors actually necessary? Are medical remedies real?"

Doktor Gorda lived to a ripe old age. He was buried in Ostroh among the great men [of the town]. He had one daughter, who was called "Khanele di Doktorshe," for she too worked in medicine, which she had learned from her father, the zaddik.

14. TWO GRAVES—A RABBI'S AND A BEADLE'S—NEXT TO ONE ANOTHER

A

Around three hundred years ago, there was a rabbi by the name of Rebbe Dovid Tsvi Auerbach who lived in Shargorod.* He was a great Talmudic scholar, but also a very fussy and irascible man.[28]

---

*H. A. Krupnik relates a different version of this tale in *Reshumot*, new series, 1:137.

The rabbi would rise every morning at dawn and pray by himself until *Barukh she-amar* [Hebrew, "Blessed is He who spoke," which opens the *Pesukei de-Zimra* section of Shakhrit, the morning prayer service]. He then learned and waited for Moshe Shamesh [Beadle] to come tap on his window and say, "Rabbi, the congregation is waiting!" At that point, Rabbi Dovid Tsvi broke away from his learning, quickly slipped into one sleeve of his cloak [because one arm was wrapped in tefillin], and rushed into the study house, where the congregation was holding at [the prayer] *"Barukh she-amar."*

And it went on like this year in and year out for a long time. The rabbi, Reb Dovid Tsvi, was stringent about praying in a group, and he never prayed alone.

On the Sabbath of the Torah portion of *Shemos* [the thirteenth Torah portion overall and the first in the book of Exodus], the *Parnes-Khoydesh* [Hebrew, the president of the community council for the month] made preparations for his son who was getting married to be called up to the Torah as was the *minhag* [custom] from time immemorial. He sent Moshe Shamesh to invite all the finest residents of the town. The beadle was so preoccupied with his work that he forgot to call the rabbi in time for prayer. As usual, the community waited a while, and then, when they saw that the rabbi was not coming, they surmised that he was, God forbid, not in the best of health and they stopped waiting and resumed their praying. Once they had gotten to [the prayer] *"Barchu,"* the beadle realized what he had forgotten to do. With great fear for the old rabbi, he ran to him and tapped on the window as he was accustomed to doing: "Rabbi, the congregation is waiting!" And Rabbi Dovid Tsvi did as was his custom and quickly threw on his cloak and hurried over for prayer. The beadle followed behind. When the rabbi approached the study house and heard the community saying *"Barchu,"* he became so enraged with the beadle that he began to rebuke him. And when the beadle tried to make up excuses, the rabbi reprimanded him even more severely, smacked the beadle on the cheek, rushed inside the study house, and stood in his usual spot next to the Torah ark, wrapped himself in his prayer shawl, and began to pray. His praying, however, which had always been full of *hislayves* [spiritual ardor] and *dveykes* [mystical ecstasy], was now cold and without *tam* [purpose or flavor].

B

At that time, it was the custom to call the rabbi up to the Torah every Sabbath for the "third" [*aliyah* or "ascent"]. And so too on this Sabbath, the rabbi went up to the Torah for the third, recited the blessings with great *kavone* [intention], and focused on hearing and repeating every word that the *baal koyre* [the Torah reader] chanted. He was reading the Torah portion *"Shemos,"* when suddenly, the rabbi became very frightened when he heard the *baal koyre* read: "When he went out the next day he found two Hebrew men fighting. He said to the wrongdoer: 'Why do you strike your fellow?'" (Exodus 2:13). The rabbi was standing there, terrified. When he repeated after the *baal koyre* word for word: "Wrongdoer why do you strike your fellow?" all of the scattered Talmudic and Midrashic aphorisms that are related to the biblical verse floated before his eyes: "Rabbi Hanina says: He who slaps his friend's cheek is just like someone who slaps the cheek of the Shekhinah [the Divine Presence]" (BT Sanhedrin 58); "Resh Lakish [Shimon ben Lakish] says: He who raises his hand against his friend, even if he does not hit him, is called wicked" (Midrash Rabbah 15); and many other such aphorisms.

It became clear to him during the reading that he had done a great injustice and that Heaven was trying to tell him that he is a sinner. . . . How would he be able to look the beadle in the face now? How could he, the sinner that he is, continue being the rabbi and spiritual guide of his community? For the Gemara explicitly states: "If a rabbi does not resemble an angel, then one must not listen to any *toyre* [teachings], which comes out of his mouth." (BT Moed Katan 17). However, he soon regained his composure and thought [to himself]: *Today is the Sabbath and you are not supposed to worry. God will have pity.* The *baal koyre* finished the Torah portion, the rabbi made the second blessing, descended from the *balemer* [synagogue platform], finished praying, went home, and stayed in the spirit of the Sabbath until the end of Havdalah.

C

Every *motsei Shabbos* [Saturday night], the beadle would go to the rabbi and inquire about who needed to be summoned to a lawsuit or some other mission of the rabbinical court. Just like on any other *motsei Shabbos*, the beadle went to the rabbi's house. His heart was pounding. He expected the rabbi, who was such a stickler, to punish him for causing him to be late for prayer. As soon as the rabbi caught sight of him, he called [the beadle] into his private study and, with tears in his eyes, began to beg him to forgive him for striking him. He would not be able to show his face before the community if he did not forgive him for his wickedness, the rabbi [said].[29]

However, the more the rabbi begged him, the more confused the beadle became. He could not comprehend how the rabbi, that Talmudic scholar and stickler, to whom the whole city was subordinated, trembling at his every word—how he, the rabbi, was standing there, pleading with tears and entreaties, that he, the beadle, that boor, should forgive him. On the contrary, the guilty one was surely he, not the rabbi!

The beadle broke out into tears. He sobbed and begged the rabbi to have mercy on him and his household and not to remove him from his service. He was prepared to accept any punishment that the rabbi wanted to impose on him, just so long as it did not mean the loss of his livelihood.

"Rabbi! I didn't, God forbid, mean anything bad by it! I got distracted by my heavy workload. Rabbi, have mercy!"

He bawled hot tears like a small child.

They stood facing each other like that for more than an hour. The rabbi begging the beadle to forgive him, and the beadle begging to atone before the rabbi. No matter what he did, however, the rabbi was unable to convince the beadle to forgive him.

The next day, Sunday, the entire town of Shargorod was going around saying: the old rabbi is not here! They had already searched for him in the study house, the ritual bath, the cemetery, the society for visiting the sick, the poorhouse, and in other communal places—but he was nowhere to be found.

They knew that the rabbi would not leave without good reason. He must have stumbled in some way and gone into exile to seek a *tikun* [redress]. Everyone was upset that their spiritual leader had abandoned them, and they hoped that the Lord would take pity on their orphaned community and bring their rabbi, the zaddik, home.

D

Rabbi Dovid Tsvi had, indeed, gone into self-imposed exile. He was constantly on the move, wandering from city to city and village to village. Soon enough, his beautiful gray hair and elegant beard became overgrown; his clear, genteel face grew wrinkly and gaunt; his clothing became ragged and tattered—even so, one could still see the Talmudic scholar in him, and, everywhere he went, he was given respect.

Three years passed like this.

And, at the end of the three years, the rabbi said to himself: I've been wandering for three years already and nothing has happened to me that could be considered a punishment for my great sin. So it must then be the will of God, may He be blessed, that I should receive my punishment in the very place that I sinned, for it is written, "In the place of justice, wickedness was there" (Ecclesiastes 3:16). For this reason, I will return home and await my punishment there. And he who opens the gate to those who knock with repentance, will see my suffering and not abandon me in my old age.

On the Friday evening of the Torah portion *Shemos* [lit., Names; the first parshah in Exodus] before the Sabbath candles were lit, he returned to Shargorod. He went into the big study house, where he had prayed all the years he had served as rabbi of the town, set his small bundle in the anteroom, and quietly settled down to pray in a corner near the furnace, full of hope that the days of his suffering would soon come to an end.

No one recognized him. They thought he was just another beggar. After *Kabbalas Shabbos* [lit., Welcoming the Sabbath; the evening prayers for welcoming the Sabbath], the beadle, as was customary at the time, paired the poor guests with wealthy congregants. He sent the more distinguished poor people with distinguished congregants and the simpler ones with simple congregants. The beadle approached the rabbi and said: "Sir, you will eat dinner tonight at the home of the *parnes* [elected member of the Jewish community council]. He's heading over there now. Follow him."

Reb Dovid Tsvi followed the *parnes*. He accompanied him into his home, said "Good Shabbos," and after [singing] *Sholem Aleichem* [traditional table song in which one greets the Sabbath angels], they made *kiddush* [blessing of the wine], sang *zmires* [traditional Sabbath hymns], and shared *divrei toyre* [insights into the Torah]. Seeing how learned his guest was, the *parnes* said to him after dinner: "How will you go out in such a freezing cold night to look for the *hakhnoses-orkhim* [lodge for wayfarers] for shelter. You know it is pretty far from here. Why don't you just spend the night here and, God willing, we will go together to the study house tomorrow morning for prayer and you will eat the other two Sabbath meals at my place."

A bed was made in the dining room and, tired, Reb Dovid Tsvi lay down to sleep.

E

In Shargorod, the Sabbath on which the Torah portion "Shemos" fell was designated for joyous occasions, mainly for weddings. On the Sabbath morning, the beadle went and invited the wife of the *parnes* and her young daughter-in-law—who had married her son three years prior (her wedding was the reason for what happened to the rabbi)—to a wedding of one of the most distinguished Jews of the city. The beadle did not dillydally for people were waiting to lead the bride into the synagogue. They quickly drank the Sabbath chicory and busied themselves with dressing in their Sabbath clothing. When it was time for the young daughter-in-law to put on her jewelry, she discovered that her pearl necklace, which was a gift from her mother-in-law, was missing. She specifically remembered placing the necklace under the tablecloth next to the silver candlesticks, the night before, and now it was no longer there.

People whispered that the servant might have stolen it. But the *parnes'* wife responded:

"No! That cannot be. She has served us for twenty years and raised my children. We rely on her as we would on a kosher Jewish daughter. No, she would not do that. She would not steal from us."

"Perhaps it was the coachman, the horse driver then?" they said.

"No way! It is, after all, the Sabbath today and he does not come on the Sabbath!" the man of the house informed them.

"Perhaps the old guard, the janitor, who comes to heat the furnace?"

"That also cannot be," countered the *parnes*. "He has been my favorite servant for so many years now. I can vouch for him!"

In a nutshell, there was a great commotion. The daughter-in-law was crying, and the mother-in-law was comforting her. The servants were searching in every nook and cranny of the house. The *parnes*, Reb Dan, was calming everyone and telling his daughter-in-law to go buy herself another pearl necklace and imploring [them]: "Stop crying. Do not be upset. Today is the Sabbath. You are not allowed to be upset, much less cast a suspicious eye on the innocent!"

And Reb Dovid Tsvi sat to the side the whole while, reciting Psalms. Meanwhile, one of the servants approached Reb Dovid Tsvi and asked him: "Mister [lit., uncle], did you happen to see where the pearls went? Did you notice anything earlier? After all, you've been sitting here alone the whole time!"

Reb Dovid Tsvi answered humbly and with a broken heart that he did not see the pearls. It was true that he had not moved from his spot the whole time, but he did not see anyone take them.

The servants began to whisper: "Perhaps the visitor did it?"

In the midst of them all, the beadle quickly rushed in and started yelling: "Hurry up! The bride and all the women are waiting for you to lead her into the synagogue. The community is also waiting to pray, so hurry, please, and get out there!"

And when they told him that the pearl necklace was missing, he yelled in anger: "Nu, so what! It will go fine without the pearls. The *parnes*' daughter-in-law will be treated with great honor even without the pearl necklace. Come! The community is waiting! We must not delay!"

Meanwhile, he heard them exchanging whispers about the poor old man. The servants were suspicious of him. He chimed in: "It makes sense that it would be his handiwork. For who other than he could have taken it? Let me talk to the half-witted Jew. I know their kind. They can pretend to be as innocent as a newborn child!"

Moshe Shamesh ran up to Reb Dovid Tsvi, grabbed him by the beard, and said harshly: "Mister [lit., Reb Yid], I know your kind and your thieving ways. Hand over the pearl necklace at once. If not, I will give you the beating that you deserve!"

And before Rabbi Dovid Tsvi could say a word, the beadle raised his hand and struck him a blow on the cheek and was about to strike him again. That is when Reb Dovid Tsvi arose to his full height, grabbed the beadle by the hand, and yelled: "Stop, Moshe Shamesh! I do not deserve more than one blow!"

Everyone was shocked. They looked at the visitor in terror. Reb Dovid Tsvi looked at everyone with open bright eyes. Holiness emanated from his face. He grabbed Moshe Shamesh by the shoulder and said with great harshness: "Moshe Shamesh! You should know that Dovid Tsvi, who is the rabbi of Shargorod and the surrounding area, is still alive! I am the rabbi of Shargorod and, therefore, I order you, with my rabbinic authority, to return immediately the pearl necklace, which you stole this morning, when you went to invite the women to lead the bride into the synagogue!"

Moshe Shamesh stood there as if he were about to be hit by a lightning bolt. He broke out into a loud wail and admitted taking the pearls. The temptation was too great. For when he arrived in the morning, the large house was empty, the pearl necklace was sticking out from underneath the tablecloth, and he was thinking that the visitor was asleep. He continued to sob. The rabbi hugged him and ordered him to stop crying: "It is forbidden to disturb the Sabbath." He ordered everyone to hurry up so as not to delay the community's prayers. He went into the study house in his tattered clothing and took his place of honor, which had remained empty for the full three years [that he was gone]. Once again, he was called up to the Torah for the third *aliyah* and the entire city rejoiced over their rabbi's return.

F

The next day, Rabbi Dovid Tsvi met with the elected community officials and leaders and told them why he had gone into exile and what happened to him in the course of those three years. He urged them not to remove Moshe Shamesh from his position and also asked them not to punish him for the theft.

Reb Dovid Tsvi no longer wanted to hold the office of rabbi on account of having sinned so greatly. He had his son-in-law take over the rabbinate. From then on, he was no longer involved in communal affairs and devoted himself to learning Torah and worship. He lived a long, fruitful life, and Moshe Shamesh remained with him to the very end.

When he felt that his end was near, he called a meeting with the leaders of the community and instructed them that Moshe Shamesh should take care of his burial, and, after one hundred and twenty years [a euphemism for long life], he was to be buried in close proximity to his grave.

In fact, both graves are located so close to one another that it is as if they were embracing. The gravestones [are] now half sunken [in the earth]. The inscriptions have been washed away by years of rain. However, the tale of the rabbi and his beadle is still fresh in the memory of the old folk of Shargorod, from whose mouths I heard and recorded the tale.

15. THE SHTIBL ON THE GRAVES OF THE POLONNOYER PREACHER, *TOLDOS YAAKOV YOSEF*, AND A RICH PHILANTHROPIST

In the old cemetery of Polonnoye, over the graves of the two giants of the Hasidic world: Rebbe Yehudah Leyb, the *Mochiach* [preacher], and Rebbe Yaakov Yosef, the author of the famous book *Toldos Yaakov Yosef*—disciples of the Baal Shem Tov—stands a single shtibl, concerning which the Jews of Polonnoye tell the following wondrous tale.[30]

During the time of the "Preacher," a well-respected man lived in Polonnoye, a rich Jew who used to give a lot of money to charity. When he approached old age, he began to think about getting a grave.

One day in the [Jewish] month of Elul, when he was visiting the graves of his relatives in the old cemetery, he noticed the graves of the martyrs who were killed by Khmelnytsky in the years 1648 and 1649. A desire stirred in him to be buried next to them. So, he went to the burial society and entreated them to prepare a grave for him beside the martyrs of Polonnoye. They explained to him that the cemetery had been closed for many years now and that there was no more vacant land. The rich man told them that if they were to find room for a grave, he would fund a new fence for the old cemetery and would also give a generous sum of money to the community treasury. They searched and found a small plot of land, large enough for one grave. They gave it to him and made a note in the pinkes for him to be buried there.

The rich man was beside himself with joy. He would go to the cemetery every day, recite eighteen chapters of Psalms, and give as much charity as there were verses in those eighteen chapters of Psalms. Every *erev rosh chodesh* [the day before the first of the month and a minor holiday], he laid coins around his burial plot and gave them to the poor. This is how he took pride in his grave [lit., eternal inheritance], by praying and giving charity.

It is said that when the Polonnoyer preacher felt that his time was near, he went to the rich man and told him: "I can see that your burial plot beams with a special holiness. I request that you give it to me, and I promise you that when your time comes, I will make room for you." The rich old man agreed. And in the year 5530 (1770), when Rebbe Yehudah Leyb, the preacher, passed away, he was buried in the rich man's plot.

This is the text on the headstone:

> Here lies the holy man, righteous and upright, a teacher of righteousness to his people, the great rabbi and scholar, wondrous and distinguished in Torah and in Hasidism. The teacher, rabbi, and preacher, our master and

rabbi Yehudah Leyb son of rabbi Yehkhiel Mikhel, who passed away on the twenty first of Tevet in the year 5530.

The closest friend of the preacher was Rebbe Yaakov Yosef Ha-Cohen, known as the "Toldos." Twelve years after the passing of the preacher, when it came time for the Toldos to leave the world, he too went to the rich elderly man and said to him: "Rebbe Yehudah Leyb, the 'Preacher,' may the memory of the righteous be a blessing, and I were lifelong friends. Therefore, after my death, I would like to be buried with my friend. And so I kindly ask you to let me lie in rest next to him and I too will promise you, that when your time comes, we will make space for you between us!"

The rich man agreed to this, and, in 5542 (1782), once Rebbe Yaakov Yosef passed away, he was laid to rest next to his friend, the preacher, in the rich old man's burial plot. This is the text on his headstone:

> Here lies a man who was full of life and accomplishments, pious and humble, a man of God, he shall be called holy [Isaiah 4:3], the rabbi of our community, the *gaon*, our lord and teacher, Yaakov Yosef son of our teacher Tsvi Kohen Tsedek, author of the book *Toldos Yaakov Yosef* and the book [*Ben*] *Poras Yosef*...

Since the headstone was half sunken [in the earth], the date was no longer visible. People erected a single shtibl, a single ohel, over both of them.

The Polonnoyer Jews say that when the rich man died, the burial society fulfilled the promise made by the two zaddikim and brought him for burial in the old cemetery to the shtibl of these two holy men. Once there, they noticed that the two graves had moved apart and that there was space between them for the rich man. Right after the burial, both graves once again moved closer to one another like before.

※ ※ ※

By the way, in the old cemetery of Polonnoye there was a large stone. People say that Khmelnytsky's henchmen used it to sharpen their swords and knives before beginning their bloody slaughter of the Polonnoyer Jews.

16. BRIDE AND GROOM GRAVES

In many shtetls of Podolia and Volhynia, next to the town's synagogues were hilly mounds surrounded by a fence, which were called *khosn-kale-kvorim* [bride and groom graves]. Almost the same legend is told everywhere, that in the years 1648 and 1649, when Khmelnytsky and his bands marched through

Podolia and Volhynia and annihilated entire Jewish communities, among the victims were a bride and groom who were murdered together with the entire wedding procession and all of their in-laws in the synagogue courtyard during their wedding. The bride and groom were buried in the same place where they were murdered—that is, right beside the synagogue. A custom was introduced soon afterward that before being led to the *khuppah* [marital canopy] in the synagogue courtyard, every bride and groom, along with their families, would walk around the anonymous grave seven times. After the wedding, the Klezmer musicians would play a *freylekhs* [a lively circle dance], and the bride and groom and their families would dance in a circle around the hilly mound to entertain the murdered bride and groom who lay there.

Next to the great synagogue of Nemirov could be found a grave of a bride and groom on which there was a headstone. Regarding this grave, the Jews of Nemirov relate the following extraordinary incident that took place in 1648.*

One of the most well-respected Jews in Nemirov threw a banquet for all the poor people in town a day before he was to lead his only daughter to the *khuppah* [wedding canopy]. While the poor were making merry and wishing everyone "mazel tov," the Cossacks stormed into Nemirov like wild devils. They took control of the city and went on a murderous rampage. The groom hurried to save his bride, and they managed to escape to the great synagogue through a narrow alleyway. Many Jews were already gathered there to shelter themselves from the murderers, for the synagogue was built as a fortress and enclosed by a thick wall. Alas, the synagogue was not spared from the calamity. The Cossacks surrounded it on all sides, stormed the walls, and broke through. The bride and groom made it out of the synagogue alive and escaped to the nearby river, where they found a fishing boat. They got in the boat and made their way through the water without paddles. The murderers spotted them, however, threw rocks at them, and several of them jumped into the water and swam toward them with the intent of catching them alive. When the bride saw that they would soon reach them, she said to her groom: "As you obviously see, the murderers will soon have us in their clutches. If I were certain that they would spare you and keep you alive for my sake, I would choose to live for both of our sakes. However, I am so afraid that they will kill you and keep me alive in order to torture me in the same way that they have always tortured the women of our people whom they have found pleasing. Therefore, I would rather die with you, than live a life of shame without you. And, if your love for me is truly strong, then do not reject

---

*This is also mentioned in vol. 5 of Chaim Gurland's book *Le-Korot ha-Gezerot be-Yisrael* [vol. 1–6, Kraków, 1887–1892].

Figure 3.6. And as mighty as a lion (wood carving by Shloyme Yudovin).

me and let us sanctify God's name together. I would rather be swallowed into this abyss here and remain pure than fall into their unclean hands."

The groom hugged his bride and they both jumped into the raging waters.

Three days after the Cossacks left the city, the few surviving Jews found their washed-up bodies. They buried them next to the synagogue and made a hilly mound over their grave.

And at their first yahrzeit, they put up a headstone with the following text:

> Beloved children and infants, women and men:
> Loving brides and grooms, pious souls,
> Who had everything during their lives,
> Were to be led to an adorned wedding canopy
> After their deaths, the river bed was too small to contain them,
> They were not slaughtered, but rather drowned.
> Their bodies were separated, but their souls were bound for eternity.
> The 19th of Sivan, 1648.

17. THE HILL OF CURSES

It is worth talking about another hill in Nemirov: The Hill of Curses. It is fenced in and located in the center of the Nemirov marketplace. And what follows is what is told about it.

There was a rabbi in Nemirov who everyone in the region called Rabbi Yaakov Yosef the preacher.[31] He could not stand wrongdoings, and he did not treat anyone with kid gloves. As a result, he made many enemies who had been on the receiving end of his sharp words.

Once, right before the Sabbath, his opponents grabbed him, placed him on a wagon full of trash and led him far away from the city. He had no other choice but to keep the Sabbath in an open field. He returned to Nemirov the following Sunday afternoon and came to a stop in the marketplace, among the non-Jewish wagoners, who had come from the surrounding villages with their women and children to shop for their needs and sell their products. Rabbi Yaakov Yosef stood in the middle of the marketplace, as if on a hill, and cursed Nemirov with his loud, brazen voice: that it may no longer be prosperous and that the entire marketplace may become overgrown with grass.

The peasants at the market were terrified by his appearance and by the curses of this *Rabbin* [Russian, rabbi]. The news of a "Holy *Rabbin*" swearing angry curses in the middle of the Nemirov marketplace quickly spread throughout the villages of the entire region. The peasants stopped going to the fairs in Nemirov, and it was not long before the marketplace became overgrown with grass.

A picket fence was placed around the spot in the marketplace, where the preacher had, according to legend, stood and cursed. And it was called "The Hill of Curses," and very tall wild grasses grew there.

It is said that, later, when the preacher settled in Shargorod, where he served as the town rabbi, the Jews of Nemirov came to him and asked for his forgiveness. He forgave them and rescinded the curse. However, the place where he had stood and cursed remained fenced in. Jews and even Christians were careful not to get too close [to the site], for they believed that the preacher's curse still hovered over the hill.

18. HOLY ROCK IN LEKHEVITSH

Next to the great synagogue of Lekhevitsh, there is a big rock on which the Jews of Lekhevitsh would burn their *skhakh* [green branches used to cover the sukkah], as a result of the following true story.

A group of Lekhevitsh *misnagdim*, headed by Reb Yisroel Leybl Navaredok [Novogrudok], who was the author of a book against Hasidism titled *Sefer HaVikuah*, kidnapped the Hasidic rebbe Rabbi Motele Lekhevitsh and flogged him on this rock.[32] The Hasidim of Lekhevitsh issued an appeal for Reb Motele's Hasidim living in other cities to come to the rebbe on Sukkot and bring along with them Reb Yisroel Leybl's *Sefer HaVikuach*. A large number of Hasidim came to Lekhevitsh for Sukkot. The day after Sukkot, they took the *skhakh* from the rebbe's sukkah as well as the *skhakh* from other sukkahs, built a large fire, and tossed Reb Yisroel Leybl's *misnagdic Sefer Ha-Vikuach* into it.

The stone became holy as a result of Reb Motele Lekhevitsh having been flogged on it. People got married beside [the rock], delivered eulogies there, and continued to burn the *skhakh* on it.

19. THE GRAVE OF A RABBI WHO MARRIED A GIRL FROM KORAH'S LAND

I want to close *Headstones, Graves, and Tombs* with a bizarre tale that we heard in Ostroh about the grave of a rabbi, a student of the Maharsha, on whose headstone, according to the testimonies of old folk in Ostroh, the following text was engraved:

> Here lies the rabbi and zaddik, Reb Asher son of Chaim, who safely entered and left the land of the Korahites...

There is nothing left of the headstone, but the old folk in Ostroh assured us that the text on the headstone and the entire tale about the rabbi who lay beneath it, Reb Asher, was recorded in the communal pinkes, which perished in one of the many fires that struck Ostroh. It is the following remarkable tale and is worth relating.

The Maharsha ran a large Yeshiva in Ostroh, where many Talmudic prodigies learned, among them a substantial number of married [students], whose souls yearned after Torah-study.

Not far from Ostroh lived a rich Jew, who used to subsidize the Yeshiva generously and financially supported the Yeshiva's poor students. He had an only daughter who was a bright girl and very beautiful. When it was time for her to get married, he made a match for her with a rabbi's son from a nearby town, who was a Talmudic prodigy from a distinguished lineage. The rich man decided to provide all the needs for the young couple until his son-in-law received rabbinical ordination and became a rabbi. They signed the *tnoim* [conditions of the engagement] and scheduled the marriage for the Sabbath after Shavuot [The Festival of Weeks, on which Jews celebrate the giving of the Torah].[33] Right after Passover, they began preparing the costly wedding. Tailors made the best clothing; waiters baked the finest pastries, fruit cakes, and tarts. They built a gigantic pavilion [decked] with brand-new tables and chairs; they hired several music bands—and everything was done generously and with no expense spared. Nearly all the Jews in Ostroh were invited to the wedding. The Maharsha also came with his students, the yeshiva boys. Among them was a certain prodigy, a Talmudic genius, whose name was Asher. When he saw how beautiful and wealthy the bride was, he grew envious and thought to himself: "Wouldn't it be fairer if I were to become the rich man's son-in-law?" And his brain began working to find a way to sabotage the match, so that he could become the rich man's son-in-law.

In those days, it was customary that before the bride's *badekns* [veiling], the old women would shave her head and cover her in a silk veil. If the bride were found to be promiscuous, the elderly women considered it a mitzvah to let the groom know, by making a knot on the top of the veil that would let him know what kind of person the bride actually was. Asher, the prodigy, managed to make one of these "knots of shame" on the bride's veil, and when the groom went to veil his bride and noticed the knot of shame on the veil, he ran out shrieking and told his parents. No amount of arguing helped. The groom's family pulled out, the bride was left in a state of shame, and an air of Tisha be-Av [Ninth of Av, a very sober fast day commemorating the destruction of the First and Second Temples in Jerusalem] reigned in the rich man's house.

When the prodigy realized the *khurbn* [destruction] that he had caused, he was struck by a feeling of remorse.[34] His conscience began to torment him. He could no longer return to the yeshiva. He, therefore, decided to set out into the world in self-imposed *golus* [exile]. He began to wander from city to city and from village to village, then traversed unfamiliar fields and forests, roads and trails. One day his wanderings took him into a thick forest, where he could find no way out. Night fell, and it became pitch dark, truly "darkness that may be felt [Exodus 10:21]." And from all sides came the wild roars of ferocious animals. A great terror overcame him. Where could he escape to in the thick darkness? With outstretched hands, he began to set out at God's mercy, among the trees, until he fell into a pit of some sort, rolled downward, and hit a wall and lost consciousness.

And imagine how astonished he was when he awoke from his fainting spell and found himself lying in a clean, nicely made bed. Above him was standing a handsome tall Jew, who was smiling good-naturedly and speaking to him in *loshn-koydesh* [the holy language, i.e., Hebrew]. Based on his speech, it became clear to him that he was in *"Korkha,"* the land of the children of Korah, whom the earth had swallowed up for being agitators and quarreling with Moses.[35] And the wall that he had hit after rolling was actually the gate to the land of *Korkha*, and his host, having heard the knock in the middle of the night, had opened the door and brought him into his home, unconscious.

The man from *Korkha* took great care of the Talmudic prodigy. He gave him food and drink, dressed him in new clothing, and brought him *seforim* [religious books] to learn. The prodigy quickly acclimated to the new way of life and, when the man of the house offered him his daughter in marriage, he quickly agreed and married her.

Several weeks passed and the prodigy was reminded of what had happened to him and the great sin that he had committed and that was the reason for his going into exile, for his becoming a *na venad* [wanderer, from Genesis 4:14]—and, now, he was sitting here in comfort, married, and enjoying life. He fell into a deep depression and wandered about as if in *olam hatohu* [the World of Chaos, from Genesis 1:2]. He thought about how he could go to his rebbe, the Maharsha, confess everything, and ask for advice on how to repent.

His wife noticed his sadness and begged him to tell her the secret of what was bothering him. He cried bitterly and told her about his great wrongdoing, which only his rebbe, the Maharsha, could help him fix, for he would certainly find a *tikun* [repair] for his great sin. His wife, out of great tenderness for him, said that if he swore to come back to her, she would bring him to his rebbe, the Maharsha. He swore. She opened the gate to the land of *Korkha* before him, gave him a kiss, and laid her hands over his eyes; he felt himself lifting into the air, and, in the blink of an eye, he was standing before the Maharsha's door. With a loud cry, he fell down before his rebbe in his house and told him all the details about what had happened at the wedding, how he had embarked on a life of exile, and how he had rolled into the land of the Sons of Korah, got married there, and vowed to his wife that he would return to her. He sobbed, "Rebbe, save me from my great sin! Give me some way to repent!" The Maharsha hugged him and said: "The only *tikun* for you is to marry the shamed bride, who is still a virgin. As for your wife from among the Sons of Korah, we will have to issue a *get* [a divorce] and the court will declare your vow to her null and void."

The Maharsha immediately informed the rich man that he had chosen a husband for his daughter, who was among his best students, and ordered him to go make the necessary arrangements for the wedding.

And the Maharsha called to order a *bes din* [court], which issued a *get* and decreed that, according to the law, the daughter of the Sons of Korah must come and receive the *get* from her husband [according to the Halakah, the wife must physically accept the *get* for the divorce to be valid]. And she did as ordered. The court also nullified his oath to her.

Asher the prodigy's wedding with the shamed bride, the rich man's only daughter, was celebrated in great splendor and glory. The inhabitants of Ostroh, including the Maharsha and the whole yeshiva, came [to the wedding] and celebrated with the bride and groom.

After the wedding, the Maharsha ordained the prodigy, Asher, and he became rabbi in one of the prayerhouses in Ostroh and served in the rabbinate for the rest of his life.

As stated earlier, the tale was recorded at the time in the communal pinkes and certified with the Maharsha's signature, may the memory of the righteous be a blessing. And after Rabbi Asher's death, he was buried in the old cemetery and the aforementioned headstone was placed there.

TO SECTION 3

Figure 3.7. The "small roof" over the Baal Shem Tov's grave in Medzhibozh.

Figure 3.8. The Besht's study house.

Figure 3.9. The interior of the Besht's study house.

Figure 3.10. Gravestone from Nemirov—weeping birds and hares.

Figure 3.11. Gravestone from Zhitomir, 5512 (1752), lions and birds.

Figure 3.12. Gravestone from Starokonstantinov, 5609 (1849), a pot with flowers.

Figure 3.13. Tulchin. A woman's gravestone on which a bear is visible.

Figure 3.14. Gravestone from Starokonstantinov, 5610 (1850), two fish kissing each other.

NOTES

1. On the Baal Shem Tov's career in Medzhibozh, see Rosman, *Founder of Hasidism*.
2. Rechtman employs the rabbinic phrase (e.g., Pirkei Avot 3:7–8) *mithayev be-nafsho* or "he is liable [for forfeiture] of his life."
3. Borukh of Medzhibozh (1753–1811) was a grandson of the Baal Shem Tov who established a court in Medzhibozh that became famous—and, in some circles, infamous—for its luxury; Hershel Ostropoler was a *badkhn* (jester/entertainer) and trickster figure who eventually became a fixture in the court of Borukh of Medzhibozh and inspired a host of tales, including many modern adaptations; Avrom Yehoshua Heshel of Apt (1748–1825) settled in Medzhibozh during the final phase of his life where he attracted numerous Hasidim.
4. Members of the Bick (also spelled Bik) family served as the most important non-Hasidic rabbinic leaders in Medzhibozh for many generations. Rabbi Simkhe Bick (1828–1896) served as the *rosh bet din* (head of the Jewish court) in Medzhibozh from 1863–1868.
5. On the kloyz and its relationship to the bes medresh in Eastern European Jewish society, see Rosman, *Founder of Hasidism*, 29; Reiner, "Hon, ma'amad hevrati ve-talmud torah," 287–328.
6. The Baal Shem Tov's kloyz (also referred to as his shul or bes medresh) was destroyed during World War II. After the fall of the Soviet Union, a replica of the building was erected on the site of the original synagogue in Medzhibozh by Yisrael Meir Gabbai and his organization Agudas Ohalei Tsadikim.
7. On the Baal Shem Tov and Tluste, see Rosman, *Founder of Hasidism*, 64. Lindenberg ("Ha-Baal Shem Tov be-Tluste," 37–39) discusses the different sources on the Besht's activities in Tluste, as well as his mother's grave in the old Jewish cemetery. For a photograph of the tombstone, which was damaged during World War I and reerected by "young Zionists" in the town, see p. 38. The tombstone in the photograph appears to lack some of the features in Rechtman's description (e.g., the menorah). One source states that the tombstone was standing until at least April 1944. See http://www.tovste.info/Cemeteries/JewishCemetery.php.
8. The origin of this magical practice among Eastern European Jews is unclear. On the use of bricks in a variety of magical rituals in ancient Egypt, see Roth and Roehrig, "Magical Bricks and Bricks of Birth," 121–139. As in the case of the bricks described by Rechtman, the Egyptian magical bricks were inscribed with spells (in their case, from chapter 151 of the Book of the Dead).
9. Rechtman employs the phrase *oysbayten dos rendel*, literally meaning "exchange the ducat or gold coin," to signify conversion.
10. According to Hasidic tradition, the Baal Shem Tov named his daughter Odl based on the Hebrew phrase *esh dat lamo* (a fiery law unto them), which concludes Deuteronomy 33:2. Odl was considered a *tsadekes* (righteous woman) and was said to have possessed *ruah ha-kodesh* (the holy spirit). Moshe Chaim Ephraim of Sudilkov (or Sodilovker) was the author of the important Hasidic work *Degel Mahaneh Efrayim* (Korets, 1810), which contains stories concerning the Besht, his grandfather, with whom the author lived in Medzhibozh for roughly his first decade.
11. Rabbi Yom-Tov Lipmann Heller (d. 1654) was a community leader in Central and Eastern Europe and an important Halakic authority who produced, among other works, *Tosfot (or Tosfos) Yom Tov*, a major commentary on the Mishnah. Like many rabbinic authors, Lipmann Heller became known by the title of this book. His stormy life, which he documented himself, in his work *Megilat Evah* inspired many legends.

12. Beliefs concerning reincarnation (metempsychosis) or gilgul appear in different strata of the Kabbalah and became widely diffused in Judaism in the wake of the Lurianic Kabbalah developed by Rabbi Isaac Luria (1534–1572) and his disciples, such as Rabbi Hayim Vital (1543–1620), who authored the work *Sha'ar Ha-Gilgulim* (The Gate of Transmigrations). For a survey of the phenomenon, see Scholem, "Gilgul."

13. The Lurianic idea that various ruptures—in God, the Cosmos, individual souls—must be repaired via a process known as *tikun* (repair) was taken up and modified by the Hasidic movement. See Scholem, *On the Kabbalah and Its Symbolism*, 113–128; Idel, "Multiple Forms of Redemption," 27–70. According to kabbalistic belief, the soul of an individual who had sinned would have to undergo a *tikun* to break the cycle of reincarnation.

14. Leyb Sores (i.e., Leyb the son of Sarah) was one of the most famous hidden tsaddikim of the eighteenth century and inspired numerous Hasidic tales.

15. On the Hasidic belief that the world rests on the merits of thirty-six (Hebrew, *lamed vav*) hidden righteous individuals, see Scholem, "Thirty-Six Hidden Just Men," 251–256.

16. Literally, "paupers in seven coattails," one of three phrases for poor people that Rechtman employs here to emphasize their poverty.

17. To stop an epidemic, Jewish communities sometimes conducted a "black khuppah" or wedding in the town cemetery between two poor or otherwise low-status individuals. See Weegrzynek, "Shvartze khasene," 55–68. For an example from a town visited by the Jewish Ethnographic Expedition, see Natan Rosenfeld, "Wedding in the Cemetery," 115–116. In Assaf, *Journey to a Nineteenth-Century Shtetl*, 383–384, Yekhezkel Kotik writes that in the midst of a cholera epidemic in Kamenetz, "Jews resorted to all sorts of remedies: a crippled, mute virgin was married to a blind man. The wedding ceremony was held in the graveyard in the hope that they would produce a generation of righteous offspring."

18. On the concept of the *korban ha-edah*, see BT Sanhedrin 97b.

19. Thirty-five Jews were said to have been massacred in Pavoloch by Haidamaks (paramilitary bands) during an uprising in 1735.

20. The initials of her father's name. "Ribaz" is traditionally an acronym for Yohanan ben Zakkai, the Tannaitic sage. But that is clearly not the individual intended here.

21. Rabbi Yehuda Ashkenazi, who lived during the first half of the eighteenth century, was the author of the *Be'er Heitev*, a commentary on the *Shulhan Arukh* that was included in many editions of the text. It is unclear whether Rechtman erred in recording (or remembering) the tombstone inscription, replacing "Yehudah" with "Abraham," or whether the tombstone itself contained the error. It is also possible, though unlikely, that the tombstone was referring to Rabbi Isaiah ben Abraham, the author of an earlier and much less known commentary on the *Shulhan Arukh*.

22. Haidamak attacks on Chechelnik in 1765 resulted in significant Jewish casualties. Perhaps this was the context for Reb Hershenyu's martyrdom.

23. When referring to an individual in a magic spell or curse, it is customary to refer to their personal name and the name of their mother (rather than father). A number of rabbinic sources describe the Lost Tribes of Israel as living beyond the Mountains of Darkness. In multiple places, the Zohar describes the Mountains of Darkness as a place where demons, as well as the rebellious angels Uzza and Azael, dwell. See, for example, translation and commentary by Daniel Matt in *The Zohar: Volume One*, 64.

24. A Hebrew version of this account attributed to Rechtman appears in *Pinkas Ostroh*, 65–68.

25. Dov Ber, the Maggid (preacher) of Mezeritch (d. 1772) in Volhynia was a disciple of the Baal Shem Tov and led the Hasidic movement following his leader's death.

26. The angel Raphael, whose name means "God heals," was invoked when someone was ill.

27. Asher Koretser, also known as Asher Zvi, the Maggid of Ostroh (ca. 1740–1817) was a disciple of the Maggid of Mezeritch and published *Ma'ayan Ha-Chokhmah* (Korets, 1816).

28. Presumably, Rechtman has in mind Rabbi Dovid Tsvi Auerbach (d. 1808), despite the chronological discrepancy. Hasidic tradition attributes his birth to a blessing from the Baal Shem Tov, who is also said to have served as the *sandek* (person who holds the baby) at his circumcision. Auerbach grew up to be an important Halakic authority in Mogilev and other towns in Podolia.

29. The end of the sentence is cut off. There is probably supposed to be a verb here, like "explained" or "said," as in "explained the rabbi."

30. Rabbi Yehuda Leyb, the Mochiach (lit., one who rebukes, also preacher) of Polonnoye (d. 1770) was a disciple of the Baal Shem Tov. Rabbi Yaakov Yosef of Polonnoye (d. 1782), another disciple of the Besht, became known by the title of his work *Toldos Yaakov Yosef*. Considered to be the first Hasidic book when it was published in 1780, *Toldos Yaakov Yosef* contains many teachings attributed to the Besht.

31. Rabbi Yaakov Yosef of Polonnoye served as rabbi in Shargorod and then in Nemirov prior to settling in Polonnoye. It appears that the legend has combined him with Rabbi Yehuda Leyb, the preacher of Polonnoye, and also confused the chronology of when he lived in Shargorod and Nemirov.

32. Rabbi Mordechai (Mottel) of Lekhevitsh (d. 1810) was a disciple of Levi Yitzchak of Berdichev and, later, Rabbi Shlomo of Karlin. Known by his own followers as the Saba Kaddisha (Holy Grandfather) of Lekhevitsh, he played a key role in attempting to spread the Hasidic movement in what is now Belarus, which brought him into conflict with the *misnagdim* or "opponents" of Hasidism, who considered this to be part of their territory. Grinshpan, "Rabbi Mordechai of Lekhovitsh (Ha-Saba Kaddisha)," 191–193, discusses the figure of Rabbi Yisroel of Ibnitz, an opponent of Rabbi Mordechai of Lekhevitsh who became a disciple after traveling to the town and meeting him. Perhaps this story inspired the legend recorded by Rechtman concerning another Rabbi Yisroel (in this case, of Novarodok) who opposed Rabbi Mordechai. Harkavy (*Navarodok*, 18–19) discusses Rabbi Yisroel Leybl of Navarodok and his fiery opposition to Hasidism. Harkavy notes that Simon Dubnow [*History of Hasidism, Voskhod* (November 1891), 143 (Russian)] asserted that the first appearance of the word *misnagdim* was in Rabbi Yisroel Leybl's book *Sefer Ha-Vikuach* (Warsaw, 1798).

33. Customarily, Jews refrain from marrying in the period known as the counting of the *omer* between Passover and Shavuot, except on Lag Ba-Omer (or other days depending on the community). Hence, the wedding was set for after Shavuot.

34. The word *khurbn* is traditionally used to refer to the destruction of the First and Second Temples in Jerusalem and, later, in Yiddish, to the Holocaust.

35. In Numbers 16, Korah leads a rebellion against Moses and Aaron. As punishment, the earth opens its "mouth" and swallows up Korah and his followers. This enigmatic episode inspired many midrashim (rabbinic interpretations) and legends concerning Korah himself and what happened to him. See Ginzberg, *Legends of the Jews*, 286–300.

FOUR

COMMUNAL PINKESIM

1. WHAT IS A PINKES?

The pinkes is the mirror of folklife from previous generations.¹ In a pinkes, the feelings of the folk are reflected: their joy and sorrow, the expression of their worries, and the content of their desires. Through the pinkes, we can evaluate both the individual and the communal life in its entire breadth and depth, and we can learn about the lifestyle of old: its relationship to itself, between one group and another, between one community and another as well as the Jewish relationship to the surrounding gentile world.

The pinkes was always considered to be a holy object. There was even a belief that fire could not damage a house in which a pinkes was present and that a woman in labor would never experience any difficulty giving birth there. Until very recently, there was a custom in many Ukrainian towns that when a woman experienced difficulty in giving birth, the town pinkes was brought to her and placed at her bedside as a charm.

Nearly all very old pinkesim were made from *klaf-tsvi* (deer-skin parchment) with only a small number from thick bluish paper. For their binding, beautiful leather, gilded with gold, in the same format as large Gemaras [that is, copies of the Talmud], often even longer and wider, was used. Most of the time, they were composed in a scribal hand; in some pinkesim, though, only the *takones* [rules] were composed in a scribal hand, and the remaining topics [were penned] in regular writing. The title page of a pinkes as well as the first letters of every new paragraph containing the rules were decorated with extraordinarily beautiful ornamentation and illustrations. Often, each individual page of text was adorned with a hand-drawn frame, painted with exquisite artistic images, in various color schemes. And it is truly astounding how much understanding of color and how much creative ingenuity our great-grandfathers possessed—those prayerhouse-goers of old, the "Bench squeezers."

Based on their content, pinkesim can be divided into three categories:

a. Pinkesim of different local societies, such as: Biker Khoylim [society for visiting the sick], Lines-HaTsedek [a society that provided overnight lodging and other aid], Khevre Kedishe [burial society], Noyse-HaMite [society of pallbearers], Gomle-Khesed-Shel-Emes [society for the burial of poor people], Khevre Tsedaka-Gedola [the "great" charity fund], Tomkhey-Dal [supporters of the poor; loaned money against pledges], Soymekh-Noflim [support the fallen; provided financial help to the needy], and the like.[2]
b. Pinkesim of workers' societies, such as: Craftsmen, Poaley-tsedek [righteous workers], Yegie-Kapayim [manual laborers], Association of Tailors, Association of Cobblers, Association of Hat Makers, Association of Tanners, and the like.
c. Pinkesim of entire communities, such as: Community of Ostroh and the Area, Community of Khmelnytsky and the Area, Community of Letichev and the Area, and so forth.

2. PINKESIM OF LOCAL SOCIETIES

The most widespread and commonly produced kind of pinkesim are those of the particular societies. Virtually every city and town in Ukraine kept one or several of these types of pinkesim. This was the case because every town had these societies and every one of these societies kept this type of pinkes.

The rules typical of the [societies] in this category of local pinkesim are quite similar, both in their style and prose and in their content and terminology, and mostly deal with: the organizational form of the society; the qualifications of the *muamadim* (candidates); the statutes of letting in new members; monetary matters, including: membership dues, contributions, fines, and yahrzeits; the distribution of aliyahs; the *kalpi** (elections for officials), and other duties of the individual to the society and the society to the individual.

According to the rules of the different pinkesim, the *bekhires* (elections) of every society had to take place for the most part during the intermediary working days between the first and last two days of Passover. The managers [of the

---

* *Kalpi* means ballot box. In the pinkesim, however, *kalpi* is used in the sense of elections: "Rules regarding *kalpi*" means rules regarding elections, and "Enrolling on the list of *kalpi*" means nominating to an office, and so on.

society] reserved the right to postpone the elections for another day of the year, although only for important reasons.

The elections, themselves, were run in a variety of ways: for example, according to one set of pinkesim, the assembled chose three or five arbitrators among themselves, and those arbitrators selected officials; according to another set of pinkesim, the old officials selected the arbitrators; according to a third set of pinkesim, the community selected the arbitrators from among the old officials themselves; and, according to a fourth set of pinkesim, the arbitrators determined only the *reshime* (list) of *muamadim* (candidates) and the entire society determined the fixed number of officials from among themselves.

Being admitted into a society as a member was not so easy. One had to pass through various stages until one could qualify for acceptance as a full-fledged member of this or that society. And, even after one passed through all the stages, one often had to wait for several years to be admitted into a society, because the number of newly admitted members was always stringently restricted by all the societies. In certain societies the restriction was to such a degree that only two new members were admitted a year. Many other societies stopped accepting new members after the fifteenth of Kislev.[3]

That said, it is important to note that children were accepted into certain societies because it was a mitzvah to do so. But, under no circumstances were more than two [children] admitted in the course of a year.

The fact should also be stressed that Talmudic scholars, especially the kind who studied *poskim* [decisors of Jewish law], were treated as an exception. They were often accepted regardless of the limit, and they were always favored over the other candidates.

There is actually a rule in a pinkes from the city of Medzhibozh that states: "If the number of new members has reached capacity, he, who studies *poskim*, and wants to be admitted [in the society], should be accepted."

An exception was also made for someone who was dangerously ill and wanted to join the society as a way of getting cured. In such cases, however, the managers [of the society] reserved the right to reject or to demand a larger payment.

Every event that took place in the society, such as, the acceptance of a new member, a fine, an inheritance, a feast, a dispute, election results, or rabbinical lawsuits, was punctiliously recorded in their pinkes by the specially appointed scribe and certified with seals by the managers [of the society].

In the pinkes of the *khevre kedishe* [burial society], the prices for digging a grave were even noted. For example, in the pinkes of the *khevre kedishe* of Letichev, it is recorded: "The price of a grave for an adult [dug] during the summer [costs] two *piatakes* [five-kopeck coins] and, during winter, three *piatakes*. For a minor [dug] during summer, one *piatake*, and [dug] during winter, one and a half *piatake*."

A person found in violation of the society's rules was treated very strictly. Such a person was harshly punished. If he did not comply with the punishment, he would be persecuted up to the point of excommunication, and often he was even actually excommunicated.

The different societies' punishments were always meted out with the help of the community leaders: the rabbis, judges, and sextons. The communal religious authorities were happy to help out to ensure the rules of the societies were followed to the letter [as the biblical verse states], "he who breaks a fence, a snake shall bite him" [in Ecclesiastes 10:8].

If a rule was hard to observe because life in the fraternal society had changed, or because of other unavoidable circumstances, the rule was either modified or, more often than not, discarded. However, this was only done with the agreement of the entire society. The pinkesim of the different kinds of local societies contain many instances of changing or repealing old rules and putting new ones in their place.

3. WORKERS' PINKESIM—SPECIAL SOCIETIES

A

Pinkesim from workers' societies were not so available in the smaller cities and towns of Ukraine. The expedition, nonetheless, managed to locate several of these precious workers' pinkesim. It is impossible to overestimate the immensely important material concerning the former life of workers that these special pinkesim contain.

On the title page of these pinkesim, which usually bears the name of the workers' society, typically there is either a relevant verse from the Tanakh or a quote from the sages of the Mishnah and Gemara, which demonstrates the importance of being a laborer. On the title page of the "tailors' *pinkes*" of Lutsk the following biblical verse is found: "If you eat the toil of your hands, you are to be praised, and it is good for you" (Psalms 128:2); "You shall be happy in this world and it will be good for you in the World to Come" (BT Berakhot 8a). And in the communal pinkes of the cobblers, tanners, and hatmakers from the town of Mikolayev, which was famous for its pelt and fur caps, which were brought to the largest fairs, in the most far off locations—written on the title page of their pinkes was this aphorism from the sages of the Mishnah and Gemara: "The man who lives by the fruits of his labor is greater than the man who fears Heaven" (BT Berakhot 8a).

The rules recorded in these pinkesim deal with issues that are directly related to their trade, such as regulating prices and settling disputes between workers and their bosses; issues related to internal organization and general interests, such as preventing dishonest competition and *shatnez* [biblically prohibited clothing made from a combination of linen and wool]; and also issues related to the religious needs of the fraternal society, such as the study house, the rabbi, *aliyahs* [being called up to read from the Torah], elections, donations, fines, and religious lawsuits.

As with other fraternal societies, workers' elections generally took place during *khol hamoed* [the intermediate days between the first and last two days of Passover and Sukkot], in multiple ways: sometimes by arbitrators and sometimes by direct election.

Besides the regular officials, who were selected in every other fraternal society (e.g., parnassim, trustees, tzerufim), the workers also chose a special council [consisting] of seven [members], which had the absolute right to speak and negotiate on behalf of the workers in all matters.

These seven closed deals and signed contracts, regulated prices, gave permission to workers to become proprietors, punished defiant [members], and even reserved the right of excommunication. In a word, everything having to do with the life of the fraternal society and its interests was run according to the discretion of those seven members. All of their dealings and decisions were meticulously recorded in the pinkes and confirmed with their signatures.

I attempt to offer in the following several characteristic rules, which we managed to see in the workers' pinkesim.

In the "tailors' *pinkes*" of the city of Lutsk from the year 1721 (5481) (the pinkes was reprinted in "Ha-Melits" from the years 1878–1879), there is a rule concerning *shatnez*. A gathering of the entire fraternal society of tailors, headed by the town rabbi, made this rule. The rule reads in Yiddish translation:

> Being that the prohibition of shatnez is very great and, because of our many sins, a considerable number of tailors were recently found in violation of the prohibition of using a nonkosher canvas. Therefore, the aforementioned assembly convened and unanimously decided that the council of seven shall at the beginning of every new year, in the [Hebrew] month of Tishrei, give the canvas lease to a man of integrity. The price shall also be determined by the seven. And it shall be announced in every house of prayer: that so and so holds the canvas lease for the entire year and everyone must, under the threat of excommunication, purchase canvas from him only.

The rule also stipulated that the leaseholder of the canvas franchise must be a religious Jew and that he must see to it that the kosher canvas is only produced by Jews. He even had the sole authority to choose the workers who would weave the canvas under his supervision. As said earlier, all tailors were obligated to buy canvas from only him and pay the cost, which was determined by the seven. If it turned out that someone violated the rule and bought canvas from somewhere else, he would be harshly punished. For instance, if he were a member of the fraternal society of tailors, he would be immediately removed from the society and declared unfit to be a tailor until he submitted himself to the rule and signed the pinkes to this effect; if he were not a member, the council of seven would turn to the leaders of the community and to the rabbis of the city and demand that they punish the violator in accordance with the law concerning a rebel, that is someone who rebels against a judgment of a *bes din* [rabbinic court]. The community and court gladly helped the workers' societies in such cases.

Generally speaking, the question of "wool and linen" occupied a very important place in the workers' pinkesim, mainly in the pinkesim of tailors and hatmakers.

B

The work hours were regulated in a nearly modern manner. According to a rule in the same pinkes, no one, even a self-employed man, and much less someone else's worker, was allowed to work late into the night. On the eve of the Sabbath or of a holiday, one had to stop working at two in the afternoon. If, however, someone was forced to work later than the set time, on account of a wedding or because the magnate of the city or the local nobleman needed the work done—in such cases, one was required to give two groschens of charity for every additional hour he worked and to pay the worker for his labor even when he was employed for the year.

Also, no one was allowed to accept more work than he could do on his own and assign it to another as piecework or on a weekly basis. If someone accepted too much work, he had to hire another worker and for no less than a fourth of a year.

In the workers' pinkesim, there were also many rules that dealt with the issue of one worker competing with another. One rule posited that, if someone were called to accept a new job or to repair old work, either by a Jew or a non-Jew, and another became aware of it, beat him to it, and received the work over the original [person], it is not enough for him to surrender his entire earnings to the original craftsman, but he also has to pay a fine, per the discretion of the seven.

To avoid competition, the prices for work were regulated by the seven. From time to time, they issued lists of prices, which were written in the pinkes and were also posted in the synagogues and study houses. The lists were numbered and stated the cost of a new job and how much to alter an old garment.

The seven also had the responsibility of keeping track of the apprentices. They determined how many years an apprentice had to remain with their "teacher," what kind of housework they were obligated to do for their bosses, and how much recompense they ought to receive. The contracts, known as "Ksav mamad," between the apprentices and their bosses were drawn up and confirmed by the seven and recorded in the pinkes.

When leasing his labor to a boss, every adult worker was obligated to appear with his employer before the seven, who managed the "Ksav mamad" (agreement) and recorded [it] in the pinkes in all its details. On a quarterly basis, the boss had to pay the full wages in the presence of the seven, and this, too, was meticulously recorded in the pinkes.

If a worker wanted to be his own boss, he was unable to do so, unless he received the permission of the seven. He only received such permission if he pledged, signing his signature in a pinkes, to contribute to the fraternal society a sum of money, per the discretion of the seven, and to promise not to accept work that is cheaper than the fixed prices. If he was unable to come to an understanding with the seven, he had to pay four ducats as a partial payment, with the obligation that, during the annual gathering for the election, he would contribute the rest in accordance with the discretion of the entire assembly.

By the way, a new applicant was not officially considered a member and so was not inscribed in the pinkes until he obtained the agreement of the entire fraternal society during the annual gathering for the election.

C

Furthermore, religious interests occupy a very esteemed place in the workers' pinkesim. Nearly all workers' societies had their own study house or synagogue and their own rabbi, gabaim, sextons, and cantors.*

Being called up to the Torah and the distribution of Torah readings took place among them in an entirely different manner. Every worker had an equal right to partake in God's Torah. Among the workers' societies, not a single Torah reading was auctioned off, as in all other fraternal societies, so as not to give wealthier individuals the possibility of appearing better than poorer ones. The Torah readings were, therefore, distributed among the members according to the order of the alphabet, or from older to younger, without distinction. An exception was made only for someone who was religiously obligated [to read from

---

*Every society, when hiring a cantor, greatly insisted that the cantor be one of their own. For the cobblers, a cobbler, and for the tailors, a tailor, and so forth. Only the burial society did not have a cantor from among themselves, for an old rule posited: "It is forbidden for a person who carries out burials and for a doctor who heals the sick to stand before the prayer stand, for they cannot represent the community during the prayer of 'Refaeynu' ['Heal us,' the eighth blessing of the Shemoneh Esrei] for they receive their livelihood from the sick and the dead."

the Torah]: such as, a *baal yahrzeit* [an individual observing the anniversary of a death], a mourner, a groom, a *baal bris* [the father of a boy whose circumcision is being celebrated], or any other obligated person . . . the circumambulations with the Torah during Shemini Atzeret [the eighth day of Sukkot] and Simkhas Toyre were also conducted according to the same order.

Funds for the maintenance of the study house and synagogue were also collected from everyone equally. According to a rule in the previously mentioned pinkes [from Lutsk], a member had to give a groschen every Sabbath eve and two groschens every *erev rosh khodesh* [at the start of a new month] for the maintenance of their prayer house. A collector went around every week to the members and collected these taxes. If someone was unable to pay immediately, it was recorded as a debt and he had to settle the debt before the elections. If he did not repay his debt, the seven had the right to confiscate an item from him and pawn it off and he was not allowed to vote that year.

4. WORKERS' PINKESIM—COMMUNAL SOCIETIES

In the larger cities, where the number of workers was greater, almost every profession had its own fraternal society: Society of Tailors, Society of Cobblers, Society of Tanners, Society of Hat Makers, and so forth. All of the aforementioned societies maintained a separate pinkes; frequently, they even had their own bes medresh where they prayed, and they managed and protected their interests in an entirely independent way.

In the smaller towns, however, where the number of workers was not significant enough, communal workers' societies operated; for example, the tailors, furriers, cobblers, and tanners were merged. They would maintain only one shared pinkes.

As gleaned from these joint pinkesim, conflicts often arose between one trade and another, especially during the elections. Every trade tried to build a majority in order to get the upper hand in the council of seven. This almost always led to quarreling and often even to blows.

Communal elections were always conducted directly. This is to say that arbitrators were not depended on to choose a winner, but rather candidates were put forward from all guilds and trades and people voted directly for their preferred candidate. And it goes without saying that those who received the majority of votes were elected. It is interesting to note that the tailors almost always had the upper hand. From this it can be inferred that the tailors were the majority everywhere.

In the election lists, which were written down in the pinkesim, elections are rarely described as being "unanimous," rather [as] "majority rules," or, most commonly, "according to the ballot box"—that is, not by the show of hands but directly through [the counting of] lots for each candidate.

According to the rules of a communal workers' pinkes in Mikolayev,* the elections of cobblers, tanners, and furriers took place in the following manner: three elections were held, that is, everyone's names were jotted down on lots—for the cobblers, tanners, and furriers, respectively. The lottery tickets were placed in three different boxes and drawn from each box: two lots for the cobblers, one for the tanners, and two for the furriers. These five drawn names were the arbitrators. These arbitrators were tasked with devising the list of candidates for every office of the society, including managers, adjuncts, trustees, accountants, including a separate list of candidates for the council of seven. Once the list was formed, the members of the fraternal societies gathered and voted for each respective candidate.

5. COMMUNITY PINKESIM

The community pinkesim are the most important and valuable. When we familiarize ourselves with the content of these pinkesim, when we carefully study each affair that is recorded in them, we arrive at the delightful realization that, many hundreds of years ago, communal life was run according to an order, in almost all respects, when it came to internal Jewish matters, the relations between one community and another, and in relation to the outside world—with noblemen, dukes, and the government.

Generally speaking, the rabbis and communal leaders possessed the necessary vantage point from which, with eyes open, they could pay attention that everything done in their community was done with fairness and consideration: they made sure that charity was distributed appropriately and that no one was favored over another; they also supervised the Talmud Torahs and Yeshivas, making certain that the poor students and Yeshiva boys were not mistreated; they were very strict about the teachers and heads of the yeshiva being qualified for their offices; they made an effort to remove individuals upon whom a shadow of suspicion had fallen; they settled conflicts between individuals and entire societies; they gathered testimonies and required oaths; they brought order to communal affairs so that they would not be chaotic; they installed special dunners to collect the government's tariffs and taxes; they engaged in *shtadlanus* in

---

*Ironically, the pinkes that documented the life of the workers was not actually kept by the workers themselves but rather by the wealthiest man of the town, Zelke Zaltsman, who descended from generations of rich men.

the name of the community, sending requests and delegations to the government and dukes; they were in written contact with other communities and often worked together on behalf of the larger collective; in sum, they enacted their rules and issued proclamations, imposed fines, and even excommunicated.

All their activities and accomplishments were generally written down with great precision in the community pinkes by the specially appointed scribe and confirmed with seals of the rabbis, judges, and elected members of the Jewish community councils.

The community pinkes is completely different from other types of pinkesim of individual fraternal societies. It begins differently and has a different order. All other pinkesim usually begin with rules, which are composed in advance of the society's founding. The community pinkes, however, contains fewer rules because the community does not provide rules in advance. Rather, with every new phenomenon in communal life, with each important happening in the life of the community, the rabbis and community council members meet with the elected representative of the community, examine the situation, deal with the necessary parties, and only then issue appropriate rules according to the particular circumstances.

Even the rules concerning elections, which often come at the beginning, are also different in the community pinkesim than in the pinkesim of individual societies: individual societies had the right, for important reasons, to change election day from *khol hamoed Pesakh* to another day during the rest of the year—however, community elections must take place precisely on *khol hamoed Pesakh* and may not, for any reason whatsoever, be postponed to another day. In other societies, anyone who is nominated as a candidate for an office in the fraternal society may decline the honor without having to give a reason. By contrast, in the community, candidates are not allowed to reject nominations in order not to transgress the dictum "Do not separate yourself from the community" (Pirkei Avot 2:5).

The following rule is found in the community pinkes of Khmelnik: "Those whose names are put forward at the time of the election as a candidate are not allowed to decline; however, if one should decline, he forfeits his right to be nominated for any position in the community for a period of three years and his name shall be recorded in the *pinkes* to shame him."

As said earlier, the elections would only occur on *khol hamoed Pesakh*. The *parnas khoydesh* [an elected member of the community council] called the elections and a majority of the community members were required to participate. The election results and the names of the newly elected officials were recorded every year in the pinkes, and the old officials had to sign. Almost all election lists in the community pinkesim begin with these words: "With good luck, we will decide on arbitrators* on such-and-such a day during *khol hamoed Pesakh*, in such-and-such a year, as is customary in all communities" and in some pinkesim, "As is customary in all places where Jews are exiled."

The community elections took place in a variety of ways just like in the [elections of the] individual societies. According to some pinkesim, the assembled chose five arbitrators from among themselves who could not be relatives. The arbitrators, in turn, alone selected the old officials. According to a second pinkes, only the old officials, not the community, chose the arbitrators, and the arbitrators chose the new officials; and according to a third pinkes, both the arbitrator and the officials were selected by the entire community, according to majority rule or by the ballot box via drawing lots. In the latter case, the arbitrators only put forward the list of candidates and the community voted.

And this is more or less the order of the community elections: first, four *Roshim* [Heads] are chosen, then three *Alufim* [Champions], and finally seven *Tovim* [Good ones]. Each of the categories had a backup in case of an unfortunate circumstance [requiring them to step down]. Additionally, twelve *Parnesey Khoydesh* [Monthly officers] were selected; a *Roeh Kheshbn* (treasurer); and *gaboim* [managers] for the various institutions of the community, such as: Talmud Torahs, hospitals, *hegdesh* [poorhouse] as well as other charitable institutions, which were located in the town. Also selected were an inspector of the *takse* [tax on kosher meat], a *Makhzik Ha-Pinkes* (the guardian of the pinkes), and a special scribe for the pinkes.

The *Roshim* were the special stewards of the community. They tended to all religious needs of the community, such as: synagogues, study houses, yeshivas, and ritual baths; they determined the budgets; and they hired doctors, bathhouse attendants, and so forth.

They would also execute transactions between other communities when necessary.

The *Alufim* were in charge of the community's financial affairs. They raised necessary funds and economized and saved on expenses; they had the authority to collect taxes and hire "govim" (collectors); they also reserved the right to confiscate an item from someone who missed [their payment] or tried to dodge taxes. They kept [the item] as collateral and, if necessary, sold it to cover his debt.

The *Tovim* were the advisers regarding mundane occurrences and, most importantly, unusual ones, such as: an epidemic in the town; a tax from the duke or nobleman; a decision to build a new place of worship; to establish a new cemetery; an excommunication; a "donkey's burial" [the burying of a sinful Jew in

---

*The [originally Hebrew] word *bekhires* [elections] is rarely used.

a dishonorable place near the fence of the cemetery], and so forth. The *Roshim* would always consult with the *Tovim* and make a joint decision.

In several pinkesim, we discovered that *Shamayim* (appraisers) were also elected. The appraisers would determine how much money to demand from everyone, in accordance with their means, for the needs of the community or for government taxes.

Most community pinkesim have a rule about the "hierarchical structure" [of the community]. According to this rule, no member of the community could immediately push to become a "Rosh," an "Aluf," or a "Tov," rather he had to first start out with a low office and then advance from level to level until he obtained the higher office. And when we examined several election lists from consecutive years, we noticed that a small number of new officers were promoted every year. Those from before always remained [in office], with the only difference being that they had advanced to higher ranks: from a Rosh to an Aluf, from an Aluf to a Tov, and so forth.

An exception to advancing through the ranks was made for a learned man, a recognized Talmudic scholar, and, above all, for an ordained rabbi. In the same pinkes from Khmelnik, there is a rule that a person who studied *poskim* and whose father was already a *gabay* was permitted to be a candidate for all offices in the community, even when he did not go through the traditional order of ranks.

It is interesting to note the following rule from this aforementioned pinkes that emphasizes the particular privileges granted a Talmudic scholar:

> If someone who comes from another place settles in town and wants to become a member of the community, and if he brings a writ with him from his former community, authorized with the seals of the community leaders [confirming] that he was a member there, he must be admitted into the community as a full member. However, he loses all prior ranks from his original community. He must begin anew with the entire ranking order in the new community. A Talmudic scholar is treated differently. He is completely exempt from making his way anew through the ranking system.

6. RULES AGAINST LUXURY

The wealthy Ukrainian noblemen—who, in that period, literally bathed themselves in riches and luxury—had a powerful influence over the well-to-do Jews, who were in business with them. These rich Jews began to learn from the noblemen how to lead a rich life and behave like aristocrats. They began to furnish their homes lavishly, traveling in expensive carriages, and, most of all, throwing extravagant parties in the aristocratic fashion: with large musical bands and the most expensive foods and wines. These parties would last for several nights straight and had an unbelievably negative impact.

First and foremost, it raised the attention of the neighboring non-Jews, who would frown in disapproval and wonder where those *Zhidkes* [Slavic pejorative for Jews] got so much money to dress and act as richly [as they do]. They must be swindlers, deceivers, "Zhid-Moshennik!" [Ukrainian, thieving Jew].

Second, it negatively impacted Jews themselves. The poor did not want to lag behind the rich, so they expended great efforts to throw parties in the same fancy style, which lasted for several days. This drove the poor into great poverty and created much suffering.

Third, these wild festivities led to drunkenness, frivolity, and other debaucheries. Our spiritual leaders noticed all of this at the time. They sensed the danger that this [debauchery] posed for their communities, for they knew where such conduct could lead. They therefore waged a systematic war against such behaviors and used their influence to stop it.

And so it should come as no surprise that most of the old Ukrainian pinkesim that we saw were replete with rules, rabbinical decrees, and proclamations against this profligate lifestyle.

In the community pinkes from [the town of] Bar, there is a proclamation, which the local rabbi, the judges, and community heads of Bar issued in the year 1825 (5585) against these never ending, decadent parties. The decree [in a mix of Hebrew, Aramaic, and Yiddish] was issued and posted in every synagogue and study house:

> Listen, holy community! The honorable great and famous rabbi, head of the court and rosh yeshiva, "May his Rock and Redeemer protect him," along with the honorable wealthy *parnes khoydesh* [title given to a rich individual who provided leadership and subsidized key needs of the community for a month], "May his Rock and Redeemer protect him," and along with the honorable distinguished rabbis, the esteemed judges, "May their Rock and Redeemer protect them," so decree publicly on account of the great sins resulting from the increase in wedding feasts lasting more than one night, it is therefore ordained by the decrees of the watchers and a word of the holy ones [Aramaic phrase from Daniel 4:14] and by the rules of the sages that from this day forward no one should dare to hold a wedding feast for more than one night, and he who breaches the fence a serpent shall bite him and upon him shall be placed the curse of the rabbis without a remedy and his sin shall be too great to bear and he shall be trapped in the fortress of excommunication. And he who hosts the feast and he who leaves his house to attend the feast for more than one night will be inscribed in the *pinkes* as a sinner and all the people will hear and see and will transgress no longer.

The rabbis led this war against a luxurious lifestyle with a strong hand and great discernment and dignity. They limited the duration of each festivity and determined how many guests could be invited and decided how many dishes could be served. They even restricted the number of poor people that a host could take in and specified the foods he could serve them.

The following rules from the pinkes of the town of Bar will serve as an illustration:

a. During the *kabales ponem* of the bridegroom [reception before the wedding ceremony], whether he is local or from another town, as well as during the *rumpl* [entertainment shortly after the wedding], jam may not be given to anyone except for close relatives.
b. At a wedding feast: If the host is wealthy,* he is allowed to invite two minyanim [a minyan is ten men] in addition to relatives, religious and communal functionaries, and the poor.
c. If the host is a householder of moderate means, he may not invite strangers, only religious and communal functionaries, poor people, and relatives—but only those who are disqualified from giving testimony [against them in court, i.e., close relatives].
d. If the host is not well to do, he may invite religious and communal functionaries and relatives—but only those who are disqualified from giving testimony.
e. A rich man is allowed to invite to a circumcision feast two minyanim, including relatives, in addition to religious and communal functionaries, and the poor.
f. A householder of moderate means—only one minyan, relatives included, in addition to religious and communal functionaries, and the poor.
g. Someone who is not well to do may not, under any circumstances, hold a banquet for a circumcision. He may only serve jam, cake, and liquor.
h. During the *ben zokher* celebration following the birth of a boy or after the birth of a girl, no jams or cookies may be served.

These rules, and more, are also found in other pinkesim.

7. TRIALS AND TESTIMONY

A

All sorts of trials and court cases having to do with one individual versus another, an individual versus the community at large, and, conversely, the community at large versus an individual, are found in the various community pinkesim.

---

* The various levels of wealth were determined according to the annual taxes that everyone had to pay.

It is most interesting that the rabbis, judges, and community heads treated minor incidents just as seriously and with the same care and attention as they did major ones. If someone testified that a person tore apart religious books in the study house, and another testified that a person defamed a Jewish daughter, and a third person violated a precept of a society, the heads of the community assembled, debated the issue, subpoenaed and examined testimony, and rendered a verdict.

In a majority of cases, the verdict was to remove the offender from a fraternal society or the community: if it were a grave violation, permanently, and for a minor infraction, temporarily.

If someone were removed for a certain period of time, once the sentence was over, he was allowed to appeal to the community or the society requesting that he be readmitted. The request, by the way, had to be put into writing. The heads of the community reconvened and deliberated. If the sinner really had improved his behavior over the course of his sentence, he was generally readmitted.

By way of illustration, I cite a couple of characteristic trials taken from the communal pinkes of Letichev.

The following incident occurred on the night of Simchat Torah [holiday celebrating the completion of the annual reading cycle of the Torah] during the *hakofes* [circumambulations with the Torah scroll] in the great synagogue in the year 5486 [1725].

One of the congregants, a wagon driver, had already gotten drunk in honor of the holiday. When he was called up to the *hakofe* and a large Torah scroll [bearing] a silver crown was placed into his arms (the Torah crowns, as is well known, are covered in small, decorative silver bells and a large bell at the very top of the crown), the coachman caught sight of the large bell, heard how it sounded, and howled with excitement: "This bell would be great for my white mare!"

The congregants, who regarded his [statement] as a defamation of the Torah, tackled him and gave him a good beating, and, right after the holiday had ended, he was ordered to appear before the court for the desecration he committed. And, for his punishment, he was to be expelled from the community permanently.

Two years later, however, the wagon driver sent a written appeal to the court. The written request was recorded in the pinkes. In his appeal, he complained that since his removal from the Jewish community he had been reduced to poverty. He begged them to have mercy on him and his household and to lift the punishment and pardon him of his wrongdoing.

An assembly convened and reached the agreement that his sentence be nullified, but only on condition that he serve the community for three years and that, every year, he host a banquet for the heads of the community, rabbis, and judges. After three years, he would be considered a new member and have to proceed through the various levels from the beginning.

Another case involved someone who hid himself under the bed of a bride and groom during their wedding night. His sentence was to be bound by his hands and feet and led out of the city on a wagon carrying trash.

A butcher was punished with a monetary fine and [a requirement to host] a community banquet, for violating a rule that had been on the books for a long time, which forbade the slaughtering of goats during the summer, since their meat is harmful [during this season].

There are also plenty of trials between fraternal societies as well as between towns. The names of the plaintiffs and their testimonies were meticulously written down in the pinkes.

B

Trials and disputes between Jews are not the only type found within the pages of the communal pinkesim; also covered are those between Jews and non-Jews. In several pinkesim, I saw testimonies from gentiles [that went]: "The non-Jew [lit., uncircumcised] Ivan says such and such, the non-Jew Yevdokim such and such, and the non-Jew Yemilian such and such."

From this testimony, we learn that the Christian population of the towns held the rabbis in great esteem and submitted to their rulings.

Right up to World War I, it was not uncommon to see a Ukrainian peasant dragging a Jew to the rabbi. It even occurred frequently that two gentiles would rather rely on a rabbi to settle their disputes than on a non-Jewish court. The [Ukrainian] expressions, "Pidem do rabina" (Let's go to the rabbi), or "Do rabina ne pidem" (We will not go to the rabbi), were very frequently employed among gentiles not only in reference to a gentile and a Jew but also in reference to one gentile and another.

In the communal pinkes of Letichev, there is an agreement signed by a priest [concerning] a Jew [who] was caught breaking into a monastery. All the stolen goods were found on his person, save one expensive goblet. The priest turned to the Jewish community, who agreed to pay a certain amount of money for the goblet. Their agreement was written down in the pinkes and was signed by the heads of the community and the priest.

C

The Ukrainian peasants loved to tell wondrous tales about zaddikim and holy Jews, especially about *Rabin Srul* [Rabbi Yisroel] the Baal Shem Tov. On more than one occasion, we managed to hear these tales told by a peasant wagon driver, who conveyed us in his horse and wagon.

In Medzhibozh, an elderly peasant told us a tale about the Besht. His father, who knew the Besht personally, told him the tale when he was a small child.

"The rabbis back in the day were not like today's rabbis," so began the elderly peasant, as he swayed with his long gray forelock from right to left. "No! They were entirely different! When I was a small boy, my father *'Tsarstvo yemu nebesnoye'* (May he inherit the heavenly kingdom), told me that a great rabbi, a holy rabbi, lived among us in Medzhibozh. His name was 'Srul.' This 'Srul' was a *'spravedlivyy rabin'* [righteous rabbi] who performed *'chudesa'* (wonders).[4] His clothes were not made of silk, but of simple linen. He prayed to God under the open sky in spacious fields and in thick forests. He had a heavenly voice, for when he prayed to God and sang passionately, flocks of birds would circle above his head and sing in unison. The peasants watched over him to make sure no-one disturbed him. Once, a *'parovok'* (*sheygets*) [gentile ne'er-do-well] wanted to frighten him, but his tongue stuck to his palate and he was unable to speak. Someone else wanted to throw a stone at him, but his hand became stiff and remained frozen, outstretched. My father himself saw how 'Srul' rolled in the snow and bathed naked in a *'polonke'* (an opening made in the ice). When 'Srul' needed water, he would insert his *palke* (walking stick) in the earth, turn it, and water would appear!"

The Ukrainian peasants told similar stories about other zaddikim and Hasidic rebbes, who resided and were active in their towns. Peasants would frequently go to rabbis with requests or would bring a sick child to have a "holy rabbi" provide a blessing. Even the rich noblemen in the area would often go to the rabbi for advice in an emergency.

In Anipol, it is said that after the passing of the zaddik, Reb Zishe of Anipol, peasants would go, weeping, to his grave with their requests.[5] Once, right after Reb Zishe's passing, a peasant, whose son was being conscripted in the military, came from a nearby village. The peasant fell at Reb Zishe's grave [and implored in Ukrainian]: Рабин! Святой рабин! Як выбереш мою дытынку, Поставлю тоби хатынку![6] (Rabbi! Holy rabbi! If you get my little son [out of the military], I will build a hut [over your grave] for you!)[7]

And, lo and behold, the peasant's son was rejected for service. The peasant went to the town rabbi, told him about his vow, and requested that he build a brick ohel [a mortuary structure] at his expense over Reb Zishe's grave. The rabbi fulfilled his request and built a beautiful brick ohel and the peasant bore the entire cost.

D

Often, in a time of great difficulty, when the community lacked the necessary funds to pay for time-pressing communal needs, which could not be delayed, such as: repairing the synagogue after a fire; rebuilding the *hegdesh* [poor house], which was at the point of collapse; fixing the roof of the bathhouse to keep the rain from leaking through; or paying late government taxes. In such exceptional cases, the community would borrow money from local wealthy men and use community property for collateral (e.g., Torah crowns, silver and brass menorahs, and other valuable objects and silverware). The amount of money borrowed, as well as a complete list of the collateralized items, were logged into the pinkes and signed by both parties.

Furthermore, there were cases in which someone went to the land of Israel and entrusted the community with a sum of money, with the understanding that they [the members of the community] would regularly send him small payments as long as he were alive; and whatever was left of his fortune after one hundred and twenty years [a traditional Jewish expression for a long life] would be given to charity in accordance with his will. The entire agreement along with the will would be recorded in the pinkes.

There are a variety of agreements in the pinkesim that were made with community employees, including with the bath attendant concerning how many times per week the bath should be open; or with the doctor concerning how many times a year he should let blood—and what their respective fees should be.

In the communal pinkesim, there are also testimonies and decisions from rabbis, judges, and heads of the community regarding girls who had lost their virginity because of an accident or a rape.[8] The father of such a girl would typically bring his daughter before the heads of the community, explain the unfortunate incident to them, and confirm his testimony through eyewitness accounts. The heads of the community and the court would conduct a thorough investigation and question all the witnesses, and, if her innocence were proven beyond a shadow of a doubt, then they would record the entire matter in the pinkes. Both the community leaders and the judges signed their names and gave the girl a *ksav* [written document], which exonerated the maiden when it came time for her to marry. Incidentally, this is the origin of the folk saying: "a girl with a *ksav*."

E

One of the main responsibilities of the community was to make sure that the individual fraternal societies and associations coordinated with one another because, as I noted before, these individual societies kept independent pinkesim and devised their own rules. On multiple occasions, the rules [devised by] the fraternal societies and associations came into conflict with each other and it was not unheard of for them to completely contradict the rules of the entire community—this led to much discord and disagreements of opinion. In such cases, the community leaders were very strict. They presided over all the legal matters and forced the fraternal societies to submit to the community and change their rules accordingly.

Not all fraternal societies had their own study houses. Rather, in such towns [where individual fraternal societies were without their own study houses], it was customary that in the great synagogue and in large study houses, the honor of being called up to the Torah on certain Sabbaths was distributed to specific societies: for instance, on the Sabbath of "Bereishis" [Genesis 1:1–6:8], the members of the "Shas society" [devoted to learning Talmud] were called to the Torah; on the Sabbath when people recited "Lekh Lekha" [Genesis 12:1–17:27], which contains the verse, "And you shall circumcise the flesh of your foreskin" [Genesis 17:11], the *mohels* [ritual circumcisers] were called up; the Torah portion "Vayera" [Genesis 18:1–22:24], where people read, "And he lifted up his eyes and looked, and, lo, three men stood by him: and when he saw them, he ran to meet them" [Genesis 18:2]—belonged to the "Hakhnasas Orkhim society" [devoted to hospitality]; the Sabbath of "Mishpatim" [Exodus 21:1–24:18], where one reads, "When you lend money" [Exodus 22:24], belonged to the "Gemiles Khasodim society" [lit., "loving kindness" society that distributed noninterest loans]; the Sabbath of "Shmini" [Leviticus 9:1–11:47], where one finds the verse, "These are the creatures that you may eat among all the animals on earth" [Leviticus 11:2], belonged to the "Maykhl Kosher society," which supplied Jewish soldiers with kosher food; the Sabbath of "Ekev" [Deuteronomy 7:11–12:25], where one reads the verse, "The Lord will remove from you all illness" [Deuteronomy 7:15] belonged to the "Bikur Kholim society" [devoted to visiting the sick], and, in like manner, other Sabbaths were assigned to other societies.*

I now tell another remarkable tale that took place about a hundred years ago, during the lifetime of the rabbi Reb Moshele of Korostishev (Jews called the town Korshev).[9] The tale was meticulously recorded in the pinkes in all of its details. In Korostishev, we spoke with old folks, who had themselves witnessed this incident. The Gabay of Rabbi Moshele [or Rabbi Motele, see below], may his memory be a blessing, Reb Avrom Bloch, the elder, told us about this [incident]. (For more on him, see "Music," p. 199).[10] We also met a son of Reb Moshe-Chaim, the hero of the story, as you will later see. His son was proud of the fact that he was still living in the same house where his father had lived and that he had

---

* Rabbi Aaron Petshenik of New York told me that in Rovno the water carriers went to the leaders of the community and complained that their society, "Shoave Mayim" [water drawers], was not given a specific Sabbath to be called up to the Torah. When they were asked, "Which Sabbath do you want?" They answered, "The Sabbath with the Torah portion 'Emor' (emer)" [Leviticus 21:1–24:23].[11]

inherited the kaftan, which his father had worn when he and his rabbi committed martyrdom. What happened follows.

A plague broke out in Korostishev, may God protect us all, and people began dropping like flies. Someone ran to the rabbi, Reb Moshele, who was still a young man at the time, though already known throughout the entire region as a miracle worker, and knocked on his door, begging him to pray for the plague to stop. The rabbi, however, postponed everything [with the Aramaic phrase], "Go away today and come tomorrow" [see BT Beitzah 4a]. The plague just kept on getting worse until it reached the point of, "For there was not a house where there was not one dead" [Exodus 12:30]. The community was desperate, and all the men, women, and children went to the rabbi one morning and pleaded with him with cries and supplications. They surrounded and then stormed his courtyard, [shouting]: "Rebbe, help! We can bear no more! [lit., water has reached the soul; see King David's plea in Psalm 69:2] Rebbe, help!" Their cries reached the heart of Heaven itself.

Then the rebbe, Reb Moshele, sent for the town's sexton, Reb Moshe-Chaim, and asked him if he was prepared to risk his life for their sake.

"Perhaps, Moshe-Chaim, together we will be able to save the town from this angel of destruction!"

Reb Moshe-Chaim answered without a moment's hesitation: "I am prepared to do whatever the rebbe orders me, even to sacrifice my life!"

That very night, it is said, the rebbe and the sexton went together to the community toilet at the outskirts of town, beneath the mountain, not far from the bathhouse.

And before they took their first step down the mountainside, the rebbe warned the sexton to hold on to the rebbe's *gartel* [belt] with all his might. And to perform combinations, letter by letter, of names and adjurations [a kabbalistic method of combining letters and divine names in order to achieve a desired theurgic result], which he had taught him earlier, and, most important, not to lose focus, not even for a moment. Moshe-Chaim fulfilled his command to the letter and both [men] began their slow descent down the mountain. However, as soon as they had taken the first couple of steps, a black dog came out from behind the toilet and began walking toward them. With each step they took downhill, the dog grew larger and larger and strained upward toward them. With great *kavone* [mystical intention], the rabbi whispered holy verses in a soft voice and calculated *tserufim* [mystical combinations], and slowly, without fear, step-by-step, descended down the mountain toward the ever-growing dog. Reb Moshe-Chaim clung to the rebbe's belt, courageously following after him, and continued to concentrate on the adjurations and *tserufim*, exactly as the rebbe had instructed him to do.

The dog, which was dark as night, continued pacing toward them, and with each step [he] grew taller and taller [reaching] the heart of heaven itself. His eyes, which dripped with blood, burned in the darkness like glowing spears. It was truly terrifying. However, Reb Moshele and his sexton, were not at all frightened and, taking sure steps, guided by holy determination, they continued their journey onward, until they were level with the threatening dog.

Then, suddenly, they heard a wild, blood-curdling howl, and the giant dog began backing up, and with every step it took in reverse it began to shrink. The rebbe and the sexton did not stop. They proceeded forward with caution, step-by-step, without taking their alert gazes from the dog, which was growing smaller and smaller.

When they approached the toilet, the dog was as small as a newborn pup. The rebbe snatched him by the tail and hurled [him] into the shithole under the toilet, turned around, his face to the town, and together with the sexton, went quickly back up the mountain and did not look back.

The next day the plague subsided.

Figure 4.1. An old wooden synagogue (wood carving by Shloyme Yudovin).

8. THE PINKES AS A HISTORICAL MEMORIAL BOOK

The pinkes was also the community's memorial book. Every incident, no matter how small or large, which took place in the life of the community, would be carefully recorded in the pinkes for posterity. If a plague broke out, may God have mercy on us, and someone composed a special prayer—both the event and the prayer were recorded in the pinkes; if something out of the ordinary took place, such as: a denunciation of the community [to the authorities], or an evil decree by the government, there was always someone who would take the opportunity to compose a lament or a rhymed poem—and the lament or poem was memorialized in the pinkes; if a new field was measured [by the town] to become a cemetery, or a new fence was put up around the old cemetery and new customs were instituted, or special rules were established and special prayers prayed—all of this found a place in the community pinkes: as a memorial for future generations.

In the community pinkesim, there are tales about *dybbukim* [malevolent spirits that take possession of a living body], gilgulim [reincarnations], imps, devils, and spirits; tales about *baale shem* [lit., masters of the name, i.e., shamanistic healers], *baale moyfes* [miracle workers], *lamed vovnik zadikim* [the thirty-six hidden righteous men of Jewish lore, who keep the world afloat], as well as your run-of-the-mill Hasidic rebbes; tales about religious skeptics and heretics, desecraters of the Sabbath in public; and informers and wicked men, who were excommunicated, driven from the town, or after their death were given a shameful burial [lit., "donkey's burial"] near the cemetery fence [the traditional location for problematic graves].

Historical events were also recorded including massacres, persecutions, blood libels, decrees from dukes, and defamations as well as sudden acts of rescue and salvation.

Among the historical events that have pride of place in the Ukrainian pinkesim are those sad incidents with a connection to two bloody epochs: the earlier one of [Bogdan] Khmelnytsky (Takh veTat [5408–5409], i.e., 1648–1649) and the later one of [Ivan] Gonta, (1768, i.e., 5528).[12]

A great number of lamentations and mourning songs are in the pinkesim, which tell of the devastations, acts of terror and cruelty, which the wild Haidamaks [Cossack-led paramilitaries] perpetrated in these periods; there are long lists with the names of martyrs; and there are many versions of a specially rendered "El-Male-Rachamim" [God full of mercy, a prayer said at someone's grave, yahrzeit, and other occasions], which the rabbis and sages of that time composed in memory of the martyrs.

Many cities and towns composed their own megillahs, which tell of the miracles that happened to the inhabitants in those bleak days [and] how they were saved and came out unscathed. The miracle day was generally celebrated in the towns as a second Purim, in almost every detail. For instance, there was a fast the day before, and, in the evening, people gathered in the synagogue to hear the rabbi read their special megillah, and then they made merry the entire next day.

In the year 5553 (1792), when the Russian soldiers laid siege to the city [of Ostroh] and shot at it, putting everyone in grave danger, suddenly a miracle occurred, and the city was saved. The rabbis, members of the local council, and leaders of the community of Ostroh at that time recorded the whole event and the miracle in a megillah, and they concluded by prescribing rules for how to keep this day holy for subsequent generations. They specified what special prayers were to be prayed and what customs should be observed on that day and imposed a holy obligation on every resident to always observe these rules, all the days of his life, even if he moved out of the city.

I reproduced the full text of "Megiles-Nes-Ostroh" [The Megillah of the Miracle of Ostroh] in an earlier chapter on the Maharsha's synagogue (see p. 58) [actually found on p. 61 of Rechtman's book]. I now present the rules listed in the megillah, which will also give you a good idea of how other communities maintained the holiness of their own miracle days and how they customarily behaved on them. I now present these rules in Yiddish translation:

> And it was decided *with the council of the upright and the congregation* [Psalms 111:1], by the important elders and leaders of our community (Ostroh), as well as of Krasnegure and Mezeritch-katan, and by rabbis and Torah scholars, jointly with the head of the rabbis, the great light Asher-Tsvi, the preacher of righteousness and teacher of justice for our community [d. 1817], that:
>
> *We should* establish a permanent law that the two days, the sixth and seventh of the month of Tammuz, must remain an eternal memorial and should never depart from our mouths and from the mouths of our children and all the residents of our town, in order to relate it to the ears of our children and their descendants and to remind them every year of the miracles that happened during those two days.
>
> *We should* accept it upon ourselves to strengthen the words of their outcry, which they shouted at that time and entreated in a loud, weeping voice—men, women, and children—from the evening of the fifth day of the month of Tammuz to the morning of the seventh day, with tears and supplications.
>
> *We should* close up all the shops early on the sixth day of the month of Tammuz and not reopen them until all five books of Psalms are recited in every synagogue.

On the sixth day we must not pray in a separate minyan, not even in the *vosikim* [Jews who get up very early in the morning to pray in a minyan], but rather only in established synagogues.

We should fast on the sixth day until *mincha-gedola* [the afternoon prayer] is over. No one may consume food, save a pregnant woman or a wet nurse. However, those who are not entirely in good health, or who are not yet 18 years of age, can exempt themselves from fasting by [giving] charity.

At *shir shel yom* [Psalm of the day] [said] at the close of the morning prayer, we must recite Psalm 116: "I love that the Lord should hear."

The following day, the seventh day of Tammuz, should be a day of happiness and of *shushan ve-simcha* [rejoicing described in the story of Esther]. We shall throw banquets like those [celebrated on] Purim, we shall dress in our Sabbath clothes, refrain from reciting *takhanun* [supplicatory parts of the morning and afternoon weekday prayers], and refrain from fasting, even for a yahrzeit.

We have taken all of this upon ourselves and on our children and on everyone who is here with us in the town. It is a sin for anyone to ever change the order year in and year out, regardless of whether you live in the city or have settled in another.

(Under these [rules] are the signatures of fifty-eight rabbis, community council members, and leaders.)

These kinds of local megillahs were generally composed on parchment in scribal writing and decorated with various paintings and fitting ornamentation. The initials of the various chapters were illuminated; a poem could often be found in which the initials of the first verses spelled out the name of the author.

The following "El male rakhamim" is found in the communal pinkes of Khmelnik in memory of those murdered by Khmelnytsky in the years of Takh veTat:

> God full of mercy who dwells in the heights provide true rest under the wings of the Shekhinah for the souls of those murdered in the holy communities of Khmelnik, Fadharfish (Pogrebishtsh), Tulchin, Polino, Bar, Humiia (Uman?), and Konstantinov and the rest of the approximately three hundred holy communities in the countries of Russia, Ukraine, Lithuania and Volhynia. Sages, scribes, leaders of the people, masters of understanding, shield bearers in the war of Torah, in its study and in its teaching, and at their head the *geonim* [geniuses] our teacher and rabbi Yekhiel Mikhel son of our teacher and rabbi Eliezer, and our teacher and rabbi Hayim, and our teacher and rabbi Yitzhak, and our teacher and rabbi Shlomo the son of our teacher and rabbi Shmuel HaLevi, and our teacher and rabbi Azriel son of our teacher and rabbi Yaakov

Yitzhak, our teacher and rabbi Eliezer son of our teacher and rabbi Yekusiel, our teacher and rabbi Moshe son of our teacher and rabbi Yonasan, our teacher and rabbi Yisroel, our teacher and rabbi Lazer, our teacher and rabbi Yaakov, our teacher and rabbi Shimshon of Ostropol, and after these I am unable to list them exactly but there are so many more, and who is able to count the rest of the men, women, boys and girls, in their thousands and tens of thousands? This is not hyperbole but rather a truthful and faithful account, for their blood was spilled like water during the years Takh veTat in the sixth millennium since the world was created. For the sake of martyrdom, they did not turn away from you [see Psalm 80:19] *Hear O Israel the Lord is God the Lord is One* [the Shema prayer] Screaming and crying, they leaped into rivers and lakes and were suffocated in the waters. Calamity upon calamity [Ezekiel 7:26], destruction upon destruction [Jeremiah 4:20], the dead were laid out flat in a field and the living were thrown into a grave, may they be considered as a sin offering and a guilt offering before you. May their final rest be honored with the merit of Rabbi Akiba and his comrades who were slaughtered [during the Bar Kokhba Rebellion of 132–135 CE], until their end, on a day on which everything is good, long, and restful [in the World to Come]. And they shall avenge the men of blood and lower them into the deepest pit [Psalm 55:24]. And by the merit of those martyrs you shall gather the dispersed as with a shovel and a fan [Isaiah 30:24]. And so in clear language they will answer and declare everything in public, Amen.*

In Starokonstantinov, this type of Purim was celebrated for seven days in [the Jewish month of] Iyar and a special megillah was read. According to the megillah, their town was saved in the following way.

---

*In *Yeda Am*, Tevet, 1950, 5–6, p. 23, the following, "El Male Rakhamim for Twelve Cities" (on the martyrs of Takh ve-Tat), is printed, with a note that A. Litvin recorded it in 1912 from an torn old prayer book in Nesvich. The substance of the text, however, is abbreviated compared to our own. On account of this, the list of cities and the sages is longer and more detailed. One text fills in the other:

> God full of mercy who dwells in the heights, provide true rest under the wings of the Shekhinah for the souls of those murdered in Nemirov, the fine and great, Bortshofka, Varkhivka (Verkhifke), Prohbishtsh, Tulchin, Plinai, Bar, Hhomiah (perhaps Humiia-Uman), Konstantinov, Nahrl (Narol), Vladivo, Krasnik, Shibershina (Shtshebershin) and the rest of the holy communities in their number in the provinces of Russia, Ukraine, Lithuania, Podolia, and Volhynia, sages and scribes, leaders of the nation, masters of understanding, shield bearers in the war of Torah, in its study and in its teaching, and at their head the *geonim* our teacher and rabbi Yekhiel Mikhel son of our teacher and rabbi Eliezer, and our teacher and rabbi Hayim son of our teacher and rabbi Abraham, teacher and rabbi Shlomo the son of our teacher and rabbi Shmuel HaLevi, our teacher and rabbi Yitzhak son of our teacher and rabbi Eliezer, our teacher and rabbi . . . son of our teacher and rabbi Yekusiel,

When the Haidamakas, led by Khmelnytsky, approached Starokonstantinov, evening had just fallen, and the sun was just about to set. The congregation had gathered in the great synagogue and was praying and wailing.

The gray-haired rabbi stood up and announced in a loud voice that every member of the community should return to his own home, wrap themselves in white [garments], and return to the synagogue without delay.

The congregation obeyed him and it was not long before everyone was back in the synagogue, cloaked in white, some in *takhrikhim* [burial shrouds], others in a *kitl* [white garment worn by men on Yom Kippur, by a groom at his wedding, and after death], and the women and older children in white bedsheets.

Right after sunset, when darkness had begun to fall, the rabbi ordered everyone to spread out across the entire city and to remain there motionless.

And so, when Khmelnytsky entered the city with his band and saw these white figures, they took them for corpses. A great dread fell upon them, and they hastily retreated.

In the pinkes of Starokonstantinov, the following remarkable incident was also recorded: before Passover, someone abandoned a dead Christian child in the great synagogue and made a blood libel.[13] The rabbi and several community leaders were taken into custody. And then, one of the community leaders died. The rabbi ordered that they should give the deceased a request for the Master of the Universe to rescue them from this misfortune. They did as instructed. In their request, they lamented the evil government, which framed Jews and issued

---

our teacher and rabbi Azriel son of teacher and rabbi Yaakov Yitzhak, our teacher and rabbi Moshe son of our teacher and rabbi Eliezer son of our teacher and rabbi Yaakov, our teacher and rabbi Shimshon son of our teacher and rabbi ... and after these I am unable to list them exactly but there are so many more, and who is able to count the rest of the men, women, boys and girls, in their thousands and tens of thousands? This is not hyperbole but rather a truthful and faithful account, for their blood was spilled like water during the years Takh veTat in the sixth millennium since the world was created. For the sake of martyrdom, they did not turn away from you [see Psalm 80:19] Hear O Israel the Lord is God the Lord is One. Screaming and crying, they leaped into rivers and lakes and were suffocated in the waters, calamity upon calamity [Ezekiel 7:26], destruction upon destruction [Jeremiah 4:20], the dead were laid out flat in a field and the living were thrown into a grave, may they be considered as a sin offering and a guilt offering before you. May their final rest be honored with the merit of Rabbi Akiba and his comrades who were slaughtered [during the Bar Kokhba Rebellion of 132–135 CE], until their end, on a day on which everything is good, long, and restful. And they shall avenge the men of blood and lower them into the deepest pit [Psalm 55:24]. And by the merit of these martyrs he shall gather the dispersed as with a shovel and a fan [Isaiah 30:24]. They shall answer and declare everything in public, Amen.

evil and harsh decrees against them, and they concluded with the verse, "When you sweep away the evil government from the earth" [from the third blessing of the Amidah on Rosh Hashanah and Yom Kippur].

Someone was present there who informed on the Jews. The authorities went and opened the grave and removed the written request. The rabbi and all the other prisoners were sentenced to be hanged for rebelling against the government.

This incident as well as the names of the rabbi and the community leaders were all written in the pinkes for the sake of posterity.

In Medzhibozh, the eleventh of Teves is celebrated as a miracle of Purim and a separate megillah is read.

The "Purim of Medzhibozh" is observed in the following manner.

On the tenth of Teves, on the eve of their Purim, in the evening after the fast, everyone gathers by two gravestones, which stand abreast, in the old cemetery. On one headstone, the name Mordechai was engraved, and on the other [the name] Esther.

There, near these two gravestones, the "Megillah of Medzhibozh"—which gives a lengthy account of how these two [figures], Mordechai and Esther, rescued their community from destruction—is read aloud.

And here is, more or less, a summary of the megillah: Mordechai was a poor tailor and his wife Esther helped him out at work. When the Haidamakas had encroached on Medzhibozh and all the Jews had bolted themselves in the great synagogue, which was designed as a fortress, Mordechai and Esther quietly snuck out of the synagogue, and they both, in full agreement, risked their lives. And, in their wisdom, they managed to save the city because of a creative stratagem.

They did the following: Mordechai and Esther took two large drums and stationed themselves behind the gate at the entrance of the city. When they saw the murderous soldiers approaching the gate, they both began to bang loudly on the drums, drumming nonstop with their full force, and, at the same time, making a clamor, yelling at the top of their voices, as if an entire regiment of soldiers were standing there. And their scheme worked: the Haidamakas, hearing this racket, thought that a host of soldiers were about to attack them—so they quickly withdrew.

In Olyka, the twenty-sixth of Sivan is the miraculous day when their city was rescued from Khmelnytsky.

The small town of Olyka, which neighbors Ostroh, a "city and mother in Israel" [i.e., an important Jewish cultural center], was surrounded by a fortress, which Count Radzivilov had erected. Cannons, now old and rusty, had been built into the walls of the fortress.

Khmelnytsky and his soldiers drew near and shot at the city. The fortress was at the point of collapse. The Jews [of Olyka] had given up all hope and had already said the *vidui* [confession], when suddenly a miracle took place: these rusty old cannons began firing. A great terror took hold of the murderers, and, willy-nilly, they scurried in all directions, leaving behind many of their weapons and a lot of casualties.

In honor of this great miracle that saved the Jews of Olyka from an almost certain death, the gaon and zaddik Rebbe David HaLevi Segal, the rabbi of Ostroh, famous for his book *Ture Zahav* [The Gates of Gold] ("TaZ")—who had previously survived the massacres of Ostroh and escaped to Olyka—authored a long poem in rhymes that he called "Slikhes of Olyka" [The Penitential Prayers of Olyka].

The Jews of Olyka would fast for half a day on the twenty-sixth of Sivan. They prayed the afternoon service together, recited the "Slikhes," authored by the TaZ, and celebrated heartily afterward.

I now reproduce only the last four verses of the [Hebrew] "Slikhes of Olyka," in which the initial letters of every verse spells out the name of the author: David HaLevi:[14]

> *My beloved is ruddy and white* [see Song of Songs 5:10]. *Strangers have cursed you and you are in a pure shelter*
> *Like a hero who cannot save [anyone] for eternity, How long, O Lord? Will you forget me forever?* [Psalms 13:2]
> *And even so I lay my horn in the dust* [a sign of mourning, see Job 16:15], *the Divine Presence, what does it say: my head and my arm are in pain* [see Mishnah Sanhedrin 6:5]
> *My glory turned away, my radiance and the light of my eyes turned away. How long will you continue to conceal your face from me My Lord?* [Psalms 13:2]
> *The blood of your pious ones will you not redeem? The attribute of mercy shall you not desire for us?*
> *From the presence of the Lord, my holy God. How long shall I take counsel in my soul, my Lord* [Psalms 13:3]
> *Will you remember my complete love? All of your servants shall go down and gather in the banishment and illuminate the darkness*
> *How long shall my enemy be exalted over me, my Lord?* [Psalms 13:3]

Further, in the pinkes of Nemirov, there is a list of martyrs who were killed during the gruesome massacres of Khmelnytsky.

Much has been written about the destruction of Nemirov. To this day, hundreds of tales tell of the martyrdom and great self-sacrifice, which the Jews of Nemirov, above all young girls, showed at the time; how girls threw themselves into raging waters so they would not fall into the hands of the defilers; more than once we hear about a beautiful girl of Nemirov, with whom a Cossack had fallen in love, who duped him into thinking that she possessed an incantation that protected her from being shot by a rifle. The Cossack believed her, fired a shot, and to her great happiness, she fell dead. And there are scores of other such stories and cases. Traces of them are found in the communal pinkes of Nemirov, in the "*kines*" [lamentations], as well as in the special megillahs.

In the great synagogue, we found hanging on the western wall a lamentation of the martyrs of Nemirov from the year TaKh [1648], written on parchment, and framed in a large beautifully woodcut frame. The author of this lamentation was the "Tosfos Yom-Tov" [Rabbi Yom Tov Lipman Heller] (1579–1654), who was rabbi in Nemirov for several years.

There was also an "El Male Rachamim" hanging [in the synagogue] for the "Victims of Nemirov and the surrounding area, in the year TaKh," by the gaon, our teacher, Sheftel Segal [maybe Rabbi Shabtai HaKohen, 1622–1663, the Shach, of Vilna, who designated the date of the massacre in Nemirov as a day of mourning], may his memory be a blessing.

In the pinkes of the community, there is a special prayer and an "El Male" in memory of the soul of the holy gaon, our rabbi Yekhiel Mikhel [Katz, d. 1648].

It is said of the martyr, Reb Yekhiel Mikhel, that in those saddest days, when the slaughter knife was literally lying at his throat, he kept encouraging the Jews of Nemirov to pray and [commit] martyrdom, to not give up hope, and, most important, to keep the Jewish faith, since the Cossacks spared Jews who promised to convert to Christianity. Rebbe Yekhiel Mikhel went among the Jews, strengthened their faith, and did not allow them to convert.

When the great massacre began, Reb Yekhiel Mikhel and his elderly mother hid themselves in the cemetery, with the mindset that if they were, God forbid, to die, at least it would be in a Jewish cemetery. The murderers did in fact find them [hiding] among the graves. Other Jews, who were also hiding behind gravestones in the same cemetery and survived, related afterward that when Yekhiel Mikhel spotted the murderers with their sharp knives, with their desire to slaughter him and his mother, he begged them to kill them another way, as long as they do not slaughter [the term *shekhitah* is employed here, as it is in the following biblical verse] them, and, in the meantime, he whispered the verse: "You shall not slaughter it and its offspring in the same day," Leviticus 22:27]. The murderers were "good-natured" and granted him this request: he also implored them to spare his mother, and, likewise, his mother implored them to spare her son. The bloody murderers bound the mother and son to each other and then beat them with a stick until they took their last holy breath.

Reb Yekhiel Mikhel's wife survived. After the Haidamakas left Nemirov, she provided a proper Jewish burial to him [Reb Yekhiel Mikhel] and his mother in the old cemetery. There is a brick *tsiyun* [tombstone] over the grave of this zaddik and martyr Rabbi Yekhiel Mikhel, may his memory be a blessing.

In Polonnoye, there is an "El Male Rachamim" hanging in the great synagogue on the western wall in memory of the martyr Rebbe Shimshon Ostropolyer [d. 1648], who was, as the Jews of Polonnoye assure us, their rabbi in the years, Takh Ve-Tat.

Rabbi Shimshon was a scholar of the exoteric and the esoteric, devoted to the study of the Zohar and delving into the books of the Kabbalah. By means of various *tserufim* and *gematrias* [numerological associations], he determined that the *khurbn* [catastrophe, destruction] wrought by Khmelnytsky was the first sign of the [final] Redemption. The name Khamil (which is how Jews referred to Khmelnytsky) alludes to this: the *notarikon* [mystical technique by which initial or final letters of words are combined to form new linguistic units] of Khamil is: *Khevlei moshiach yehyu lakhem* [They shall be for you birth pangs of the messiah, BT Sanhedrin 98a]. The *gematria* of *khevlei moshiach* is *Takh* (408). He also identified many other abbreviations and *gematrias* that prove this is the first sign of the Redemption.

Rebbe Shimshon and his entire community were martyred in the following way: when the murderers drew near to Polonnoye and had already begun to smash open the city gates, Reb Shimshon went out into the city and called everyone to come to the great synagogue dressed in burial shrouds and wrapped in prayer shawls. Once the synagogue was filled with men, women, and children, and their cries reached the heart of heaven, Reb Shimshon stood before the lectern, speaking first with great passion about martyrdom, and then reciting the *vidui* [confession of sins] in a loud voice, and everyone repeated after him word for word. While they were in the middle of saying confession, the Haidamakas broke into the synagogue, and Reb Shimshon and his entire holy community perished in holiness and purity.

The Jews of Polonnoye established this unfortunate day, the sixteenth of Kislev, as a collective fast day. They all gathered in the study houses, remembering the souls of the entire community, who were killed so tragically, and reciting the special "El Male Rachamim," in which the martyr, Rebbe Shimshon Ostropolyer, is specifically mentioned.

We also saw similar "lamentations," "slikhes," and "El Male Rachamim," in Bar, Tulchin, Yaltushkov, Uman, Korostitshev, and Brailov.

※ ※ ※

One hundred and twenty years after Khmelnytsky [Ivan] Gonta led a bloody campaign that laid waste to hundreds of well-established Jewish communities throughout Ukraine and also left behind just as many bloody footprints in scores of local pinkesim. Long lists of Gonta's victims can be found in the records books as well as special "El Male Rachamims" written in their memory. There are also lamentations and megillahs, which speak of Jewish martyrdom and self-sacrifice; of the terrible, cruel torments that our grandfathers and great-grandfathers underwent.

There is a widespread legend that soon after the evil decrees of Takh Ve-Tat, after the massacres of Khmelnytsky, a great *zaddik nister*, one of the hidden *lamed vovnik zaddikim*, traveled to what remained of the Jewish settlements in Ukraine and decreed on pain of excommunication that they should abandon that blood-soaked land, Ukraine, and settle in other lands. The *nister* warned that those who stayed would be excommunicated. They would render themselves guilty, and the biblical verse would apply to them and come to pass: "He is after all flesh and his days shall be a hundred and twenty years" (Genesis 6:3). And, as is well known, Gonta's *khurbn* [lit., destruction or catastrophe; same word used to refer to the destruction of the two Temples and to the Holocaust] came exactly one hundred and twenty years after Khmelnitsky's *khurbn*.

The expedition managed to find important material, both written and oral, concerning the period of Gonta in Starokonstantinov, Balta, Smiela, Zhitomir, and Uman. Incidentally, two printed books, which were soaked in Jewish blood spilled during the Gonta massacres, were found in the great synagogue of Uman. The first book is *Levush Ir Shushan* by Rabbi Mordechai Yoffe [d. 1612], the Baal Ha-Levushim, and the other is *Shnei Lukhot Habrit* by Reb Yeshaya Ha-Levi Horowitz, the Shelah.[15] These two blood-soaked books were treated with great sanctity and stored in the holy ark with the Torah scrolls.

THE WIDOW AND HER DAUGHTER AND GONTA'S DOWNFALL

Among the hundreds of tales about the miracles and wonders that took place in the days of Gonta, there exist a significant number that depict, in varying versions, the downfall of his soldiers as well as his own miserable end.

I now relate a tale I heard from an elderly man in Brailov, Reb Yekusiel Segal, a grandson of the late rabbi of Brailov, the gaon and zaddik Rabbi Avraham-Moshe Segal, may a zaddik's memory be a blessing. He is the author of the book *Mayim Kodashim*, a commentary on Seder Kodashim [the fifth book of the Mishnah]. The book was published in Mezshirov in the year 5550 [1790]. We were photographed* on the porch of the house where Reb Yekusiel lived, and in which his grandfather, the "Mayim Kadoshim," had also lived. Reb Yekusiel

---

*See the photograph in Section 4.

assured me that his father had watched the tale being recorded in the local pinkes, which was lost in a fire a few decades back.

And the elder Reb Yekusiel gave the following account:

> When Gonta, may his name be blotted out, arrived in Brailov, he asked the first person [he came across]: Where is a tavern located? For it was well known that his *modus operandi* was that in every city, before he began his murdering and slaughtering, he would get his Haidamakas drunk, so that not a single bit of mercy was left in them, and when he saw that they were good and plastered, he kicked off his bloody sport of plundering, looting, and murdering.
>
> In those days, a young widow ran the tavern in the city and her only daughter, who was a very beautiful girl, lent her a hand. The widow was herself a beauty, with a luminous face and graceful manner.
>
> And so, when Gonta caught sight of this gorgeous widow, he was enchanted by her beauty. He proceeded to sweet-talk her and, after several glasses of whiskey, told her that she really needed him and that he wanted to take her as his lawfully wedded wife; he promised her a huge wedding with a military procession as was fitting for a heroic Cossack leader such as himself.
>
> With no other choice, the widow pretended to be happy over his declaration of love, and said that she was more than happy to [get married] on one condition: he must spare the city of Brailov and make sure that nothing bad happens to anyone. Gonta immediately issued a stringent order not to harm anyone. He even assigned a squadron of Haidamakas to preserve order in the city.
>
> *And then at midnight* [quoting from the Passover Haggadah]—the elder Reb Yekusiel continued—A messenger came and reported that the Poles were making an assault. Gonta and his soldiers abandoned the city in great haste and engaged the Polish soldiers in battle. Meanwhile, Brailov breathed a sigh of relief and enjoyed this respite. The widow, however, did not stop crying and wailing, for she knew very well that when this murderer returned, he would carry out his devilish plan. He would defile her and perhaps her daughter too. Her fear of the imminent danger greatly troubled her and, out of great desperation, both the widow and her daughter agreed to take their own lives, so that they would not fall into his impure, murderous hands! They both went into the cellar of their tavern. The mother slit her only daughter's throat with her own hands and then killed herself.

The old man, Reb Yekusiel, grew suddenly silent and pondered how he could search in his memory to link this disjointed series of events. He, however, soon gathered himself and said:

> We have a great God who pays the wicked for his deeds! In that battle [against the Polish], the wicked Gonta, may his name be blotted out, and his whole

army, were captured by the Poles, and they got the death they deserved, may they be gone forever. Gonta himself, that great oppressor, was tortured to death in the most awful of ways: he was skinned alive; his flesh was torn apart by iron combs; and then, finally, a searing-hot, iron crown was placed on his head while people joked that they were crowning him the Polish *król* (Polish, king).

The good news of Gonta's downfall spread with lightning speed throughout all the Jewish settlements of Ukraine. Everyone thanked and praised God for this great miracle. In Brailov the good news reached us as well, almost that same day, and we were so happy. We all gathered in the great synagogue and recited the entire *Hallel* [Psalms of joy and thanks] collectively.

When we realized that the widow was not there among the congregation, the rabbi sent for her. It was only then that we discovered what had happened to her and her daughter.

A great sadness took over the entire city. Everyone cried and lamented the widow's tragic end, for she originally meant to sacrifice herself in order to save the Jews of Brailov from a sure death, and then committed martyrdom with her only daughter so that they would not fall into impure hands.

She and her daughter were accompanied to the old cemetery with great honor and there both were buried in a single grave. And this entire incident—Reb Yekusiel concluded—was recorded in the communal *pinkes* in eternal remembrance.

Figure 4.2. Agile like the deer (wood carving).

TO SECTION 4

Figure 4.3. The title page of the communal pinkes of Berdichev (taken from "Yeda Am").

Figure 4.4. The house of the Mayim Kedoshim in Brailov. On the porch, with his grandchild. The old man recounts, and A. Rechtman records.

NOTES

1. The word pinkes (Hebrew, *pinkas*) derives from a Greek word meaning "notebook." Jewish communities or certain communal organizations (e.g., the burial society) employed the term to refer to a book in which they recorded important events and other notable information for posterity. The town pinkes was treated with great reverence by community members, as detailed by Rechtman and confirmed by other sources from Eastern Europe, for example, Leybl Shiter, "What Is a *Pinkes*?" in Kugelmass and Boyarin, *From a Ruined Garden*, 51–53. After the Holocaust, many of the *yizker bikher* (memorial books) published to commemorate now destroyed Eastern European Jewish communities were given the name "Pinkas" or "Pinkes," in homage to the earlier tradition of the town pinkes. Simon Dubnow, the great Russian Jewish historian, drew extensively on pinkesim—which he also collected—in his historical research. More recent scholarship has included Petrovsky, "Newly Discovered Pinkassim of the Harkavy Collection," 32–35; Berkovitz, *Protocols of Justice*. Today, the most important collections of pinkesim are located in the Vernadsky Library in Kiev, the library of the YIVO Institute in New York, and the National Library of Israel, which along with the Central Archives for the History of the Jewish People in Jerusalem, has made some pinkesim available digitally.

2. For a description of similar societies in a single community, see Nadav, *Jews of Pinsk, 1506–1880*, 454–458.

3. In some communities, the members of the *khevre kedishe* would fast and recite *selikhes* (penitential prayers) on the fifteenth of Kislev. See Gelbard, *Otsar Ta'amei Ha-Minhagim*, 568.

4. Here, Rechtman portrays the peasant as employing Slavic religious terms to describe the Baal Shem Tov.

5. Rabbi Meshulum Zisha (a.k.a. Zusha or Zusya) of Anipol (d. 1800) was a disciple, along with his brother, Rabbi Elimelech of Lizhensk, of Rabbi Dov Ber, the maggid of Mezeritch (next to whom he was buried in Anipol). His life of poverty, piety, and wandering inspired many Hasidic legends.

6. Rechtman included the Ukrainian text in the original rather than transliterating it as he typically did.

7. The Ukrainian word *xatinka* means "hut" or "shack." Rechtman glosses it with the Yiddish *shtibl*, which typically refers to a small synagogue or prayer room but can also refer to a structure—also called an ohel—built over a grave.

8. Communal pinkesim frequently recorded cases of girls who accidently lost their virginity—a phenomenon known as *mukat ets* (Hebrew, woodstruck)—in order to prevent problems when the girls later sought to marry. Freeze (*Jewish Marriage and Divorce in Imperial Russia*, 36) quotes one such entry: "Let it be recorded this day of the mishap that occurred to so-and-so, the daughter of so-and-so. By an act of heaven she fell from the stove and impaled herself on a sharp-edged bedpost standing nearby. There was blood on that spot and blood on the bedpost. Therefore, lest it be questioned, God forbid, in the future should there not be a sign of virginity, we, the undersigned have inscribed this event in this *pinkas* as evidence of accidental loss of virginity."

9. This is a reference to Rabbi Moshe of Korostishev (1789–1866), the second of the eight sons of Mordechai (Mottel) of Chernobyl, the founder of the Twersky Hasidic dynasty that spread throughout Ukraine during the nineteenth century. In 1838, Rabbi Moshe had a son, whom he named Mordechai (Mottel), in honor of his own father who had passed away in 1837. He, in turn, was the father of a second figure known as Rabbi Moshe of Korostishev, who was named after his grandfather. This second Moshe of Korostishev had a son whom he named Mordechai (Mottel).

10. This is an error. It is actually located on page 249 in the Yiddish.

11. Rechtman glosses the Hebrew *emor*, meaning "speak," with the Yiddish *emer*, meaning water bucket or pail. Evidently, when the water carriers heard the name of the *parshah* recited in Hebrew they mistook it for the Yiddish word and assumed that it had to do with their profession. In fact, the Torah portion actually concerns the *kohanim* or priests. Given the low social status of the water carriers, their identification with this particular *parshah* was ironic.

12. Ivan Gonta (d. 1768) was a leader of the Koliyivshchyna, a Cossack uprising against Polish rule in Ukraine. He was involved in the massacre of the Jews of Uman in 1768 that would later inspire Rabbi Nahman of Bratslav to settle in the town. Gonta became the subject of numerous legends and is one of the heroes of the Ukrainian nationalist, artist, folklorist, and writer Taras Shevchenko's epic poem "Haidamaky," published in 1841.

13. The blood libel refers to the centuries-old antisemitic lie that Jews murder Christian children in order to use their blood to make matzah, the unleavened bread eaten on Passover, or for other ritual purposes. For a survey of the phenomenon, see Dundes, *Blood Libel Legend*.

14. On the TaZ in Olyka and the *slikhes* (*selichot*) he composed, see Buneh, "Ha-TaZ be-Olyka," 64–68.

15. Rabbi Mordechai Yoffe (d. 1612), known as the *Levush*, was a major Halakic authority who incorporated kabbalistic and philosophical elements into his legal works, including *Levush Ir Shushan* (1598). Rabbi Yeshaya Ha-Levi Horowitz (d. 1630), an important legal scholar and mystic also known as the Shelah, was the author of the influential work *Shnei Lukhot Ha-Berit* (1648).

FIVE

TALES ABOUT NIGUNIM [MELODIES] AND PRAYERS

1. THE ORIGIN AND SIGNIFICANCE OF NIGUNIM

Music was very important to the Ukrainian Jews, especially to the Hasidim. Through music and melody, they sweetened their difficult and bitter lives. When a Hasid went to his rebbe for a holiday, the best gift he could bring back to his fellow Hasidim was a new tune. The Hasidim in the shtibl quickly grasped the tune and sang it with great joy, *dveykes*, and *hislayves*. It did not matter whether you were rich or poor—all were equal when they sang.

For Hasidism, music was not merely a spiritual pleasure but also a form of holy worship whose sanctity reached the supernal realms and could even influence the ministering angels.

"Music is the language of the soul, as well as of the ministering angels!" exclaimed Rebbe Shneur Zalman of Liady.[1] The angels above are influenced by people below: "The supernal beings are only awakened by the Jewish people, who are the root of all and the principle of thought. When Israel sings, the angels also possess the power to sing."[2]

The place of learning together was taken by singing together. Learning Torah is a sacred obligation, and consulting a holy book is a great mitzvah, but "with one holy tune, one can relay the content of entire bookshelves, for the language of melody is concise."

The Besht (other sources say Rebbe Nahman of Bratslav) once explained to his inner circle the reason why his method of Hasidism draws opposition. He did so in the following way: "I am likened to one who sings a melody and people get so caught up that they lose themselves in an ecstatic dance. Onlookers, who cannot hear the melody, wonder to themselves: *why are they dancing?* That is precisely the reason why *misnagdim* [opponents of the Hasidim] are surprised that you are so attached to me—for if they do not hear the melody, they cannot understand the dancing!"

"Music originates from beneath the Throne of Glory, which is saturated with praise and exaltation. Souls also originate beneath the Throne of Glory and they know the songs and sing them constantly. Once they are born, souls forget those songs. However, when a human soul comes into contact with the pure music that originates underneath God's throne, the person is reminded of the origin from whence it came!"[3] For this reason, Hasidim maintain that pure, unadulterated music necessarily produces true happiness and joy.

Rebbe Pinkhes Koretser, one of the Besht's companions, was intolerant of sad tunes. In this same vein, Rebbe Nahman of Bratslav would not let his Hasidim grow sad through melancholic tunes. He even arranged the special prayer, which his Hasidim would recite before singing:

> Protect us, God, from tear filled and sad tunes—from tunes that are sung mainly by the wicked, in order to draw others to themselves. Be merciful and shelter us from their grasp, for you know the kind of damage they do with their tunes and how greatly they can harm virtuous Jews. So come to our aid and see to it that we merit pure and holy happiness through joyful music; through song that draws the heart to you and to your Torah and to the true *zaddikim* ... and help us, so that with the strength of the true *zaddikim* we may elevate all the tunes from the wicked ... and transform them into tunes of happiness.[4]

Further, it is said that Rebbe Nahman of Bratslav said the following to his disciples: "How do you pray? Can you serve God with words only? Come, for I will show you a new way: not with words, not with speaking, but with song! We will sing and the Lord will understand us!"

The melodies and wording of the prayers of our grandfathers and great-grandfathers that were transmitted to us, are in the category of Oral Torah. Since no one could read musical notation, naturally no one recorded any of the complicated tunes or lyrics. Thus, they were kept from being forgotten only because they were always sung: on Sabbath and festive occasions in the home, or at the *tishn* [Hasidic gatherings] held by rebbes, both in joy and, God forbid, in sorrow. Such is how all the wonderful, uncorrupted songs were transmitted orally from one generation to the next, until we inherited this enormous treasury of music. Melodies upon melodies, and every melody has its significance, pedigree, and origin.

Figure 5.1. An old wooden synagogue (wood carving by Shloyme Yudovin).

2. THE RECORD PLAYER IN THE BES MEDRESH [STUDY HOUSE]

The Ethnographic Expedition devoted great efforts to the work of collecting, recording, and classifying the [Jewish] musical heritage. To this end, the famous musician from Moscow and composer of Jewish folk music, Yoel Engel, and the musician Z. [Zisman] Kiselgof, one of the pioneers of Jewish folk music, and the author of several songbooks, originally participated in the expedition, although just for a short time.[5] And when these two musicians had to break away from the expedition, we continued collecting and recording, on our own, a great number of songs and tunes with a phonograph on wax cylinders. The records were then sent off to Petersburg and Jewish musicians put them into musical notation. One of [these musicians] was the composer Lazar Saminsky, who worked for some time on the aforementioned recorded song collection and brought them critical acclaim.[6]

The melodic and lyrical material that we recorded on our phonograph was very diverse: traditional melodies and *zmires* [songs] for holidays and Sabbath ("Havdole" [the ritual separating the Sabbath from the week], "Got fun Avrom" [God of Abraham], "Eliyahu Ha-Novi" [Elijah the Prophet]); songs and melodies from the *kheder* (about the rebbe, the angry rebbetzin, and yeshiva boys); melodies from Hasidic dynasties; *musar* [ethics] melodies; melodies with words, which were passed down with great holiness in the name of *zaddikim* of previous generations, such as: the melody and song that the Baal Ha-Tanya [Master of the Tanya; Shneur Zalman of Liady] used to sing before reciting *toyre* [his teachings], "All the angels and all the seraphs ask where is God?" the "[*tikkun*] *hatsos*" [kabbalistic prayer recited after midnight in mourning of the Temple's destruction], melody of the Besht; the Apter Rov's melody of "*dveykes*" [cleaving to God or the *zaddik*; religious ecstasy], or his song "Harey ani lefanekha ke-khli male busha u-khlima!" ["Behold I am before Thee like a vessel filled with shame and confusion," BT Berakhot 17a]—Oy, father, I am ashamed; the Shpoler Zeide's "Kol bayaar anokhi shomeya, aym [should be 'av'] le-banim kore" [I hear a voice in the forest, a father calls to his children] in Hebrew, Yiddish, and Ukrainian; Reb Borukhl Medzhibozher's "Zagray mini kozatshenko"; the now well-known but previously obscure songs by Rebbe Levi Yitskhak of Berdichev: "Der Kadish" [The Kaddish], "Du-du" [You-You], "Mayn tate zikhrono levrokhe" [My Father, May His Memory Be a Blessing]—and hundreds of other sacred songs and melodies.

We also collected a great many songs that celebrate or mourn out-of-the-ordinary local events. Occurrences that happened in one's own shtetl, for example: an unlucky love, a fire, a drowning,* a person who froze to death, a convert, a murder victim, an informer; historical songs about pogroms, evil decrees, blood libels, persecutions; songs about *Khapunes* ["kidnappers" of Jewish children to serve as soldiers in the Russian military during the reign of Czar Nicholas I], "Czar Nicholas' Soldiers" [i.e., the child soldiers known as "cantonists"]; songs about Czar Nicholas, and so on.

The bes medresh was our go-to place for recording melodies, prayers, and songs. We brought along the phonograph that we were traveling with and, once prayer had ended, set the case on a long wooden table. The assembled Jews would gather around us. We opened the case and explained the deep wisdom that lay within this wondrous machine. Meanwhile, one of us would sing some well-known tune into it, immediately transpose the "membrane," and play back exactly what had been sung into it. We used to cough or laugh intentionally in the middle of singing and the cough or the laugh would then be heard distinctly [when we played it back]. This was always a big hit with every one and it did not

---

*It is worth noting that in nearly every shtetl that had a river, there was a deeply rooted superstition that the river demanded an annual human sacrifice.[7] And, until someone drowned, the Jews of the town were extremely careful when bathing in the river. They avoided going in too deep, and would not dunk, let alone go for a swim.

take long before many of the gathered Jews wanted to sing something into [the phonograph].

In the eyes of these simple Jews, the phonograph seemed like one of the seven wonders of the world and [Thomas] Edison, its inventor, a great genius. It is truly astonishing just how popular the name Edison was among these Jews. Wherever one went, people knew of him and told remarkable tales and legends about him. It was, therefore, no great wonder that [these Jews] reacted to his invention of the phonograph with such heartfelt enthusiasm.

Even the rabbis, who were usually very concerned about maintaining their status; for whom it was beneath their dignity to be impressed by material things, and whose initial attitude toward the phonograph was, naturally, a reserved one, with a bit of disdain for an object that was created for the common folk—even they eventually dropped their dignified opposition and joined everyone else in taking pleasure in the remarkable object, the strange instrument, the phonograph.

Indeed, in most cases, it would be the rabbi himself, who would good-naturedly turn to his gathered Jews and call on one of them to sing into [the machine]: "Reb Chaim!" the rabbi would holler with a kind smile, "Reb Chaim! We are all well aware of your singing voice. Nu, get over here, sit down right there, and sing one of your 'best of the best' into it. You know what, Reb Chaim? Sing the 'Gerer Nigun' [The Gerer Rebbe's Niggun], and let's see how it 'plays back.'"

"Reb Berl! I shouldn't have to ask you. They can say what they want, but you are certainly not bashful! Get over here and sing into it your [version of] 'Marko, Marko, shtsho ti robish na yarmaku?'" (Marko, Marko, what are you doing at the fair?)

"Moshe-Ahron! Moshe-Ahron! A *badkhn* [entertainer/master of ceremonies at Jewish weddings] knows that there is no such thing as shame! For you, the public is like clay in the hands of the potter [Jeremiah 18:6; a piyut from Yom Kippur]—when you want it, people cry; when you want it, people laugh! So, I beg your pardon, but get over here and show these strangers what you know! I want them to hear either how you seat the bride, or how you sing the cheerful 'Dobridzshen!'" [Dobriden; Russian, "good morning," a standard tune at Jewish weddings].[8]

The precious, kind-hearted Jews would go along good-naturedly and for hours on end and with great pleasure sing us their finest and best songs. Practically every time, it would end with them following us in droves to our inn, where we offered them a *tikun* [here, drink] and snacks and talked late into the night.

In this manner, we managed to acquire a great quantity of authentic songs, both sacred and mundane, sung by generations of Jews. And with every city and town that the expedition visited, our treasury of music and songs grew and was enriched.

3. SUBLIME MUSIC, THE KOROSTISHEVER ZADDIK AND THE PHONOGRAPH

Hasidim and mystics believe that sacred music, music played with *kavone* [kabbalistic intention], is able to ascend to the supernal realms and open the "Palaces of Holiness," just as it is written in (*Zohar Tikun* 11 [i.e, *Tikkunei Zohar* 11]): "There are palaces which can only be opened by means of music."[9] Likewise, it is believed that coarse, commonplace music, that is too say, music sung without [kabbalistic] intention, has no real substance or life. This music is born dead—it resides in the material world and lacks sufficient life to rise to the supernal world.

I chose to make this brief introduction, because I want to segue into a very characteristic story about a *zaddik*'s relationship to the phonograph. An elderly man, Reb Avrom Bloch, the gabay of the late Korostishever Rebbe, Reb Motele, may his memory be a blessing, told this story to me.

As soon as our expedition arrived in Korostishev, I performed my duty and paid a visit to the rebbe, a grandchild of the great *zaddik*, Reb Moshele of Korostishev, one of the eight sons of Reb Motele Tshernobiler. His gabay, the esteemed older gentleman by the name of Reb Avrom Bloch, was an acclaimed musician. He had a large repertoire of melodies, which were sung at the *tishn* that Reb Motele Tshernobiler himself had hosted. The current rebbe, who, incidentally, was also named Reb Moshele, invited us to visit him and let us bring along our phonograph. We arrived after the Sabbath was over with our record player and, as usual, showed off its tricks: we recorded ourselves before coming, played it back, and then requested that the elder Reb Avrom, the gabay, sing something from those old melodies of yesteryear.

Reb Avrom took a moment to think, looked around at the rebbe and his household, who were all sitting around the table, dressed in their Sabbath best, then turned to us and said more or less the following:

> "As soon as I saw this machine of yours over here, it reminded me of a story that took place many decades ago: the rebbe, Reb Motele, our rebbe's holy father, may his memory be a blessing, was a young man at the time. And you, rebbe," he said to his rebbe with a grin, "were just a boy at that point." The rebbe, Reb Motele, may his memory be a blessing, was a good

friend of mine and used to chat with me when he was in the mood. I still remember it as if it were yesterday that a Jew came to town with a similar machine that was able to sing and talk on its own. And whenever we gave the man a coin, he turned on the machine and played cantorial pieces, ditties and other foolishness. This wondrous machine became the talk of the entire town and it was said that a genius had invented it. The news soon reached the rebbe, Reb Motele, may his memory be a blessing, who sent me to invite over the Jew with this 'novelty.' That happened right after the Sabbath. The rebbe put on his Sabbath kaftan. The rebbetzin and her children dressed up in their Sabbath clothing. Someone covered the table with a new tablecloth and everyone took to their seats. When this Jew arrived, he placed his 'novelty' in the very center of the table, inserted black, rubber tubes in the rebbe's ears and into all of our ears, turned something inside of the machine, and suddenly we heard Jews reciting the blessing for the new moon, 'So I dance before you' [part of the text of the blessing] and 'Sholem Aleykhem, Aleykhem Sholem.'[10] Afterward, we heard someone singing lamentations for Yom Kippur. Then suddenly, the rebbe jumped up, as if he had been bitten by a snake, and yanked the rubber tubes out of his ears. He stood and began to pace back and forth, evidently disturbed, stopped right next to me, laid both hands on my shoulders, staring me straight in the face, and said: 'Avrom! Try singing something, a melody or a prayer, right into the machine, but do it with all your heart and soul and sublime holiness!' I began to shake and stutter from fright, 'Rebbe! You want people to mock me too?' The rebbe stared right into my face again, pulled his hands away from me, shook his head no and cried, 'Help, Avrom! Where does one get hold of the great man!' and shortly afterward went into his private study.

"The rebbe's words confounded me and gave me great heartache. I, however, did not have the courage to go straight to the rebbe myself and ask him the meaning of his statement. I gave the Jew with the 'novelty' a ruble and he went on his merry way.

"I couldn't sleep a wink the entire night. The rebbe's words, may his memory be a blessing, ate away at me. At the break of dawn, I quickly ran to the rebbe, having already made up my mind to ask him to explain the significance of his cryptic statement. When I entered the rebbe's study, I found him pacing back and forth from one corner to another. It was a clear sign to me that he was in great distress. Once the rebbe saw me, he repeated in a melancholic voice, his words from yesterday: 'Help, Avrom! Where does one get hold of the great man!' I could no longer control myself and burst into tears: 'Rebbe!' I sobbed, 'I could not sleep the entire night! Have pity, Rebbe, and tell me the meaning of your holy words.' The rebbe put me at ease and said the following: 'The Baal Shem Tov, may his merit protect us,' once came into a study house and yelled: 'Help, Jews! The study house is full of prayer and it's suffocating,' and then offered this explanation: 'Pure prayers, those uncontaminated by strange thoughts, do not remain in the study house below, but rather they rise into the heights and soar straight into Heaven, to the storehouse of prayer. On the other hand, improper, defective prayers cannot be elevated, rather they are left to wander here, below, in the study house. And that,' the rebbe concluded, 'Is the secret of this 'novelty,' invented by Edison. Simple, vulgar words and inappropriate music reside in his machine. That's why I asked you, Avrom, to sing a pure, uplifting, holy prayer into his machine. Yet, when you refused, I screamed out: 'Help, where does one get hold of the great man!' according to how it is rendered in the holy Zohar: 'the words of a great man ascend into heaven'; and then Edison would have been the fool."

* * *

The [Hasidic] court of Korostishev was renowned for its outstanding, original architecture. Famous artists, architects, and painters would travel great distances to paint and copy this building, as an exceptional model of old architectural style.

And how beautiful and original the extraordinary building was from the outside, so exquisite and magnificent, and the inside was just as original. The walls and the ceiling were covered with rare paintings by an anonymous artist that depicted: "the four seasons of the year," "the seven planets," "the Exodus out of Egypt," and the like—in short, a rich combination of colors full of charm and naivete.

The gabay, the elderly gentleman Reb Avrom Bloch, showed me many antiques, an inheritance from previous generations. Among them, an old manuscript, containing commentary on the Torah, written on deer parchment, with a verse from the Pentateuch followed by Rashi, and then a translation into Arabic. So it went, verse by verse. A second manuscript, which consisted of kabbalistic combinations of letters based on the single verse "Shema Yisroel . . . "; and in the center of the residence stood a large silver Hanukkah menorah that Reb Avrom said the late rebbe, may his memory be a blessing, inherited from his father-in-law, who was a *kohen*. In his city, people considered it an honor that his father-in-law was the *kohen* for a *pidyen-haben* [redemption of the firstborn son].[11] For years, he collected the silver coins (five silver rubles equivalent to five shekels, which are mentioned in the Pentateuch), which he would receive for the *pidyen ha-ben*, in a special container. When the container became full, he went to Zhitomir to a famous goldsmith who made the Hanukkah menorah from the silver rubles. The Hebrew date and the name of the goldsmith were inscribed on the menorah stand.

4. THE SHALESHUDES [SABBATH THIRD MEAL] AND *MELAVE-MALKE* [USHERING OUT THE SABBATH QUEEN] AMONG BRATSLAV HASIDIM, AND THE *EYNKL* [GRANDSON] WHO PLAYED FIDDLE

When the expedition visited Berdichev in the year 1913, there could still be found around sixty to seventy families of Bratslav Hasidim.[12] They were a self-sustaining and isolated community; they were not allowed to participate in a single communal activity and were not admitted into any local societies. One did not marry into their fold and generally avoided them at all costs.

However, among themselves, the Bratslav Hasidim lived in peace and harmony. They literally shared the bread from each other's mouths. One man's joy was everyone's joy, and one man's sorrow was everyone's sorrow.

Happiness was the linchpin of their community: "And you shall indeed be joyful" [Deuteronomy 16:14, traditionally connected to the holiday Shemini Atzeret], always be happy and never permit sadness. Their rebbe, Reb Nahman of Bratslav,* always warned that even tears that one sheds during a time of trouble should come from the *source of happiness* and not, God forbid, from the *source of sadness*: "Weeping," said Reb Nahman, "is an acronym for: 'In your name, they rejoice all day'" (Psalms 89:17). They prayed in their own synagogue, which was located in a "yamke" [a kind of basement apartment], a few steps down, so that the windows were at about the same level as the sidewalk. The Bratslav Hasidim had their own style of prayer. They say it originated from Reb Nahman himself. During prayer, they would dance and bounce all over the place, always in the spirit of "All my bones shall say" [Psalms 35:10]. In the heat of prayer, they would mix in many Yiddish and goyish words.

Every Bratslav Hasid was accustomed to setting aside a brief period of time each day for solitary meditation. Wherever he found himself, be it at home, at work, or even on the train, he would steal away for several minutes. He hid in a corner, covered his face, concentrated his thoughts on *Le-shem yikhud kudsha berikh hu* [for the purpose of the unification of the Holy Blessed One] and, at the same time, recited a short prayer from the *tefilas ha-hisdavkus* [prayer of

---

*Reb Nahman of Bratslav (Rosh Chodesh Nisan, 1772 to 18 Tishrei, 1810) was a great-grandson of Reb Yisroel Baal Shem Tov (the son of Feyge, who was the daughter of Odl, the Besht's daughter). In 1798, Reb Nahman took a trip to the land of Israel and spent about a year there in Tiberias. In 1800, he settled in Bratslav and, in 1810, after a fire, moved to Uman, where he died at thirty-eight and was buried. His Hasidim traveled great distances to Uman for Rosh Hashanah to visit their rebbe, whom they thought of as if he were still alive and whose place they did not fill with another rebbe.

cleaving to God].[13] The style and text of this prayer was not a traditional one, and it was neither static nor uniform. Rather, during *hisdavkus* each would say what he was feeling at that moment, in his own words and style—that is, precisely in his own language. According to tradition, this is how the rebbe, Reb Nahman, conducted himself, and he ordered his students to conduct themselves in this way: "*Tefilas ha-hisdavkus* must come from the depths of one's heart and necessarily be in the language that one normally speaks, not in the holy tongue. For in Hebrew, it is difficult to speak from the heart, since we are not accustomed to speak in the holy tongue."[14]

Regarding the verse, "And I shall remove the heart of stone from their flesh, and I shall give them a heart of flesh" (Ezekiel 11:19), the Bratslav Hasidim indicate that *lev basar* [heart of flesh] possesses the same letters as Bratslav.

As mentioned earlier, they isolated themselves from everyone, just as everyone kept away from them. For a stranger who was not one of them, it was very difficult, almost impossible, to be admitted into their circle. They simply would not have it. They eventually explained to us that this was done to prevent any unpleasantness from taking place on the part of these strangers, who were known to come ostensibly to pray together, but who would then provoke conflicts that sometimes led to bloody beatings.

With much difficulty, patience, and perseverance, we, Jews from far away, succeeded in gaining their trust, and very soon we were even considered like one of them. We prayed in their synagogue, were called up to the Torah on the Sabbath, and ate the Sabbath meals with them.

Everyone celebrated Shaleshudes [the third Sabbath meal] together in the synagogue.[15] Each person brought a couple of servings of food, which they casually placed on the table. Once everyone had arrived, some accompanied by their wives, who, incidentally, had a separate entrance to the women's section, they prayed the afternoon prayers and quickly took their spots around the table. They ate the food that everyone brought and fulfilled the mitzvah of Shaleshudes with all its festivities, music, and song. They began by singing these *piyutim* [liturgical poems]: "Bnei Heichala" [Children of the Palace] and "El Mistater" [Concealed God]. Then they recited "Ta Chazi" [Come, See] and moved to wordless music, to their own inherited Bratslav melodies.[16]

In between melodies, people also spoke words of Torah, related a story or a parable, repeated an original Torah insight, an aphorism, or simply a good word, and everything [derived] from the rebbe, Reb Nahman—"the wellspring of wisdom is a flowing stream" [Proverbs 18:4].[17] And then they continued singing. They sang with blazing spiritual intensity; and, in the heat of their enthusiasm, stood up and broke into a dance—"They will praise His name in dance" [Psalms 149:3].[18] While dancing, they sang the words from the Zohar over and over: "The

Torah was given with a melody; the Divine Presence—with a melody; Jews will go out from Exile with a melody."*¹⁹

And so, in the darkness of the synagogue, they and their shadows danced in a tight circle. For hours on end, they elevated their spirits and transcended the desires of the flesh, truly [penetrating] the depths of the soul.†

That same Saturday evening, we celebrated *melave malke* in the residence of one Reb Hillel, who was a great-grandchild of Reb Nahman of Bratslav, and was a well-liked, kind-hearted person. Tall, with a long blonde beard, his *yikhes* [lineage] illuminating his good-natured, smiling face, he was a scholar with rabbinical ordination. However, he did not involve himself with the rabbinate but rather made a living in business.

The Bratslav Hasidim gathered in his house for the *melave malke*.²⁰ Right after Havdalah, Reb Hillel played a number of tunes on his fiddle, which he had inherited from his great-grandfather, Reb Nahman (who, by the way, loved to play fiddle during *melave malke*). Reb Nahman explained this in the following way: the feast of *melave malke* is called "the feast of King David,"‡ and King David, the sweet singer of Israel [2 Samuel 23:1], famously played fiddle: "David's harp!"²¹

Reb Hillel told us that his [great] grandfather, Reb Nahman, would say that, by virtue of the fiddle, one can reach the "wellspring of song" and draw handfuls from it. One need only know how to play [the fiddle] correctly. Pedatsur§ revealed secrets of the Torah with his fiddle.²² It is just a shame that he did not know what he was revealing.

Reb Nahman also, by the way, recounted how his great-grandfather interpreted the verse, "I shall sing songs to my God as long as I exist" [Psalms 104:33], which relates to music, by means of a parable.

"In the whole world," Reb Nahman said, "There is but one holy Jewish melody that contains the entirety of the Jewish people. In the soul of every

---

*Reb Nahman Bratslav used to say: Why do Hasidim dance? Because they rise above materialism, above worldly concerns, when they dance, and if even just a bit, that too is good.

† It is worth noting that when An-sky watched the Bratslav Hasidim dance, he was so enraptured that he sent a telegram to [Konstantin] Stanislavski, of the Moscow Art Theater, which at the time was in the process of preparing An-sky's mystical drama *The Dybbuk* for the stage, and asked him to send his ballet master to Berdichev, so that he could see how Hasidim dance.²³ And, indeed, Stanislavski's ballet master came several days later from Moscow, and we all spent a Sabbath with the Bratslav Hasidim and watched how they danced during the Shaleshudes.

‡ It is told in the Talmud [BT Shabbat 30a] that, in response to King David's prayer to God: "God, reveal my death and how much longer I will live" (Psalms 39:5), it was revealed to him that he would die on the Sabbath. For this reason, he used to praise God every Saturday night and rejoice over the fact that he would live to see another week.

§ A famous fiddler in Zhitomir, who used to play at the weddings of Hasidic rebbes.

individual, of every single Jew, there is a small piece of this collective melody, a mere spark. The *zaddik* gathers all of these scattered, individual sparks and sings the melody of the world—with wholeness. When the *zaddik* sings the collective melody with a sense of wholeness and with mystical intention, he awakens all the individual parts and makes them sing. They sing with him with all their heart and he gladdens their souls. So when a person's soul detects the part of a melody, which is related to its root, then the entire person is elevated and sanctified, and he feels that he is a part of the great song of the Jewish people. And this is the interpretation and meaning of the verse: 'I will sing'; 'with my being,' with my own part, with the spark that is in my soul and which relates only to me."

"There are three kinds of melodies," Reb Nahman once said, "A melody that *one sings* during prayer, a melody that *causes* one to pray, and a melody that turns one into a *praying person*" [italics in original].

The congregation at the *melave malke* sang wonderful Bratslav melodies. Each melody more beautiful than the other. And the entire time Reb Hillel held forth on the fiddle. They told stories about Reb Nahman of Bratslav, about the persecutions he went through, about the great feuds he waged—first with the Shpoler Zeyde [Grandfather of Shpola] and then later on with the Savranyer Zaddik—and also about his trip to the Land of Israel.[24]

Reb Hillel said that when Reb Nahman returned from his trip to the Land of Israel (in 1799), he told his closest followers: "My dear children! I brought you a gift from the land of Israel and its name is *mahloyke* [feud]!" And later, when he began to be persecuted greatly, Reb Nahman repeated to them: "No, my dear children! That's not what I meant! I meant that people will not let me sit on a Jewish '*prizve*' [bench]!"[25]

And this is how the Bratslav Hasidim passed the time at Reb Hillel's house: with music, song, and conversation about Torah, until the woman of the house gave a call from the kitchen. We all washed up, sat at the set table, and relished the hot red beet borsht they had served us.

While eating, they sang "zmirot le-motzei shabbat" [traditional songs for the close of the Sabbath], recited the special "Atkinu [Seudata]" [a kabbalistic poem composed by Rabbi Isaac Luria] in honor of King David: "Prepare the feast of faith, the fourth feast for King David," and they finished off with a dance.

By the time we left, the roosters had already crowed at the third watch of the night.[26]

※ ※ ※

And at the home of the handsome, remarkable Bratslav Hasid, Reb Hillel, we recorded from him and his close associates, hundreds of penetrating aphorisms

Figure 5.2. And strong as a lion (wood carving by Shloyme Yudovin).

and wonderful tales, which were passed down over several generations by word of mouth. We recorded Reb Hillel playing fiddle and scores of Bratslav melodies and prayers, which he and his close associates sang.

By the way, we purchased many valuable objects from Reb Hillel for the Jewish Ethnographic Museum, among them: a manuscript by Reb Nosen, Reb Nahman's disciple; a crystal chandelier, which hung, according to family legend, in Reb Nahman of Bratslav's private study; a white silk *zshopitse* [long coat] fashioned with white brocaded flowers; a wide white silk belt, made from the same fabric, as well as a metal Hanukkah menorah.

5. A MELODY THAT EXPLAINS SECRETS OF THE TORAH (THE RABBI'S MELODY)

Hasidim believed that a melody sung with mystical intention often explains profound secrets of the Torah. They said that Rebbe Shneur Zalman of Liadi, the founder of Chabad Hasidism, the Baal Ha-Tanya and author of *Shulchan Aruch Ha-Rav*, always sang this [Yiddish and Aramaic] hymn before sitting down to learn:

> All the angels, all the seraphim,
> Ask where is God?
> Oy vey! What does one reply to them?
> *No thought can grasp him at all* ... (three times)

> All peoples, all nations of the world,
> Ask where is God?
> Oy vey! What does one reply to them?
> *There is no place devoid of Him* . . . (three times)
> (There is a third stanza that I cannot remember.)²⁷

According to tradition Rebbe Shneur Zalman authored ten melodies that parallel the ten *sefirot* [divine aspects]. One of the melodies was widely disseminated among the Hasidim, and it is known as "The Rav's Melody."²⁸ The following tale is told about this melody, which is sung to this day in Jewish communities throughout the world.

One Sabbath, the "Rav," Rebbe Shneur Zalman, was saying *toyre* [teachings] to his Hasidim at his *tish* [lit., table, i.e., gathering]. While he was speaking, he noticed a strange old man sitting across from him whom he had never seen before. The man was tense and staring straight at the rebbe's mouth. [It looked as if he did not want] to miss a single word of the Rebbe's teaching. He was all ears and focused toward the Rebbe with his entire being. However, it turned out that he was unable to grasp the Rebbe's teaching, filling his face with profound sorrow.

Afterward, the Rav went into his private study and sent for the stranger. He asked him if he understood his earlier remarks. The man broke into tears and, despairing, replied that he could not grasp his holy words. With tears in his eyes, he explained that he was orphaned at a very young age. His poor mother could not afford to keep him in cheder that long, so he had to lend a hand and became a craftsman. By the time he became an adult and got married, he could not find the time to study Torah. He had to provide for his wife and children. He satisfied himself with reciting Psalms, yet even the Psalms, which he recited every day, he could not understand too well. And now, in his old age, with his children already married off, his heart yearned to learn Torah. Even so, he was laughed at among the learned Jews in the study house: "I have heard, rebbe, that you befriend all people, so I came to you and sat at your table like everyone else. My happiness knew no bounds; I felt like a somebody. But when you started to teach *toyre* and I did not understand a lick, I grew bitter and my joy vanished. Rebbe! Holy Rebbe! What can I do to become worthy of being your disciple and understand your *toyre*?"

The man dropped his head and his tears ran through his beard. Reb Shneur Zalman placed his right hand on the man's shoulder and said to him in a gentle voice: "Stop crying! It's the Sabbath. And you're not supposed to be sad on the Sabbath! Today, at my *tish*, I explained the Baal Shem Tov's approach to Hasidism. If you were unable to understand via words, I shall help you to understand via music. I will now sing a melody for you which contains the entire approach of the Baal Shem Tov."

And Rebbe Shneur Zalman began to sing a melody with great sweetness. One "movement" after the other. The man listened with all his heart and soul. He stood, as if frozen, and did not move an inch. The further the melody progressed, the brighter his face beamed. He radiated happiness and a joyful warmth coursed through his every limb. When the Rav finished the melody, the radiant Jew cried out blissfully: "Rebbe, I understand! I get it! I feel that I am now worthy to be your student!"

From that moment on, the man of Liady made it a rule to sing this melody after each time he taught *toyre*, in case there was someone present who did not fully grasp the words of his teaching. He would reexplain his *toyre* by means of the melody that is known to this day as "The Rav's Melody."

* * *

The expedition successfully recorded many songs and melodies that were associated with wondrous tales and legendary events: I recount in the following pages several of these legends having to do with melodies.

In the various cities that we visited, we recorded with our phonograph the melodies and songs connected to the legends that follow, and in due course sent them off, together with all the rest of the ethnographic material, to the Ethnographic Museum in Petrograd. Let us hope that they are preserved in their entirety there.

6. THE BESHT'S "THE LORD REIGNS, HE IS CLOTHED IN MAJESTY" [PSALM 93] AND MENDEL HIS CHAZAN

This was recorded by the Ethnographic Expedition in Medzhibozh, in the year 1913. It was sung by the town rabbi Chaim Bick, now a rabbi in New York; he also told us the following tale, which we recorded at that time.[29]

A rich lumber merchant from Pilyava, a small shtetl not far from Medzhibozh, provided *kest* [room and board] for his son-in-law, who was devoted to Hasidism. His name was Mendel. A couple of times a year, Mendel would travel with his father-in-law to Medzhibozh, to receive a blessing from the Besht and to drink from the pure wellspring of Hasidism.

After his father-in-law died, and it was time for Mendel to look for a way to make a living, he went to Medzhibozh and sought the advice of the Besht concerning what he should do to best provide for himself and his family. The Besht listened to his request and ordered him to spend the Sabbath with him, to pray in his synagogue, to listen to his mode of prayer, and, most important, to remember the melody of the new [version of] "The Lord reigns, He is clothed in majesty," which the Besht himself would sing that Sabbath for the first time ever.

Mendel humbly obeyed. At *kabbalas shabbos* [lit., Welcoming the Sabbath; Friday night prayer service], as soon as the Besht began singing his new [version of] "The Lord reigns, He is clothed in majesty," Mendel became all feeling, all ears, and felt the sacred tones of this melody engraving themselves forever into his burning mind. For the entire Sabbath, his senses were tensed and prepared to receive the Besht's style of prayer.

On Saturday night after Havdalah [the ritual separating the Sabbath from the week], the Besht sent for Mendel, closed the door to his private study, and said the following to him: "Mendel! During *kabbalas shabbos*, you heard my new [version of] 'The Lord reigns, He is clothed in majesty,' and I will now sing it for you again. But make sure you are concentrating, so that you can absorb [the melody] and sing it back."

Mendel answered with great humility: "Rebbe, I feel that I absorbed your holy melody the first time I heard it. I know it already."

And, in the midst of talking, he began to sing, "The Lord reigns, He is clothed in majesty," with great spiritual feeling and intense enthusiasm, exactly as the Besht had sung it during *kabbalas shabbos*.

The Besht was captivated by his sweet voice and greatly impressed by his precise rendering [of the melody]. He said to him: "Mendel, become a chazan, and in my synagogue no less," to which Mendel immediately and with great happiness agreed.

When they were saying their goodbyes the Besht gave him his hand, pulled him toward him, and whispered into his ear: "You shall make a living from *khazones* [cantorial work] for the rest of your life. And you should know that the last time you pray will be when you are pushed away from the *omed* [synagogue lectern]."

And Mendel became the regular chazan in the Besht's synagogue. The new [version of] "The Lord reigns, He is clothed in majesty" won instant fame and was sung by the many Hasidim who used to come from near and far to visit the Besht in Medzhibozh.

After the Besht died, Mendel Chazan hired a choirboy and traveled to cities and towns to pray on the Sabbaths in their synagogues. His reputation as the "Baal Shem Tov's Chazan" preceded him, and, in every city that he visited, people treated him with respect, let him lead the Sabbath services, and afterward generously compensated him.

And, just like that, Mendel Chazan and his choirboy wandered from city to city, until they finally arrived in Lizensk, the city of the rebbe, Reb Elimelekh of Lizensk, who was the most outstanding pupil of the rebbe, Reb Dov Ber, the Maggid of Mezeritch, who succeeded the Besht. So, just as Mendel Chazan was accustomed to doing in every city and town he came to, he went directly to the local rabbinical authority, the rebbe Reb Elimelekh, to request permission to lead the Sabbath prayers in the synagogue. The Rebbe Elimelekh looked down on chazans, especially chazans with choirboys, and he never allowed a nonlocal chazan to go before the *omed* of his synagogue. However, when Mendel came to him, Reb Elimelekh could not turn him away all together on account of his respect for the Besht, and so he permitted him to lead prayer, but only on Friday night.

And as soon as Mendel Chazan began the prayer service for welcoming the Sabbath, Rebbe Elimelekh's spirit was stirred and uplifted. He felt a sweet ecstasy down in the depths of his soul, and, by the end of *kabbalas shabbos*, when Mendel began to sing with his choirboy, "The Lord reigns, He is clothed in majesty," in the tune of the Besht, Rebbe Elimelekh suddenly felt himself losing vitality as if his soul were about to depart. He was so shaken up that he jumped up and dashed over to the chazan, shoving him aside with both hands and standing before the *omed* himself. He finished *kabbalas shabbos* and prayed the evening prayers.

Right after prayer ended, Rebbe Elimelekh approached the humiliated Mendel Chazan and asked him to forgive him for his insult and explained that he had to behave in such a manner for, had he waited a second more, his soul would have departed from the great sweetness [of Mendel Chazan's singing]. He invited the chazan and his choirboy over for the Sabbath and bestowed great honor on them.

At the close of the Sabbath, during *melave malke*, the rebbe Reb Elimelekh asked the chazan to tell, as is customary among Hasidim, a tale about the Besht, as well as how he merited becoming his chazan.

Mendel began by speaking at length about how he had gone to the Baal Shem Tov for advice on how to make a living; how the Besht had him master his new version of "The Lord reigns, He is clothed in majesty"; how after the Sabbath he had shut both of them inside his private study, where he sang him the melody again; and, finally, how the Besht had ordered him right then and there to become the chazan of his synagogue.

And, what is more, Mendel added the following tale, which he heard from the Besht that same Sabbath during Shaleshudes.

A duke built a palace for several years straight. [It was] a magnificent building. One time, when a zaddik went to go pray, a heavy downpour suddenly broke out, hail fell, and a powerful windstorm began to blow. So the *zaddik* sheltered himself from the storm in the not-yet-completed palace. When the windstorm subsided and the rain had stopped, the *zaddik* left the palace. And then as soon as the zaddik reached a [safe] distance, the palace cracked and collapsed.

And then the Besht gave the following explanation: that the whole point of the building was to protect and strengthen the zaddik through the brief duration of the storm, and that as soon as the building carried out its mission, it performed its tikkun [redemptive purpose], and there was no longer any reason for its existence; therefore, it collapsed.

Mendel caught his breath and continued with a deep sigh: "When the Besht ordered me to become his chazan, he also told me while we were saying our goodbyes that the last time I pray will be when I am pushed away from the *omed*. For this reason, know that I have completed my mission on earth, I have performed my tikkun, and now my time has come."

The Rebbe Elimelekh understood that the chazan was in the same category as the palace and that, through the spiritual inspiration that he had awakened in him, through the great joy that he had brought him with the Besht's melody of the "The Lord reigns, He is clothed in majesty," which comes from the [heavenly] palace of music and song, the chazan's soul had fulfilled its purpose and performed its tikkun and would for this reason soon abandon his material body.

And that is what happened. The next day, the chazan died. The rebbe Reb Elimelekh, accompanied him to the cemetery, ordered the choirboy to sing the "The Lord reigns, He is clothed in majesty," at his open grave, and, after covering the grave, he alone recited kaddish for him.

It is said that three days later the choirboy went to the burial society and requested that a grave be prepared for him next to the chazan because Mendel Chazan had come to him in a dream and told him that he was being invited to welcome the Sabbath in *gan eden* [the heavenly paradise], so that he could sing the Besht's "The Lord reigns, He is clothed in majesty," in honor of the rebbe Reb Elimelekh, and that he, Mendel Chazan, does not want to stand before the *omed* without his choirboy.

When the Rebbe Elimelekh was told this, he understood that he, too, was being summoned to the *kabbalas shabbos* in the heavenly paradise. So, he ritually purified himself [for burial], laid in his bed, and gave up his soul.

7. *VE-LA-MALSHINIM* [MAY THE SLANDERERS; BLESSING AGAINST HERETICS] FROM BEFORE THE GALLOWS

In Belaya Tserkov [Russian, White Church] (Jews referred to the city as "Sadeh Lavan," [Hebrew, White Field] or "Shvarts Tume" [Yiddish, Black Impurity]), people slandered the town chazan and his choirboys, claiming that in the [town's] great synagogue, while praying "The Giver of Salvation" [a traditional prayer for the government] on the Sabbath, the chazan and his choirboys had cursed the czar rather than blessed him. The chazan and his choirboys were put in jail and sentenced to death by hanging.

Execution day was set for a Sunday. A crowd of peasants traveled with their wives and children from the local villages to watch the condemned Jews, the "Anti-Christs," get hoisted onto the prepared gallows. It is said that, while the chazan and his choirboys were being led to the gallows, they sang on their final journey: "May the slanderers have no hope," from the weekly *Shmone-esre* ["eighteen benedictions" or Amidah prayer]. And they sang with great sadness and heartache. The chazan's voice carried into the open space of the Belaya Tserkov market and above everyone's heads and the choirboys accompanied [him], their voices saturated with sadness, and they continued to sing, until they approached the gallows.

And then a miracle took place. The music moved the hearts of the peasants and their wives. Sobs were heard everywhere. The hardened hearts of the judges grew softer and then they rescinded their prior judgment on the spot and let the chazan and his choirboys go free.

The Jews of Belaya Tserkov memorized this [version of] "May the slanderers" and sang it at every opportunity on both joyous and sorrowful [occasions].

8. THE SHEPHERD'S MELODY

In Pilyava, a tiny shtetl in Podolia, there lived a *zaddik*, in the time of Gonte's massacres (in 1769), whose name was Rebbe Leyb.[30] The Jews of Pilyava told many tales about their Reb Leyb: his circumspection, humility, and piety. They even believed that on account of [Reb Leyb's] merit, their town had survived Gonte and his bloodthirsty soldiers.

Rebbe Leyb was devoted to his fellow Jews. He loved everyone the same and had no favorites. In Pilyava, he so loved to say the following, that it had become an aphorism: "A partial *zaddik* loves partial sinners; a complete *zaddik* loves complete sinners." He had a large number of Hasidim and many students.

His work used to bring him to Jewish settlements, where he would encourage village Jews to send their children to study Torah.

It is said that once when he was traveling with several of his students, they passed by a gentile shepherd boy, who was blowing on a pipe. As they got closer and Reb Leyb could hear the melody that the shepherd boy was playing, he ordered the horse and wagon to come to a halt and listened attentively to the melody coming from the shepherd's pipe. Once the shepherd stopped playing,

Rebbe Leyb ordered that he be given several coins to replay that same melody. This was done several times until the zaddik Rebbe Leyb and his students began to grasp the melody and could reproduce it. And when Rebbe Leyb and his students were finally able to reproduce the entire melody exactly, the shepherd boy began to get confused and eventually started to play an entirely different melody.

Reb Leyb struck his pony, and they were off. At that moment, he also made an aside: "Certainly, the shepherd will never again be able to play this melody on his pipe." Later, he explained what he meant to his fellow travelers:

> The Levites sang this very melody in the Holy Temple [in Jerusalem]. However, it was once damaged by an evil thought that a Levite had while singing. As a result, the melody was defiled and could not ascend to the [heavenly] Palace of Song. It, therefore, remained hovering here in the Material World; and then the shepherd caught it in his pipe. But now that we have mastered this melody, we have, by playing it with proper intention, repaired and redeemed it from the gentile shepherd and that is the reason why the shepherd boy forgot it right away and could no longer play it.

The melody, which is called "The Shepherd's Melody," quickly became famous all over Pilyava and the surrounding area.[31] Everyone knew it, and it was sung at weddings, circumcisions, and all joyful occasions and holidays.

9. "THE GIRLISH MELODY" IN NEMIROV

Years ago, when "pańszczyzna" [Polish, serfdom] was still the law of the land in Ukraine, and the peasants were the serfs of princes and dukes, there lived an evil, bloodthirsty duke in Nemirov. He flogged his peasants, ripped off pieces of their skin, beat them mercilessly just for the fun of it, and, for the slightest infraction, hung or shot them.

And he greatly persecuted the Jews of Nemirov, literally bathing himself in their blood. One time, the cruel duke passed a decree that on his birthday [the Jews] must present him with three of the most beautiful Jewish girls in Nemirov—girls who had never known a man.

The Jews took this evil decree strongly to heart. They prayed and fasted, but, alas, no remedy could be found to nullify the evil decree. When the day of reckoning, which the duke had set, arrived, lots were cast, and the three girls, on whom the dreadful lots fell, were led off with cries and laments to the duke's castle.

It came to pass that when the duke and his guests were drunk on wine and in good spirits, he ordered the Jewish girls to be escorted in—completely naked.

Figure 5.3. An old wooden synagogue (a wood carving by Shloyme Yudovin).

As soon as the girls had stepped over the threshold, one of them began to sing a heart-wrenching song. Her song touched everyone. The duke and his drunken guests remained seated as if in a trance. They listened attentively to the exceptional style of singing, which they had never heard before, and, when the girl finished singing, they applauded her at length, lavished the girls with expensive gifts, did not lay a finger on them, and with great pomp and fanfare sent them home.

And the city of Nemirov was relieved. They rejoiced and thanked God for the miracle. They quickly learned the "girlish melody," as it was referred to, and it was sung joyfully at all happy gatherings.

10. REBBE DOVIDL OF TALNE SAYS KADDISH [MOURNER'S PRAYER] FOR AN OPERA SINGER

Rebbe Dovidl Talner, one of Rebbe Motele Tshernobiler's eight sons, author of the books: "Mogen Dovid," "Birkas Dovid," and "Kehilas Dovid," among others, held music in extremely high regard.[32] It is well accepted among Hasidim that Rebbe Dovidl was a regular visitor to the [heavenly] "Palace of Music" and that, through his personal cantor Reb Yosele (he was actually called "the rebbe's Yosele"), about whom it was believed that he was to the Talner what the Golem was to the Maharal of Prague—that through him, Rebbe Dovidl drew melodies directly from the [heavenly] "Wellspring of Music," which is located in the middle of the [heavenly] "Palace of Music."

The "rebbe's Yosele" would bring a new melody every Sabbath and rehearse it with the Hasidim at the *tish*. When the Hasidim returned home, they brought the melody back to their locales, and soon enough the whole lot of Talner Hasidim were singing the melody wherever they lived.

In all, the chazan Reb Yosele introduced around five hundred different melodies.

I recount a notable tale here concerning the power of a Talner melody, which we recorded during our visit to Talne.* It goes like this.

[There was once] a childless Talner Hasid from the small shtetl of Rakitno. After Rebbe Dovidl gave him a blessing, the man had a baby boy and [the rebbe] ordered him to name the child Meyer. He was a precocious child and while still in infancy demonstrated a great penchant for music. His crying was calmed by music. He was raised on music, and, well before he could recognize the form of the letter aleph, he could already repeat his mother's lullabies and even [knew] his father's Sabbath songs.

His father beamed with pride and was merely waiting for his musically gifted son to mature a bit before taking him to the rebbe for a blessing: that his voice should be strong, clear, and sweet but, above all, dedicated to God's work.

Alas, his father passed away before he could merit bringing his little Meyerl to the rebbe.

As soon as Meyerl had grown up a little, his widowed mother put him in the service of Reb Meir Polishuk, the chazan of the "Talner Synagogue" in Belaya Tserkov (Shvarts Tume), to be a choirboy. Polishuk was one of the most famous chazans in the entire region. From the start, he became aware of Meyerl's prodigious skills and took him under his wing and let him sing solo. His singing amazed everyone, and [they] showered him with great love and admiration.

Due to all the fanfare, Meyerl grew prideful and thought of himself as if he had an illustrious pedigree. He no longer listened to the chazan and behaved impudently with the other choirboys. He would play tricks on them and tormented not only the choirboys but even the chazan himself. The chazan, however, would bite his tongue, withhold his anger, lovingly put up with his

---

*Pini Minkovsky mentions this event in his memoir *From the Story of My Life* in the first volume of *Reshumot*, Odessa, 1914 [sic], p. 102.[33]

shenanigans, and always forgive him, all because of his wonderful singing; that is, until Meyerl played such a dirty trick that the chazan became enraged and lost all his patience.

This happened during the time of *slikhos* [penitential prayers]. Preparations for the Days of Awe were already in progress. Meyerl took the chazan's "Slikhe" [sing., penitential prayer], with the musical notes, and right before the prayer "Hear our voice," jotted down the following disgusting words: "The chazan loves a shikse!" While reciting "Slikhes," when the chazan came to [the point] "Hear our voice" and realized the trick Meyerl had pulled on him, he could no longer turn a blind eye to his insolent behavior. He drove him away right before the Days of Awe.

So Meyerke left for Kishinev and became one of Nisi Belzer's choirboys. However, he did not conduct himself any better with Nisi.[34]

One Sabbath, Nisi and his choirboys had come to Talne, for the rebbe Reb Dovidl, who, as said previously, was a lover of music, especially cantorial music, had invited them, so that he could enjoy their music. In the rebbe's honor, Nisi prepared a new "ke-bakarat [roeh edro]" [a liturgical piece with the words from the biblical verse "Like a shepherd inspecting his flock," Ezekiel 34:12] and taught Meyerl the solo. However, when the time came for his solo, Meyerl did not sing the prepared "ke-bakarat," but instead one of his own "Ha-ben yakir li efrayim" ["Is Ephraim a dear son to me?"; Jeremiah 31:19].

The rebbe was overjoyed by Meyerl's singing and asked him to sing again. The entire time that Meyerl was singing, Reb Dovidl sat pensively, not taking his eyes off of Meyerl. It was obvious that the music touched him. Once Meyerl finished singing for the second time, Reb Dovidl called him over, praised his singing and gave him a blessing that the merit of his beautiful and holy music should protect him in all of his hardships.

Nisi Belzer could not forgive Meyerl for undermining him and not singing the "Kevakores" that he had taught him. So, he too drove him away from his presence.

For a while no one heard anything more of Meyerl. No one knew what had become of him. Sometime later, it was discovered that he had completed the conservatory in Kiev and ultimately become a singer in the Kiev Opera and even married a singer from the same opera company—a Christian.

Then, one day, Meyerl crossed paths with a Talner Hasid in Kiev. Meyerl recognized him immediately. He hugged him and asked about the rebbe. When the Hasid reminded him of his [rendition of] "Ha-ben yakir li efrayim," Meyerl's face beamed with joy.

It is said that soon after his encounter with this Hasid from Talne, Meyerl became greatly depressed. For entire days, he went about lost in thought, full of sorrow and bitterness, until he became so melancholic that he left his gentile wife.

Once, in the middle of singing a well-known aria, which he always did so well, while the orchestra was accompanying him and the conductor stood, waving his baton, Meyerl suddenly saw the rebbe, Reb Dovidl, standing in the place of the conductor. He was conducting him with the baton and ordering him to sing: "Ha-ben yakir li efraim." Meyerl obeyed the rebbe and, with his high voice, he began to sing the same "Ha-ben yakir li efrayim," which he had sung years earlier for the rebbe when he was a choirboy.

There was a great uproar. The curtains went down. The orchestra stopped playing. Everyone screamed for him to stop. Meyerl, however, heard and saw no one. He continued to sing his [rendition of] "Ha-ben yakir li" with great enthusiasm and rapture—until he was carried off the stage by force.

As a result, he lost his esteemed, artistic position. He was expelled from the opera and left Kiev. For a period of time, he wandered about from city to city—ragged, unkempt, and disheveled, to the point that he was unrecognizable—often hungry and reduced to begging for a bit of bread.

After years of wandering around in this condition, he came back to Talne and stayed in the poorhouse with all the rest of the poor people.

Rebbe Dovidl Talner had a custom to invite over all the poor people in the city for Shaleshudes. On that Sabbath, Meyerl came with all the other poor people to the rebbe Reb Dovidl for Shaleshudes.

While the Shaleshudes hymns were being sung, Meyerl suddenly jumped up and yelled out: "Rebbe, I want to sing!" When the Hasidim looked at him, they took him for a complete lunatic, may God protect us, and wanted to remove him from the table. As they were doing this, they heard the voice of the rebbe Reb Dovidl say:

"Jews, don't touch him! Leave him be! It is Meyerl the singer! Meyerl wants to sing! Let him! Meyerl has repented and is searching for a tikkun [spiritual redress], so let's all help him get it! Let him! Let him sing and may the merits of his singing protect him!"

Meyerl sang his "Ha-ben yakir li efraim" from the Days of Awe—and he sang with so much sweetness, that everyone stood where they were as if enchanted. Not taking his eyes off of him, Rebbe Dovidl asked Meyerl to sing the song again just like before and afterward called him over and asked him to stay with him in Talne.

At the end of Shabbos, Reb Dovidl told his inner circle: "His soul has received its *tikkun*, but his body cannot recover."

Meyerl did not live to the end of the year. Rebbe Dovidl accompanied him to his eternal rest and personally said kaddish over him for the entire year.

11. THE DYBBUK-MELODY OF TALNE

The town chazan of Vishnevets was an elderly Hasid whose voice was well past its prime. Many of the congregants were dissatisfied with how he prayed and asserted that it was high time for a new chazan to be appointed. However, the Talner Hasidim pushed back. The city went on like this for a while, silently quarreling over the chazan.

Then, one day, the chazan's voice became very hoarse and, after some time, even many of the Talner Hasidim agreed that it was time for a new chazan.

So, as is the custom among Jews, they came to an agreement with the old chazan and he gave his consent, though he had no choice but to give it. A new chazan was hired. He was a brilliant young singer, who was extremely pious to boot. The whole city loved the sweetness of his beautiful praying and respected him greatly for his piety and virtue.

The former chazan, whom they had gotten rid of, could not stand his demotion. He considered the new chazan an encroacher and was jealous and hateful toward him. When the Days of Awe arrived, the disgruntled old chazan grew greatly ill and on the eve of Rosh Hashanah passed away.

Everyone regretted his death and many of his old enemies felt deep down that they had something to do with his untimely passing. The new chazan, the pious young man, also felt restless and went about in a daze, tense and upset—and felt that he, too, had been a cause of heartache for the chazan, which might have brought about his untimely death.

Then, something unlucky happened to the new chazan: the first day of Rosh Hashanah, before Musaf [the additional Sabbath and holiday service], when it was time for him to begin his [version of] "Hineni" [Behold me of little merit, trembling and afraid], which he had rehearsed with his choirboys—all of a sudden, he went blank and forgot his prepared [version of] "Hineni." He shuts his eyes, tries to remember—but, to no avail—he cannot remember. Suddenly, the late chazan flashed before his eyes, and "Behold me of little merit, trembling and afraid," issued from his throat, but not the one he had rehearsed rather the one the old chazan had sung in years past. The congregants immediately recognized the voice to be that of the old chazan and also recognized his version of "Hineni."

The new chazan collapsed. The choirboys circled around him, lifted him up, and wanted to take him out of the synagogue. He fought back with extraordinary might, escaping their grasp. He dashed to the *omed* and the hoarse voice of the old chazan angrily tore at his throat, complaining: "I am still the chazan of this city! This is my *omed*, so I will say 'Hineni . . .' in my style and tune!"

Faint, the young chazan was taken home, and one of the householders prayed musaf in his place.

Soon after Rosh Hashanah, the young chazan was brought to the rebbe, Reb Dovidl, in Talne. Rebbe Dovidl shut himself and the chazan in his private study and ordered him to sing his [version of] "Behold me of little merit, trembling and afraid!" He obeyed. However, the hoarse voice of the late chazan was heard. Reb Dovidl, now livid, said angrily:

> Music must be sweet and pleasant, and there must be sweetness in prayer, especially during the Days of Awe, when one prays [the verse] in "Behold me of little merit, trembling and afraid," "May it be your will, awesome God, that my voice may go unhindered and not become hoarse, that it may grow in strength like the sound of the shofar." A prayer leader must be able to persuade the Master of the Universe with his voice; and in order to be convincing, you need a more beautiful and better voice than yours. Go back to your eternal rest and let your replacement pray in his own beautiful, sweet voice, so that he can intercede on behalf of his congregation of Jews!

A drawn-out whine became audible. Reb Dovidl continued in a gentle whisper and without any anger. He said more or less the following: "Listen to my words and hear the sayings of my mouth [Hebrew, play on Proverbs 4:20]. Listen up cantors, the young one and the old one, pay close attention to the 'Behold me of little merit, trembling and afraid,' which I am about to sing for you with my own tune. Pay attention and learn this new melody for both your sakes!"

Then, Rebbe Dovidl began to sing his [version of] "Behold me of little merit, trembling and afraid" in a pure voice and with a new tune. The more he sang, the more powerful his voice became with great *deveykes* [mystical ecstasy] and sweetness. And when Reb Dovidl finished off with "He hears prayer" [part of the Amidah prayer] he lifted up his moist eyes, reached out both his hands, and said with great tenderness:

"Now, purified ghost, return at once to your rest. This melody shall open all gates for you and loosen all bolts. Your soul will receive its full redress and I assure you that you will merit to sing this melody before the righteous in paradise!"

Reb Dovidl approached the young chazan, stared deep into his eyes, embraced him and said: "Well then, let's now try to sing my 'Hineni' in unison. The old chazan is no longer here. He will never again appear before the *omed*!"

Then, Reb Dovidl began to sing his "Hineni" again. The young chazan sang along in his own clear young voice, which had returned to him and which sounded even clearer and purer than before.

For many years, the Talner Hasidim sang this melody, which they referred to as "The Talner's Dybbuk-Melody."[35]

12. IMPURE MUSIC AND RABBI YOSELE, THE REBBE'S, DEMISE

Although Reb Yosele, the Talner Rebbe's chazan, merited to live to a ripe old age, his death was nonetheless very tragic: he was buried alive in a mass grave along with many other important townsmen in Novomirgorod, on Lag Ba-Omer 5679 (1919) by [Ataman Nikifor] Grigor'ev's murderous bandits.[36]

After the passing of Reb Yosele's rebbe, Reb Dovidl Talner [he] was asked to be the chazan of Reb Yokhntse [Yohanan] of Rachmistrivka, the younger brother of Reb Dovidl.[37] And when, a few years later, Reb Yokhntse passed away, Reb Yosele stayed with Reb Yokhntse's eldest son, Reb Dovidl, in Zlatopol.[38]

The town of Novomirgorod was located on the other side of the Zlatopol River. Reb Yosele's daughter, Devorah Leah, and his son-in-law, Nakhum Spivak, resided there with their four children.

Reb Yosele set out on a journey to spend Lag Ba-Omer with his children in Novomirgorod. However, as soon as he crossed the bridge, he fell into the hands of the Grigor'evtsy, who had already occupied Novomirgorod.

Reb Yosele, his son-in-law, Nakhum, and many other important men of the city, were forced to dig themselves a mass grave.

Devorah Leah witnessed how her father, husband, and other important Jews were hurled into the mass grave that they had dug for themselves and were buried alive.[39]

As the grave was being filled, Reb Yosele said the *vidui* [confession] with everyone and then began to sing one of his holy melodies with great *deveykes*. And he did not stop singing the entire time the grave was being filled. Eyewitnesses would later say that the melody could still be heard from within the grave for some time afterward.

* * *

Hasidim and mystics, who always seek to discover the ultimate source and reason for everything, also looked for the source of Reb Yosele's sin, which had led to his tragic death. They searched and searched and eventually hit on a moral defect, which Reb Yosele had brought about unknowingly. And even though it was done unintentionally, the sin had such large-scale, public impact, that it was said this was the reason his punishment was so merciless and tragic: "The Holy One Blessed be He deals strictly with those around him like a thread of hair" (Babylonian Talmud Yevamot 121b). The following is what was concluded.

Reb Yosele prayed for many years for the old rebbe, Reb Dovidl Talner, may the memory of a *zaddik* be a blessing. The last time that the elderly Reb Yosele led prayer during the Days of Awe at Rebbe Dovidl's [court] in Zlatopol, hundreds of Hasidim assembled for the honor of hearing him. On the eve of Rosh Hashanah, when the sun had already begun to set, the great synagogue was packed with people praying, and Reb Yosele returned from ritual immersion [in the mikveh] with his entourage of fine Hasidic men. They were ascending the steps of the synagogue, when, suddenly, the sound of church music and the babbling of priests could be heard in the distance. A long procession of priests in their *haylike shmates* ["holy rags"] soon appeared. The procession stretched over the entire span of Synagogue Street.

This was a funeral procession for the late prince, who was being brought for burial in the cemetery.

Since the prince was a very wealthy man, his heirs spent a lavish amount of money to bring the bishop in person and a large choir of famous singers all the way from the "Guberniye" [Russian, governorate], and their song reverberated over Synagogue Street on the eve of Rosh Hashanah as the sun was setting.

When Reb Yosele's entourage of distinguished, pious Jews caught sight of the procession and heard the priestly babble and church music, they immediately turned their heads away to keep themselves from defiling their eyes, plugged their ears with their fingers to keep from hearing the impure babbling, and quickly, quickly, as if driven by a whirlwind, rushed into the synagogue.

However, Reb Yosele, the blessed musician that he was, remained in his spot outside and listened attentively to the music, which drew closer and became clearer and more distinct. He stood as if in a trance, until the procession passed, turned onto another street and the music disappeared. Then, Reb Yosele, as if awakened from a dream, hollered with excitement: "Ahh, they have a bass! He is a remarkable singer." He quickly ran into the synagogue, pulled the prayer shawl over his head, and stood before the *omed*.

Hasidim say that Reb Yosele, although in his old age, surprised everyone during the Days of Awe with his novelties and superb singing.

Once the Days of Awe were over, Reb Dovidl Zlotopolyer told his disciples: "The entire Heavenly Host knows that the only *yetser haro* [evil inclination] that has power over Yosele is music. Music endangers his soul. So Yosele is certainly at fault!"

It was inferred from his statement that [Yosele's] singing during the Days of Awe was blemished by the church music, which he heard on the eve of Rosh Hashanah at dusk, and for this reason a [heavenly] accusation was aroused against him.

And the *katigor* ["accuser" or "prosecutor"] was victorious.

13. THE MELODY OF CREATION

The Talner Hasidim sing a cheerful melody, which they refer to as "The Melody of Creation." How the melody came to be and the reason for its name is told in the following way.

When the great study house was in the process of being built, people realized that there was not enough money left to finish the building.

So, the community organized a great feast, a big benefit, with all sorts of delicacies, with the best foods, and the most expensive liquors. All the residents of the city were invited to the banquet. And it happened that when the guests had drunk their fill and were satiated, happy, and favorably predisposed, the town rabbi got them to pledge to complete the study house's construction. They honored the pledge and each promised to donate as much as he could, each according to his ability: "Some more and some less."

At this mitzvah feast, the famous singer, Reb Yosele-the-Rebbe's, the Talner Rebbe's permanent chazan, was also present. Reb Yosele entertained the guests with his voice, as he knew how. He sang various melodies and Sabbath hymns, which were a great crowd-pleaser. The audience could not get enough and kept begging for more. When the tired Reb Yosele refused to sing anymore, a person in the audience, one of the up-and-coming town notables, stood up and with

Figure 5.4. Pallbearers at a funeral (wood carving by Shloyme Yudovin).

the ease of someone wealthy, drunkenly called out the following words: "If Reb Yosele will improvise a brand-new melody for five minutes straight, I promise to pledge 18 x 18 more rubles for the completion of the study house."

Reb Yosele propped up his head with both hands and at the same time covered his ears, to keep from hearing the noise around him, and, with closed eyes, he sat pensively for a few minutes. Then he stood up and began singing a brand-new, cheerful melody. His singing was so joyful and full of burning enthusiasm that everyone began to dance.

The wealthy man kept his word and paid the full amount of his pledge right then and there. Reb Yosele then sang the new melody, which he himself dubbed "The Nigun of Creation," over and over until the whole audience mastered it.

The melody was later sung at the dedication of the study house and when the Torah scrolls were brought into the new building.

14. WHY ONE SINGS IN A TREMULOUS VOICE DURING PRAYER

Some fifty years ago, in my hometown of Proskurov there lived a Chernobler "grandson" by the name of Reb Motele. He had his own minyan of Hasidim who resided at his house. One of his grandchildren, Dovidl, a child of his son Avremele, was my age. We both learned with the same *melamed* [teacher]. Because of my friendship with Dovidl, I became a part of the rebbe, Reb Motele's household, and prayed in his prayerhouse.

Reb Motele was mostly on the road, collecting money from his Hasidim, who lived in cities both near and far, while his son, Reb Avremele, held down the fort: he collected petitions from his followers and led communal gatherings.

Reb Motele was a wonderful singer and loved to pray at the *omed*. He had inherited his sweet, spiritually moving style of prayer from the Chernobler Hasidic dynasty. And even though he was well into his seventies, his voice was as clear and pure, as powerful and lively as ever. Even when he presided at his *tish*, he himself led his Hasidim in song and got everyone to sing along.

Reb Motele was tenderhearted and truly good-natured. He was all smiles. He horsed around with his grandchildren a lot, played all sorts of tricks on them, and they all ended up rolling on the floor laughing, himself included.

I still remember fondly how he would pinch my cheeks with two fingers when he tested Dovidl and me on the weekly Torah portion.

While leading *tishn* [gatherings with his Hasidim], instead of offering his *toyre* [teachings], he would tell us magnificent tales, offer ingenious explanations of biblical verses, and in such an eloquent way. He loved to throw in a witty saying and, by doing so, always gladdened his Hasidim, just as he was always full of joy.

The *rebetsin* was his second wife. A sister of his first wife. He proceeded sister after sister.

His first wife, Chaya, was reserved, sweet, and thoughtful. No one ever heard a loud word from her. She venerated him and took great care of him. His second wife, her sister, was named Brukhe. She was the complete opposite of her sister. She was always angry, was loud, made scenes, and simply tormented him. Reb Motele, however, accepted all of her abuse good-naturedly, always remained calm, and never betrayed any sign of anger. She would yell and rant, and he would just look at her with a calm smile.

Except for this one time, when she annoyed the hell out of him, and he reproached her: "Now look, your sister, may her memory be a blessing, was named Chaya and was a *brukhe* [blessing]; your name is Brukhe and you are a *chaya* [animal]."

I remember to this day many of his tales, aphorisms, and subtle arguments. I now give you an example of a characteristic parable, which relates directly to the topic at hand—that is, to music. Reb Motele posed a difficult question:

> "It is difficult to understand at first the reason why, when we go before the Master of the Universe to pray for our children and for good health and livelihood, common sense dictates we should speak to the Lord above clearly and straight from the heart. So why then do we not behave according to [common sense] and, in fact, do the complete opposite? Instead of straightforward, heartfelt communication, we speak in fragments, minced and distorted, just like crazy people. Before we even utter a whole word, we make all sorts of off-the-wall sounds. We make noise and we sing: 'ay ay ay' and 'oy, oy, oy.' Just imagine what would happen if we went before a king of flesh and blood and began our request with 'ay ay ay, oy oy oy, my lord ha ha ha, hu hu hu king.' The king of flesh and blood would no doubt have us thrown out for impudence, and perhaps he would punish us as well. So, if one ought to speak to a king, a mere mortal, with clear and intelligible speech, think how much more one should speak to the King of Kings, the Holy One, Blessed be He. One would have to be all the more mindful in how one speaks to him. So why then do we clown around and sing in a tremulous voice as we do? What a solid question!" he concluded, "I will, however, tell you a tale about a king and a prince, and you should be able, God willing, to resolve the question on your own."

"What is this comparable to?" Rebbe Motele began his story, "to a king, who had an only son, whom he loved with all his heart. Indeed, their very souls were connected one to the other. [The king] saw himself in him and lavished gifts on him. When the prince grew up, the king entrusted him with the keys to his treasuries.

"And it came about, just as the biblical verse states, 'And Jeshurun grew fat' [Deuteronomy 32:15], that because life was so good for the prince, he began to abandon his father's ways and turn away from his commandments.

"What is more the spoiled prince did not treat the king's ministers with respect. He stopped honoring them properly and mocked and abused them at every turn. Out of their humiliation and persecution, came resentment … they hated his guts.

"And when the king saw that his only son had completely turned from the straight and narrow, and did not keep his father's commandments, he decided to distance himself from him and to banish him from his home. He called his officers and ordered them to carry out his decision. The disgruntled royal officers, who had been waiting a long time for such an opportunity as this, jumped at the king's order, and drove the prince away from his father's house.

"The exiled prince began wandering. He found no place to rest anywhere. He was hungry and lacked the bare necessities needed to survive. He began to regret his bad deeds and yearned for his father's house. He sent letters full of humility and supplications, and begged his father, the king, for his forgiveness and pardon, for him to have pity on him, and to at least provide him with his daily necessities. His letters, however, never reached his father, the king, because the evil, disgruntled royal officers intercepted the letters and prevented the king from getting them.

"The prince rightly understood that his father's ministers, [the prince's] enemies, were to blame for his father's silence. They wouldn't let his requests reach his loyal father, so he came up with an ingenious plan: he took a blank sheet of parchment, the kind which he always used to write his letters. On the parchment, he scribbled and jumbled together unintelligible tangles and confusing lines and doodles and, in the middle of all this chaos, within every jumble, he mixed in a word of request. And he sent this letter to his father.

"And when the king's ministers saw the confusing script, they did not intercept the letter, but rather brought it straight to the king and showed him how his son mocks and ridicules him. However, the king, a father who ached for his child, took a good look at his son's letter, and between every jumble, within the scribbles, he picked out all the words and pieced together his son's supplication. He granted him mercy and provided for him.

"The moral," Reb Motele concluded, "is crystal clear: we make noise and sing tremulously while praying, so that the accusers among the ministering angels, in other words our mortal enemies, do not understand our prayers. They believe we mock our heavenly Father. They deliver our disjointed prayers to our Father, our King. He, however, has already pieced together our supplication from among the unintelligible, fragments of prayers, and 'As a father pities his children,' so too He pities us and provides us with a livelihood, 'Bread to eat and clothes to wear.' And God willing, we will soon, 'Speedily and in our days,' merit the final redemption, amen!"

NOTES

1. Rabbi Shneur Zalman of Liady (d. 1812) also known as the Alter Rebbe, the GRaZ, the Rav, the Rebbe RaShaZ, and the Baal Ha-Tanya, after his most famous work, the *Tanya* (*Likkutei Amarim*), was a disciple of the Maggid of Mezeritch and the founder of the Chabad-Lubavitch branch of the Hasidic movement.

2. Rechtman quotes these lines in Hebrew and then translates them into Yiddish. Although he attributes them to Rabbi Shneur Zalman of Liady, Gashuri ("Nigunim ve-zemirot le-Shabat") identifies Rabbi Dov Ber, the Maggid of Mezeritch, as the composer.

3. Rechtman is citing Gashuri, *La-Hasidim Mizmor*.

4. This appears to be a reference to Idelsohn, "Ha-Neginah ha-Hasidit," 74–87.

5. On the prolific musical careers of Zisman Kiselgof (1878–1939) and Yoel Engel (1868–1927), see Loeffler, *Most Musical Nation*, 67–93, 159–162.

6. On the life and work of Lazar (Lazare) Saminsky (1882–1959), see Loeffler, *Most Musical Nation*, 11, 178–186.

7. This fear was probably rooted in local Slavic beliefs in malevolent water spirits such as the male *vodyanoy* and the female *rusalka*, who were said to drown swimmers.

8. On the musical repertoire of the traditional Eastern European Jewish wedding, including the *dobriden*, see Feldman, *Klezmer*, 146–154.

9. The quote is from *Tikkunei Ha-Zohar* 11, where it appears in a somewhat different form than what Rechtman provides here. Written in Aramaic, *Tikkunei Ha-Zohar* consists of seventy commentaries on *Bereshit*, the first word of the Torah. First printed in Mantua in 1588, it is traditionally attributed—like the *Zohar* itself—to the Tannaitic sage Rabbi Shimon bar Yohai, though many scholars argue that it was likely composed in the medieval period.

10. The blessing or sanctification of the new moon (Hebrew, *kiddush levana*) is a nighttime ritual traditionally performed outdoors. Grounded in BT Sanhedrin 42a, it became a favorite of the Kabbalist Isaac Luria and his disciples, who added other elements to the ritual.

11. *Pidyon ha-ben* or "redemption of the first born," is a commandment first mentioned in Exodus 13:13–16, Numbers 3:45–47, and elaborated on by later legal authorities (e.g., *Shulhan Arukh, Yoreh Deah* 305). In the ritual, the father of a firstborn male child born by natural means (i.e., not by cesarean section) must "redeem" the baby by giving five silver shekels or its current equivalent to a Kohen. If the father of the child is a Kohen or Levite, himself, or if the mother is the daughter of a Kohen or Levite, then the ritual is not performed.

12. Rabbi Nahman of Bratslav (1772–1810), a great-grandson of the Baal Shem Tov, became an important Hasidic leader in his own right whose followers remained intensely committed to him following his early death from tuberculosis. His grave in Uman became a site of pilgrimage and remains so to this day, especially on the holiday of Rosh Hashanah. During the nineteenth century, his Hasidim were sometimes persecuted by the followers

of other Hasidic leaders. On this phenomenon, see "'Happy Are the Persecuted': The Opposition to Bratslav Hasidim," in Assaf, *Untold Tales of the Hasidim*, 120–152.

13. Under the influence of the Kabbalah, Hasidim sought to unite different aspects of God and to cleave to the Divine, phenomena signified by the terms *yichud*, *devekut*, and *hitdavdut*.

14. *Sefer Lekutei Moharan*, pt. II, 25. *Sefer Likutei Moharan* (pt. I, Ostrog, 1808; pt. II, Moghilev, 1811) was Rabbi Nahman of Bratslav's most important work. Rechtman's Yiddish translation contains some differences from the Hebrew original. Green (*Tormented Master*, 145) discusses this passage within the wider context of Rabbi Nahman's attitudes toward praying in one's vernacular.

15. Also known as *Shalosh Seudot* or *Seudah Shelishit*, Shaleshudes is the "third meal," customarily eaten on the afternoon of the Sabbath. Many Hasidic groups place great importance on celebrating the Shaleshudes meal.

16. There are a number of kabbalistic traditions associated with Shaleshudes, including the singing of *zmiros* (songs) with mystical significance, such as "Bnei Heikhala," composed by Rabbi Isaac Luria. On the role of music in Rabbi Nahman of Bratslav's teachings, see Smith, *Tuning the Soul*.

17. The first letters of the Hebrew words in this biblical phrase spell out the name "Nahman."

18. On the importance of dance among Bratslav Hasidim, see Fishbane, "To Jump for Joy," 371–387.

19. The reference is to *Tikkunei Zohar*, Tikkun 21, 51b.

20. The *melave malke* or *melaveh malkah* ("escorting the queen") refers to the meal traditionally eaten on Saturday night following the end of the Sabbath. Many kabbalistic beliefs and practices are associated with the ritual.

21. The *melave malke* is also known in Aramaic as *seudata de-david malka meshikha* or "the feast of David, King Messiah."

22. It is unclear who Rechtman has in mind.

23. Konstantin Stanislavski (1863–1938) founded the Moscow Art Theatre in 1898.

24. On the bitter conflict between Rabbi Nahman of Bratslav and Rabbi Aryeh Leib of Shpola (ca. 1725–1811), a much older Hasidic leader known as the Shpoler Zeyde ("Grandfather of Shpola") and Saba Kadisha ("Holy Grandfather"), see Green, *Tormented Master*, 100–110. On the tension between Rabbi Nahman of Bratslav and Rabbi Moshe Zvi of Savran (1775–1837), who became the rebbe in Berdichev following the death of Rabbi Levi Yitzhak and who also later served as rabbi in Uman, see Green, *Tormented Master*, 130n48.

25. On Rabbi Nahman of Bratslav's journey to the land of Israel, see Green, *Tormented Master*, 63–93.

26. According to Jewish tradition, the night is divided into *ashmurot* or "watches." See, for example, Exodus 14:24, 1 Samuel 11:11, etc.

27. Somewhat different versions of this song are attributed to different Hasidic rebbes.

28. The "Rav's Nigun," also known as the "Alter Rebbe's Nigun," the "Nigun of the Four Stanzas," and the "Nigun of the Four Worlds," is widely considered to be the most important nigun in the Chabad repertoire. On different aspects of this wordless nigun and when it is peformed by Lubavitchers, see Koskoff, *Music in Lubavitcher Life*, 88–91.

29. On Chaim Bick's life, see "Rabbi Chaim M. Bick, 76."

30. It is likely that this tale is about Rabbi Leyb Sarah's (i.e., Leyb son of Sarah), a *zaddik nister* (hidden *zaddik*) and disciple of the Baal Shem Tov. Rabbi Leyb Sarah's inspired many

stories, including one connected to a second figure, Rabbi Yitzhak Isaac Taub of Kaliv (see below), whom he discovered singing a nigun that he had adapted from a shepherd's song.

31. The tradition of the Hasidic *zaddik* who hears a gentile shepherd singing and thereafter transforms the melody into a holy nigun—a process that was understood kabbalistically as elevating the divine spark embedded in the tune—was linked to a number of figures, including, most famously, Rabbi Yitzhak Isaac Taub of Kaliv (1744–1828), the first Hasidic rebbe in Hungary.

32. Rabbi David of Talne (1808–1882), one of the eight sons of Rabbi Mordechai (Mottel) of Chernobyl, became an important rebbe in his own right. See Radensky, "Rise and Decline of a Hasidic Court," 131–170. In act 1 of An-sky's play *The Dybbuk*, one of the characters mentions Rabbi David of Talne.

33. The essay was actually published in 1919. See Freeze and Harris, *Everyday Jewish Life in Imperial Russia*, 61.

34. On Nisi Belzer, one of the most famous Eastern European cantors of the nineteenth century and his relationship to Rabbi David of Talne, see Radensky, "Rise and Decline of a Hasidic Court," 139–143.

35. For a different version of this tradition, see Mekler, *Fun rebbins hoyf*, 135–141; English translation in Neugroschel, *Dybbuk and the Yiddish Imagination*, 362–366.

36. Nikifor Grigor'ev (ca. 1885–1919), known by the title "Ataman" or "warlord," was a paramilitary leader who fought for various sides during the Russian Civil War in Ukraine and who oversaw multiple pogroms against Jews, including in Novomirgorod. For a description of the 1919 pogrom in Novomirgorod, see Heifetz, *Slaughter of the Jews in the Ukraine*, 141–142. Heifetz writes, "The episode in Novo-Mirgorod contains the tragedy of all Ukrainian Jewry, who live scattered thinly in many towns and villages of beautiful Ukraine. Novo-Mirgorod is a symbol."

37. Rabbi Yohanan of Rachmistrivska or Rotmistrovka (1816–1895), one of the eight sons of Rabbi Mordechai (Mottel) of Chernobyl, established his own dynasty.

38. Rabbi David of Zlatopol (d. 1915) became a Hasidic rebbe with many followers.

39. For Devorah Leah's own account of her father's life and death, see Rosenblatt, "Tokhter fun barimten Talner," *Forverts*, April 23, 1942.

SIX

EXORCISMS, CHARMS, AND REMEDIES

"Reb Yohanan used to come and sit by the gates of the ritual bathhouses and declare: When Jewish women gaze upon me after ritually bathing themselves, they will have children just as beautiful as I. The rabbis asked him: does the rabbi not fear an evil eye? He responded: I am descended from Joseph's children, who were immune to an evil eye, just as it is written: 'A fruitful bough is Joseph, a fruitful bough by the spring (Genesis 49:22). Rabbi Abahu commented on this [verse]: don't read *by the spring*, but rather *to the eye* (*"Ayin"* means [both] *eye* and *spring*). Reb Yosi ben Khanina added (it is inferred that Joseph was impervious to an evil eye): 'And they shall multiply like fish in the midst of the land' (Genesis 48:16) (It is also written about Joseph), Just as the fish of the sea are surrounded by water and an evil eye has no power over them, so too an evil eye shall have no power over Joseph's children. And if you prefer, one can put it this way: his eye did not seek to lust after that which did not belong to him (Joseph did not want to sin with Potiphar's wife), therefore an evil eye shall have no power [over him]."

([Babylonian Talmud] Berakhot 20, Yiddish translation by Dr. Yaakov Meir Zalkind.)[1]

1. INCANTATIONS MUST NOT BE TAUGHT TO ANYONE

I purposely chose to quote this longer passage regarding an *ayin-haro* [evil eye], even though there are plenty of much briefer sayings and descriptions in the Gemara [Aramaic section of the Talmud] regarding a wide range of evil eyes. I did so for two reasons.

First, simply to show that the belief in the power of the evil eye (*ayna-bisha*) dates back to hoary antiquity, perhaps well before the Talmudic period.[2]

Second, and this is the central reason, because the passage from the Gemara that I have cited above discusses Joseph the Righteous and deduces from biblical verses that Joseph and his offspring are impervious to evil eyes. And, as you shall see from the incantations that I reproduce below, the name Joseph the Righteous appears in practically all of them. This certainly reflects the influence of the Gemara text; hence, I quoted it at length.

According to the Talmud, the evil eye is itself a very dangerous affliction and can also cause all sorts of other terrible illnesses. The Talmud, therefore, contains a wide variety of cures and remedies for how to protect or heal oneself from an evil eye* as well as how to prevent illnesses from developing as a result of its influence.

This belief in the power of a good eye [euphemism for an evil eye],[3] as well as in the cures and remedies used to fight against it, has persisted unbroken over the generations, from antiquity to the present day. When the Ethnographic Expedition traveled through the cities and towns of Ukraine, we saw how deeply rooted and widespread these beliefs were as well as the large number of female and male exorcists who made use of all sorts of remedies and cures passed down from previous generations as a kind of inheritance.

In every city and town of Ukraine, there were old women, whom one turned to in every time of trouble and in every case of misfortune. Almost every pregnant woman, especially those pregnant for the first time, was in their care. People even believed that they were able not only to predict the child's gender but to influence whether the child would be a boy or girl.[4]

The old women knew a variety of incantations, charms, and remedies "tested out" for any emergency. They could ward off a "good eye," a toothache, a sprained foot, an abscess, a "rose" [a severe skin disease known as erysipelas], a dog bite, epilepsy, and other afflictions; they performed *kishuf* [magic] with knives, socks, and hair combs; and they spilled wax [and] lead, "rolled eggs" on [the body of] a frightened person, tore the hem of undershirts, and performed hundreds of other cures and remedies.[5]

---

*[Here Rechtman provides the original Aramaic followed by a Yiddish translation.] If someone enters a city with the fear of an evil eye, he should put the thumb of his right hand into his left hand, and the thumb of his left hand into his right one, and say the following: "I, so and so, the son of so and so, descend from Joseph's children, who are immune to an evil eye" (BT Berakhot 20:5).

The expedition successfully recorded and collected a significant number of incantations, charms, and amulets for a wide variety of illnesses.

It was very challenging to get our hands on this type of material. The female exorcists were dead set against teaching anyone, even close relatives, their incantations, remedies, or charms because there was a belief that as soon as one taught an incantation or gave a charm to someone who did not believe in its efficacy, it would immediately lose its power. There even existed the danger that one who had recited the incantation would be hurt the next time they attempted to use it.

We employed various means to extract these incantations from female exorcists. Often, one of us would pretend to be sick, lie in bed, and have someone send for a female exorcist. Sometimes, she spilled wax, [and], other times, she exorcised a "good eye," or what have you. One of us sat in a corner, and, as much as we could catch, recorded her incantations. In almost all cases, the photographer was able to take pictures.

More than once, An-sky went to one of these old women and poured out his heart about his bitter luck: [he] told her that he had been a man of means, a businessman, who had been reduced to nothing, left without a penny to his name or a source of income, hence, the meaning of his visit. He had come to request that she impart some of her incantations, as well as her cures and remedies, in hopes that they would put him back on his feet. At the same time, An-sky made

Figure 6.1. Pallbearers at a funeral (wood carving by Shloyme Yudovin).

it abundantly clear that he did not intend, God forbid, to freeload but was prepared to spend several rubles. An-sky's broken voice and fluent speech proved to be quite effective. The old women gave in and showed mercy, while haggling all the while, so as to maximize their profits. At last, an agreement was reached, and An-sky recorded the incantations that they had entrusted to him.

I was present for one such negotiation. An-sky brought me along, claiming that I [was] his nephew [and] did all his writing for him, since he was not so great a writer and his vision was failing. I remember that while we were taking our leave of the old woman, she asked God to bless An-sky with livelihood and wished him all the best.

2. FEMALE EXORCISTS (OLD WOMEN)

In order to give [the reader] a good sense of the incantations and charms the female exorcists used (more on male exorcists later), I now quote some of the most typical and widespread incantations.[6] The texts themselves are written in Yiddish and Ukrainian and target an "evil eye," [or] any general illness. I also describe the old women's modus operandi [in performing their incantations].

For an evil eye (very widespread) [in Yiddish]:

> Three wives are sitting on a stone. The first says that (...) has an evil eye, the second says: "no," and the third says: "It should go back from wherever it came." If a man did something wrong to him (her), may his hair fall out of his beard; and if a woman did something to him (her), may her teeth fall out and her breasts sag. Just as the sea does not have a road, and fish and moths do not have kidneys, so too may you (...) be free of all evil eyes and all sickness. May the three wives intercede on your behalf and may you be blessed forevermore. Just as Hezekiah was healed of his sickness, may God send you a complete recovery for all of your limbs and for your entire body. Tfu! Tfu! Tfu (Spit three times and bow).—Chaya Bela Shapiro, Starokonstantinov

We recorded several variations of this incantation.

A second incantation for an evil eye [in Yiddish]:

> With the help of Almighty God, who heals the sick, may He heal you (...) of all ailments, sicknesses and tribulations, which have come upon you—whether it was sent to you from the evil air, or cast upon you from an evil person's glance, whether from a man or woman, young or old. May it have no effect on your body, nor on your heart, nor on your lung. Then, Elijah the Prophet came across the angel "Ashtrikhu" [see, Ashtribu]. Elijah asks the angel: where do you want to go? The angel responds: I want to go to (...) and sit at his (her) bedside and infiltrate his (her) veins and all of his (her) limbs.

I want to eat his (her) flesh and drink his (her) blood. Elijah the Prophet chanted: just as you do not have permission to drink up all the ocean's water, so should you have no permission to damage his (her) body or a single one of his (her) limbs. If someone from among the men and women of the world has given you an evil eye, may it not harm you, whether by day or by night. And just as the evil eye had no effect on Joseph the Righteous' children, may it also have no effect on you. And before one can count to nine, may the Lord, Blessed be He, heal you and may you be healthy and whole, amen, selah.—Sore Grinberg, Proskurov

Female exorcists often rendered their incantations in a mix of Yiddish and Ukrainian, or entirely in Ukrainian.

It is truly astounding that, despite Jewish insularity and segregation from their gentile surrounding neighbors and in spite of the hostility that the Jews harbored toward the belief in *Yoyzl* [diminutive for Jesus], the Jewish folk masses and even religious Jews manifested a great trust in folk charms, exorcists, fortune-tellers, sorcerers, and, most of all, Tatars.[7] It was not uncommon for people to call a gentile exorcist or go to a Tatar. A sick person was often transported [to these healers] from miles away. Additionally, a special messenger was often sent to a Tatar [in place of the sick person], so that [the Tatar] could exorcise the sickness in absentia. In such a case, the proxy brought the Tatar an object belonging to the sick person, such as an adult's shirt or a child's swaddling cloth. The Tatar then chanted over the object and the sick person wore it until he recovered.

I now relay two incantations in Ukrainian that Jewish exorcists used. [For these two, Rechtman provides the Ukrainian original followed by a Yiddish translation.] I heard the first [incantation] from a professional exorcist in my hometown Proskurov, and I recorded the second one from Khaykele Twersky,* may her memory be a blessing, in the Sholem Aleichem Houses in New York.

For an evil eye:

Evil eye, I cast you out of the neck, the forehead, the chest, the shoulders, the spinal cord, the joints, the fingers, the stomach, the back, the feet, the knees, from under the knees, [and] out of the entire body. Whether you are an evil eye, a spirit sent [from the beyond], or a spirit of chronic illness; whether you come from one's eyes or from one's thoughts; whether you are a 24-hour [problem], a 12-hour one, or a 72-hour one; whether you are [active] by day or

---

*Khaykele Twersky, may she rest in peace, [was] a very learned woman, the daughter of the Hasidic rebbe Reb Motele Shpikover, the wife of the rebbe Reb Nakhumtse Trisker, who was killed in Hitler's ovens, may God avenge his blood [and] the mother of the Hebrew writer Yohanan Twersky.

commandments; by the sun and moon; by the angels, who reside with the Lord our God in Heaven; by the stars, which are in the sky of the Lord our God, may His Name be Blessed; by the nine generations and nine Torah scrolls; by the ten commandments and by the ten *sefirot*. Whether the sickness entered the house, or came with the wind, or with the rain, or in the crow of the rooster, or from demons. May You, the Lord our God, heal him of [all illnesses] right here and now, due to the merit of our patriarchs: Abraham, Isaac, and Jacob, and due to the merit of Moses, Aaron, David and Solomon; and due to the merit of our matriarchs: Sarah, Rebecca, Rachel and Leah, Miriam the Prophetess and Queen Esther. May the Lord send a complete cure this very hour. Amen, Selah.—Hinde the Bath Attendant, Proskurov

The preparations for an exorcism and the ways in which the female exorcists conducted themselves during the incantations were diverse and extremely interesting: they made all sorts of grimaces, opening their eyes wide, wrinkling their noses, [and] blowing with their lips. Some barked like dogs, crawled on all fours, bleated like lambs, turned in circles, [and] hopped around the bed [of the sick person] on one foot. They also used an assortment of tools, such as: a knife, a comb, a sieve, a sock, and often even a wagon wheel.

The majority of exorcists, before they recited their incantations, washed their hands seven times. After each washing, the exorcist placed her hands on the sick person's head. When she completed the seventh washing, she did not remove her hands from [his] head until she was completely finished. After the exorcism, she usually licked the sick person's forehead seven times and spit three times after each licking, wetting her finger with the sick person's saliva, or with his urine, and dampening his forehead with the fluid.

On the other hand, some would take medicinal herbs, tossing [them] in a glass of water to steep. While the bitter herbs were steeping and the water changed color, the exorcist washed her hands repeatedly and recited her incantations. Usually, a colored liquid would come from the bitter herbs. Upon finishing her incantations [the exorcist] would fill her mouth with the fluid and, through a sieve, spray the face of the sick person three times in a row.

In Letichev, there was an exorcist by the name of Gnendl, who made a name for herself all over the region. When we visited Letichev and heard about her good reputation, I was the one chosen to act sick and lay in bed. We sent a special messenger, a respected resident of Letichev, to ask her to come [to us]. It was considered an honor for her to attend to someone. First, because she did not accept monetary payment. Second, because she was already very old and barely mobile. She hailed from a family with an august lineage consisting entirely of rabbis and *zaddikim* and did her work as a good deed.

by night; whether you came from the road or from the other side of the border. I cast you out of (...). Whether you came from aristocratic, *Tsigaynerishe* [Roma], English, or Jewish eyes; whether you are from a woman or a man, a girl or a child, or from a calf, I exorcise you out of the bones, out of the blood, and out of the entire body. You may not rejoice here. You may not take root here. You may not torment this white body. You may not drink this red blood. You may not break these yellow bones. I cast you out of (...) and cast you into the reeds, to the mud pits, to the blue sea, to the stony mountains. That is where you shall rejoice. You shall take root there and bury yourself in sand and cover yourself with stones. Go from God's face at once and from everything else which is sacred.—Hinde the Bath Attendant, Proskurov

Khaykele Twersky, may she rest in peace, told me that she heard the following incantation from an eighty-year-old woman, who raised the children of her father, the Shpikover Rebbe, in his court.

For an evil eye:

The first time is for good luck:

I have come to (...) in order to cast out an evil spirit. I command you out, I shout you out, I drag you out, I chop you out. You are not to be here, to live it up, to suck out its red blood and to break its white bones. Go to the black sea, where hens will not go, where geese will not honk, where a dog will not bark. That is where you must be and that is where you will live it up.

The second time is for good measure:

[repeat incantation]

The third time's the charm:

[repeat incantation]

The incantation was typically chanted three times. Afterward [the exorcist] leaned over the sick person and whispered in his ear: "Ni hori, ni bori, ni kori." She then spit three times and started to yawn vigorously.

Khaykele Twersky, may she rest in peace, also told me a short incantation for a "good eye," where the entire household is called together. They form a circle around the sick person's bed, holding each other's hands, and the eldest says: "so and so the son (daughter) of so and so has an evil eye." And the surrounding people shout: "Oh my, oh my, oh my, a transgression."

This is done ten times, and everyone yawns all at once.

For an Ordinary Sickness [in Yiddish]:

In the name of the Lord God of Israel, send your angel Refuel to heal this sick person, (...), of all his illnesses and pains. I swear [this] by the name of almighty God, may His name be blessed, as well as by all of His

Our messenger told her that I was a Talmudic scholar with a fine pedigree [and] the son of a rabbi at that. [I] had come to town to do a mitzvah but had suddenly fallen ill. This brought her to me.

First off, she sent everyone out [of the room]. When we were all alone, she fumigated the room with incense that she had brought along with her. Then, she ordered me to take off my undershirt. Taking the shirt, she made various gestures over it, murmured incantations, washed my forehead with it, and placed the shirt by my bedside. Then, she took out a new penknife, held it over the incense, and laid it under the pillow.

Then she washed her hands seven times and, between each washing, did everything imaginable, without taking a moment's rest: she made grimaces, pulled me by the ears, laid on top of me, and constantly mumbled gibberish. Even today, I am still amazed by how drained I felt from the whole affair, which seemed to have dragged on for an eternity. When she finally finished her never-ending incantations, she took the small knife out from under the pillow, clipped my fingernails from my left hand,[8] the hand used for tefillin, took a piece of soft bread and kneaded the fingernails into [it], handed it to me and told me to feed it to a black male dog (because a female dog only helps females). I should do so for three days straight: trimming my fingernails with the little knife, kneading it into soft bread and feeding it only to a black dog. She told me to put my shirt back on and not to remove it for three days.

In Shepetovka, a Jewish woman, speaking extemporaneously, related something that had happened to her:

> In the first years after her marriage, she was unable to have children. Every time she got pregnant, she would miscarry. This continued for several years straight. She traveled to doctors, but they could not help her. That is until a certain exorcist, an old woman, gave her this charm:
> She told her to get a black cat without a single white hair. In the evening, before going to bed, she should pluck out several of the cat's hairs, singe them on hot coals, and inhale the smoke through her nose. She should keep her mouth closed. This she should repeat for seven evenings straight. Then, on a night with a full moon, she should take the cat to the river and spit three times at the moon and seven times in the river; tie a stone around the cat's neck, toss it into the river and run home quickly, without turning around to glance.

And the Jewish woman assured me that it helped her. Afterward, she gave birth to several children who grew up to be strong and healthy.

3. MALE EXORCISTS (OLD MEN)

Older women were not the only ones who knew the secret of incantations, charms, and cures. Rather, in many cities and towns throughout Ukraine, there were also old men who were no less expert in the profession. They knew various incantations and had a slew of charms for any occasion. Fewer people placed their trust in the "old men," however, than in the "old women," and they turned to them less frequently.

Furthermore, the style of the old men's incantations differed entirely from those of the old women. They differed in content and, most important, in language. Whereas female exorcists recited their incantations in Yiddish, Ukrainian, or a mixture of both, male exorcists almost exclusively used *loshn koydesh* [Hebrew], the sacred language of the holy Torah and, often, the language of the Zohar [Aramaic] as well.

The old men derived their knowledge in the main from ancient manuscripts, or rare sacred texts, which had been passed down for generations.

In Derazhnya, at the residence of Reb Yisroel Shraybman, a Gemara teacher, I saw one such manuscript, containing incantations, charms, cures, and adjurations. He told me that the holy book had come from a long line of *zaddikim* and that the incantations and adjurations themselves had been thoroughly tested [for their efficacy]. Reb Yisroel Shraybman won fame throughout the entire region as a miracle worker and people traveled great distances to enlist his services.

He considered the manuscript to be very holy and would not let it out of his sight for a minute, let alone allow someone to remove it from his residence. He, however, let us photograph the manuscript at his house for a certain sum of money.

I now relay several incantations and charms from his manuscript [written] in a mixture of Aramaic and Hebrew. [Rechtman provides the Hebrew/Aramaic text that is translated below.]

The first incantation, for an evil eye, is recited three times. So that this "male" incantation in Hebrew can be compared with the "female" incantations in "jargon" [Yiddish], I've translated it into the latter:

An Incantation for an Evil Eye:

> I adjure you, all kinds of evil eye: a black eye, a heavy eye, a narrow eye, a wide eye, a straight eye, a crooked eye, a round eye, a sunken eye, a bulging eye, a male eye, a female eye, an eye of a mother and daughter, an eye of a daughter-in-law and mother-in-law, an eye of a young man, an eye of an old man; all

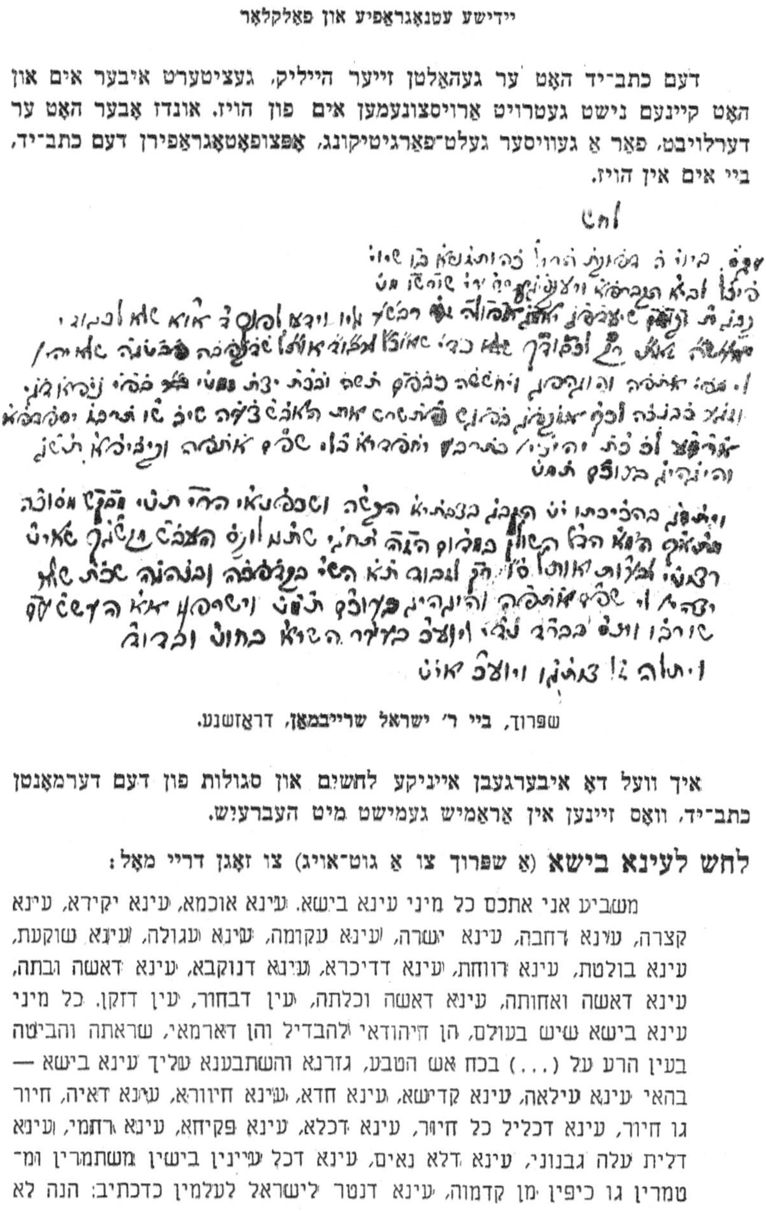

ייִדישע עטנאָגראַפֿיע און פֿאָלקלאָר

דעם כתבֿ־יד האָט ער געהאַלטן זייער הייליק, געצִיטערט איבער אים און האָט קיינעם נישט געטרויט אַרויסצוגעמען אים פֿון הויז. אונדז אָבער האָט ער דערלויבט, פֿאַר אַ געוויסער געלט־פֿאַרגיטיקונג, אַפּצופֿאָטאָגראַפֿירן דעם כתבֿ־יד, בײַ אים אין הויז.

שפּרוך, בײַ ר׳ ישׂראל שרײַבמאַן, דראָזשנע.

איך וועל דאָ איבערגעבן אייניקע לחשים און סגולות פֿון דעם דערמאַנטן כתבֿ־יד, וואָס זײַנען אין אַראַמיש געמישט מיט העברעיִש.

לחש לעינא בישא (אַ שפּרוך צו אַ גוט־אויג) צו זאָגן דרײַ מאָל:

משביע אני אתכם כל מיני עינא בישא. עינא אוכמא, עינא יקידא, עינא קצרה, עינא דחבה, עינא ישרה, עינא עקומה, עינא ועגולה, עינא שוקעת, עינא בולטת, עינא רווחת, עינא דדיכרא, עינא דנוקבא, עינא דאשה ובתה, עינא דאשה ואחותה, עינא דאשה וכלתה, עין דבחור, עין דזקן. כל מיני עינא בישא שיש בעולם, הן דיהודאי ולהבדיל והן דארמאי, שראתה והביטה בעין הרע על (...) בכח אש הטבע, גזרנא והשתבענא עליך עינא בישא — בהאי עינא עילאה, עינא קדישא, עינא חדא, עינא חיורא, עינא דאיה, חיור גו חיור, עינא דכליל כל חיור, עינא דכלא, עינא פקיחא, עינא רחמי, ועינא דלית עלה גבנוני, עינא דלא נאים, עינא דכל עיינין בישין משתמרין ומטמרין גו כיפין מן קדמוה, עינא דנטר לישראל לעלמין כדכתיב: הנה לא

Figure 6.2. Incantation from Reb Yisroel Shraybman of Derazhnya.

eyes, which exist in the world, both from a Jew and, pardon the comparison, from a gentile, who casted an evil eye upon ... by the natural power of fire, I issue a decree and adjure you, evil eye, by the eye of the Lord above, by the holy eye, by the only eye, by the pale white eye, by the eye of the kite bird, white in whiteness, the eye which is entirely white, a destructive eye, an open eye, a merciful eye, an eye with a cataract, an unpleasant eye, an eye that all evil eyes watch out for, escaping and hiding from its glance among the owls, an eye that constantly keeps watch over the Jews, just as it is written in scripture: "Indeed, he who watches after Israel neither slumbers nor sleeps" (Psalms 121:4) and again: "Behold, the eye of God is upon those who fear him, upon those who hope for his compassion" (Psalms 33:18). I, therefore, by the eye from the Lord above, the open eye, summon and order all evil eyes to leave this house, this area, and (...), and that they shall have no power over (...), neither by day nor by night, neither between day and night nor between night and day, neither while awake nor in one's dreams; nor in a single part of the 248 limbs and 365 veins [of the human body]; and that (...) shall be guarded, sealed off, protected, rescued, sheltered, and put at peace from every kind of evil eye, just as it is written in scripture: "You are my hiding place, you shelter me from hatred, you encircle me with songs of refuge, selah" (Psalms 32:7). Selah, refuge of songs with me encircle you hatred from me shelter you place hiding my are you.

The last verse from the Psalms is said in reverse. And here are two very interesting short incantations from the same manuscript:

When a child bleeds after circumcision:

"Indeed, you desire truth about that which is hidden; teach me wisdom about secret things." [Psalms 51:8] The benefactor of masters, slaves are bound. He planted a garden for the man. [Cf. Genesis 2:8] Moses split the sea. [Cf. Exodus 14] "And the fountains of the deep and the windows of the heavens were stopped up and the rain from the heavens was confined." [Genesis 8:2] So the veins of the tender boy, the circumcised, shall be stopped up and his blood confined.[9]

When you come across a dog, you should say:

"Dog, dog, I am Jacob's son. You are Esau's dog. If you bite me, wolves will tear you to pieces."

And here are a few characteristic charms from the same manuscript:

For love:

If you should become unloved, you should take a hot bath. When you begin to sweat profusely, collect the sweat from your face into a glass, stir the drops of sweat into water, or into another beverage, and give it to drink to the person whose love you seek.

To find out whether a person away in a distant land is still alive:

Get an egg from a black hen, which was laid on a Wednesday. Then, go to the well on a Thursday and while drawing water, say: "I am drawing this water for the sake of (so and so)." Bring the water home in a sealed container and after midnight by the light of the moon pour the water into a clean pot. Take the egg in your right hand, hold it over the pot and say: "With this [egg], I want to know whether (so and so) is alive." Immediately, crack the egg and pour it into the water. If the [contents of] the egg forms into [something resembling] a head, floating in the center of the water, it is a sign that the person is alive; if, however, [the contents] sink to the bottom of the pot, it is a sign that the person is no longer alive.

For fever:

Capture a live black spider. Then, while it is still alive, place it into the two halves of a walnut shell and glue the halves shut with resin, or with sealing wax, so that it looks like a whole round nut. Cover the nut with the live spider inside with white linen and sew it together with black thread. The sick person should carry the spider around his neck for seven days straight.

In the manuscript, there were other similar, and truly fantastic, charms and cures for all sorts of possible and impossible, common and uncommon, natural and unnatural illnesses and calamities that could befall a person.

There were also adjurations and spells for how to protect oneself against dybbuks, demons, spirits, and garden variety "evil beings," a real treasure trove of ethnographic material.

※ ※ ※

We located an unusually valuable manuscript in Letichev belonging to Reb Zalman Shlomovits, a distinguished elder who had once been, as he boastfully put it, a great businessman. He held leases to mills and rivers, leased orchards, and did business with rich noblemen whom he had in his pocket.

The name of the manuscript was "Sefer Khokhmat Shlomo" [The Book of Solomon's Wisdom], and its owner, Reb Zalman, attributed it to King Solomon himself. From what he told us, the book appears to have been passed down from King Solomon, going from one generation to the next, until his father passed it on to him.

By the way, he was certain that the fact that his last name was Shlomovits (Shloyme'vits) constituted clear proof that he descended from King Solomon.

The book was written on parchment in an ancient scribal hand and was dedicated solely to demonology: with adjurations, names, and spells for demons and spirits.[10]

Figure 6.3. An old wooden synagogue (wood carving by Shloyme Yudovin).

The manuscript was made up of 120 pages. Every page bore the picture of a different demon or spirit. Beneath each figure, the demon was named, and what his role was, which names and spells could force him to appear, and which ones could bring him back were given. It is interesting to note that some spirits and demons appeared mild, nice, and even with a loving smile, while the majority were painted with evil grimaces, wild eyes, and hairy paws ready to do harm.

On no account would the old man, Reb Zalman, allow his manuscript, which he considered to be extremely holy, to be duplicated; and selling it was certainly out of the question. We could barely convince him to let us photograph the manuscript at his house for a generous sum of money; on top of that, he wanted to sit there and receive a copy of all the photographs taken. And, basically, this is how we succeeded in making a copy of his rare manuscript, which is located among the other treasured objects that the ethnographic expedition collected.

4. PROFESSIONAL FEMALE MOURNERS AND WAILERS

In addition to the usual type of female exorcists that existed in every city and town, there were also, although in much smaller numbers, a remnant of a rarer type of old women: klogmuters, or professional mourners,* whose work, whose calling it was to weep and lament and to make others do the same.[11]

If someone passed away, may God protect us, they came wailing and mourning. If someone became gravely ill, they "moved heaven and earth," "opened the Torah Ark," and "wailed at graves." And they did all of this with professional expertise. They used to burst into a synagogue with a great clamor, with a heartrending lament, throwing open the doors of the Torah Ark, putting their heads inside, kissing the "Torah Scrolls," breaking into bitter laments and crying and pleading at the top of their lungs for a speedy recovery. When "wailing at graves," they went with tearful lamentations all the way to the cemetery and spread themselves over the graves of the sick person's relatives. They moved heaven and earth, stirring the dead from their rest to knock on the Gates of Mercy and intercede on behalf of the sick person.

In the case of an orphaned bride, the mourners would lead her on the wedding day to the graves of her parents. They would wish her father and mother mazel tov, invite them to the wedding, cry their eyes out that the devoted father and mother would not merit to accompany their dear child to the wedding canopy, list the bridegroom's merits, and beg the parents to intercede on behalf of the couple.

During the month of Elul, they spent entire days at the cemetery. When people would visit the graves of their relatives, they would hire them to mourn their kin. The female mourners would ask the name of the deceased and his or her mother's name and then, without any special preparations, would suddenly break out into a heartrending lament, hitting themselves on the head, beating at their breasts—and improvising original *tkhines* [supplicatory prayers, often for, and sometimes by, women] and other prayers. And they would proceed in this way from one grave to the next, shedding tears, wailing and lamenting, singing the praises of the deceased and pleading for mercy on behalf of the living.

The female mourners never made use of published *tkhines* or prayer books. They thought up all of their chants on the spot, so to speak—impromptu. One woman began and the other repeated after her. Sometimes, they would go on at great length, and sometimes not. It usually depended on the payment they received or expected to receive. If they were given a pretty penny, they would let loose: they would wail dramatically, recount more praises, raise their voices, and draw out their lamentations. For less money, they would make less of a show.

---

*Female and male professional mourners alike are mentioned as early as the Tanakh; for example, "Call the female mourners to come" (Jeremiah 9:16). In Talmudic times, professional male and female mourners were hired for funerals to sing lamentations and get the bereaved relatives to cry and lament along with them (Moed Katan 8:28).

Not uncommonly, when generously compensated, they would go to the extreme: wailing even more, throwing themselves on gravestones, and recounting the payer's virtues.

At the end of this section, you will find a photograph of three old women, "professional mourners," whom we met in the cemetery of Nemirov during the month of Elul. We shadowed them for the entire day and recorded their improvised lamentations and poetic verses. By the end of the day, we paid them generously and recorded different versions of their chants [used] for a wide range of mundane and special occasions.

This material will certainly be a great addition to the treasury of folklore and ethnography that the expedition assembled.

5. ADMONITIONS AND ADJURATIONS TO EXORCISE A DYBBUK

A

"Af a *mayse* fregt men nisht keyn *kashe*!" [Yiddish, Regarding a tale one does not ask any questions] goes an old Yiddish saying, and it is understandable why— kashe and mayse are polar opposites. Whereas kashe comes from reason, logic, and reality, mayse necessarily begins where reason ends. Kashe originates in the brain, and mayse in the heart. Kashe asks: how is this possible? Whereas mayse knows no bounds. It is, therefore, self-evident why one does not ask a kashe [a question], which is entirely concerned with reality, about a mayse [a tale], which is entirely concerned with fantasy.

And, indeed, the folk's fantasy and power of the imagination spin a tale in an array of colorful gradients that reach the highest spheres of the supernal world, on the one hand, and the lowest depths of the realm of impurity, from evil spirits, demons, and dybbuks, on the other. During its journeys, the ethnographic expedition accumulated a rich collection of supernatural tales about demons, ghosts, evil spirits, and above all dybbuks, which are stubborn spirits that possess human bodies and will not leave without a fight. The expedition recorded a great number of adjurations and spells that were used to drive out these stubborn spirits by force.[12]

We copied the tale that I present here from an old manuscript that belonged to the rabbi, Reb Daniel Slabodiansky, of Khmelnik. He initially refused to let us copy the manuscript, because he held to the tradition that if a skeptic examined it, that person could, God forbid, be harmed. Therefore, he did not want any of us to look at the manuscript, for he did not want to feel personally responsible for anything bad that might happen to us because he had violated the commandment, "Do not place a stumbling block before the blind" (Leviticus 49:14) [should be Leviticus 19:14].

An-sky, however, twisted his arm until he relented, and he let me copy the manuscript in its entirety at his house.

I still have in my possession the copied text of the special prayer, as well as the texts of the [rabbinical] proclamations, which are found in the following pages; and on the basis of a few surviving notes, I have restored the rest of the tale, which goes more or less like the following.

In 1748, a young man in Khmelnik, a small town in Podolia, suddenly showed signs of "epilepsy." He would collapse to the ground three times a day: at the morning prayers, the late afternoon prayers, and the evening prayers. With his face to Heaven, he would pound his fists on his heart and confess, in a voice not his own, grave sins he had supposedly committed.

His parents brought him to great doctors, to wonder-working rebbes, and—pardon the comparison—to Tatars. But no one could help him. And, soon enough, his parents died from great heartache. And so, the sick boy, the orphan, who was left to fend for himself, set off in search of a cure. *Maybe God would take pity...!*

For three years, he led a life of wandering and exile. He went from one rebbe's court to another, but no remedy could be found for his terrible illness.

And so, at the end of three years, the defeated boy returned to his hometown of Khmelnik more broken and sicker than ever; and, because there was no one there to give him a helping hand, he was forced to stay in the local poorhouse.

Meanwhile, in those days there was a pious Jew in Khmelnik, by the name of Reb Yeshayele, who lived in a small wooden house outside the town. Those in the know understood that he was a hidden *zaddik* who undertook secret missions to help Jews in times of need. Therefore, he was seldom at home.

Once, when returning home for the Sabbath, Reb Yeshayele came across the young man as he was having one of his seizures, laying on the ground, beating on his chest, and listing his sins and transgressions out loud. Reb Yeshayele stopped, examined him closely, and declared:

"A dybbuk dwells in this boy. I shall not rest until, by the grace of God, I drive out this dybbuk. I trust that the Lord will show me how to cast [the dybbuk] all the way to the 'Mountains of Darkness' and thereby save this miserable wandering soul."[13]

After the Sabbath was over, Reb Yeshayele went to the town rabbi, Rabbi Shmuel, the author of the book *Tiferet Shmuel* and asked him for help in his holy mission to drive out the dybbuk.[14] The rabbi, who knew Reb Yeshayele and was well aware of his concealed righteousness, agreed to help him as much as possible. He authorized him in the name of the rabbinical court and the holy community of Khmelnik to take whatever measures he deemed necessary.

Early the next morning, Reb Yeshayele went to the poorhouse, accompanied by the town rabbi, judges, and several distinguished God-fearing Jews. They all formed a circle around the possessed boy and Reb Yeshayele began to speak:

> Dybbuk, whoever you are! By the power of the rabbinical court and the leaders of this holy community, who are presently standing around you, I am warning you to leave the body of Shmuel ben Chaim voluntarily. You must do so without causing him any further pain, or harming anyone else in the process, including those who are present and those who are not. We promise to do our part by praying on your behalf, that you should be purified of all of your sins and transgressions and that your soul should be redeemed.... However, if you do not comply, then I warn you that I shall have no choice but to prosecute you to the fullest extent of the Law: with oaths, with excommunications, with vows and even curses. I will expel you as far as the "Mountains of Darkness" and you will be doomed thenceforth. This is my first warning to you. Mark my words and take heed! Now listen as I repeat to you again for a second and third time, that we will make good on our promise to cleanse and repair your soul, so that it should be fully restored. We will learn Torah *in your name*, offer prayers and charity *in your name*, and study the Mishnah everyday according to the order of the letters *in your name*. I will take it upon myself to fast for an entire year, except on the days when *takhanun* [Hebrew, "supplication," a daily prayer] is not recited [i.e., on the Sabbath and holidays], and I will say *Kaddish* for you three times a day for an entire year. Dybbuk, whoever you are! Take heed of my warning and believe in my promise!

The young man violently jerked forward suddenly as if he were about to tear everyone to shreds. His loud laughter rumbled through the entire poorhouse and his insolent voice roared: "Ha ha ha! I laugh at you and your warnings! As long as I am inside the boy, I have nothing to fear. I don't care what you have to say! I am here to stay!"

All of a sudden, the wild laughter ceased, and a muffled wail sobbed from within him: "Where should I go? Where can I seek shelter? A soul that has been banished from all the worlds like myself? No! I will not obey! I'm here to stay and I will not budge!"

Following the impudent words of the dybbuk, Reb Yeshayele, standing in the same spot in the poorhouse before everyone, repeated the earlier warning another six times—yet every time he told the dybbuk to leave the young man's body voluntarily, or else he would be compelled to expel him by force, the dybbuk stood his ground stubbornly.

Reb Yeshayele grew impatient waiting for an answer. He motioned to his companions, and they all silently filed out of the shelter.

B

When Reb Yeshayele realized that he could not convince the dybbuk to leave peacefully, he began to make preparations for the first exorcism to force the spirit to submit to his authority. At the request of Reb Yeshayele and the rabbinical court, twenty-one God-fearing Jews assembled. The selected Jews ritually purified themselves for seven days—they fasted every day except on the Sabbath, removed themselves from their wives, prayed with special mystical intentions as instructed by Reb Yeshayele, ritually bathed [in the mikveh] three times a day, before each prayer, and avoided discussing mundane matters.

At the end of the seven days, the rabbinical court, Reb Yeshayele, and the twenty-one God-fearing Jews all gathered in the great synagogue. It was Thursday, the twenty-second day of the Jewish month of Tevet, in the Jewish year 5515 (1755). The poor boy was brought in, his hands and feet bound in thick rope, and he was led to the *balemer* [a synonym for the bimah, the platform on which the Torah is read], where the rabbinical court, Reb Yeshayele, and the twenty-one Jews were gathered. Reb Yeshayele divided the twenty-one purified Jews into three groups of seven. He gave one group seven shofars and the second group seven black candles; the third group he ordered to remove seven Torah scrolls from the ark.

But, before they could open the holy ark and remove the Torah scrolls, the town rabbi cried out to wait. He bent over the young man, who was bound in rope, and said to him in a sobbing, broken voice:

> Dybbuk, whoever you are! I, the town rabbi, am also gravely warning you, by the authority of the Torah, which the holy community has invested in me, that we are about to prosecute you to the fullest extent of the Law and can show no mercy! I implore you to have mercy upon yourself and not force us to take a stand against you with adjurations and possibly also with excommunications. I urge you with great entreaties not to make us remove the sacred Torah scrolls from their usual place in the holy ark, not to perform a commandment as is customary, but for the sake of a banishment, to curse and excommunicate you! Repent! Stop the stubbornness and keep us from dishonoring the Torah scrolls. Do this not for our sake, but for their sake. Our blessings will thereby protect you and our prayers to the Master of the Universe will bring you forgiveness, atonement, and redemption. Dybbuk, whoever you are, repent!

The rabbi broke out into loud sobs.

When the rabbi had quieted down, the young man jolted forward. In one fell swoop, the rope around his hands and feet broke, and he roared with great might: "All the tempests of the world can't defeat me and you can't possibly right all my wrongs. My sins are great and they are so many in number they cannot be reckoned. Here I am and here I will remain!"

All were now certain that the stubborn dybbuk was impervious to positive measures. There was no other choice but to bring the exorcism to bear. And so, the rabbi slowly got down from the bimah, wearily made his way to the holy ark, opening it with trembling hands. He returned, his face soaked in tears, and loudly proclaimed for all to hear:

> Gentlemen! In the name of this holy community and the Jewish court, I pray that the Torah scrolls forgive us for the discomfort we are going to bring them by driving out this insubordinate spirit who refused to follow the order of the court. As God is our witness, we greatly admonished the dybbuk numerous times and implored him not to bring us to this point of disrespecting the holy Torah scrolls. However, it appears that this is the will of the Creator of the World. And so, with the power of the Torah that has been invested in me, I am proclaiming for all to hear that I am removing any bit of responsibility for any offence brought to the Torah from our holy community, and I pray that the sacred Torah scrolls will forgive us—and if we shall falter, may the Lord, Blessed be He, protect us from any punishment!

The rabbi himself removed seven Torah scrolls and placed them in the hands of the seven Jews who were waiting, prepared for action. The seven Jews went to the bimah with the seven scrolls in hand. The seven black candles were lit [a standard part of the exorcism ritual]. Reb Yeshayele gave a signal and all seven shofars were blasted all at once [another standard part of the ritual]. With that, the first exorcism began.

Reb Yeshayele silently combined the holy names [of God] and between combinations, he pronounced all sorts of curses, adjurations, and excommunications. The entire gathering repeated the curses out loud word for word. Between one excommunication and the next, all seven shofars blasted at once. Suddenly, in the middle of the shofar blasts, a muffled sob became audible, which turned into a loud roar that began to disparage and blaspheme Reb Yeshayele and to abuse everyone else present with the worst calumnies.

Meanwhile, the last rays of the setting sun began to expire on the synagogue's long windows. The time for the afternoon prayers had arrived. Reb Yeshayele ordered the Torah scrolls to be returned [to the ark], the shofars to be set aside, and their white garbs to be removed. He himself stood before the *omed* and led everyone in prayer. With much heartache, he recited the eighteen benedictions and after each blessing the congregation answered with fear and trembling, *borukh hu u-vorukh shemoy—umeyn* [Blessed is He and Blessed is His Name—Amen].

Then, Reb Yeshayele announced that another exorcism would, God willing, be performed immediately after the Sabbath. This time, however, it would not be held in the great synagogue but would be moved to the old study house and all were commanded to be present.

And so, everyone said the evening prayers and with heavy hearts returned home.

C

Oddly enough, the young man began to improve after the first exorcism. For all of Friday, the dybbuk left him alone. Even during the Sabbath, the time he usually suffered the most, the young man remained peaceful: he prayed with everyone, ate all three festive meals calmly, said grace in a group, and even took a nap peacefully.

But then, once the Sabbath was over and *Havdalah* had ended, the young man collapsed in the middle of the study house and the dybbuk cried out in a weak voice like a person on the edge of death, pleading: "Have mercy on me! Evil spirits and demons will pounce the moment I abandon this innocent body and will tear me to shreds! I can see the Angels of Destruction glaring at me with their flaming eyes! No! I can't leave the kosher body of the lad. Not when I'm safe here from their grasp!"

His cry rang out through the entire study house.

Reb Yeshayele approached him, crouched down, and said in a soothing voice: "Dybbuk, whoever you are. Tell me your name and your mother's name, so that with God's help I can personally compose a special prayer to repair your soul. I will ask the Master of the Universe to protect you from the Angels of Destruction who are pursuing you with their outstretched nets!"

"Shmuel ben Rivke!" sobbed the young man as he stood up.[15]

D

Everyone came the following afternoon to the old study house. They brought along the bound man and placed him on the bimah, directly facing the Torah ark. Reb Yeshayele ordered the ark to be opened and unrolled a sheet of parchment. Upon opening the ark, he began to pray the special prayer, which he had penned the night before in scribal writing on a sheet of deer skin.

And this is the text of the prayer [Here, Rechtman provides the prayer in Hebrew followed by a Yiddish translation]:

> Master of the Universe, Merciful Father, Lord of Forgiveness, God our King! You are full of mercy and grace, showing compassion to all Your creatures. We come before You with prayer and supplication, entreating You to display

an abundance of goodness and act with indulgence toward this spirit that has united with and invaded the young man Shmuel son of Rivke, and gives him no rest. We beseech you, Merciful Father, to lessen Your judgment against him, because, even though he deserves harsh punishment, You are a gracious God. Act compassionately towards him, so that *no banished soul shall remain banished from Him* [2 Samuel 14:14]. Consider our prayers, as they ascend before Your Throne of Glory. Remember all the merits and good deeds that he once did, as well as those of his parents. Add up all of our prayers that they should ascend to You like incense and be pleasing like a fragrant odor. Shower Your mercy on him and forgive him of all sins, which he personally committed against You, as well as those he committed through others. Consider our prayers as if he himself were praying them. Guard and protect him from all destructive spirits that threaten him on all sides; and do not listen to the accusers, who are demanding judgement. Rather, give him true rest, on the condition that he will stay away from the young man and will bring no harm to anyone else, whether a male or a female. With Your great compassion, have mercy on him, shelter him, give him peace and tranquility, and repair his soul. Lord our God, our Creator, and our Redeemer! May You, who heed the prayers of Your people Israel, heed our prayer, and our words should be favorable to you, our God, our creator and our redeemer, amen!

The congregation silently repeated the prayer word for word and concluded with an amen that traveled over the study house like a deep sigh.

Reb Yeshayele turned his face to the young man and said to him in a gentle and calm voice:

Shmuel ben Rivke! I am now promising you again, in the name of the rabbinical court and in the name of this holy community, that if you voluntarily leave this young man's body, we will pray the prayer you just heard everyday for an entire year, except on the days when *takhnun* is not recited. We will also make absolutely sure to keep our previous promises, that is: to learn the Mishnah every day in your name and to recite Psalms for the entire year. I myself shall, God willing, say *rabonen kaddish* [rabbis' kaddish] after each time that I learn Mishnah as well as *kaddish yosem* [orphan's kaddish] for an entire year! Rest in peace and harm no one else!

The dybbuk broke into a wail and begged: "Let me look for another resting place in the world. Only then will I heed you and vacate the young man's body. I can now see thousands and tens of thousands of Angels of Destruction before me, which are waiting for the moment when I leave the young man, so they can trap me in their domain, torture me and tear me to pieces. So, how could I possibly leave my current fine home, before I have found another place of refuge where I can hide from them?"

Reb Yeshayele consoled him:

> Have no fear, Shmuel ben Rivke! Our public prayer will keep all Angels of Destruction and demons at bay. A public prayer is never returned empty handed. The Lord, Blessed be He, will protect you and guard you from the evil spirits, which are waiting to spring on you, and He will return your sinful soul to its lofty source. We, ourselves, are willing to wait until tomorrow afternoon. At that time we will reconvene right here in the same study house. You will publically sanctify the name of Heaven on this holy *bima* and will vacate the young man's body. The Creator of the Universe will therefore forgive you of your sins and you will be purified for good. If, however, you should rebel and reject my good counsel, I am warning you for the last time, that I will rise up against you, with all the harshness of the law, and with even greater and more powerful adjurations and excommunications than up until now; with such that have never before been heard. I will be forced to invoke the holy names [of God], to stir you and those who are in charge of you, both in Heaven and on earth, to drag you from the young man's body by force. At that point, you will be doomed and will be barred from this world and the next!

E

By the afternoon of the following day, the old study house was packed. All the Jews of the community gathered, including their leaders. The young man's hands and feet were rebound, and he was placed on the bimah across from the Torah ark. Reb Yeshayele unrolled the parchment and read the prayer, which he had composed earlier. The congregation silently repeated the prayer word for word. Everyone then said kaddish and Reb Yeshayele proclaimed in a loud voice: "Shmuel ben Rivke! In the name of this holy community, I am treating you more lightly than the letter of the law requires. Nevertheless, I warn you that you must immediately leave the young man's body through his pinky toe. If you do not, I am gravely warning you for the last time, that I will come against you with adjurations, excommunications, and curses, which have never before been heard, and I will deliver you into the hands of the *Sitra Ahra* [Aramaic, 'Other Side,' i.e., the realm of evil] for eternity."

A deathly silence permeated the entire study house. No one spoke. All eyes were fixed on the *balemer*, where the young man was placed, and all ears were attuned, waiting to hear what the answer would be. *Would he obey? Or continue to be stubborn?* Reb Yeshayele was standing stooped over, his head a little to the side, as if he were straining to hear a whisper, or a murmur, in the deafening silence. Alas, not a peep from anywhere. It was as if the dybbuk had become mute.

Reb Yeshayele was sure that this was an act of defiance. He lifted his head with great determination, opened his arms, and rose to his full stature. Stretching and straining to heaven, he gave the congregation a bold stare as if he were reassuring himself that the entire community of Jews, which were assembled there, believed like him that victory was in their grasp. His beaming face was shining like the light of seven days [see Isaiah 30:26] and with his right hand he pounded the table. In the deafening silence, the unexpected blow resonated in everyone's hearts like a distant echo from a concealed and secret world. Then, the clear voice of Reb Yeshayele declared in a manner that was at once frightening and encouraging:

> To the holy community of Khmelnik and to the rabbinical court! What we could not achieve by peaceful means, we will, God willing, accomplish with coercion. Mark my words that after today we will expel the insubordinate dybbuk from the young man's body and cast him to the other side of the deserted and desolate Mountains of Darkness. First, we must extinguish all menorahs, remove the seven Torah scrolls [from the ark], and station throughout the entire study house seven people with black candles and seven with shofars in their hands. Then we will begin our final exorcisms.

Everyone did as they were told, and Reb Yeshayele wrapped himself in his prayer shawl. The black candles were lit, and, in the half darkness, all seven shofars blasted at once. And the voice of Reb Yeshayele could be heard performing all sorts of adjurations and excommunications. And like such seven times over. The shofars blasted seven times, and Reb Yeshayele adjured and excommunicated the dybbuk seven times. And, after each round, everyone else recited with great fear and trembling—amen.

Suddenly, a blood curdling cry rang out in the study house and the sobbing dybbuk could be heard begging:

> Jews! Be merciful and do not drive me out today! I will submit to you later! I will leave! But I ask that you grant me another twelve days. After twelve days, I promise you that I will keep my word and will leave the body of the young man exactly as instructed. Merciful ones who are children of merciful ones! Take pity on me just as you have taken pity on the young man. I promise never again to enter his body, so long as you keep your word to me. But I would also like to add these requests: as soon as I depart, I want you to sit shiva for me; to observe the mourning customs for the full thirty days; to say kaddish for me not only in the great synagogue but in all the holy places in Khmelnik, and to revoke all of the excommunications that you have placed on me.

Reb Yeshayele answered without mincing words: "No! We will not relent until you are forced out of the young man—by today!"

The dybbuk continued to beg: "Have mercy! I cannot leave right now! I must wait a little! Leave me alone, if not for twelve days then at least for twelve hours. Trust me that I will not go back on my word and will do exactly as you instruct! Trust me and leave me in peace."

Reb Yeshayele answered him: "We will oblige you only if you swear by the name of God to leave the young man's body in exactly twelve hours."

"Oh no!" the dybbuk burst into more sobs. "How can I be expected to swear when I am not even allowed to mention His holy name. If only I were allowed to do so, I would not fear these demons. No! I can't swear, but I can give you a handshake, that in exactly twelve hours, I will voluntarily leave the young man's body."

Reb Yeshayele put his right hand in the air and at the same time said the following words: "I accept those terms and will accept a handshake from you. We will wait patiently for twelve hours, trusting that you are a man of your word and will voluntarily leave the young man's body. We only ask that you give us a sign when you are gone."

The dybbuk answered in a clear voice: "When you notice blood trickle from his pinky toe [a common place for a dybbuk to exit a body] and a small hole form in one of the window panes, you'll know that I am gone."

Reb Yeshayele drew back his outstretched hand, nodding his head in agreement. He ordered the Torah scrolls to be returned to the ark immediately, the black candles to be extinguished, and the shofars to be put away. With measured steps, he descended from the bimah. Darkness blanketed everyone's faces. Reb Yeshayele, who was dressed in his prayer shawl and *kitl*, took a position before the *omed* to lead the afternoon prayers. After the afternoon and evening prayers, everyone went home, and the young man was brought back to the poorhouse where he stayed the entire time. On Tuesday, exactly twelve hours after the handshake had taken place, the young man suddenly awoke at the crack of dawn with a wild sob. He tore himself from his bed, violently went from room to room, and pounded on the doors with great force. Everyone scurried from their beds in terror. They were all frightened by his insanity and crept alongside the wall in the direction of the window in order to jump outside. Then, all of a sudden, the young man tumbled to the ground. He began to wheeze as if he were about to die and with his last bit of strength, cried out: "Get away from the window! I will hurt anyone who blocks the window!"

And, as he was talking, the sound of shattering glass could be heard. A small round hole the size of a coin formed in a windowpane on the eastern wall, and a thin stream of blood trickled from the young man's pinky toe.

It is a miracle! The dybbuk kept his word!

F

The good news traveled through the entire city like lightning. The whole town gravitated to the old study house, where the rabbis, judges, and community leaders had come earlier. The young man was brought there as well. Everyone prayed with great fervor and recited the special prayer that Reb Yeshayele had composed. The young man said the first kaddish, and everyone thanked God profusely for the great miracle. Then, the rabbi and judges got onto the bimah and the rabbi declared in a shaken, yet intelligible voice:

> In the name of the rabbinical court and in the name of this holy community, I declare publicly that the dybbuk, Shmuel ben Rivke, fulfilled his promise completely; he kept his word and handshake and has departed us at the set time. We the rabbinic court, therefore, legally relieve Shmuel ben Rivke of all banishments, excommunications, and curses, which we placed on him. From this day forward, they are null and void like the dust of the earth. They should befall empty fields and desolate forests, and not a single one of them should apply to him and do any harm to him from now until eternity—amen!

And everyone in the study house repeated in unison—amen!

Right away, loyal messengers of the court announced the "Annulment of the Court" in all the holy places in the town.

G

That same night, the dybbuk appeared to the rabbi and asserted angrily:

> I fulfilled my promise to you and kept my word. I left the young man's body and have not harmed anyone else. However, as soon as I appeared in the open, thousands of demons and evil spirits encroached on me and began to chase after me. The Angels of Destruction, which were created from your excommunications and curses, are still in pursuit of me. I can find no place where I can protect myself from them—unless I once again enter the body of the young man. Therefore, I have now come to you, the town rabbi, to ask why you haven't kept your promise to me and nullified the curses you've made against me. I ask that you immediately reverse all banishments exactly as the Law instructs and put an end to the demons who are tirelessly pursuing me.

The rabbi assured him that an "Annulment of the Court" had already been announced in all the holy places, and it was made known publicly that all excommunications and curses were now null and void. This frustrated the dybbuk even more, and he asserted further: "Your annulment has no weight, because it was made unlawfully. It cannot divest the authority which was invested in the demons by means of your adjurations, because the Law as it stands, according to our sages, may their memory be blessed, commands: 'The mouth that forbade must also be the mouth that permitted.'* Reb Yeshayele decreed the adjurations, excommunications, and banishments alone, so according to the Law, he alone must also nullify the curses with his holy mouth!"

The rabbi did not tarry. . . . Without delay, he sent his servants out in the middle of the night to wake all the city's Jews and to summon each and every one to come right away to their own prayerhouse. In the dead of night, Reb Yeshayele, together with the rabbinical court and the heads of the community, went from one prayerhouse to the next and Reb Yeshayele himself announced that he was making all the adjurations, excommunications, and banishments against Shmuel ben Rivke null and void.

After each proclamation, everyone prayed the special prayer that Reb Yeshayele had composed and the young man, whom they had brought with them, recited kaddish in every one of the prayerhouses.

H

After that night, the young man began to lose his strength. He grew weaker with each passing day and soon enough was paralyzed from head to foot. It seemed as though the dybbuk had drained him of all his energy. He grew very sick and was confined to his bed with a high temperature. He mumbled unintelligible words, broke out in frightening cries, and groaned in agony.

When the situation turned life-threatening, Reb Yeshayele ordered the sick man's bed to be carried into the old study house. He hung protective amulets and charms around the man's neck and ordered a permanent guard to watch over him for thirty days and recite Psalms, learn Mishnah, and so forth.

In the study house, the young man improved and his fever went down. He opened his eyes and could recognize those around him. His speech grew more intelligible and he became better and better with every passing day. A permanent guard continued to watch over him, reciting Psalms day and night, and learning the Mishnah and other holy books.

On the last night of the thirty-day period, the young man suddenly woke up and let out a bloodcurdling scream: "Shema Yisroel!" As soon as he had calmed down, the young man sat up and explained that the dybbuk had just appeared before him in the study house and wanted to approach his bed. However, he could not get closer than two yards, even though he tried with

---

* [Babylonian Talmud] Bekhorot 36.

all his might to do so. The dybbuk proceeded to persuade him with eloquent speech to remove the amulets containing the holy names, so that he would be given authority [over him] and be able to enter him again. The young man related that the dybbuk had sought to convince him with the following sweet talk:

> "'Don't you see? For the more than six years that I've inhabited your body, you were never once sick and you never experienced any pain. Even in the bitter cold of winter, when you walked the streets half-naked and barefoot, you came out unscathed. But now that I've abandoned you, you're bedridden and suffering from agonizing pain. If you just took off the amulets and the [holy] names, I could immediately return to you, and you'd recover completely and feel no more pain!'
>
> "When I asked him," the sick young man continued, "Why don't you feel like keeping your promise? We are praying for you, learning the Mishnah according to the order of your name, and saying kaddish for you. Do our prayers have no substance? Have they done nothing for you? The dybbuk answered me:
>
> "'It's true that your praying, your learning, and your reciting *kaddish* have helped me tremendously by relieving part of my suffering. From the beginning, the Heavenly Court had decreed that I be tormented four times a day. Now, thanks to you, I am tormented only two times [a day]. True, the afflictions themselves are a lot less severe and I'm certain that they will one day cease altogether on account of your prayers. Even so, the court also sentenced me to roam about the Mountains of Darkness, in the *valley of the shadow of death*, for seventy years! Your prayers can do nothing to anul that judgment. Thirty years have already passed and another forty years are left for me to live among demons and evil spirits in the domain of Asmodeus and Lilith. I will have to look at their gruesome faces, dance their devilish dance, without any rest or tranquility, and be chased after day and night. How will I be able to endure that? I have therefore come here today to ask for your mercy. Please rescue me from their grasp and let me back into your holy body! And this time I will be there because you have decided of your own free will. And I beg you, please promise me with a handshake that you won't let anyone else drive me out of your body.'"

Shaken, the young man explained that the dybbuk had already extended his right hand to him. That's why he had suddenly been overtaken with terror and started to scream: "Shema Yisroel!" As soon as the dybbuk heard him shout "Shema Yisroel!" he disappeared in the blink of an eye.

The next day, the young man began to regain his strength. The dybbuk never again showed his face. As soon as thirty days was over, the young man made a complete recovery.

Shortly, thereafter, the young man got married and his wife gave birth to sons and daughters. He named his first son, Shmuel, in memory of Shmuel ben Rivke.

I

Reb Yeshayele's grave is located in the old cemetery of Khmelnik. The gravedigger showed us his grave. When we visited, more than half of his gravestone was already sunken in the earth and the letters were already worn out.

By the way, I should also mention that not far from Reb Yeshayele's grave was a beautiful tall gravestone on which one could still read the clear bold letters:

Here is buried the son of the doctor Reb Yaakov Leyb son of Yizhok Naftali, who passed away on the fourth of Iyar, in the year 1841

Regarding the doctor's son, we recorded a wonderful story. However, I cannot recall the tale. Who among the former residents of Khmelnik remembers it?

TO SECTION 6

Figure 6.4. Professional mourners in the cemetery of Nemirov during the Jewish month of Elul.

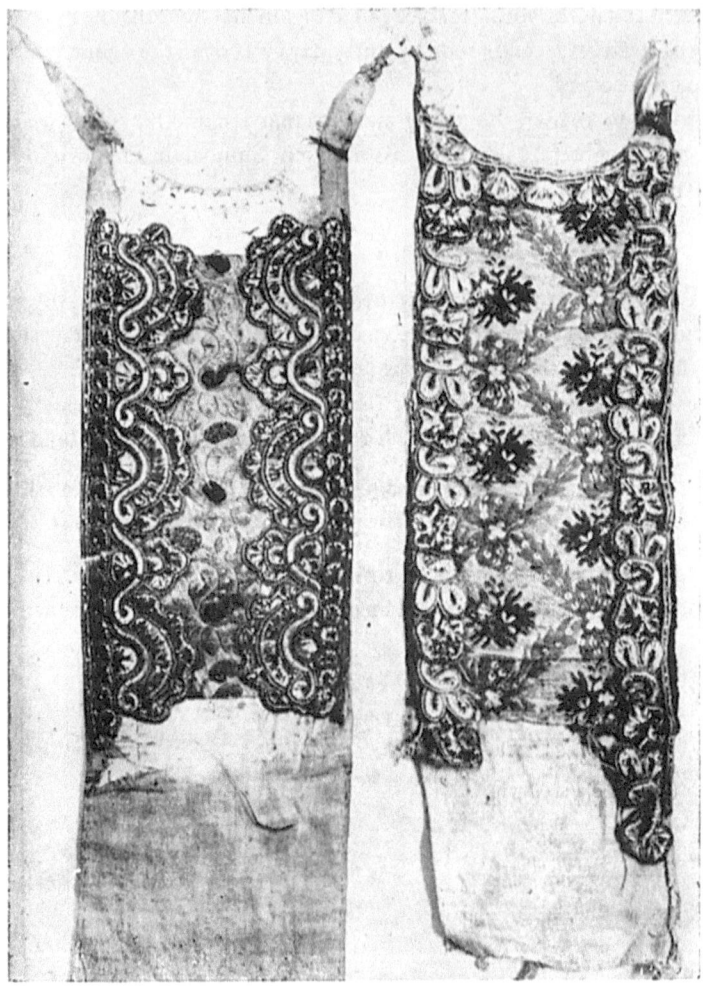

Figure 6.5. Aprons embroidered with gold and silver thread and laden with precious stones.

NOTES

1. On this Talmudic passage, see Daniel Boyarin, *Carnal Israel: Reading Sex in Talmudic Culture* (Berkeley: University of California Press, 1995), 214–215. The writer Yaakov Meyer Zalkind (1875–1937) translated tractate Berakhot of the Babylonian Talmud—where this tradition appears—into Yiddish along with several other tractates.

2. On the evil eye, see Dundes, *Evil Eye*. For Eastern European Jewish traditions, specifically, see Lilienthal, "Eyn hore," 256–271; An-sky, "Zagovory ot durnogo glaza."

3. This is an example of *lashon sagi nahor* (Aramaic, language of great light) in which a word or phrase is employed euphemistically to mean its opposite, that is, a negative phenomenon expressed in positive terms.

4. In BT Shevuot 18b, Rabbi Elazar declares, "Whoever sanctifies himself during intercourse will have male children." See Zohar 112a for a kabbalistic elaboration on this motif.

5. For example, Trachtenberg (*Jewish Magic and Superstition*, 169) writes: "During the last days prior to delivery she would keep a knife with her when she was alone ... the key to the synagogue was placed in her hand during labor; in isolated country places and villages where there was no synagogue the key to a church was borrowed for this purpose."

6. For questions from the *Jewish Ethnographic Program* connected to incantations and exorcisms, as well as notes with relevant secondary sources, see Deutsch, *Jewish Dark Continent*, 258–260.

7. Tatars—"Kadorim" in Yiddish—lived throughout the Pale of Settlement and Tatar healers were particularly popular among Jews. See "Kadorim" and "Kadorim un mekhashfim," *Yidishe filologye* 1 (1924): 163, 394–396.

8. The belief that if a pregnant woman steps on nail clippings she may miscarry appears in several rabbinic sources (e.g., BT Moed Katan 18), where it is cited to explain why clipped nails should be disposed of by burning, as well as in later Halakic literature (i.e., *Shulkhan Arukh, Orekh Haim* 260). Kabbalistic sources provide their own explanation for why nails are dangerous, linking them to the *klipot* or evil forces.

9. The Hebrew incantation quoted by Rechtman also appears—with some variations—in a number of written sources, including Kohn, *'Ot Berit, Toldot ha-milah be-yisrael mi-yeme avraham avinu 'ad ha-yom ha-zeh*, Kraków, 1903, p. 156. Unlike the other incantations in the book, Rechtman does not translate it into Yiddish. This may be because the first sentence is corrupt, substituting the word *akhat* ("one") for *emet* ("truth"), thereby rendering its meaning incomprehensible. In any case, the biblical verse being quoted, Psalms 51:8, is difficult to translate. The verse was likely included in the incantation because it contains several words with symbolic valences appropriate for the context (i.e., preventing or stopping bleeding in a circumcised boy), including *emet* (truth), as in "The seal of the Holy One Blessed Be He is truth" (BT Shabbat 55b), and *satum*, which can mean "shut up" or "blocked." Other words in the incantation also convey the desire to staunch the bleeding of the child. By contrast, incantations employed to help a woman having difficulty delivering a child refer to untying knots, opening doors, etc.

10. *The Wisdom of Solomon* is an Apocryphal Greek work composed by a Hellenized Jew in Alexandria sometime between the first centuries BCE and CE and is considered extracanonical by Jews. In 1780, a Hebrew translation with the name *Sefer Khokhmat Shlomo* was published by the Maskil (Jewish Enlightener) Naftali Hertz Wesseley (1725–1805). Despite sharing the same title, the *Sefer Khokhmat Shlomo* discussed here by Rechtman is not the same work, as its demonological content makes clear. Nor is it identical to other Hebrew books with the same or similar titles that we have been able to locate. Since antiquity, King Solomon has been associated with magic and demonology (see, e.g., the pseudepigraphic work *Testament of Solomon* and BT Gittin 68a).

11. Professional women mourners could also be found among the Russian Orthodox population in the Pale of Settlement. On the Jewish phenomenon, see Suliteanu, "Traditional System of Melopeic Prose," 291–349.

12. There is an extensive body of literature on dybbuks and their exorcism. For a survey and analysis of primary and secondary sources, see Chajes, *Between Worlds*.

13. In a wide range of Jewish sources, including rabbinic literature, Rashi, the Zohar, and Sholem Aleichem, the Mountains of Darkness were a legendary place beyond which—among other things—the ten "lost tribes" of Israel were exiled, Alexander the Great traveled in his journeys, the "fallen angels" Uzza and Azael were chained as punishment, and a host of demons dwelled. See, for example, Louis Ginzberg, *Legends of the Jews*, vol. 4 (Philadelphia: Jewish Publication Society of America, 1913), 149–150.

14. It is unclear which figure is intended here. One possibility is that the folktale anachronistically associated the story of the exorcism with Rabbi Aaron Shmuel Kaidanover (1614–1676), who was serving as rabbi in Kraków when he died in Khmelnik while attending a gathering of the Council of the Four Lands. Kaidanover was the author of the work *Tiferet Shmuel*, a commentary on various sections of the Talmud.

15. The text is a bit confusing since the young man's name is Shmuel ben Chaim and the dybbuk states that his name is Shmuel ben Rivke. It is possible that "Rivke" was the name of the young man's mother. If so, the dybbuk is responding with the young man's name.

SEVEN

SCRIBES AND SCRIBAL WRITING

A scholar may not live in a town without a scribe.
—[BT] Sanhedrin 17.

1. THE SCRIBAL CRAFT

Almost every town, no matter how small or remote, had its own *sofer stam* [scribe] [who produced] *sifre Torah* [scrolls of the Torah], tefillin [phylacteries], mezuzahs [parchment scroll with verses from the Torah placed in a case and affixed to a doorpost, see Deuteronomy 6:9].[1] Just as a town could not function without a Halakhic authority, a rabbi, to resolve technical legal questions, settle disputes, officiate at weddings for their children, and ensure that the community's functionaries were performing their holy duties faithfully, so, too, a town could not function without a scribe to meet all of the scribal needs that a Jewish lifestyle required: when a son reached bar mitzvah age, the scribe wrote tefillin for him; when a person built a new house, or moved to another location, the scribe prepared mezuzahs; or when, God forbid, an emergency took place—say someone had fallen ill, the children were under the influence of an evil spirit or were having nightmares, or whatever the case may have been—the scribe was the first on the scene and would inspect the tefillin and the mezuzahs on the doors. The scribe was also an integral part of the marriage process. Generally speaking, once the match was concluded, he would draft the engagement contract and the marriage contract, not to mention the divorce contract. Without his twelve lines of text, there could be no divorce.

Jews considered the scribal craft to be a holy profession and scribal writing itself to be the holy of holies.[2] They would refer to the Torah scroll as *dos heylikayt* [the holiness], and they would kiss the tefillin before and after using it. It should, therefore, come as no surprise that the folk imagination, above all the Hasidic inclination to mysticism, had also identified scribes among the hidden [righteous] ones [i.e., the *lamed vovnikim*, on whose merits the world rests] and wove wonderful legends about them, depicting their extraordinary holiness and righteous ways and the extreme care that they took when writing every letter, as well as the special kabbalistic techniques they employed when writing God's name.

To illustrate these points, I now mention a few of these holy scribes by name and recount some of the typical lore associated with these individuals.

Reb Yitshak Komarner

He was a student and also the personal scribe of the Baal Shem Tov, who prayed using his tefillin.[3] The care and concern that Reb Yitshak Komarner brought to his craft knew no bounds. He would shut his eyes when going out into the street so as not to see any impure thing and, while writing, would wear special white linen clothes. Each time before he wrote, he would cleanse himself in a ritual bath, and before he had to write the tetragrammaton, he would dunk himself twenty-six times (twenty-six is the numerical value of the tetragrammaton). It is also said that when he sat down and started writing, his table and stool hovered in the air, and the angel Michael would stand by his right side, drying every letter as it emerged from his quill.

After the Besht's passing, his tefillin was passed down to his grandson Rebbe Borukhl of Medzhibozh. Rebbe Borukhl proudly donned his grandfather's tefillin with great veneration. This led him to sin in a feud with Rebbe Shneur Zalman of Liady, which I recount at the end of this section.

Reb Moshe Pshevisker

It was said that whoever was worthy of donning his tefillin was worthy of seeing the Prophet Elijah. According to legend, Reb Moshe would receive word from Heaven whenever a lofty soul was about to be born who was worthy of praying in his tefillin. Reb Moshe would immediately go to work on the tefillin and continue until the child's bar mitzvah at age thirteen.

The *zaddik* Reb Yisroel of Ruzhin, who died in 1851 [he actually died in 1850], prayed in Reb Moshe Pshevisker's tefillin. After he passed away, his younger son, Reb Dovid Moshe Tshortkover inherited his tefillin. He died on Hashana Raba in 1904 [actually in 1903].

Reb Dovid of Anipol

He became a scribe at the insistence of the zaddik Reb Dov Ber, the Maggid of Mezeritch, who died in 1773 [actually 1772]. Reb Dovid had originally refused to become a scribe under the pretense that he was not worthy of such holy work. However, when the Maggid responded with sharp words and, in the end, even issued a decree [reference to Daniel 4:14] that he needed to become a "scribe in Israel," Reb Dovid yielded. He announced that he would accept his fate at the behest of the honorable rabbi on the condition that the Maggid teach him all the mystical *kavanos* [mystical intentions] of the letters and reveal to him the secret of the tetragrammaton. The Maggid ordered his disciple, Reb Shloyme of Lutsk, to teach Reb Dovid the mystical intention for each and every letter. After doing so, the Maggid himself revealed the mysteries of the tetragrammaton.

Reb Ephraim Sofer of Ostroh

It was said by Reb Pinkhes of Korets, who died in 1791 [actually died in 1790], that his pen never faltered and his ink never left a stain, for he wrote every letter and every ornamental stroke with the mystical intentions "for the sake of the unification [of God's different aspects]."

The *zaddik* Reb Refuel Bershader, one of Reb Pinkhes of Korets's star pupils, prayed in Reb Ephraim Sofer's tefillin. Reb Refuel would always say that his tefillin was a tried and true charm for curing headaches.

One of Reb Ephraim's Torah scrolls was kept in the great bes medresh [study house] in Rovno. It is said that a hundred years after the scribe's death, a missing letter was discovered in his Torah scroll. Everyone was deeply upset, and they set the scroll aside for the time being.

Meanwhile, there was a diligent student who studied in the same bes medresh where the scroll was kept. Every day he would arrive to learn well before daybreak. Once, when he arrived at the bes medresh before daybreak, as was his holy custom, he noticed a Torah scroll lying on the bimah and a very old man leaning over it. As soon as the young man approached, the old man turned to him and said, "I am Ephraim Sofer. The heavenly host granted me permission to descend in order to fix my Torah scroll. Please return the scroll to the holy ark." The young man did as he was told and when he turned around, the old man was no longer there.

2. REBBES' TORAH SCROLLS

It was seen as a great honor to be called up to read from a Torah scroll written by one of these holy scribes—people would travel great distances just to get their hands on one of their mezuzahs and would spend a fortune to acquire their tefillin.

There were well-known legal battles between heirs in which each of the sons was willing to give up a great chunk of his inheritance just to get hold of the father's tefillin that was written by one of these holy scribes.

Indeed, many of the Baal Shem Tov's own students were themselves experts in this holy craft. Several left behind Torah scrolls that they had personally written. After their deaths, these scrolls were considered to possess great holiness. They were only to be read on the most sacred day of the year, Yom Kippur, except when a famous *zaddik* came to town or when the rebbe of the Hasidim who were the caretakers of the Torah scroll visited.

I remember when I was a small child of eight years old, I was studying in Mikolayev with my teacher Isaac Malke's, who, by the way, was a wonderful storyteller. The great *zaddik*, Reb Dovid of Mikolayev, who was a longtime student of the Besht, had made Mikolayev famous in the Hasidic world. He spent his entire life there, was buried there, and his tomb was located in the old cemetery.

My teacher, Mr. Isaac, would tell us very beautiful stories about Reb Dovid and his righteousness and holy character, as well as how he came to be recognized as a *zaddik*, and the way in which he would intercede for the Jewish people. It suffices to offer the following single example.

Once before *Kol Nidre*, Reb Dovid stood before the open ark. With tears running down his cheeks, he cried, "Master of the Universe! We come to you now with prayer and supplications so that you should help us on account of our great truthfulness! We are greater truth-tellers than our fathers and grandfathers, who, when the *Days of Awe* came, would not tell the truth. They would beat their hearts [and declare]: We have been guilty; we have betrayed; we have stolen—falsehood! A bald faced lie! When we, on the other hand, beat our hearts: We have been guilty; we have betrayed; we have stolen—all of it is true! Pure truth! We beseech you, *tatenyu* [lit., beloved father, i.e., God] help us due to the merit of this pure truth, with which we stand before you now."

The Torah scroll that Reb Dovid had written himself was inherited by the great synagogue of Mikolayev, which, by the way, he had helped build. (Refer back to p. 35 for more about this synagogue.) It is said that the Apter Rov, Reb Avrom Yehoshua Heshel, who died in 1825, used to visit Mikolayev every year on a Sabbath to be called up to Reb Dovid's Torah scroll. In connection with the Apter Rov's custom, I heard an interesting tale in my teacher Reb Isaac's cheder told by an elderly woman who had known the Apter Rov personally. Her name was Estherke. She was my teacher's neighbor and a frequent guest at our cheder. I can still see Estherke's emaciated small frame standing before my eyes. She was a precious woman of just skin and bones. Her wrinkled face was radiant, and her eyes were always smiling. With walking stick in hand, she took small steps, quickly moving as if she were gliding in the air. She was always in a hurry to tend to people waiting for her [help]: be it a poor woman in childbirth, an orphaned bride, or a sick person in the poorhouse, and so on. I once heard that she had declared that she was already 110 years old, and that she had reached such a ripe old age, because of the Apter Rov, who had given her a blessing that she should live until one hundred and twenty years old. And this is what Estherke then related in detail.

When the Apter Rov used to come to Mikolayev specifically to be called up to Reb Dovid's Torah scroll, he would always lodge at her parents' house. Once, on such a Sabbath, the Apter went to pray, with his prayer shawl underneath and his long coat worn over one arm on top, surrounded by a large entourage of Hasidim, who were accompanying him to the great synagogue. Estherke, a young girl at the time, was among the crowd. On the way there, the Apter's prayer shawl slipped and began to drag on the ground. Estherke, seeing what had happened, went and lifted up the prayer shawl, to keep it from getting dirty. She walked like this all the way to the synagogue. When the Apter Rov noticed Estherke holding his prayer shawl, he bent down and removed it from her hands, pinched her cheek, and said with a loving smile, "For being such a good child and protecting my *tallis*, you shall live for a 120 years."

"My father," recalled Esther, with partially closed eyes, as she rested against her walking stick, pleasantly recalling memories from over a hundred years earlier, "My father, of blessed memory, who was standing nearby, when he heard the rebbe's blessing, swooped me up into his arms, gave me a peck on the cheek, and said: 'Go, my child, and tell your mother what the rebbe told you.' Everyone who heard the rebbe's blessing considered me a lucky girl. The news soon spread from one end of the synagogue to the other and eventually reached the women's section. And, when a little later I found my mother, she took me into her arms and covered me in kisses, her hot tears burning my cheeks, while the other women smiled lovingly."

"After the Apter's blessing, people in town started to look at me completely differently. They were happy for me and thought I was lucky. It was as if I had grown up overnight. A year later, before the Days of Awe, I was given the honor of cleaning and mending the white silk cover of Reb Dovidl's holy Torah scroll. And that's how it's been ever since, year in and year out—when the Days of Awe approach, someone brings me the white silk cover from the great synagogue, and I make sure to give it a good cleaning and examine it closely for any little blemish. I consider it a great honor to perform this *mitzvah* and I don't intend to give it up until the last Days of Awe of my life. And God will most certainly grant me ten years. The holy rebbe's blessing will, without a doubt, be fulfilled in its entirety."

Estherke grew silent. With both hands, she propped herself up by her walking stick, straightened her shoulders, took a couple steps backward, as one does during the Shmoneh Esreh prayer, said "Good day," and hurried away in her usual fashion.

Figure 7.1. And mighty like a lion (wood carving by Shloyme Yudovin).

Her deep faith in the Apter's blessing left a strong impression on us children. We had not the slightest doubt that Estherke would not only reach her promised age but that, after reaching 120, she would live even longer.

3. SCRIBAL WRITING

The expedition made it a point to call on the local scribe of every city it visited. As a result, we accumulated an impressive collection of material related to the scribal craft, including samples of calligraphy.

In addition to the rare writing samples and hundreds of unique legends we collected, the expedition succeeded in recording distinctive scribal terminology having to do with the special tools employed for making the parchment for scrolls, regular animal skin and deer skin; how and with what tools people manufactured the animal tendons or veins with which they stitched together the scrolls; the *gall* (the scribal ink); what the workshop and the primitive tools were called to make the cases and straps of the tefillin.

When the expedition arrived in Anipol, we paid a visit to the scribe, Reb Dovid Elye (whose picture we reproduce here [at the end of this section]). He was known in the entire region for his exquisite penmanship—people were in awe of the way his beautiful letters spread out and filled a line and his artistically crafted ornamental strokes and "crowns" on the seven letters known as *shatnez getz* [an acronym formed by the seven letters that must be written with ornamental "crowns"]. Reb Dovid Elye, the scribe told us that he inherited his entire style of calligraphy from his great-grandfather, who was the scribe of the

Maggid of Mezeritch, and whose name was Reb Dovid of Anipol, as we already mentioned earlier.

I now relate what he told us more or less in his own words:

> "'As was his holy custom, Rebbe Shneur Zalman of Liady, the 'Baal Ha-Tanya,' Reb Dovid Elye began, 'once went to his own rebbe, the Maggid of Mezeritch, for Rosh Ha-Shanah.'
>
> Immediately after Rosh Ha-Shanah he readied himself to return home. It was, however, his practice every year to wait until the rebbe had called him over and sent him home with a blessing. This year, too, Rabbi Shneur Zalman waited and was astonished that the rebbe did not call for him. Yom Kippur and Sukkot came and went and still the rebbe did not call him at all. Rabbi Shneur Zalman remained in shock and continued to wait. Finally, at the end of Sukkot, the Maggid sent for him, shut him in his private study, and said, 'It is common knowledge that the form of the letters, their crowns and other ornamentations were given along with the Torah to Moses, our master, at Mt. Sinai. As the Gemara says, 'When Moses ascended into heaven, he watched as the Master of the Universe sat and attached crowns to the letters of the Torah' (BT Shabbat 89). And it was stated elsewhere, 'Seven letters must have three small strokes over them and these are the letters *shatnez getz*' (BT Menachot 29). It is, therefore, imperative that the letters, crowns, and other ornamentations be written with great precision and care just like when they were [originally] given to us, so that we will not come, God forbid, to any accusation. And this is why the masters of the Kabbalah interpret the saying of Hillel the Elder, 'And one who uses the crown of Torah, perishes' (Pirkei Avot 4:7), as meaning that anyone who writes the crowns of the Torah in a way they should not will die. They make sense of this [interpretation] with God's answer to Moses, 'In many generations from now, one Rabbi Akiva Ben Yosef will come, who will, on the basis of every jot and tittle, expound on mountains of laws' (BT Menachot 29). Therefore, if one stroke is off in the slightest, this person could, heaven forbid, misinterpret God's Torah. For 'Rabbi Zeira said: even a small error in writing the Torah can destroy the world ... *ekhad* [one] could, God forbid, become *aher* [other]' (*Vayikra Rabbah* 19:2). 'So you clearly see' concluded the Maggid, 'as I have just described, that you must be very careful to write all the letters and ornamentations of the Torah here below just like the Torah that lays before the Creator, may he be blessed, there above and which was, as it is known, given to us via Moses from Sinai. However, due to our many sins, numerous scribes in our time have deviated from the old, correct scribal path and have begun to invent their own writing styles. On account of this, a great accusation has been leveled against these innovating scribes this year before the Heavenly Court. Therefore, I entreat you, Shneur Zalman,

to take it upon yourself to repair these errors and to restore the scribal writing so that it is identical with the letters of the Torah as they were transmitted to us from Sinai, in order that the harsh accusation become null and void.'

Rebbe Shneur Zalman obeyed and went into isolation for several days. He shut himself in a room, and *bidkhilu u-rekhimu* [Aramaic, with fear and love, i.e., with great care] worked zealously day and night to perfect every last detail of the scribal letters of the Torah. He rounded them, sharpened the corners, made them bolder—and with great diligence, perfected every crown and jot.

Rebbe Shneur Zalman brought the letters to the Maggid. He rolled out the parchment on which the letters were written and the Maggid became overjoyed. His face beaming, he lifted his eyes to Heaven with a smile and affectionately embraced Rebbe Shneur Zalman. 'Shneur Zalman!' he called out to him enthusiastically, 'A voice from Heaven has just now announced that the accusation has been annulled. You can now go home in peace!'

And on that very day, the Baal Ha-Tanya [another name for Rabbi Shneur Zalman, based on his most famous book, the *Tanya*] departed."

"'While on his way home' continued Reb Dovid Elye, 'Rebbe Shneur Zalman passed through Anipol. It was the dead of night. All the houses were dark, save for one shtibl [small house of prayer] in which a light could be seen. Rebbe Shneur Zalman walked up to the shtibl and looked through the window as Reb Dovid the Scribe, whom he knew well, sat bent over a table, engrossed in writing. He silently slipped into the shtibl and, so as not to disturb the scribe in his holy work, decided to wait until Reb Dovid stopped writing. All of a sudden, Shneur Zalman realized that Reb Dovid was writing the very same letters and ornamental strokes that he himself had just shown the Maggid. He could not believe his eyes. A fear overcame him as he knew this was impossible. Reb Dovid simply could not have been in Mezeritch with the Maggid. Out of fright, Shneur Zalman's teeth began to chatter uncontrollably. Hearing a commotion, Reb Dovid looked up and was happy to see his important visitor. But when he noticed Shneur Zalman trembling, he grew worried and asked what was wrong with him. Reb Shneur Zalman gained control of himself and answered, 'I was wondering whence you learned this new way of writing the letters of the Torah? Who revealed it to you?' Reb Dovid replied, 'Be calm. There are no secrets involved. Reb Zishe* sent for me yesterday and explained that the Heavenly Host had announced that from this day forward the form of the

---

*Reb Zishe [or Zusya] of Anipol, who was a brother of Reb Elimelekh of Lizhensk and a student of the Maggid of Mezeritch, died in 1800.

letters must be just like this. At the same time, he demonstrated each and every letter. Nu, I am now writing the letters, just as Reb Zishe showed me yesterday.'

'From then on,' concluded Reb Dovid Elye, 'The writing style of my grandfather, Reb Dovid of Anipol, may his memory be for a blessing, was adopted in almost all the Jewish communities. And above all, we, his grandchildren, have been extremely careful that our writing should be like that of our grandfather. We are strict with ourselves not to deviate even one hairbreadth from his path.'"

Reb Dovid Elye then demonstrated for us the difference between his letters and those of other scribes, which differed in some respects from Reb Dovid of Anipol's style of writing.

Later, Reb Dovid Elye brought us to a Jew who had a workshop for making the cases and straps of the tefillin, as well as the animal tendons or veins employed to stitch the parchment sheets of a Torah scroll together. We took a photograph of the Jew at work and bought an entire set of tools from him for the Jewish Ethnographic Museum.

4. REB BORUKHL OF MEDZHIBOZH, THE "RAV," AND THE BESHT'S TEFILLIN

I cannot resist telling an interesting story about a heated disagreement between Rebbe Borukhl of Medzhibozh, the grandson of the Besht, and Rebbe Shneur Zalman of Liady, the "Baal Ha-Tanya," which Hasidim explain, caused the Besht's tefillin to become ritually unfit.

We recorded this story in an old-age home in Vinnytsya. I can still picture the scene in my mind: more than ten elderly Jews sitting around a long table with us among them. An-sky explained in a gentle voice, full of his signature warmth, as only he was capable of doing, the reason for our visit. He told them about how Baron Gintsburg of Petersburg, a rich Jew with government connections, had given thousands of rubles to preserve Yidishkayt, and how we were traveling at his expense and in his name. The old men listened in astonishment, and, soon enough, we won them over and they began to do the talking.

I remember how one of the old men, who had a modest build and a bent back, a short bushy beard and a good-natured, smiling face, narrated in a half-playful tone the following tale of a bizarre incident involving Rebbe Borukhl of Medzhibozh and Shneur Zalman of Liady; and he depicted this incident with so much grace and expressiveness, in a fine scholarly Yiddish, that so delighted An-sky that he did not want to miss a single word. I recorded the story word for word exactly as it was being narrated, including the heckles from the several old men who could not tolerate that the narrator had placed Rebbe Shneur Zalman on a higher pedestal than Rebbe Borukhl.

It is simply a shame that I am unable to convey his language, his idioms, his intonations and, most important, his detailed, wonderful depiction of this incident involving these two great men in Reb Borukhl's private study and the incendiary dispute that took place there.

At any rate, the following is the gist of what the old man told us.

Rebbe Borukh of Medzhibozh was a very fussy and irascible person. He prided himself on being a grandchild of the Baal Shem Tov and prayed in his grandfather's tefillin. He thought he was better than his peers and showed no one respect. He had only one chair in his study, so that no one who entered could sit down in front of him. At every opportunity he went around boasting about himself: 'I was sent here to be in charge of the *zaddikim*.'

"As you can see, Reb Borukhl thought too highly of himself," the old man said with a grin. "So it's no wonder he was a curmudgeon who would get angry over the littlest thing."

As mentioned earlier, he kept himself at a distance and did not fraternize with any of the other *zaddikim* and rebbes of his generation. He made no exceptions, even for Rebbe Shneur Zalman of Liady—the "Rav," the star disciple of the Maggid of Mezeritch, the great scholar, author of his own Shulhan Arukh, the Baal Ha-Tanya. When Reb Shneur Zalman began spreading the teachings of Chabad—[an acronym] which stands for "wisdom," "understanding," and "knowledge"—Reb Borukhl dismissed the entire school of thought and its founder, the "Rav."

"It's a matter of common knowledge," the old man noted with a wise expression. "Hasidim and mystics know perfectly well that Rebbe Shneur Zalman gained admittance into the highest of government circles, winning the esteem of rulers and princes alike. From them, he would very often hear of evil decrees being planned against the Jews by the government."

News once reached him from completely reliable sources that a decree was in the works to grab small Jewish boys for conscription in the military. His informant tipped him off that the decree could be thwarted with a *khabar* [Ukrainian/Yiddish, bribe], but it had to be done as soon as possible.

Rebbe Shneur Zalman knew very well that without the help of Rebbe Borukhl, who wielded great influence in the Hasidic world and had many wealthy followers to boot—that, without him, he would be unable to collect the large sum of money that was needed. So, he immediately sent a special messenger with a sealed letter to Reb Borukhl, informing him of the impending danger facing Jewish children and requesting that he raise enough money among his closest followers to thwart the decree. The messenger returned with a sealed letter from Reb Borukhl, in which he responded that Heaven had not informed him of a decree to make Jewish children into soldiers. This answer made Reb Shneur Zalman's Lithuanian blood boil, but he possessed enough wherewithal to know that anger would get him nowhere. So, he sent another messenger, who brought him the same news of impending doom. And again, Reb Borukh sent him back with the same response, that Heaven had not informed him of a decree to make Jewish children into soldiers.

The old man, the narrator of our tale, cleared his throat as if Rebbe Borukhl's answer were stuck in it. As he narrated the story, several other old men—who could not stand the way he was disparaging the great rebbe, Reb Borukhl—heckled: "Give me a break!" "What a bunch of lies," "Look how he's babbling," and so forth. Nevertheless, the good-natured old man would just smile and carry on as if they were not talking about him. He stared at the angry faces of the old men and, with a knowing smile, continued his story.

"You undoubtedly think that Reb Shneur Zalman gave up! Think again! The Litvak [Lithuanian Jew] grew even more livid from Reb Borukhl's smug response. He dropped everything he was doing and went to Reb Borukhl himself. And after several days, he arrived in Medzhibozh."

"Hasidim and mystics, who were privy to the following events, related afterwards, that when Shneur Zalman came to Reb Borukhl, he saluted him by putting his hand to his forehead, in true soldier-like fashion, and said: 'Reb Borukh! The government is planning an evil decree, may God protect us all, to capture little Jewish boys in order to conscript them into military service. However, I am certain that we can stop the decree by bribing the government. Therefore, I have come to you so that you can raise money in order to anul the decree.' Rebbe Borukh turned to the 'Rav' and responded harshly: 'But Heaven has not informed me of a decree to turn Jewish children into soldiers!' The 'Rav' quickly dropped his hand from his forehead. His boiling Lithuanian blood began to seethe and, sure enough, he spit out, as if from a loaded pistol, several angry words: 'Rebbe Borukh! You're going to pay for this! I'm warning you!' Reb Borekh darted from his chair and yelled at the 'Rav' right in his face: 'You insolent Litvak! Do you know to whom you are speaking? You are speaking to Borukh, a grandchild of the *Baal Shem Tov*, of blessed memory. I pray in my grandfather's holy *tefillin*!' This response made the 'Rav's' Litvak blood boil even more. He was practically on fire. He forced himself in the direction of the door, tore off the knob, angrily throwing it to the ground, and nonchalantly said: 'Nu? Just because your tefillin are the Baal Shem Tov's, you think they can't be rendered unkosher?!' He jimmied the door open with his foot and without saying a goodbye he strode over the threshold."

"The very idea petrified Reb Borukh. What!? Damaged tefillin!!! He prays in damaged *tefillin*!!! He grew hysterical. He began to scream like someone bit by a snake, 'Call Hershl Sofer at once!' And when the scribe opened the tefillin for the head, one could clearly see that a letter was missing, a '*Yud*' had come off. Reb Borukhl leaped into the air as if stuck with a burning spear and he screamed in a voice not his own, 'What!? The Litvak took a *yid* [a letter][4] from my *tefillin*? I will take a *yid* [Jew] from his children!'"[5]

"Reb Borukhl's bitter words," the old man said with a deep sigh, "soon became a reality due to our many sins. One of the Rav's children left the fold. Some even say that he converted, but that is a complete lie. He would soon repent and punish himself in terrifying ways: he would tie his feet to the bath house ceiling and hang there upside down every night until the morning."

* * *

The old man added these interesting details to the story of Shneur Zalman's visit to Reb Borukhl:

"The next day, when the 'Rav' wanted to make a pilgrimage to the Besht's grave, Reb Borukhl kept him out of the cemetery by ordering all the entrances locked."

"A few days later, a Jew from a nearby village came to Reb Borukhl, and asked him to be the *sandek* [the man who holds the baby] at his child's circumcision. Reb Borukhl said to him, 'There is an important visitor in town, a rabbi. Go and invite him as well.' The Jew went to Shneur Zalman and told him matter-of-factly, 'The Rebbe, Rabbi Borukh told me that I should invite you to my son's circumcision.' The 'Rav' replied, 'After you pick up Reb Borukh, come and fetch me.' And that's exactly what happened. The 'Rav' sat in the sled next to Reb Borukh and neither of them looked at the other or uttered a single word."

"In the middle of the trip, the 'Rav' suddenly said to the driver, 'Make a right turn because soon there will be a deep pit in the snow and we might, God forbid, capsize.' When Reb Borukhl heard this, he commented mockingly: 'Look at the Litvak trying to show off that he is an expert in geography—We know that too!'"

"At this, the Rav's Litvish blood immediately started to boil and he jumped off the sled, grabbed a handful of snow, and quickly turned to Reb Borukh: 'If you like, I will show you in this handful of snow the four elements—earth, water, wind, and fire.'"

"Rebbe Borukhl grabbed him by the hand and gave a frightful shriek: 'No! No! There is no need!'"

"Later, Reb Borukhl said that he had already seen the element '*esh*' (fire)."

Figure 7.2. Reb Dovid Elye, the scribe of Anipol.

NOTES

1. The Hebrew acronym "stam" refers to the first letters of the Hebrew words *sifre Torah*, *tefillin*, and *mezuzot*.
2. Because of its importance, the scribal craft inspired its own Halakic literature. Among the most important works devoted to the topic were *Sefer Keset Ha-Sofer* (Ofen, 1835) by Rabbi Shlomo Ganzfried (1804–1886) of Ungvar and *Mishnat Sofrim* (part of the *Mishna Berurah*, vol. 1, Jerusalem, 1884) by Rabbi Israel Meyer Kagan (1839–1933), the Chofetz Chaim.
3. Other sources identify the Baal Shem Tov's personal scribe as Reb Tsvi Sofer. See, for example, Wertheim, *Law and Custom in Hasidism*, 265–266n31.
4. *Yid* is how the tenth letter of the Hebrew/Yiddish alphabet is pronounced in southern variants of Yiddish; *yud* is how it is pronounced in the northern variant spoken by Rabbi Shneur Zalman.
5. This is an allusion to the tradition that Rabbi Shneur Zalman's son, Moshe, converted to Christianity. On this episode, see "Apostate or Saint? In the Footsteps of Moshe, the Son of Rabbi Shneur of Lyady," by Assaf, in *Untold Tales of the Hasidim*, 29–96.

BIBLIOGRAPHY

Abramson, Henry. "Russian Civil War." *YIVO Encyclopedia of Jews in Eastern Europe.* Available at https://yivoencyclopedia.org/article.aspx/Russian_Civil_War.
Alexander, Yonah, and Kenneth Myers. *Terrorism in Europe.* New York: Routledge, 1982.
Altshuler, Mort. "The First Tzaddik of Hasidism: The Zlotchover Maggid and His Circle." *Jewish Studies Quarterly* 11, nos. 1–2 (2004).
An-sky, Sh. *Der Yudisher Khurbn fun poylen galitsye un Bukovina, fun tog-bukh 1914–1917.* In *Gezamelte shriften in fuftsen bender* [a.k.a. *Khurbn Galitsye*], vols. 4–6. Vilna-Warsaw-New York: Farlag "An-sky," 1921–1928.
———. "Zagovory ot durnogo glaza, boleznei i neschastnykh sluchaev sredi evreev severno-zapadnogo kraia." *Evreiskaia Starina* 1 (1909).
Apter-Gabriel, Ruth. "Solomon Borisovich Iudovin." *YIVO Encyclopedia of Jews in Eastern Europe.* Available at https://yivoencyclopedia.org/article.aspx/Iudovin_Solomon_Borisovich.
Assaf, David. *A Journey to a Nineteenth-Century Shtetl: The Memoirs of Yekhezkel Kotik.* Detroit, MI: Wayne State University Press, 2008.
———. "'My Tiny, Ugly World': The Confession of Rabbi Yitzhak Nahum Twersky of Shpikov." *Contemporary Jewry* 26 (2006).
———. *Untold Tales of the Hasidim: Crisis and Discontent in the History of Hasidism.* Waltham, MA: Brandeis University Press, 2011.
———. "Viduyo shel Reb Yitzhak Nahum Tversky mi-Shpikov." *Alpayim* 14 (1997).
Bar-Itzhak, Haya. *Jewish Poland: Legends of Origin, Ethnopoetics, and Legendary Chronicles.* Detroit, MI: Wayne State University Press, 2001.
Beizer, Mikhail. *The Jews of St. Petersburg: Excursions through a Noble Past.* Philadelphia: Jewish Publication Society, 1989.
Berkovitz, Jay. *Protocols of Justice: The Pinkas of the Metz Rabbinic Court 1771–1789*, 2 vols. Leiden, Netherlands: E. J. Brill, 2014.
Berlin, Moisei. *Ocherk etnografii evreiskogo narodonasileniia v Rossii.* Saint Petersburg: V. Bezobrazova, 1861.

Beukers, Mariëlla, and Renée Waale, eds. *Tracing An-sky: Jewish Collections from the State Ethnographic Museum in St. Petersburg.* Zwolle: Waanders Uitgevers; Amsterdam: Joods Historisch Museum, 1992.

Biber, Menachem Mendel. "Gedolei Ostroh." In *Pinkas Ostroh*, edited by Benzion Hayim Ayalon-Baranick. Tel Aviv: Be-hotsa'at irgun olei Ostroh be-Yisrael, 1960.

———. *Sefer mizkeret le-gedole Ostroh.* Berdichev, Ukraine: Hayim Yaakov Sheftel, 1907.

Boyarin, Daniel. *Carnal Israel: Reading Sex in Talmudic Culture.* Berkeley: University of California Press, 1995.

Brisman, Shimeon. *A History and Guide to Judaic Dictionaries and Concordances.* Hoboken, NJ: KTAV, 2000.

Buneh, Mordechai. "Ha-TaZ be-Olyka." In *Pinkas Ha-Kehilah Olyka*, edited by Kalman Burshtayn. Tel-Aviv: Irgun Yotse Olyka be-Yisrael, 1972.

Buxbaum, Yitzhak. *The Light and Fire of the Baal Shem Tov.* New York: Continuum, 2006.

Cashman, Greer Fay. "Not Just for Old Times' Sake: Daniel Galay's Opera, Adapted from An Extraordinary Folktale, Show How We Can Live Yiddish, Even Today." *Jerusalem Post*, January 23, 2007.

Chaban, Matt. "At Bess Myerson's Former Home, Shades of a Bronx Utopia." *New York Times*, January 12, 2015.

Chajes, J. H. *Between Worlds: Dybbuks, Exorcists, and Early Modern Judaism.* Philadelphia: University of Pennsylvania Press, 2011.

Deutsch, Nathaniel. *The Jewish Dark Continent: Life and Death in the Russian Pale of Settlement.* Cambridge, MA: Harvard University Press, 2011.

———. *The Maiden of Ludmir: A Jewish Holy Woman and Her World.* Berkeley: University of California Press, 2003.

Dubnow, Simon. *Ob izuchenii istorii russkikh evreev I ob uchrezhdenii russko-evreiskogo istoricheskogo obshchestva.* Saint Petersburg: A. E. Landau, 1891.

Dujovne, Alejandro. *Una historia del libro judío: La cultura judía argentina a través de suseditores, libreros, traductores, imprentas y bibliotecas.* Buenos Aires: Siglo XXI Editores, 2014.

Dundes, Alan, ed. *The Blood Libel Legend: A Casebook in Anti-Semitic Folklore.* Madison: University of Wisconsin Press, 1991.

———. *The Evil Eye: A Casebook.* Madison: University of Wisconsin Press, 1981.

Feldman, Walter Zev. *Klezmer: Music, History, and Memory.* New York: Oxford University Press, 2016.

Fishbane, Michael. *The Kiss of God: Spiritual and Mystical Death in Judaism.* Seattle: University of Washington Press, 1994.

———. "To Jump for Joy: The Rites of Dance According to R. Nahman of Bratslav." *Journal of Jewish Thought and Philosophy* 6 (1997).

Freeze, ChaeRan. *Jewish Marriage and Divorce in Imperial Russia.* Waltham, MA: Brandeis University Press, 2001.

Freeze, ChaeRan, and Jay Harris, eds. *Everyday Jewish Life in Imperial Russia: Select Documents, 1772–1914.* Waltham, MA: Brandeis University Press, 2013.

Gashuri, Meir Shimon. "Bet ha-midrash al shem 'rabi volf ha kodesh.'" In *Sefer Lutsk*, edited by Nahum Sharon. Tel Aviv: Irgun Yotse Lutsk be-Yisrael, 1961.

———. "Der lutsker alter un nayer bes-oylem." In *Sefer Lutsk*, edited by Nahum Sharon. Tel Aviv: Irgun Yotse Lutsk be-Yisrael, 1961.

———. *La-Hasidim Mizmor.* Jerusalem: Haver Hovavim Shel Neginat Hasidim, 1936.

———. "Nigunim ve-zemirot le-Shabat." *Mahanayim* 85 (1964).
Gelbard, Shmuel Pinchas. *Otsar Ta'amei Ha-Minhagim: Rite and Reason, 1050 Jewish Customs and Their Sources*. Petach Tikvah: Mifal Rashi, 1998.
Giller, Pinchas. *Reading the Zohar: The Sacred Text of the Kabbalah*. New York: Oxford University Press, 2001.
Ginzberg, Louis. *The Legends of the Jews*, vol. 3. Philadelphia: Jewish Publication Society, 1968.
Goldberg, J. J. "David Twersky, Political Journalist and Peace Activist, Dies at 60." *The Forward*, July 18, 2010.
Goldberg, Sylvie Anne. "Paradigmatic Times: An-sky's Two Worlds." In *The Worlds of S. An-sky: A Russian Jewish Intellectual at the Turn of the Century*, edited by Gabriella Safran and Steven Zipperstein. Stanford, CA: Stanford University Press, 2006.
Grade, Chaim. *Tsemakh Atlas*, vols. 1–2. Los Angeles: Yidish Natsionaln Arbeter Farband, 1967, 1968. Published in English as *The Yeshiva*. Translated by Curt Leviant. New York: Macmillan, 1977.
Green, Arthur. *Tormented Master: A Life of Rabbi Nahman of Bratslav*. Tuscaloosa: University of Alabama Press, 1979.
Grinshpan, Avigdor. "Rabbi Mordechai of Lekhovitsh (Ha-Saba Kaddisha)." In *Lekhovitsh: Sefer Zikaron*, edited by Yisroel Rubin. Tel Aviv: Hotsa'at Igud Yotsei Lechovitsh, 1949.
Gur Aryeh (Pikangur), Yitzhakh. "An-sky, Ha-Ish Umafal Hayav." *Yeda-Am* 2, nos. 4–5 (1954): 115–119.
Harkavy, Alexander. *Navarodok: Ir historiye un ir hayntiger leben*. New York: Grayzel, 1921.
Heifetz, Elias. *The Slaughter of the Jews in the Ukraine in 1919*. New York: Thomas Seltzer, 1921.
Heschel, Abraham Joshua. "Di mizrekh-eyropeishe tkufe in der yidisher geshikte." *YIVO Bleter* 25, no. 2 (1945).
———. "Reb Pinkhes Koritser." *YIVO Bleter* 33 (1950).
———. *The Sabbath*. New York: Farrar, Straus, and Giroux, 1951.
Horeker, N. L. "Liova Fradkin—L. M. Shteyn." In *Yovel bukh tsu L. M. Shteyns finf un tsvantsik yorikn yubiley fun kultur-gezelshaftlekhe tetikeyt*, edited by Y. Kh. Pomerants and A. Pravitiner. Chicago: Sholem Aleykhem Folk Institut, 1938.
Horowitz, Brian. *Jewish Philanthropy and Enlightenment in Late-Tsarist Russia*. Seattle: University of Washington Press, 2011.
Horowitz, Elliot. "The Early Eighteenth Century Confronts the Beard: Kabbalah and Jewish Self-Fashioning." *Jewish History* 8, no. 1–2 (1994).
Idel, Moshe. "Multiple Forms of Redemption in Kabbalah and Hasidism." *Jewish Quarterly Review* 101 (Winter 2011).
Idelsohn, Abraham Zvi. "Ha-Neginah ha-Hasidit." *Sefer Hashanah: The American-Hebrew Year Book* 1 (1931).
Ilon, Ben-Tsiyon. "Ostroh birat Volin ve-ha-galilot: Zikhronot mi-pinkas ostroh ha-yashan." In *Pinkas Ostroh*, edited by Benzion Hayim Ayalon-Baranick. Tel Aviv: Be-hotsa'at irgun olei Ostroh be-Yisrael, 1960.
"Jews Slain in Ukraine." *New York Times*, September 14, 1919.
"Kadorim." *Yidishe filologye* 1 (1924).
"Kadorim un mekhashfim." *Yidishe filologye* 1 (1924).
Kan, Sergei. *Lev Shternberg: Anthropologist, Russian Socialist, Jewish Activist*. Lincoln: University of Nebraska Press, 2009.
Katskah, Moshe. "Batei-tefilah u-vatei-midrash be-Dubno." In *Dubno: Sefer Zikaron*, edited by Y. Adini. Tel Aviv: Hotsaat Irgun Yotsei Dubno be-Yisrael, 1966.

Kirshenblatt-Gimblett, Barbara. "Theorizing Heritage." *Ethnomusicology* 39, no. 3 (1995).
Klier, John. "The Gintsburg Family." *YIVO Encyclopedia of Jews in Eastern Europe*. Available at http://www.yivoencyclopedia.org/article.aspx/Gintsburg_Family.
Kohn, Samuel. *'Ot Berit, Toldot ha-milah be-yisrael mi-yeme avraham avinu 'ad ha-yom ha-zeh*. Kraków: J. S. Fuchs, 1903.
Koskoff, Ellen. *Music in Lubavitcher Life*. Urbana: University of Illinois Press, 2001.
Kugelmass, Jack, ed. *Between Two Worlds: Ethnographic Essays on American Jewry*. Ithaca, NY: Cornell University Press, 1988.
Kugelmass, Jack, and Jonathan Boyarin. *From a Ruined Garden: The Memorial Books of Polish Jewry*. Bloomington: Indiana University Press, 1998.
Lilienthal, Regina. "Eyn hore." *Yidishe filologye* 1 (1924).
Lindenberg, Gabriel. "Ha-Baal Shem Tov be-Tluste." In *Sefer Tluste*, edited by G. Lindenberg. Tel Aviv: Hotsa'at irgun yotsei Tluste ve-ha-svivah, 1965.
Litvak, Olga. *Conscription and the Search for Modern Russian Jewry*. Bloomington: Indiana University Press, 2006.
Loeffler, James. *The Most Musical Nation: Jews and Culture in the Late Russian Empire*. New Haven, CT: Yale University Press, 2010.
Lukin, Benyamin. "'An Academy Where Folklore Will Be Studied': An-sky and the Jewish Museum." In *The Worlds of S. An-sky: A Russian Jewish Intellectual at the Turn of the Century*, edited by Gabriella Safran and Steven Zipperstein. Stanford, CA: Stanford University Press, 2006.
———. "An-ski Ethnographic Expedition and Museum." *YIVO Encyclopedia of Jews in Eastern Europe*. Available at https://yivoencyclopedia.org/article.aspx/An-ski_Ethnographic_Expedition_and_Museum.
Mark, Yudel, and Judah Yoffe. *Groyser verterbukh fun der yidisher shprakh*. New York: Yiddish Dictionary Committee, 1961.
Mekler, Dovid. *Fun rebbins hoyf: Fun Chernobyl biz Talne*, vol. 2. New York: Jewish Book Publishing Company, 1931.
Michels, Tony. *A Fire in Their Hearts: Yiddish Socialists in New York*. Cambridge, MA: Harvard University Press, 2009.
Milamed, Susan. "Proskurover Landsmanshaftn: A Case Study in Jewish Communal Development." *American Jewish History* 76, no. 1 (September 1986): 40–55.
Moshe Ginzburg zayn lebn un tetigkayt. Paris: Aroysgegebn fun di fraynd fun M. Ginzburg, 1935.
Nadav, Mordechai. *The Jews of Pinsk, 1506–1880*, edited by Mark Jay Mirsky and Moshe Rosman. Stanford, CA: Stanford University Press, 2008.
Nathans, Benjamin. *Beyond the Pale: The Jewish Encounter with Late Imperial Russia*. Berkeley: University of California Press, 2002.
Nedava, Yosef. "Some Aspects of Individual Terrorism: A Case Study of the Schwartzbard Affair." In *Terrorism in Europe*, edited by Yonah Alexander and Kenneth Myers. New York: Routledge, 1982.
Neugroschel, Joachim, ed. *The Dybbuk and the Yiddish Imagination: A Haunted Reader*. New York: Syracuse University Press, 2000.
———, ed. and trans. *The Enemy at His Pleasure: A Journey through the Jewish Pale of Settlement during World War I*. New York: Metropolitan Books, 2002.
Opalski, Magda. "Regina Lilientalowa." *YIVO Encyclopedia of Jews in Eastern Europe*. Available at http://www.yivoencyclopedia.org/article.aspx/Lilientalowa_Regina.

Petrovsky, Yohanan M. "Newly Discovered Pinkassim of the Harkavy Collection." *AVOTAYNU* 12, no. 2 (Summer 1996).

Petrovsky-Shtern, Yohanan. *Jews in the Russian Army, 1827–1917: Drafted into Modernity*. New York: Cambridge University Press, 2008.

Plunz, Richard. *A History of Housing in New York City*. New York: Columbia University Press, 2016.

"Rabbi Chaim M. Bick. 76. Led Brooklyn Congregation." *New York Times*, May 26, 1964.

Rabinovitch, Simon. "Positivism, Populism, and Politics: The Intellectual Foundations of Jewish Ethnography in Late Imperial Russia." *Ab Imperio* 3 (2005).

Radensky, Paul. "The Rise and Decline of a Hasidic Court: The Case of Rabbi Duvid Twersky of Tal'noye." In *Holy Dissent: Jewish and Christian Mystics in Eastern Europe*, edited by Glenn Dynner. Detroit, MI: Wayne State University Press, 2013.

Rechtman, Abraham. "A tsol minhogim un zeyre folkstimlekhe tamim un bataytn." *YIVO Bleter* 42 (1962): 249–265.

———. "Bazilier Rebbe." In *Khurbn Proskurov: Tsum ondenken fun di heylige neshomes vos zaynen umgekumen in der shreklikher shkhite, vos iz ongefirt gevorn durkh di haydamakes*. New York: Levant, 1924.

———. "Foreword." In *Khurbn Proskurov: Tsum ondenken fun di heylige neshomes vos zaynen umgekumen in der shreklikher shkhite, vos iz ongefirt gevorn durkh di haydamakes*. New York: Levant, 1924.

———. "Mi-dor holekh: Reshimot etnografyot." *Luah Ahiever* 2 (1920): 329.

———. *Yidishe etnografye un folklor: Zikhroynes vegn der etnografisher ekspeditsye, ongefirt fun Sh. An-ski*. Buenos Aires: YIVO, 1958.

Reiner, Elchanan. "Hon, ma'amad hevrati ve-talmud torah: Ha-Kloyz ba-hevrah ha-yehudit be-Mizrah Eiropah ba-meot ha-17–ha-18." *Tsiyon* 58 (1993).

Rejzen, Zalman. *Leksikon fun der literatur, prese, un filologye*, vol. 4. Vilna, Lithuania: Vilner Farlag fun B. Kletskin, 1929.

Rosenblatt, Devorah Leah. "Tokhter fun barimten Talner khazn shraybt tzum 'forvertz' vegn ir tatn." *Forverts*, April 23, 1942.

Rosenfeld, Natan. "The Wedding in the Cemetery." In *Pinkas Ha-Kehilah Olyka: Sefer Yizkor*, edited by Natan Livneh. Tel Aviv: Hotsaat Irgun Yotsey Olyka be-Yisrael, 1972. Hebrew.

Roskies, David. "An-sky, Sholem Aleichem, and the Master Narrative of Russian Jewry." In *The Worlds of S. An-sky: A Russian Jewish Intellectual at the Turn of the Century*, edited by Gabriella Safran and Steven Zipperstein. Stanford, CA: Stanford University Press, 2006.

———. *S. Ansky: The Dybbuk and Other Writings*. New Haven, CT: Yale University Press, 2002.

———. "S. Ansky and the Paradigm of Return." *The Uses of Tradition: Jewish Continuity in the Modern Era*, edited by Jack Wertheimer. New York: Jewish Theological Seminary of America, 1999.

Rosman, Moshe. *Founder of Hasidism: A Quest for the Historical Ba'al Shem Tov*. Berkeley: University of California Press, 1996.

Roth, Ann Macy, and Catharine Roehrig. "Magical Bricks and Bricks of Birth." *Journal of Egyptian Archaelogy* 88, no. 1 (2002).

Safran, Gabriella. *Wandering Soul: The Dybbuks Creator S. An-Sky*. Cambridge, MA: Harvard University Press, 2010.

Scholem, Gershom. "Gilgul: The Transmigration of Souls," in *On the Mystical Shape of the Godhead: Basic Concepts in the Kabbalah*. New York: Schocken Books, 1991.

———. *On the Kabbalah and Its Symbolism*. New York: Schocken Books, 1965.
———. "The Tradition of the Thirty-Six Hidden Just Men," in *The Messianic Idea in Judaism and Other Essays on Jewish Spirituality*. New York: Schocken Books, 1995.
Schwartz, Barry. "'Hanoten Teshua': The Origin of the Traditional Jewish Prayer for the Government." *Hebrew Union College Annual* 57 (1986).
Schwarz, Jan. *Survivors and Exiles: Yiddish Culture after the Holocaust*. Detroit, MI: Wayne State University Press, 2015.
Sefer Zikaron Radzivilov, edited by Yaakov Adini. Tel Aviv: Hotsa'at Irgun Yotsei Radzivilov be-Yisrael, 1966.
Sergeeva, Irina. *Arkhivna spadshchina Semena An-s'kogo*. Kiev: Dukh i litera, 2006.
Shapiro, Marc. "Torah Study on Christmas Eve." *Journal of Jewish Thought and Philosophy* 8 (1999).
Shenderay, Moshe. "A bukh vos iz a sefer." *Di Yidishe Tsaytung*, July 13, 1958.
Sherira, Shmuel. "With An-sky on His Travels." *Davar* (November 8, 1940). Hebrew.
Shiter, Leybl. "What Is a *Pinkes*?" In *From a Ruined Garden: The Memorial Books of Polish Jewry*, edited by Jack Kugelmass and Jonathan Boyarin. Bloomington: Indiana University Press, 1998.
Smith, Chani Haran. *Tuning the Soul: Music as a Spiritual Process in the Teachings of Rabbi Nahman of Bratslav*. Leiden, Netherlands: E. J. Brill, 2010.
Stanislawski, Michael. *Tsar Nicholas I and the Jews: The Transformation of Jewish Society in Russia, 1825–1855*. Philadelphia: Jewish Publication Society, 1983.
Stein, Sarah Abrevaya. "Illustrating Chicago's Jewish Left: The Cultural Aesthetics of Todros Geller and the L. M. Shteyn Farlag." *Jewish Social Studies*, n.s., 3, no. 3 (1997).
Suliteanu, Gisela. "The Traditional System of Melopeic Prose of the Funeral Songs Recited by the Jewish Women of the Socialist Republic of Romania." *Folklore Research Center Studies* 3 (1972).
Taubman, Howard. "Theater: Mostel as Tevye in 'Fiddler on the Roof.'" *New York Times*, September 23, 1964.
Tcherikower, Elias. *Di ukrayner pogromen in yor 1919*. New York: YIVO, 1965.
Teter, Magda. "Ger Tsedek [Righteous Convert]." *YIVO Encyclopedia of Jews in Eastern Europe*. Available at http://www.yivoencyclopedia.org/article.aspx/Ger_Tsedek.
Trachtenberg, Joshua. *Jewish Magic and Superstition: A Study in Folk Religion*. Philadelphia: University of Pennsylvania Press, 2004.
Twersky, Yohanan. *He-Hatzer ha-Pnimit: Korot mishpahah*. Tel Aviv: N. Tverski, 1954.
Veidlinger, Jeffrey. *In the Shadow of the Shtetl: Small-Town Jewish Life in Soviet Ukraine*. Bloomington: Indiana University Press, 2013.
Weegrzynek, Hanna. "Shvartze khasene: Black Weddings among Polish Jews." In *Holy Dissent: Jewish and Christian Mystics in Eastern Europe*, edited by Glenn Dynner. Detroit, MI: Wayne State University Press, 2013.
Weinreich, Beatrice Silverman. *Yiddish Folktales*. New York: Schocken, 1988.
Weissler, Chava. *Voices of the Matriarchs: Listening to the Prayers of Early Modern Jewish Women*. Boston: Beacon, 1999.
Wertheim, Aaron. *Law and Custom in Hasidism*. Hoboken, NJ: KTAV, 1992.
Yerushalmi, Yosef Hayim. *Zakhor: Jewish History and Jewish Memory*. Seattle: University of Washington Press, 1996.
YIVO RG 3, folder 2934.
YIVO RG 677, folder 65.

Zavadivker, Polly. *1915 Diary of S. An-sky: A Russian Jewish Writer at the Eastern Front*. Bloomington: Indiana University Press, 2016.

Zevin, Shlomo Yosef. *Sipure Hasidim al ha-Torah: A Collection of Inspirational Chassidic Stories*. New York: Mesorah, 1980.

Zinberg, Israel. *A History of Jewish Literature: The Haskalah Movement in Russia*, vol. 11. New York: KTAV, 1978.

Zipperstein, Steven. "Underground Man: The Curious Case of Mark Zborowski and the Writing of a Modern Jewish Classic." *Jewish Review of Books* (Summer 2010).

The Zohar: Volume One. Translation and commentary by Daniel Matt. Stanford, CA: Stanford University Press, 2004.

INDEX

Abramson, Henry, 6
agile like the deer (wood carvings), 62
  fig. 2.1, 68 fig. 2.2, 90 fig. 2.4, 124 fig. 3.2,
  138 fig. 3.4, 200 fig. 4.2
Agudas Ohalei Tsadikim, 165n6
Aharon Doktor Gorda, 139–43
Akiva (Rabbi of Pavoloch), 126–27
Alt-Konstantin [Starokonstantinov], 106
  fig. 2.16, 162 fig. 3.12, 164n3.14, 193–94,
  198, 243
Alufim [Champions], 178
Amalgamated Clothing Workers of
  America, 9
Amidah prayer (*Shmone Esre*), 141, 174, 223
amorets [ignorant person], 136–37
amputated fingers, 66
amulets, 265, 266
angels, 133, 139–40, 145, 166n23, 167n26,
  243–46, 270n13, 272
animals: in synagogue decoration, 61, 62
  fig. 2.1, 68 fig. 2.2, 90 fig. 2.4, 95, 99
  fig. 2.9, 124 fig. 3.2, 138 fig. 3.4, 200
  fig. 4.2, 217 fig. 5.2; used by female
  exorcists, 246, 247
Annulment of Court, 264–65
anonymous artists, 60, 66, 152, 212
An-sky, 2, 52 fig. 1.6; cheder experience of,
  3; death of, 14, 48; ethnographic work
  of, 22, 27, 43–44; health of, 45–46, 48;
interview skills of, 34, 58–59, 77, 242–43,
  255, 279; *Jewish Ethnographic Program*
  (life cycle questionnaire), 2, 5–7, 23, 27,
  44, 45 fig. 1.1; Libernson correspondence
  with, 36n3; Lutsk pinkes gifted to, 71;
  personality of, 34, 43–44, 45–48, 71,
  279; Rechtman's relations with, 5–6, 14,
  43, 45–48, 47 fig. 1.2, 49 fig. 1.3; Relief
  Committee for the War-Victims, 2, 43,
  54 fig. 1.8; secular Jewish culture, 10, 48.
  See also Ethnographic Museum; Jewish
  Ethnographic Expedition
apprenticeships, 173–74
Apter Rov, 27, 33, 116, 208, 274–75
Aramaic language, 24, 33–34, 348
arbitrators for elections, 170, 172, 176, 178
Argentina, Yiddish culture in, 16–19, 18, 39n75
art in synagogues, 60–62, 65–66, 212
Aryeh Leib of Shpola (Shpoler Zaide), 208,
  216, 238n24
Asher, son of Chaim, 155
Asher [Talmud prodigy], 156–58
Asher Tsvi, Rabbi, 81
Asher Zvi, the Maggid of Ostroh, 141, 143,
  167n27
Ashkenazi, Yehuda, 132, 133, 166n21
Ashtribu (angel), 243
Assaf, David, 30
Auerbach, Dovid Tsvi, 143–49, 167n28

293

INDEX

ayin-haro (evil eye), 241
ayna-bisha (evil eye), 241

baale moyfes, 189
Baal Ha-Levushim. *See* Yoffe, Mordechai
Baal Ha-Tanya (Shneur Zalman of Liady).
  See Shneur Zalman of Liady (Baal Ha-Tanya)
baal shem, 189
Baal Shem Tov (Besht), 23, 26, 33; advice given by, 88, 120–21, 219–20; blessings given by, 167n28, 220; at dedication of Mikolayever synagogue, 65; descriptions of, 183–84, 203n4; disciples of, 63, 88, 109n4, 112n54, 167n30; in dreams, 115, 117, 119; grave of, 114, 115–16, 119, 120, 158 fig. 3.7; kloyz of, 116–17, 159 fig. 3.8, 3.9, 165n6; in Medzhibozh, 114, 116–17, 159 fig. 3.8, 3.9, 165n6, 184; miracles attributed to, 88, 119–20, 184; Moshe Chaim Ephraim Sodilkover (grandson), 119, 165n10; music of, 208, 219–22; Odl (daughter), 119–20, 165n10; opposition to, 205–6; peasants' tales of, 183–84; personal scribe of, 272, 283n3; Rebbe Liber the Great and, 72–73; Sore [Sarah] (mother of Besht), 117; tales about, 26, 183–84, 221; tefillin of, 272, 279–80; travels of, 21, 23, 87.
  See also Borukhl, Rabbi (of Medzhibozh)
Bach (Sirkis, Yoel, Rebbe), 84, 112n47
badkhn, 165n3, 209
baldakhin [ceremonial canopy], 108 fig. 2.18
Balta (town), 198
Banco Israelita del Rio de la Plata, 16
Bar (town), 181, 197
bar mitzvah, 272
Baron of Port Arthur (Moshe Ginsburg), 62
Barukh, Reb, 71
bath attendants, 30, 245
bathhouses, 71, 94, 185
Bazilier Rebbe (Yosef Dovid Shmilovitch), 4, 7
beadles, 78, 144–49
beards, 73, 110n26
beautiful young man (legend), 25, 131–32
Be'er Heitev (Ashkenazi), 132, 133, 166n21
bekhires (elections), 169–70, 172, 175–79
Belaya Tserkov (city), 222–23

Belzer, Nisi, 227–28, 239n34
Berdichev, 26, 72–75, 110n25, 119–21, 125, 167n32, 208
Berdichev cemetery, 125, 201 fig. 4.3
Berlin, Moisei, 56n3
Bershader, Refuel, 273
bes medresh, 69, 109n1, 110n20, 208
beys din [Jewish Court], 129, 130, 157, 165n4
Biber, Menachem Mendel, 111n32, 111n38, 112n46
Bick, Chaim, 21, 219–20
Bick, Simkhe, 116, 165n4
Bick (Bik) family, 21, 116, 165n4, 219–20
Biker Khoylim, 169, 186
bimah, 99 fig. 2.9, 137, 257
black candles, 257, 258, 262, 263
black *chuppah*, 125, 166n17
bleeding from the pinky toe, 261, 263
blessings from rebbes, 167n28, 220, 226, 227, 274–76, 275, 277
Bloch, Avrom, 186, 210–12
blood libels, 70–71, 189, 193, 203n13
bodies, desecration of, 126–27
Borukhl, Rabbi (of Medzhibozh): court of, 165n3; half of love brick on grave of, 116, 117, 119; Hershel Ostropoler in court of, 116, 165n3; nigun of, 208; Shneur Zalman of Liady's feud with, 272, 279–82; tefillin of the Besht passed to, 272, 280; temperament of, 280–82
Boyarin, Jonathan, 22
Brailov, 90–91, 197, 198–200, 202 fig. 4.4
Bratslaver Hasidim: dancing of, 215; language of, 26; melave-malke (escorting the queen, meal following the Sabbath) with, 213, 215–16, 238n20; music of, 214, 215, 217–18; prayer of, 213–14; shaleshudes with, 213, 214–15, 238n15; solitary meditation of, 213–14; synagogue of, 212, 213; *tefilas ha-hisdavkus*, 213–14, 238n13; Uman, 197, 198, 203n12, 213, 237n12, 238n24. *See also* Nahman of Bratslav
Breslauer's Kloyz (Dubno), 92–94, 100 fig. 2.10
bricks, 65, 118, 119, 165n8
Brisman, Shimeon, 11
broken windowpane, 263

Brukhe (wife of Reb Motele), 235
Buber, Martin, 33
burials: of Asher [Talmud prodigy], 158;
  of body parts, 66; bricks, 118; burial
  shrouds, 115, 193; burial societies *(Hevra
  Kadisha)*, 34, 71, 83, 121, 130, 150, 169–70,
  174, 203n3, 222; donkey's burial, 178–79;
  funeral processions, 86, 121, 123 fig. 3.1,
  232, 253; Gomle-Khesed-Shel-Emes, 169;
  live burial, 128, 131; of martyrs, 200; mass
  graves, 127, 231; melodies beyond the
  grave, 231; of Mendel the Chazan, 222;
  price of graves, 171; recorded in pinkesim,
  171, 200; social status, 150–51, 169; of
  Yekhiel Mikhel [Katz] and mother, 196–97
burial societies *(Hevra Kadisha)*, 34, 71, 83,
  121, 130, 150, 169–70, 174, 203n3, 222
butchers, 77, 78, 183

candidates *(muamadim)* for elections, 169,
  170, 175, 177, 179
carpenters, 115–16
ceiling murals in synagogues, 94–95, 212
cemeteries, 28; adjacent family plots, 83;
  admittance to, 282; arrangement of
  burial plots, 83, 116, 117, 121, 149–50,
  178–79, 189, 222; burial of Maharsha
  (Shmuel [Eliezer] Eydels), 83; burial
  societies *(Hevra Kadisha)*, 34, 71, 83,
  121, 130, 150, 169–70, 174, 203n3, 222;
  churches adjacent to, 86, 134–36;
  establishment of, 178; funding for,
  150; grave of Baal Shem Tov (Besht),
  114, 115–16, 120, 158 fig. 3.7; graves of
  misnagdim, 116; *Hevra Kadisha*, 34;
  Jewish Ethnographic Expedition visits
  to, 116; during Khmelnytsky massacres,
  196; *klogmuters* (female professional
  mourners), 28–29, 253–54, 267
  fig. 6.4; location of gravesites, 83,
  116–17, 120–21, 149–50, 178–79, 189,
  203n5, 222; pinkes of Berdichev
  cemetery, 201 fig. 4.3; re-interment of
  martyrs in Jewish cemeteries, 127; study
  houses in, 94; tombstone inscriptions,
  33, 42, 69, 71; visits to, in Elul, 28, 150,
  253, 254; weddings in, 166n17
cemetery caretakers: as source of legends, 95

Central Union of Polish Jews in Argentina
  (Tsentral-Farband fun Poylishe Yidn in
  Argentine), 16
Chabad Hasidism. *See* Shneur Zalman of
  Liady (Baal Ha-Tanya)
Chaim son of Chaya who was born in his
  mother's grave, 128–31
charity: collection of, 13, 76, 79, 141, 234;
  promises of, 150, 185; societies for, 169;
  tithing for, 77
charity boxes, 133
charms, 241, 265
Chaya (wife of Reb Motele Shpikover),
  235, 244
chazanim: attraction to church music, 232;
  choirboys, 220–23, 226–27, 228, 229;
  compositions of, 237; death of, 231–32;
  of fraternal societies, 174; of the Talner
  Hasidim, 225–27, 231, 233–34, 239n32; of
  Vishnevets, 229–30
Chechelnik, 134–38, 136–38, 166n22
cheder education, 3, 4, 33, 207
Chernobyl Hasidim, 30, 203n9, 210, 225–26,
  239n32
childbirth, 78; childbirth after death,
  129–30, 131; death of mothers in, 129–30;
  female exorcists, 247; infant mortality,
  87–88, 119–20, 124; infertility, 226, 247;
  miscarriages, 247, 269n8; *pidyen-haben*,
  212, 237n11; prediction of child's gender,
  29, 241, 269n4; pregnancy, 87–88, 119,
  129–30, 241, 247, 269n8; talismans for,
  34, 120, 168, 241, 269n5, 269n9
children: apostasy of, 282, 283n5; cheder
  education, 3, 4, 33, 207; childlessness,
  128, 226–27, 247; circumcision, 87–88,
  108 fig. 2.18, 119, 167n28, 175, 181, 186,
  250, 269n9, 282; as illegitimate, 129–30;
  infant mortality, 87–88, 119–20, 124;
  as members of societies, 170; military
  conscription of, 4, 66, 109n15, 185, 208,
  280; naming of, 119–20, 131; orphans, 29,
  253, 255–67; paternity of, 129–30; *pidyen-
  haben*, 212, 237n11; poverty of children of
  zaddikim, 125; revival of dead children,
  120, 131; sick, peasant children brought
  to rabbis, 184; thumb sucking, 124, 125;
  Torah learning, 78

choirboys, 220–23, 226–27, 228, 229
Christianity: conversion to, 118, 165n9, 196; intermarriage, 227; priests, 69–71, 94–95, 139, 232; *Yozyl* (Jesus), 77, 244
Christians: in Pale of Settlement, 26; rabbis used as mediators, 183; relations with Hasidim, 26
Christmas eve, 77, 78, 111n33
chuppah (wedding canopy), 125, 152
churches, 127; adjacent to Jewish cemeteries, 134–36; construction of, 69, 72, 88, 134–38; destruction of, as punishment, 86; priests, 69–71, 94–95, 139, 232; synagogues, 72, 89; wood carvings in, 62
circumcision: Baal Shem Tov (Besht), 87–88, 119–20, 167n28; being called up to the Torah in honor of, 175, 186; celebrations of, 175, 181, 224; Elijah's seat, 108 fig. 2.18; fathers of the boy, 87–88, 175, 181; incantations for, 250, 269n9; miracles associated with, 87–88, 119–20; mohels [ritual circumcisers], 186; sandak at, 167n28, 282; sources (Tanakh, Talmud) related to, 250, 269n9; stopping bleeding after, 250, 269n9
Cobblers, Association of, 169, 175
combinations of names of God, 258
communal leadership, 67, 110n18, 176–77
communal pinkesim: martyrs recorded in, 116, 127, 189, 194–96
communal pinkes of Letichev, 182–83
communal pinkes of Nemirov, 195–96
communal workers' pinkes (Mikolayev), 176
community pinkesim: communal leadership roles recorded in, 176–77; communal miracle day observances, 190–91; community megillahs in, 190; elections, 169–70, 172, 175–79; hierarchical structure, 178–79; law cases in, 181–83; miraculous tales recorded in, 186–89; pogroms recorded in, 189–98; privileges of Talmud scholar, 179; rules against luxury, 179–81
community pinkes of Bar (town), 181
community pinkes of Khmelnik, 177

Conference on Jewish Material Claims against Germany, 16
Congress for Jewish Culture, 14
construction equipment, 110n19
contracts (Ksav mamad), 173–74
conversion bricks, 118
conversion of Jews, 118, 165n9, 196, 282, 283n5
cooperative worker housing projects. *See* Sholem Aleichem Houses (*Sholem Aleikhem Hayzer*)
council of seven of workers' societies, 172, 173–74
Count Lubomirski, 75, 92
Count Potoski, 88–89, 112n55
Count Tipinitsky, 63–65
craftsmen societies, 169
crowns on letters (*shatnez getz*), 276, 277–78
Culture League [*Di Kultur Lige*], 48
"The Culture of the Shtetl." *See Life Is with People*
curses, 122–23, 141, 153–54, 166n23, 180, 282

dancing of the Bratslaver Hasidim, 215
David, King, 215, 216
David of Talne (Dovidl Talner), 225–29, 232, 239n32
Days of Awe, 64, 109n11, 227, 229–30, 232, 274, 277
death, 34, 71, 83, 121; and the afterlife, 122; burial shrouds, 115; childbirth after, 129–30; church construction disrupted by the dead, 135–38; cursing the dead, 122; dates of, 71, 119, 134, 139; of duke's daughter, 132; funeral processions, 86, 121, 123 fig. 3.1, 232, 253; infant mortality, 87, 88, 119–20; kaddish, 131, 134, 222; kiss of God, 83, 112n45; *klogmuters* (female professional mourners), 28–29, 253–54, 267 fig. 6.4; *Oylem Ha-Emes* [afterlife], 122; of Reb Yosele (the rebbe's Yosele), 231–32; request to God given to the dead, 193–94; revival of the dead, 86; of sinners, 80, 122–23; soul, departure of, 116; talking to the dead, 121, 137–38; as tikkun, 222; *vidui* (confession before death), 116, 195, 197, 231; yahrzeit

observances, 122, 133, 153, 175; of zaddikim, 71, 73, 85, 86, 121, 132, 184–85, 222, 272
deer motifs, 62 fig. 2.1, 68 fig. 2.2, 90 fig. 2.4, 95, 124 fig. 3.2, 138 fig. 3.4, 200 fig. 4.2
Degel mahaneh Efrayim (Sodilkover), 165n10
demons, 166n23, 251–52
depression, motif of, 157
Derazhnya. *See* Shraybman, Yisroel, Reb
Der Forverts, 18–20
determination if person is alive (incantation), 251
Devorah Leah (daughter of Reb Yosele), 231
dibukkim [malevolent spirits]. *See* dybbuk
Di Idishe Tsaytung (periodical), 18, 19
Di Presse (periodical), 18
doctors, 139–41, 139–43, 185, 267–68
dogs, in incantations, 245, 246, 247, 250
Doktor Gorda, 139–43
Doktor Zamler (pseud. for Rechtman), 13–14, 38n57
donkey's burial, 178–79, 189
Dos Naye Lebn (periodical), 20
Dov Ber, the Maggid of Mezeritch. *See* Maggid of Mezeritch
Dovid Elye (scribe of Anipol), 272–73, 276–77, 279, 283 fig. 7.2
Dovid Moshe Tshortkover, 272
Dovid of Anipol, 277, 279
Dovid of Mikolayev (Rebbe), 63–64, 109n7, 274–75
Dovid the scribe (Anipol), 278
dreams, 67, 115, 117, 119, 121, 127
Drohobitsher, Itzikl, Reb, 87–88
drowning, 208, 237n6
Dubno, 92–93, 100 fig. 2.10
Dubnow, Simon, 1, 3, 5, 56n3, 167n32, 202n1
duke of Mezeritch, 66–68
Dvorkin, Ben, 21
dybbuk, 42, 251; amulets against, 265, 266; appearance of, 265; exit of, 261, 263–64; exorcism of, 255–57, 259, 260, 261; kaddish for, 256, 260–62, 265, 266; name of, 259, 260, 261; speech of, 256, 257–58; tales recorded in community pinkesim, 189
The Dybbuk (An-sky), 46, 215, 239n32

Edison, Thomas Alva, 32, 209, 212
education: bes medresh, 69, 110n20, 208; cheder, 3, 4, 33; for learning Yiddish culture, 8, 9, 48; *talmud-toyre* (Talmud Torah), 63, 176, 178; yeshivot, 22, 76, 78, 176. *See also* Torah study
Egyptian magical bricks, 165n8
elections *(bekhires)*, 169–70, 172, 175–79
Eliezer Liber ha-Gadol, 72–75, 110n25
Elijah's seat, 108 fig. 2.18
Elijah the Prophet, 73, 243–44, 272
Elimelekh of Lizensk/Lizhensk, 203n5, 220–22
El-Male-Rachamim, 134, 189, 191–93, 196, 197, 198
Elul, cemetery visits in, 28, 150, 253, 254
embroidered aprons, 268 fig. 6.5
employment regulations of workers' societies, 173–74
Engel, Yoel, 42, 207
Ephraim Sofer of Ostroh, 273
epileptic boy from Khmelnik, 255–67
Esterke (Hasidic woman), 27, 33
Esther gravestone (martyr's grave), 194
Estherke (Mikolayev), 274–76
Ethnographic Museum, 46–47, 48, 53 fig. 1.7, 66, 71, 77, 96–98, 217, 279
evil eye *(eynhore, ayin-haro)*, 29; good eye as euphemism for, 241, 242, 245, 269n3; incantations against, 241, 243–45; incantations of male exorcists against, 248–50; sources related to, 240, 243; Talmud on, 241
excommunications, 77, 172, 178, 180, 182–83, 198
exile, 146–49, 156, 198, 255
Exodus from Egypt, 31
exorcism: Annulment of Court, 264–65; black candles in, 257, 258, 262, 263; completion of, 263; of dybbuk, 255–57, 259, 260, 261; male exorcists, 29, 248, 249 fig. 6.2; preparation for, 246, 247, 257; shofar blowing, 257, 258, 262; Tatars (Kadorim), 26, 244, 255; tools of, 29, 244, 246, 247, 257, 258; Torah scrolls in, 257, 258. *See also* female exorcists
eynhore (evil eye), 29

fasting, 79, 87, 197; as acts of piety, 115; communal observances, 80–81, 191, 195, 197; for forgiveness, 131; *Hevra Kadisha* (burial societies), 203n3; Megilas Nes Ostroh [The Scroll of the Miracle of Ostroh], 190–91; on Mondays and Thursdays, 115, 133; in preparation for exorcism, 256, 257; before Second Purim observances, 194; VaYekhal (Torah reading for fast days), 79

female exorcists: charms of, 247; childbirth attended by, 29, 247; documentation of treatments, 30, 242–43, 246–47; effectiveness of treatments, 247; expedition members as subjects for, 30, 242–43, 246–47; hand washing, 246, 247; incantations of, 243, 244–47; languages of, 26, 243–45, 244, 248; *opshprekherke* (women exorcist and healer), 29–30; payment of, 242–43, 246; practices described, 241, 243, 245–46, 247, 269n5; preparation of, 246; recording of, 242–43; refusal to teach incantations, 30, 242; remedies of, 29; reputations of, 246, 247; spitting, 243, 245, 246; tools of, 29, 244, 246, 247

female professional mourners *(klogmuters)*, 28–29, 253–54, 267 fig. 6.4

fever, cures for, 251

Feyge (granddaughter of Besht), 119–20, 213

fiddle players, 215, 216, 217

Fiddler on the Roof, 19, 24, 39n84

Fikangur, Yitzhak, 5, 37n19, 42, 43

final confession, 116, 133, 195, 197, 231

fingernails, clipping of, 247, 269n8

fires, 60–62, 82, 133–34, 155

"Five Books of the Pentateuch" (sons of Yekhiel Mikhl Zlotshever), 109n4

flogging of Hasidim, 154–55

Fonye, 66, 110n16

food and food customs: blessings before eating, 122; food offered by An-sky to the old men, 58; at happy occasions, 181; for Jewish soldiers, 186; kashrut, 4, 70, 77, 178, 186; on the Sabbath, 87, 147, 213, 214–15, 216, 228, 238n15

fraternal societies: conflicts between, 175, 183; coordination between, 185–86; council of seven in, 172, 173–74; distribution of Torah honors, 174–75, 186; elections *(bekhires)*, 169–70, 172, 175–79; joint pinkesim, 175; membership in, 170–71, 182–83; punishments meted out by, 182–83; rules of, 13, 169–73, 170–71, 172, 173, 175–77, 185–86; study houses of, 174, 186

Freeze, ChaeRan, 203n8

funeral processions, 86, 121, 123 fig. 3.1, 232, 253

fur trade, 122, 171

Gabbai, Yisrael Meir, 165n6

gaboim, 178

Gaiviker, Naum, 37n24

Galay, Daniel, 23

gan eden, 222

Gashuri, Meir Shimon, 110nn20–21

gematria, 17, 197, 214

Gemiles Khasodim, 186

gentile exorcists, 244

get [divorce document], 84, 157

gilgulim, 122, 166n12, 189

Ginsburg, Shaul, 56n3

Gintsberg, David, Baron, 5

Gintsberg, Naftali Hertz, Baron. *See* Jewish Ethnographic Expedition

Gintsburg, Vladimir Horacevich, Baron, 5, 55 fig. 1.9. *See also* Jewish Ethnographic Expedition

Ginzburg, Moshe (Baron of Port Arthur), 62, 109n6

"girlish melody," 224–25

"girl with a ksav" [folk saying], 185

"The Giver of Salvation" (prayer for the government), 223

Gladshteyn, Yankev, 10, 11

Gladstone, Renée (Reyzl), 5, 8–11, 10, 14, 16, 37n45

Gnendl (exorcist in Letichev), 246

goats, slaughtering during the summer, 183

God: combinations of names of, 258

goldene keyt (golden chain) of tradition, 35

golus [exile], 146–49, 156

Gomle-Khesed-Shel-Emes, 169
Gonta massacres, 28, 189, 197–99, 203n12
Gorman, Rachel, 109n2
Grade, Chaim, 11, 21–22
gravediggers, 267
graves: burnt bricks on, 118; *khosn-kale-kvorim* [bride and groom graves], 151–53; lamps over, 120; maintenance of, 95, 110n21, 120; of married couples, 116; mass graves, 127, 231; peasants at graves of zaddikim, 185; petitions *(kvitlekh)* left on, 33, 114, 117–18, 120, 122; pilgrimages to, 110n21; praying at, 124; *shtibl over*, 114–15, 116, 132–33, 151; written requests to God in, 193–94; of Yeshayele (of Khmelnik), 267
Great Reb Liber's Synagogue, 72–75
Grigor'ev, Nikifor, 231, 239n36
Grinberg, Sore (Proskurov), 244
Groyser verterbukh fun der yidisher shprakh (Great Dictionary of the Yiddish Language), 11–12, 24
gzeyres takh ve-tat. *See* Khmelnytsky massacres

"Ha-ben yakir li efrayim" (Jeremiah 31:19), 227, 228
Haidamaks, 28, 166n19, 166n22, 189, 193, 194, 196, 199
Hakhnasat kalah, 13
hakhnoses-orkhim, 147–48, 186
"Ha-Melits," 172
Hands of Aaron, 66, 94
hand washing, 246, 247
harassment of ethnographers, 3, 36n10
Harbin, China, 6
Harkavy, Alexander, 167n32
Hasidic court of Korostishev, 212
Hasidim, 3; Apter Rov, 27, 33, 116, 208, 274–75; Bratslaver Hasidim, 26, 112n54; Chabad Lubavitch, 32; contact with Christian neighbors, 26; courts of, 165n3; embrace of, 85, 87; hasidic melodies, 207, 208–9, 219; influenced by contact with neighbors, 26; influence of Kabbalah on, 238n13; kidnapping of, 154–55; *kvitl/kvitlekh* (written requests), 33, 114, 117–18, 120, 122; language of, 25, 26; Maiden of Ludmir, 111n27; misnagdim, 87, 116, 139–41, 154–55, 167n32; music of, 205, 208, 209, 210; in Ostroh, 86–87; as patriarchal, 27; Reb Motele (Chernobler grandson) of Proskurov, 234; Ruzhin Hasidim, 30; Stolin Hasidim, 30; as storytellers, 235–36; tales about, 26, 183–84, 221; Talner Hasidim, 225–29, 230–34, 239n32; Twersky Hasidic dynasty, 10–11, 30–31, 203n9, 233, 244; women, 27, 30, 235; zaddik who hears a gentile shepherd boy singing, 223–24, 239n31. *See also* Baal Shem Tov (Besht); Maggid of Mezeritch; Shneur Zalman of Liady (Baal Ha-Tanya)
Hat Makers, Association of, 169, 173, 175
headstones, 143 fig. 3.5; artwork on, 117, 160 fig. 3.10, 161 fig. 3.11, 162 fig. 3.12, 163 fig. 3.13, 164n3.14; of Asher [Talmud prodigy], 158; condition of, 83, 110n21, 149, 151; death dates on, 71, 119, 134, 139; inscriptions on, 33, 42, 69, 71, 76–77, 83, 86, 119–20, 125, 128, 131–34, 138, 149, 151, 153; memories of, 155; from Nemirov, 160 fig. 3.10; positioning of, 117; shapes of, 128, 139; Starokonstantinov, 162 fig. 3.12, 164n3.14; Tulchin, 163 fig. 3.13; for women, 117, 163 fig. 3.13, 164n3.14, 194; of Yehiel Michel, 197; from Zhitomir, 161 fig. 3.11
healers: doctors as, 142–43; prayers for healing, 141; Raphael (angel), 140, 167n26; recorded in community pinkesim, 189; Tatars (Kadorim), 26, 244, 255; women as, 27, 29–30, 34
Hebrew language: account of Jewish Ethnographic Expedition in, 13–14; inscriptions on synagogues, 79; in Jewish Ethnography and Folklore *(Yidishe etnografye un folklor)*(Rechtman), 24; in manuscripts, 348
hegdesh [hospice], 178
Heller, Yom Tov Lipmann *(Tosfos Yom Tov)*, 112n54, 121, 165n11, 196

Hershel Ostropoler, 116, 165n3
Hershenyu, Reb (Chechelnik/
    Tshitshelnik), 33, 134, 136–38, 166n22
Hershl Sofer, 282
Heschel, Abraham Joshua, 14, 24
Heshel, Abraham Joshua (Apter Rov)
    (1748–1825), 33, 116, 165n3, 274–75
Hevra Kadisha (burial societies): cantors
    for, 174; fasts of, 203n3; graves prepared
    by, 170, 222; gravestones erected by, 83;
    pinkesim of, 34, 169, 170
Hillel (Reb), 215, 216, 217
Hill of Curses (Nemirov), 153–54
Hinde/Hilde the Bath Attendant
    (Proskurov), 30, 245
"Hineni" prayer, 229–30
Hirsh Leyb, 116
History of the Jews of Warsaw (Shatzky), 14
Holocaust, 7, 14, 17, 28, 167n34, 202n1
Horodetsky, Shmuel Abba, 27
Horowitz, Yeshaya Ha-Levi (Shelah), 198,
    204n15
hospitality, 58, 146–47, 186

Immigration Act (1924, United States), 8
imprisonment of Jews, 126–27
incantations: for circumcision, 250, 269n9;
    efficacy of, 30, 242, 247, 248; against
    evil eye *(eynhore, ayin-haro)*, 243–44;
    of female exorcists, 243; for good eye,
    245; against illness, 241; Joseph the
    Righteous in, 240, 241, 244; languages
    of, 243, 244–46, 248, 269n9; of male
    exorcists, 249 fig. 6.2; manuscripts of,
    248, 249 fig. 6.2; modus operandi of,
    243–44; recordings of, 30, 34, 241–44;
    spitting in recitations of, 243, 245, 246;
    teaching of/transmission of, 30, 242;
    three wives (incantation), 243; Yiddish
    as language of, 243–46
incantations, languages of, 26
incantations of male exorcists:
    reproduction of, 248
In poylishe velder (In Polish Woods)
    (Opatoshu), 10
inscriptions on headstones, 33, 42, 69, 71,
    76–77, 83, 86, 119–20, 125, 128, 131–34, 138,
    149, 151, 153

International Workers Order (IWO), 9
Ish Yemini (pseud. for Rechtman), 13–14,
    38n57
IWO (Instituto Cientifico Judio), 16, 17–18,
    39n75

Jesus *(Yozyl)*, 77, 244
Jewish Academy (St. Petersburg), 5
Jewish calendar: cemetery visits in Elul, 28,
    150, 253, 254; commemoration of miracle
    at Ostroh synagogue, 79–82; dates of
    societies' elections, 169–70, 171; dates of
    weddings, 155, 167n33; death dates, 71, 83,
    86, 119, 134, 139; headstones, dates on, 71,
    119, 134, 139; second Purim celebrations,
    79, 81, 111n36, 190, 191, 192–94
Jewish Committee for the Relief of War
    Victims. *See* Relief Committee for the
    War-Victims
Jewish Court *[beys din]*, 129, 130
Jewish Ethnographic Expedition, 12;
    conversations with local residents,
    58, 209–10; destruction of records, 35;
    founding of, 42, 55; grave of Yeshayele
    (of Khmelnik) viewed by, 267; hasidic
    melodies collected by, 207, 208;
    Hebrew language account of, 13–14;
    Jewish Ethnographic Program (life
    cycle questionnaire) of, 2, 5–7, 23, 27,
    44, 45 fig. 1.1; members as subjects
    for exorcisms, 242–43, 246–47;
    phonograph recordings made by, 2, 42,
    207–9, 210–11, 212, 219; reception of, 2,
    20–23, 58–59, 183–84, 208–10, 242–43,
    246–47, 272, 279–82; *as visnshaft* (dry
    scholasticism), 20. *See also* dybbuk;
    exorcist headings; music; sound
    recordings; synagogues
Jewish Ethnographic Program (life cycle
    questionnaire), 2, 5–7, 23, 27, 44, 45
    fig. 1.1
Jewish Ethnography and Folklore *(Yidishe
    etnografye un folklor)*(Rechtman). *See
    Yidishe etnografye un folklor* (Jewish
    Ethnography and Folklore)(Rechtman)
Jewish folk remedies. *See* exorcist headings
Jewish girls, 185, 203n8, 224–25
Jewish Historical-Ethnographic Society, 42

Jewish National Workers Alliance
  (Nationaler Yidisher Arbeter Farband), 9
Joseph the Righteous, 240, 241, 244

kabbalah, 34, 112n53, 122, 133, 166nn12–13,
  197, 218, 223–24, 239n31, 277
kabbalas shabbos [prayer service
  welcoming the Sabbath], 147, 207, 216,
  220, 221, 222
kaddish, 5, 131, 134, 222, 256; for an opera
  singer, 228; for dybbuk, 256, 260–62, 265,
  266; Hasidic song, 208; recitation of by
  the rebbe, 222, 228; for women, 131
Kadorim (Tatars), 26, 244, 255, 269n7
Kaidanover, Aaron Shmuel, 270n14
kalpi (election rules), 169, 177
Kamenets-Podolsk, 117
Karaites, 110n20
kashe (use of term), 254
kashrut, 4, 70, 77, 178, 186
Katz, Aleph, 20–22
kavanos [intentions], 133, 273
ketubah, 84, 271
Khamil. *See* Khmelnytsky massacres
Khanele di Doktorshe, 143
khapunes, 65, 208
khevre kedishe. See Hevra Kadisha (burial
  societies)
Khevre Tsedaka-Gedola, 169
Khmelnik. *See* Slabodiansky, Daniel
Khmelnik pinkes, 177, 191–92
Khmelnytsky massacres, 23, 112n56;
  commemoration of rescue from,
  in Olyka, 194–95; destruction of
  synagogues, 82, 89; El-Male-Rachamim
  for martyrs of, 191–93; graves of martyrs,
  150–53; kinah (dirge) to commemorate,
  6–7; martyrdom of Mordechai and
  Esther of Medzhibozh (married
  couple), 116; martyrs of Polonnoye,
  6–7, 150, 197; in Nemirov pinkes, 196; in
  Olyka, 194–95; in Ostroh, 82, 84, 151; in
  Starokonstantinov, 192–94
khol hamoed Pesakh election day, 177, 178
khosn-kale-kvorim [bride and groom
  graves], 151–53
khuppah (wedding canopy), 125, 152
khurbn, 7, 156, 167n34

Khurbn Galitsye (An-sky), 2
Khurbn Proskurov (The Destruction of
  Proskurov), 7
kiddush levana (sanctification of the new
  moon), 211, 237n10
kidnapping, 131–32, 154–55, 208
kidush hashem. See martyrs and martyrdom
kings: tales of errant sons, 236
Kirshenblatt-Gimblett, Barbara, 23
Kiselgof, Zusman, 42, 56n5, 207
kishuf [magic], 241
kitl/kitlen, 63, 109n9, 263
Klezmer musicians, 152
klogmuters (female professional mourners),
  28–29, 253–54, 267 fig. 6.4
kloyz, 92–93, 92–94, 100 fig. 2.10, 109n1,
  116–17, 159 fig. 3.8, 3.9, 165n6
knives, 247, 269n5
knots (motif), 156, 269n9
knots of shame on wedding veils, 156
kol-bo (prayerbook), 43
Kol Nidre, 63, 64, 109n11, 274
Korahites, 155, 167n35
korban edah [communal sacrifice], 125–26,
  166n18
korban olah [burnt offering], 133
Korets, 138–39
Koretser, Asher, 141, 143, 167n27
Koretser, Pinkhes, 86–87, 206
Korkha [land of Korah], 156–57
Korostishev, 103 fig. 2.13, 104 fig. 2.14,
  186–88, 197, 203n9, 210, 212
Korostishev synagogue, 103 fig. 2.13, 104
  fig. 2.14
Kotik, Yekhezkel, 166n17
Krements synagogue, 108 fig. 2.18
Ksav mamad (contract), 173–74
ksav [writtten document], 185
Kugelmass, Jack, 22
kune (prison cell), 82
kvitl/kvitlekh (written requests to a Hasidic
  rebbe), 33, 114, 117–18, 120, 122

labor cooperatives, 8–10, 30–31
lamed vavnik zaddikim [Thirty-Six
  Righteous], 123, 166n15, 189, 198, 272
lamentation of the martyrs of Nemirov, 196
lamps, 102 fig. 2.12

Land of Israel, 4–5, 185, 213, 216
law cases, 67–68, 139, 182–83
leaseholds, 172–73, 174
lecterns, 64, 98 fig. 2.8, 102 fig. 2.12, 104 fig. 2.14, 122
Lekhvitsh synagogue, 154–55
Letichev. *See* Shlomovits, Zalman
Letichev pinkesim, 170, 182–83
letter of Thanksgiving (Maharsha synagogue (Ostroh)), 79–82
Levi Yitzhak of Berdichev, 110n25, 119, 120–21, 167n32, 208
Levush Ir Shushan (Yoffe), 198
Leyb Baal Parnose, 123–24
Leyb Sores, 123, 166n14, 239n30
Libernson, Moisei Solomonovich, 36n3
Liber the Great, Rebbe, 72–75, 110n25, 125–26
Lichtenbaum, Abraham, 39n75
life cycle questionnaire (Jewish Ethnographic Expedition), 2, 5, 7, 23, 27, 44
Life Is with People, 18, 24
Lifshitz, Joseph, 17
Lilientalowa [Lilienthal], Regina, 56n3
Lines-HaTsedek, 169
literacy, 16–20
Litvin, A., 192
Lizensk, 203n5, 220–22
longevity (120 years), 112n60, 122, 149, 185, 275–76
long voyage motifs, 128
"The Lord reigns, He is clothed in majesty" (Psalm 93), 220, 221, 222
loshn-koydesh/loyshen kodesh (holy language), 24, 117–18, 156, 248
loss of virginity *(mukat ets)*, 185, 203n8
love bricks, 33, 118, 119
love potions (incantation), 250
Loyfer, Haya-Sarah, 110n21
Ludmir (Vladimir-Volynsk), 75, 111n27
Ludmir synagogue, 75
Luria, Isaac, 237n10
Lutsk: blood libel in, 70–71; cemeteries of, 71, 110n23; church construction in, 69–70; Jewish population of, 110n20; pinkesim of, 171; study house of Rebbe Yehudah the Martyr, 69; visit of Jewish Ethnographic Expedition to, 110n20
Lutsk synagogue, 97 fig. 2.7, 99 fig. 2.9

Ma'ayan Ha-Chokhmah (Koretser), 167n27
Maggid of Mezeritch: disciples of, 85, 203nn4–5, 220–22, 273; Doktor Gorda, 139–41; influence of, 110n17, 167n25; scribes of, 272–73, 276–77. *See also* Shneur Zalman of Liady (Baal Ha-Tanya)
magic spells, 122–23, 137–38, 166n23
Maharsha (Shmuel [Eliezer] Eydels), 155; condemnation by shtetl resident, 77–78; death and burial of, 83; excommunication of shtetl resident, 77–78; as head of yeshivah, 76, 78; inscribed stones of, 76–77; on *nitl nakht*, 77, 78, 111n33; in Ostroh, 75, 76, 78, 79–83; scholarship of, 76; tale of Asher [Talmud prodigy], 156–58; yeshiva of, 76, 78
Maharsha synagogue (Ostroh), 79–83, 100 fig. 2.10
Maiden of Ludmir, 111n27
Makhzik Ha-Pinkes (guardian of the pinkes), 178
male exorcists, 29, 248, 249 fig. 6.2, 251
Malke, Isaac, 274
manuscripts, 212; acquisition of, 248, 252; demons in, 251–52; examination of, 254–55; of incantations, 248, 249 fig. 6.2, 250; transcription of, 34, 79–80, 248, 252
Marek, Peysekh, 56n3
Mark, Yudel, 12
marriages: to Christians, 227; divorce, 84, 157; forced marriage, 199; *get* [divorce document], 84, 157; holy rock in Lekhevitsh as site of, 155; *ketubah*, 84, 271; to a Korahite woman, 156–57; matchmaking, 155–56; of orphans, 29, 253; proof of virginity, 185, 203n8; remarriage, 235; Torah learning after, 84; Torah portions before, 144, 147. *See also* weddings

martyrs and martyrdom, 28, 69–71, 110n22; Akiva (Rabbi of Pavoloch), 126–27; Bazilier Rebbe (Yosef Dovid Shmilovitch), 4, 7; of the beautful young man, 131–32; burial of, 116, 127, 132–33; in communal pinkesim, 189, 191–92, 200; El-Male-Rachamim, 134, 189, 191–92, 196, 197, 198; El-Male-Rachamim for, 134, 189, 191–93, 196, 197, 198; final confession of, 116, 133, 195, 197, 231; girls as, 195–96, 200; Gonta massacres, 197–98; graves of, 69, 150–53; headstone inscriptions, 69, 132–34; of Hershenyu, Reb, 134, 136–38, 166n22; of Khmelnytsky massacres, 7, 195–97; killed by fire, 133; lamentation of the martyrs of Nemirov, 196; Martyrs of Pavoloch, 126–27, 166n19; of Mordechai and Esther of Medzhibozh (married couple), 116, 194; of Polonnoye, 150, 197; of Reb Yosele, 231; recorded in community pinkesim, 189; self-sacrifices of, 133; women, Jewish, in Pale of Settlement as, 28; women as, 28, 73, 98, 151–53, 195–96; young men as, 131; zaddikim as, 125–26

Martyrs of Pavoloch, 126–27, 166n19

mass graves of martyrs, 127, 231

matzah baking, 85

Mayim Kedoshim (Yekusiel Segal of Brailov), 91, 198–99, 202 fig. 4.4

Maykhl Kosher society, 186

mayse (tale), 254

"May the slanderers have no hope" (prayer), 223

Medzhibozh: Baal Shem Tov (Besht) in, 114, 116–17, 159 fig. 3.8, 3.9, 165n6, 184; Bick (Bik) family in, 21, 116, 165n4; Jewish Ethnographic Expedition in, 219–20; martyrs, 116; pinkes of, 170; Second Purim in, 194

Megilas Nes Ostroh [The Scroll of the Miracle of Ostroh], 79–82, 111n36, 111n38, 189, 190–91

Megilat Evah (Yom Tov Lipmann Heller), 165n11

Megillah of Medzhibozh, 116, 194

megillahs, 33, 79–82, 116, 165n11, 189, 190–94

Megillas Medzibozh (Megillah of Medzhibozh), 116

Mekhilpoli synagogue, 105 fig. 2.15

Melamed (teacher), 234

melave-malke (escorting the queen, meal following the Sabbath), 213, 215–16, 221, 238n20

melodies: of the Besht, 220, 221, 222; of Bratslaver Hasidim, 214–16, 225–26; drawn from heaven, 225–26; language of, 217; "The Lord reigns, He is clothed in majesty" (Psalm 93), 220, 221, 222; sources (Tanakh, Talmud) related to, 207–9, 220, 221, 222, 230, 236; of Talner Hasidim, 230–31, 233–34

"The Melody of Creation" (Talner Hasidim), 233–34

membership in societies, 170–71, 182–83

Mendel Chazan, 219–22

menorahs, 82, 94, 117, 212, 217

Der Mentsh, 44

Meshulum Zisha of Anipol, 203n5

messiah, 5, 197

Meyerl (legend of childless Talner Hasid), 226–28

Mezeritch synagogue, 66–68, 110n17

Mezshirov, 198

mezuzahs, 271

Michael (angel), 272

Michel, Tony, 20

mikhtav patuah, 111n39

Mikolayever synagogue, 63–65, 63–66, 65, 98 fig. 2.8

Mikolayev/Mikulaev, 4, 7, 32–33, 63, 109n7, 171, 176, 274

Mikolayev pinkesim, 171, 176

mikveh (ritual bath), 35, 73, 115, 178, 232, 257, 272

military conscriptions, 4, 65, 109n15, 185, 208, 280

mincha (afternoon prayer), 73

Minkovsky, Pini, 226

minyan, 117, 126, 137, 144, 181

miracles: childbirth after death, 129–30, 131; commemorations of, 79–82; discovery of grave of Sore [Sarah] (mother of Besht), 117; end of plague, 125–26; "girlish melody," 224–25; in Olyka, 84; rescue from Khmelnytsky, 194; savior of chazan and choirboy in Belaya Tserkov, 223; survival of children, 124–25
miracle worker (*poel-yeshues*), 118, 187–88
Mirele's Synagogue (Brailov), 90–91
misnagdim, 87, 116, 139–41, 154–55, 167n32
mizrekh-vant (eastern wall), 85, 109n10, 113n62
Mlinov, 21
mochiach (preacher), 150, 167nn30–31
Mogilev, 132–33
mohels [ritual circumcisers], 186
monasteries, 138–39
Mordechai and Esther (Medzhibozh cemetery), 116, 194
Mordechai gravestone, 194
Mordechai (Mottel) of Chernobyl, 203n9, 210, 239n32
Mordechai (Mottel) of Lekhevitsh (Saba Kaddisha), 167n32
Moshe Chaim Ephraim of Sudilkov (Sudilovker), 165n10
Moshe of Korostishev (Moshe-Chaim), 186–88, 203n9, 210
Moshe of Pshevisker, 272
Moshe Shamesh [Beadle], 144–49
Moshe Zalyozink's Monastery, 139
Moshe Zvi of Savran, 238n24
Motele (melamed in Proskurov), 3
Motele Lekhevitsh, 154–55
Mountains of Darkness, 138, 166n23, 255, 256, 262, 266, 270n13
mourning practices: in Elul, 28, 150, 253, 254; *klogmuters* (female professional mourners), 28–29, 253–54, 267 fig. 6.4; yahrzeit observances, 122, 133, 153, 175. *See also* kaddish
muamadim (candidates) for elections, 169, 170, 175
mukat ets (girls' loss of virginity), 185, 203n8

murals, 102 fig. 2.12
music, 35; of Bratslaver Hasidim, 214, 215, 217–18; David of Talne as lover of, 225–26, 227; of Hasidim, 205–6, 209; influence of secular music on hasidic music ("The Shepherd's melody"), 223–24, 239n31; Klezmer musicians, 152; of the Sabbath (*zmires*), 147, 207, 216. *See also* songs; sound recordings
Muslim Tatar healers, 26
Musterverk series, 16, 17, 39n75

Nahman of Bratslav: on collective melody of the Jewish people, 215–16; conflict with Shpoler Zaide, 216, 238n24; on fiddle music, 215; Hasidism of, 205–6, 213–14; in Land of Israel, 216; mother of, 119; Noson of Nemirov, disciple of, 112n54; his prayer before singing, 206; *Sefer Lekutei Moharan*, 214, 238n14; Uman, 197, 198, 203n12, 213, 237n12, 238n24
nekitat hefetz, 113n61
Nemirov: anti-Semitic violence in, 225–26; communal pinkes of, 195–96; duke of, 224–25; "girlish melody," 224–25; Hill of Curses, 153–54; Khmelnytsky massacres in, 73, 189, 195–96; *khosn-kale-kvorim* [bride and groom graves], 151–53; martyrs of, 195–96; Noson of Nemirov, 112n54
Nemirov pinkes, 195–96
Nemirov synagogue, 88, 101 fig. 2.11, 102 fig. 2.12, 112n54, 196
ner tamid [eternal light], 120
Neugroschel, Joachim, 22
Niger, Shmuel, 15
nigle [exotic Torah], 122, 132, 197
nigunim, 42, 209, 223–24, 233–34, 239n31
"The Nigun of Creation" (Talner Hasidim), 233–34
Nikolayev. *See* Mikolayev/Mikulaev
Nikolayevski soldiers, 65, 109n15
the *nister* (Velvele of Zhitomir), 121–23
nister [esoteric Torah], 122, 132, 197
nitl nakht (Christmas eve), 77, 78, 111n33

noblemen, 179; anti-Semitic violence of, 225–26; beautful young man and the duke's daughter, 131–32; Brailov, duke of, 90–91; carriages of, 131; churches built by, 134–36; Count Potoski, 88–89; Count Tipinitsky, 63–65; death of, 128; disturbed by the Jewish dead, 135–36; duke of Mezeritch, 66–68; as evil, 127; influence on rich Jews, 179–80; informants against Jews, 77, 78, 126–27; Lubomirski, Count, 75, 92; mortality motif, 72; palaces of, 131; persecution of Nemirov community, 224–25; punishment of, 127–28; relations with rabbis, 67–68, 89, 94, 109n13, 128, 134–36, 184; synagogues funded by, 59, 64–68, 89, 95
non-Jews: attempted destruction of synagogues, 79–82; in community pinkesim, 183; conversion to Judaism, 112n55; disputations with Jews, 69–71, 94–95; melody of gentile shepherd boy transformed into nigun, 223–24, 239n31; ohel (tomb) built by, 114–15, 184; rabbis as mediators, 183; rebuilding of synagogues, 89; reconstruction of synagogues funded by, 64–68; relations with Jews, 88–89, 93–94, 180, 183–84, 244; tributes to zaddikim, 26, 184; on wealthy Jews, 180
Noson, of Nemirov, 112n54
notarikon, 17
Novomirgorod, 231, 239n36
Noyse-HaMite, 169

oaths, 93, 94, 113n61, 157
Odl (daughter of Besht), 119–20, 165n10, 213
ohel (tomb), 114–15, 120–21, 184, 203n7
old-age homes, 25, 126, 279
Olyka, 72, 84, 110n24, 112n49, 194–95
120 years (longevity), 112n60, 121, 122, 149, 185, 198
Opatoshu, Yosef, 10, 15
opera singer, legend of, 226–28
Orah Torah *(Toyre shebalpe),* 29, 31, 34–35, 41–42, 56n2, 206
"Or Ha-Meir" (Velvele of Zhitomir), 121–22

Oricom Press, 8
orphans, 29, 253, 255
Ostroh, 35, 111n33; Asher Zvi, the Maggid of, 141, 143, 167n27; cemetery in, 83, 128, 131, 139, 143; Doktor Gorda, tale of, 139–43; Ephraim Sofer of, 273; fires in, 155; Hasidim in, 86–87, 141, 143, 167n27; inscribed stones of, 76–77; Khmelnytsky massacres in, 82, 84, 151; Maharsha (Shmuel [Eliezer] Eydels) in, 75, 79–83; Megilas Nes Ostroh [The Scroll of the Miracle of Ostroh], 79–82, 111n36, 111n38, 189, 190–91; priests in, 86; Purim of, 79, 81, 111n36, 189; siege of, 79–80; Yaakov Yosef [ben Yehuda] (Reb Yevi), 85–86, 112n50; yeshivah of Maharsha (Shmuel [Eliezer] Eydels), 76, 78
Ostroh synagogue, 79–83
Ostropolyer, Shimshon, 197
Oylem Ha-Emes [afterlife], 122
Der oytser fun der yidisher shprakh (Thesaurus of the Yiddish Language), 11

pallbearers, 123 fig. 3.1, 143 fig. 3.5, 169, 233 fig. 5.4, 242 fig. 6.1
pańszczyzna (serfdom), 63, 224–25
parchment, 79; books written on, 251–52; communal megillahs, 191; lamentations written on, 196; pinkesim, 34; prayers written on, 125, 261; scribal use of, 271, 276; Torah scrolls, 43, 44, 212, 271
parnes, 147, 148
Parnesey Khoydesh, 178, 180
Parnes-Khoydesh, 144
Passover, 10, 85, 88, 126, 169, 171, 177
Pavoloch, 126–27, 166n19
peasants, 26, 63, 74, 183–84
Pedatsur (fiddle player), 215
Peretz, Isaac Leib, 18
Perezhitoe [Experience], 42
periodicals in Yiddish, 16–20
Peter the Great Museum of Anthroplogy and Ethnography, 43
Petshenik, Aaron, Rabbi, 186
phonograph recordings, 2, 42, 207–9, 210–11, 212, 219

physical punishment, 143–46, 148–49, 154–55
pidyen-haben [redemption of the first born], 212, 237n11
pigs, law of the dead pig in Poland, 70
Pikangur, Yitzhak, 5, 37n19, 42, 43
Pikaver Rebbe, 121
Piliave (town), 33
Pilyava, 122
pinkesim, 2, 33, 202n1; accounts of Khmelnytsky massacres, 195–96; accounts of the supernatural, 189; of Berdichev cemetery, 201 fig. 4.3; blood libel accusations, 193; burial records, 150, 155; categories of, 34, 169–70, 175, 202n1; as charm in childbirth, 34, 168; collection of, 42, 71; communal miracle day observances, 190–91; decrees against luxurious lifestyles, 180–81; destruction of, 35, 126, 155, 199; disputes between Jews and non-Jews, 183; employment agreements, 173–74, 185; financial records, 169, 178, 179, 185; genealogies recounted in, 60; historical events in, 189; illustrations and ornamentations, 34, 168–69, 171, 201 fig. 4.3, 202n1; importance of, 34–35, 168, 202n1; investigations of personal status, 185, 203n8; *Makhzik Ha-Pinkes* (guardian of the pinkes), 178; martyrs recorded in, 116, 127, 189, 194–96, 195; *Megillas Medzibozh* (Megillah of Medzhibozh), 116; prayers in, 60, 189, 196, 198; scribes for, 171, 177, 178; *Shamayim* (appraisers), 179; synagogues, 60, 64; tales recorded in, 35, 156–58; testimony from non-Jews, 183; trials between fraternal societies recorded in, 183; verses from Tanakh or Talmud on title page, 171; of women's society, 13; *yizker bikher*, 7, 202n1; of Zhitomir, 127
pinkesim of societies: council of seven of workers' societies, 172, 173–74; election procedures, 169–70, 172, 175–78; financial records, 169, 178, 185
pinkes of Nemirov, 195–96
pinkes of Starokonstantinov, 193–94

Pinkhes of Korets, 273
Pinski, Dovid, 15
piyutim, 214
plagues, 125–26, 166n17, 187–88, 189
Plunz, Richard, 9
Poaley-tsedek society, 169
Podolia province, 1, 3, 223–24
poel-yeshues (miracle worker), 118
pogroms, 48, 124; books found during, 198; El-Male-Rachamim, 134, 189–94, 191–93, 196, 197, 198; Gonta massacres, 28, 189, 197–99, 203n12; Haidamaks, 28, 166n19, 166n22, 189, 193, 194, 196, 199; Hebrew words describing, 196, 198; kinah (dirge) to commemorate, 6–7; of Nikifor Grigor'ev, 231, 239n36; Petlyura's pogroms, 8; in Proskurov, 6–7, 13, 28, 35, 37n24, 51; records of, 189, 191–93, 195–96, 198. *See also* Khmelnytsky massacres
Polonnoye: martyrs of, 150, 197; Yaakov Yosef of Polonnoye, 112n54, 150, 151, 153–54, 167nn30–31
Polonnoye synagogue, 197
the poor, 78, 124–25, 141–42, 152, 166nn16–17, 169, 181, 255
Potocki, Walentyn (Count Potoski), 88–89, 112n55
Dos poylishe yidntum, 16–17
prayers, 60; Amidah prayer *(Shmone Esre)*, 141, 174, 223; of Bratslaver Hasidim, 213–14; Days of Awe, 63, 64, 109n11, 228, 229–30, 274; for the dead, 124, 131, 134; El-Male-Rachamim, 134, 189, 191–93, 196, 197, 198; in exorcism, 258, 259; "The Giver of Salvation" (prayer for the government), 223; for government officials, 64, 75, 223; for healing, 141; Kol Nidre, 63, 64, 109n11, 274; language of, 213; minyan, 117, 126, 144; petitionary prayers, 95; in pinkesim (communal record books), 189; of professional mourners, 253, 254; quality of, 115, 144, 214, 235–36; recorded in community pinkesim, 189; second Purim celebrations, 79, 81, 111n36, 190, 191, 192–94; Shehecheyanu blessing, 89, 112n57; Shema Yisrael prayer, 70,

110n22, 265, 266; before singing, 206; *slikhes* [penitential prayers], 84, 195, 197, 227; solitary meditation of Bratslaver Hasidim, 213–14; *tefilas ha-hisdavkus*, 213–14; times of, 73–74, 125, 144, 145; *tkhines/tkhinot* [supplicatory prayers], 13, 28, 253. *See also* chazanim
preacher *(mochiach)*, 150, 167nn30–31
pregnancy, 87–88, 119, 129–30, 241, 247, 269n8
price regulations of workers' societies, 173
priests, 69–71, 94–95, 139, 183, 232
the prodigy, account of, 156–57
Proskurov, 23, 28, 30–31, 51, 234, 245; Hasidim in, 234; *Khurbn Proskurov (yizker bukh)*, 7; pogroms in, 6–7, 13, 28, 35, 37n24, 51; Rechtman and, 3–7, 13, 51; women in, 30, 244, 245
public disputations between priests and Jews, 69–71, 94–95
Purim of Ostroh, 79, 81, 111n36, 189

Rabbi David of Zlatopol, 231, 239n38
rabbinical courts, 67, 256, 257, 261
rabbis: burial of, 149; community relations of, 77, 144–45, 153–54, 176–77; generations of, 85; as heads of yeshivot, 76, 78; as martyrs of Khmelnytsky massacres, 191–93; personalities of, 143–47, 153–54, 167n28, 280–82; relations with non-Jews, 69–70, 71, 89, 94, 109n13, 183; as source of legends, 91; Talmud commentaries by, 76
rabbis as mediators, 176, 183
Rabin Srul. See Baal Shem Tov (Besht)
Radzivilov, 60–61, 62, 109n2, 109n6
Radzivilov, Itsikl [Yitshak], 60, 109n4
Radzivilover Synagogue, 59–62, 97 fig. 2.6, 109n2
Raphael (angel), 140, 167n26, 245
Rapoport, Shlomo Zanvil. *See* An-sky
Rashi, 76, 83
Rav. *See* Shneur Zalman of Liady (Baal Ha-Tanya)
"The Rav's Melody" (Shneur Zalman of Liady), 217–18, 219, 238n28
Rav Yevi (Yaakov Yosef [ben Yehuda]), 85

Rebbe Leyb (Podolia), 223–24, 239n30
Rebbe Yehudah the Martyr, 69–71, 70, 71, 110n20, 110n21
Reb Hershenyu of Tshitshelnik, 33, 134, 136–38, 166n22
Reb Leyb of Piliave, 33
Reb Moshele. *See* Moshe of Korostishev
Reb Yevi, 85–86, 112n50
Reb Yokhntse [Yohanan] of Rachmistrivka, 231, 239n37
Reb Yosele (the Talner rebbe's Yosele), 225–26, 231–34, 239n32
Rechtman, Abraham, 50 fig. 1.4, 51 fig. 1.5, 53 fig. 1.7, 202 fig. 4.4; An-sky's relations with, 5–6, 14, 43, 45–48, 47 fig. 1.2, 49 fig. 1.3; arrest of, 1, 2, 36n3, 43; birthdate, 3, 36n11; correspondents of, 10–11, 15–16, 20–22; education of, 3, 4, 24–25, 275; examples of scribal craft collected by, 33–34; family of, 4–5, 7–12, 14, 16, 25, 27, 37n45; feigned illness and as subject for exorcisms, 30, 246–47; *Groyser verterbukh fun der yidisher shprakh* (Great Dictionary of the Yiddish Language), 11–12, 24; Haykele Twersky as friend of, 30–31; Hebrew language account of Jewish Ethnographic Expedition, 13–14; on Jewish customs *(minhagim)*, 12; *Jewish Ethnographic Program*, 5–6; *Khurbn Proskurov* (The Destruction of Proskurov), 7; kinah (dirge) composed by, 7; language usage/multilingualism conveyed by, 25–26, 203n11, 203nn6–7; loss of ethnographic materials by, 7–8; meeting with Sholem Aleichem, 24; memory of, 31–32, 35, 36n3, 51, 56n8, 109n2, 110n19, 167n28; nostalgia for shtetls, 48; notes and photographs of, 48; Oricom Press, 8; personal life, 3–5, 4, 10, 12, 22, 24–25, 36n11; and Proskurov, 3–7, 13, 51; pseudonyms of, 13–14, 38n57; publication of *Jewish Ethnography and Folklore (Yidishe etnografye un folklor)*(Rechtman), 15–16; readers' responses to, 21–22; recording of female exorcists at work,

Rechtman, Abraham (*Cont.*)
243; research methods of, 11–12, 25, 48, 51; residence in Sholem Aleichem Houses (*Sholem Aleikhem Hayzer*), 8–10, 30–31; scholarly Yiddish (*perldikn lomdishn yidish*) of, 25; as subject for exorcisms, 246–47; transcription errors of, 208, 237n2; travels of, 5–6, 8; Ukrainian text used by, 185, 203n6; visit with Reb Moshele of Korostishev, 210–11; *visnshaft* (dry scholasticism), 19, 20–21; women in Hasidic movement, 27; writing style of, 24–25; Yiddish language used by, 24–25, 51–52, 109n13, 203n7, 203n11. *See also* cemeteries; female exorcists; Jewish Ethnographic Expedition; scribes and scribal arts; sound recordings; study houses; synagogues; writing, culture of; *Yidishe etnografye un folklor* (Jewish Ethnography and Folklore)(Rechtman)
Rechtman, Avigdor, 4–5, 7
redemption, 197, 237
reincarnation, 122, 166nn12–13, 189
Rekhil (wife of Rabbi Yeshaya of Mogilev), 133
Relief Committee for the War-Victims, 2, 43, 54 fig. 1.8
relief organizations, 2, 6, 43, 54 fig. 1.8
repentance narratives/accounts, 143–49, 157, 167n28, 228, 236
responsa, 112n48, 132
Ribaz, 132, 166n20
Rivkah (Rechtman's mother), 27
robbers, 124
Roeh Kheshbn (treasurer), 178
ropes, possessed victim bound in, 257, 259
Rosh Hashanah, 229–30, 232, 277
Roshim [Heads], 178, 179
Roskies, David, 23
Rozhanski, Shmuel, 16, 17
rules of societies, 13, 169–73, 175–77
Russian Civil War, 6
Ruzhin Hasidim, 30

Saba Kaddisha (Mordecha (Mottel) of Lekhevitsh), 167n32, 238n24

Sabbath: as day of peace, 145, 148–49; desecration of, 85–86, 189; exorcism after, 259; food and food customs on, 87, 147, 213, 214–15, 216, 228; in *Jewish Ethnographic Program* (life cycle questionnaire), 44; melave-malke (escorting the queen, meal following the Sabbath), 213, 215–16, 221, 238n20; prayers on, 147, 220, 221, 222; Psalm 93 sung by Baal Shem Tov (Besht), 220; shaleshudes [third meal on Sabbath], 213, 214–15, 228, 238n15; as space, 24; *tishn* (Hasidic gatherings), 11, 206, 210, 218, 226, 234; visitors on, 60, 147–48, 186; weddings on, 155; work on the eve of the Sabbath, 173; *zmires* (songs) of, 147, 207, 214, 216
The Sabbath (Heschel), 24
Safran, Gabriella, 36n3, 36n10, 56n6
Saminsky, Lazar, 207
Samosenko, Ivan, 6
sandak, 167n28, 282
Sar Ha-Eysh [Prince of Fire], 133
Sar Ha-Torah [Prince of the Torah], 132–33
Savranyer Zaddik, 216
Schwarz, Jan, 16–17
scribes and scribal arts: calligraphy, 33–34, 60, 276–77, 279; crowns on letters (*shatnez getz*), 276, 277–78; holiness of, 272–73; languages of, 79; megillahs, 33, 79–82, 116, 165n11, 189, 190–94; missing letters, restoration of, 273, 282; penmanship of, 276–77; prayers against plague written by, 125; preparation of, 272; *sofer stam*, 271; visit with Dovid Elye, 276–79, 283 fig. 7.2
second Purim celebrations, 79, 81, 111n36, 190, 191, 192–95
seduction: by duke's daughter, 131–32
Sefer HaVikuah (Yisroel Leybl Navaredok), 154, 155, 167n32
Sefer Khokhmat Shlomo [the Book of Solomon's Wisdom], 251, 269n10
Segal, Avraham-Moshe, 198
Segal, David ben Shmuel HaLevi (TaZ), 84, 112n49, 195
Segal, Sheftel, 196

INDEX

Segal, Yekusiel (of Brailov), 91, 198–99, 202 fig. 4.4
servants, 85–86, 147–48
seven (number), 257, 258, 262
sextons, 122, 123, 127, 134
sgules [protective charms], 42, 73, 118, 119, 120, 125, 170
Shabbes un Yontif, 44, 45
Shabtai HaKohen (Shach), 196
shaleshudes [third meal on Sabbath], 213, 214–15, 238n15
Shamayim (appraisers), 179
Shamesh [Beadle], 144–49
Shapiro, Chaya Bela (Starokonstantinov), 243
Shargorod (town), 143–49, 146, 167n28
Shargorod cemetery, 123–24
Shargorod synagogue, 107 fig. 2.17
Shas society, 186
shatnez getz (acronym for seven Hebrew letters that require crowns when written), 276, 277–78
Shatnez [wool-linen mixture], prohibition of, 172–73
Shatzky, Jacob (Yankev), 14, 15
Shavuot, 89
Shehecheyanu blessing, 89, 112n57
Shelah (Yeshaya Ha-Levi Horowitz), 198
Shema Yisrael prayer, 70, 110n22, 265, 266
Shemos (Torah portion consisting of Exodus 1:1-6:1), 144–46, 147
Shenderay, Moshe, 19, 20–21
Shepetovka, 247
The Shepherd's melody, 223–24
Shlomo of Karlin, 167n32
Shlomovits, Zalman, 251–52
Shloyme of Lutsk, 273
Shmilovitch, Yosef Dovid (Bazilier Rebbe), 4, 7
Shmone Esre (Amidah prayer), 141, 174, 223
Shmuel (rabbi of Khmelnik), 255
Shmuel ben Chaim (epileptic boy), 255–67
Shnei Lukhot Habrit (Horowitz), 198, 204n15
Shneur Zalman of Liady (Baal Ha-Tanya), 208, 217, 237n1; account of the old man, 218–19; feud with Borukhl of Medzhibozh, 279–81; music of, 205, 208, 217–19, 238n28; perfection of scribal letters of Torah by, 277–78; Rosh Hashanah visit to Maggid of Mezeritch, 277–78
shofar blowing, 257, 258, 262
Sholem Aleichem, 18–19, 24
Sholem Aleichem Houses *(Sholem Aleikhem Hayzer),* 8–10, 30–31
Shpikover, Motlele, Reb, 235, 244, 245
Shpoler Zaide (Aryeh Leib of Shpola), 208, 216, 238n24
Shraybman, Yisroel, Reb, 248–49
Shrayer, Shmuel (later, Sherira), 2, 5, 36n8, 37n19, 42
Shternberg, Lev (L. Y.), 2, 43, 44, 56n7
Shteyn, L. M., 15–16
shtibl (tomb), 114–15, 116, 123, 132–33, 151, 203n7
Shulchan Aruch Ha-Rav (Shneur Zalman of Liady), 217
Simchat Torah, 182
singing in a tremulous voice, 235–36
Sirkis, Yoel, Rebbe (Bach), 84, 112n47
skhakh burning, 154, 155
Slabodiansky, Daniel (Khmelnik), 34, 254–55
slander, 222–23
"Slikhes of Olyka" (TaZ), 195
slikhes [penitential prayers], 84, 195, 197, 227
Smiela (town), 198
Snitkov synagogue, 105 fig. 2.15
Snyder, Timothy, 3
societies: distribution of honors of being called up to the Torah, 174, 186; labor contracts, 173–74; in large cities, 175; leadership of, 171; membership in, 170, 174–75, 182; payments to, 174; rules of, 13, 169–73, 175–77
Sodilkover, Moshe Chaim Ephraim, 119, 165n10
sofer stam [scribe], 271
Sokolsky, Esther Nelson, 9
solitary meditation: of Bratslaver Hasidim, 213–14
Somekh-Noflim, 169

songs, 26, 32; at Bratslaver shaleshudes [third meal on Sabbath], 213, 214–15; of the gentile shepherd boy singing, 223–24, 239n31; "girlish melody," 224–25; languages in, 26; of local events, 208; nigunim, 42, 209, 223–24, 233–34, 239n31; sources (Tanakh, Talmud) related to, 207–9, 220, 221, 222, 230, 236; of Talner Hasidim, 230–31, 233–34
Sore [Sarah] (mother of Besht), 117, 165n7
Sosye-Sore (mother of Levi Yitzhak of Berdichev), 120
sound recordings: in bes medresh, 208–9; Hasidic songs, 208, 217–19; publication of music, 207; reactions to, 32, 208–11; of Reb Hillel's fiddle playing, 217; Thomas Alva Edison and, 2, 32, 209, 212
sources (Tanakh, Talmud) related to: *ashmurot* (divisions of time), 238n26; Bratslaver Hasidim, 213, 214, 215; childbirth, 269n4, 269n8; circumcision, 250, 269n9; community affairs, 126, 171, 177, 186, 190; darkness, 156; death and mourning, 121, 253; destruction of churches, 86; doctors and medical care, 141; dybbuk, 265; evil eye, 240, 241, 250; examination of manuscript, 34, 254–55; exodus from Egypt, 65; exorcism, 30, 243–44, 245, 247, 260, 262; headstone inscriptions, 83, 114, 116, 151; holiness, 114, 116, 165n2; Joseph the Righteous, 240, 241, 244; on Korah, 167n35; longevity, 112n60, 198; martyrdom, 126, 166n18, 192, 193, 195, 197; miracles, 80–81, 111n40; names, 119, 165n10, 197; opulence, 180; parable of the king's son, 236; personal behavior, 112n60, 198, 209; physical beauty, 131; pidyon ha-ben, 237n11; plagues, 125, 187; prayer, 195, 209, 212, 227, 237n10, 260; on rabbis' behavior, 144–45; scribal writing, 212, 271, 273, 277; of sin, 231; songs and melodies, 207–9, 220, 221, 222, 230, 236; synagogue art, 60, 61, 66, 79, 95; title pages of pinkesim, 171; Torah readings and study, 60, 111n37, 144–45, 147, 186, 208, 214; use of language, 25, 131–32, 214; wandering, 157
spitting, 243, 245, 246
Spivak, Nakhum (son-in-law of Reb Yosele), 231
Stanislavski, Konstantin, 215, 238n23
Starokonstantinov [Alt-Konstantin], 106 fig. 2.16, 162 fig. 3.12, 164n3.14, 193–94, 198, 243
Stein, Sarah Abrevaya, 15
stepping on nails, 269n8
Stolin Hasidim, 30
stones, 76–77, 151, 154–55
stopping bleeding after circumcision, 250, 269n9
Storch, Hannah, 4–5, 12, 25, 27
storytellers: wagon drivers as, 183–84
St. Petersburg. *See* Ethnographic Museum
strangers, 146–47, 214, 218–19
study houses, 69, 92–94, 109n1, 110n20, 174–75, 186, 234
Stutchkoff, Nahum, 11, 12
Sukkot, 86, 154–55, 172
synagogues: architecture of, 32, 59–60, 72, 82–83, 94–95, 212; art in, 60–62, 65–66, 94, 196, 212; atmosphere in, 63–64; auctioning of honors, 78, 174; *baldakhin* [ceremonial canopy], 108 fig. 2.18; of Bratslaver Hasidim, 213; charity boxes in, 133; construction of, 62, 64–68, 90–91; dating of, 59, 61, 79; destruction of, 79–80, 82, 109n2, 152; Elijah's seat, 108 fig. 2.18; Great Reb Liber's Synagogue, 72–75; Hands of Aaron, 66, 94; Khmelnytsky massacres, 152; Korostishev synagogue, 103 fig. 2.13, 104 fig. 2.14; lecterns, 64, 98 fig. 2.8, 102 fig. 2.12, 104 fig. 2.14, 122; lighting of, 62, 63, 102 fig. 2.12; maintenance of, 64–65, 89–91, 175; miracles occurring in, 60–61, 79–80, 82, 112n44; *mizrekh-vant* (eastern wall), 85, 109n10, 113n62; naming of, 28, 91–92; patronage of, 62, 64–68, 72, 75, 89, 174–75; photographs of, 96, 97–108; pinkesim, 60, 64; seating in, 80, 85, 94, 109n10, 113n62; Shargorod synagogue,

107 fig. 2.17; tunnels under, 22, 82–83; women's sections in, 80, 214; wood synagogues, 60, 105, 107 fig. 2.17, 188 fig. 4.1, 207 fig. 5.1, 252 fig. 6.3; zodiac, 60, 65, 66, 109n3. *See also* Torah arks; individual headings (e.g., Korostishev synagogue)

tailors' societies, 171, 172–73, 175
Takh ve-Tat. See Khmelnytsky massacres
Talmud study, 12, 24, 170, 186
talmud-toyre (Talmud Torah), 63, 176, 178
Talner Hasidim, 225–29, 230–34, 239n32
"Talner's Dibbuk Melody," 230–31
Tanners, Association of, 169, 175
Tatars (Kadorim), 26, 244, 255, 269n7
Taubman, Howard, 39n84
taverns, 122, 137, 199
tax payments, 126, 178
TaZ (Segal, David ben Shmuel HaLevi), 84, 112n49, 195
tefilas ha-hisdavkus, 213–14, 238n13
tefillin: of Baal Shem Tov (Besht), 279–80; as cure for headaches, 273; defective tefillin, 281–82; Elijah the Prophet associated with, 272; of Ephraim Sofer of Ostroh, 273; inheritance of, 272, 279–80; missing letters from, 282; vows made while holding, 94
Tetragrammaton, 272, 273
Tevye the Milkman, 24
theft of jewelry, 147–49
three wives (incantation), 243
thumb sucking, 124, 125
Tikkunei Zohar, 210, 237n9
tikun [repair], 122, 166n13, 222, 228
tishn (Hasidic gatherings), 11, 206, 210, 218, 226, 234
tkhines/tkhinot [supplicatory prayers], 13, 28, 253
Tlust (town), 117, 165n7
Toldos Yaakov Yosef (Yaakov Yosef of Polonnoye), 150, 151, 167n30
tombs: family burial sites, 120; over graves of zaddikim, 33, 42, 83, 114–15, 115–16, 151, 158 fig. 3.7
Tomkhey-Dal, 169

Torah arks, 43, 61–62, 93, 94, 98 fig. 2.8, 102 fig. 2.12, 106 fig. 2.16, 125, 198
Torah readings, 60, 99 fig. 2.9, 144; distribution of, by workers' societies, 174–75; distribution of honors of being called up to the Torah, 174–75, 186; for fast days, 79; marking communal disasters, 60; rabbis called up for, 144–45, 149, 274–75; religious obligations for, 174–75; *Shemos* (Torah portion consisting of Exodus 1:1-6:1), 144–45, 147
Torah scrolls, 43, 61, 75, 93; Apter Rov called up to Reb Dovid's Torah scroll, 274–75; covers for, 43, 275; defamation of, 182–83; in exorcism, 257, 258, 263; vows made while holding, 94; writing of, 271, 273–75
Torah study, 141; on Christmas, 77, 78; and dybbukim, 256; funding of, 85; melodies associated with, 217–19; *nigle* [exotic Torah], 122, 132; *nister* [esoteric Torah], 122, 132; *nitl nakht* (Christmas eve), 77, 78, 111n33; "The Rav's Melody," 217–18, 219; singing, 205; study houses, 69, 92–93, 110n20, 174–75, 186, 234; Talmud scholars who study *poskim*, 170
Tosfos (Tosafot), 76, 83
Tosfos Yom Tov (Yom Tov Lipmann Heller), 112n54, 121, 165n11, 196
Tovim [good ones], 178–79
Trachtenberg, Joshua, 269n5
Trisker, Nakhumtse, Reb, 244
trufes [traditional remedies], 42
Tsemakh Atlas (Grade), 22
Tsentral-Farband fun Poylishe Yidn in Argentine (Central Union of Polish Jews in Argentina), 16
tserufim [mystical combinations], 187, 197
Tshernobiler [Chernobler], Motele [Mordechai], 203n9, 210, 239n32
Tshitshelnik (town), 33
tshuve [repentence], 122
tsiyun (tomb), 114–15, 115–16, 158 fig. 3.7
Tsukunft (periodical), 18, 20
Tulchin, 163 fig. 3.13, 197
Twersky, Abraham, 10–11, 30

Twersky, David, 10
Twersky, Khaykele, 10, 30–31, 244, 245
Twersky, Menachem Nahum, 30
Twersky, Yitzhak Nahum, 30
Twersky, Yohanan, 10, 30, 244
Twersky Hasidic dynasty, 10–11, 30–31, 203n9, 244
tzerufei-shemos [combination of divine names], 133, 187

Ukrainian language, 184, 203nn6–7, 208, 243, 244–45
Uman, 197, 198, 203n12, 213, 237n12, 238n24
United States, Yiddish culture in, 5, 8–14, 21–22, 30–31

VaYekhal (Torah reading for fast days), 79
Vaynshteyn, Sh., 53 fig. 1.7
Vayter, A. [Ayzik Meyer Devenishski], 48
Velvel (Talmud Torah teacher), 116
Velvele of Zhitomir (the *nister*), 121–23
verst, 63, 109n8
vidui (confession before death), 116, 195, 197, 231
Vilna, 47–48
Vinitse, old age home in, 25
Vinnytsya, old-age home in, 279
Vishnevets, chazan of, 229–30
visnshaft (dry scholasticism), 19, 20–21
Vohl, Velvele. *See* Velvele of Zhitomir (the *nister*)

wagon drivers, 182, 183–84, 236, 255
wanderer motif, 156, 157, 228, 236, 255
water carriers, 186, 203n11
wealthy Jews: burial of, 150–51; charity of, 85–86, 92–93, 150, 152, 155, 234; community loans from, 185; displays of wealth, 180–81; as healers, 251; as keepers of workers' pinkesim, 176; marriage of children, 152, 155–57, 156–58; sons-in-law supported by, 219–20; Ukrainian noblemen's influence on, 179–80
wedding canopy *(chuppah)*, 125
weddings: charity for *(Hakhnasat kalah)*, 13; communal rules on, 180–81; dates of, 155, 167n33; of Hasidic rebbes, 215;
knots of shame on wedding veils, 156; preparations for, 152, 155, 156; songs at, 224; Torah portions before, 144, 147
Weinreich, Beatrice Silverman, 22
Wessely, Naftali Hertz, 269n10
whiskey traders, 127
widow of Brailov, 198–200
Wiesel, Elie, 17
wife of Yekhiel Mikhel [Katz], 196–97
wills, 31, 124
women: alleged promiscuity of, 129, 156, 185, 203n8; charity collected by, 76; as ethnographers, 56n3; in Hasidism, 27, 33, 111n27, 120, 235; Haykele Twersky's recollections of, 30; headstones for, 117, 163 fig. 3.13, 164 fig. 3.14, 194; as healers, 27, 29–30, 34; *klogmuters* (female professional mourners), 28–29, 253–54, 267 fig. 6.4; knots of shame on wedding veils, 156; loss of virginity *(mukat ets)*, 185, 203n8; maintenance of tombstones by, 110n21; as martyrs, 28, 92, 98, 151–53, 195–96, 198–200; memories of the Apter Rov, 274–76; mothers, 27, 117, 120, 196; pilgrimages to graves of zaddikim, 110n21; pinkes of a women's society, 13; pregnancy, 87–88, 119, 129–30, 241, 247, 269n8; sections for women in synagogues, 80, 214; synagogues named after pious women, 90–91; *tkhines/tkhinot* [supplicatory prayers], 13, 28, 253; *zaddekes* (righteous woman), 27–28, 33, 76, 130, 165n10. *See also* childbirth; children; female exorcists
women exorcist and healer *(opshprekherke)*, 29–30
women healers, 143
wood carvings by Solomon Yudovin, 71 fig. 2.3, 130 fig. 3.3, 217 fig. 5.2; agile like the deer motifs in, 62 fig. 2.1, 68 fig. 2.2, 90 fig. 2.4, 124 fig. 3.2, 138 fig. 3.4, 200 fig. 4.2; of lions, 153 fig. 3.6, 217 fig. 5.2; of pallbearers, 123 fig. 3.1, 143 fig. 3.5, 233 fig. 5.4, 242 fig. 6.1; of synagogues, 105, 107 fig. 2.17, 188 fig. 4.1, 207 fig. 5.1, 252 fig. 6.3
wooden synagogues, 60, 105, 107 fig. 2.17, 188 fig. 4.1, 207 fig. 5.1, 252 fig. 6.3

INDEX 313

workers' pinkesim and societies, 169, 171–75
work hours regulated by workers' societies, 173
Workmen's Circle *(Der Ring)*, 8, 9
writing, culture of: incantations of women healers, 30, 34; *kvitl/kvitlekh* (written requests), 33, 114, 117–18, 120, 122; manuscripts, 3, 34, 79–80, 248–52, 249 fig. 6.2, 254–55; orality, relationship with, 35; religious texts, 33–34; tombstone inscriptions, 33, 42, 69, 71, 76–77, 83, 86, 119–20, 125, 128, 131–34, 138, 149, 151. *See also* pinkesim; scribes and scribal arts

xatinka as *shtibl* (tomb), 203n7

Yaakov Yosef Ha-Cohen, 151
Yaakov Yosef of Ostroh [ben Yehuda] (Reb Yevi), 85, 112n50
Yaakov Yosef of Polonnoye, 112n54, 150–51, 153–54, 167n30, 167nn30–31
yahrzeit observances, 122, 133, 153, 175
Yakhnes, Moshe, 120–21
Yaltushov, 197
Yanov synagogue, 107 fig. 2.17
Yayles, 64, 109n11
Yeda-Am (Israeli folklore journal), 14
Yegie-Kapayim society, 169
Yehoash Publishing Society, 21
Yehudah Leyb, the *Mochiach* (preacher), 150–51, 167nn30–31
Yehudah the Martyr (Rebbe), of Lutsk, 69–71, 110n20, 110n22
Yehuda Leyb, Rabbi (Ostroh), 85
Yekhiel Mikhel [Katz], 196–97
Yerushalmi, Yosef Hayim, 31
Yeshaya, Rabbi (Mogilev), 132–33
Yeshayele (of Khmelnik), 255–67
The Yeshiva (translation of *Tsemakh Atlas* (Grade)), 22
yeshivot, 22, 76, 78, 176
Yeskusiel of Ostroh, 35
Yidbukh (Buenos Aires Yiddish publisher), 18
Yiddish culture and language: in Argentina, 16–19, 39n75; education in, 8, 9, 48; incantations in, 243–44, 245–46; inscriptions on synagogues, 79; as language of storyteller, 279; periodicals, 16–20; in pinkesim, 172, 180, 190–91; Rechtman's use of, 24–25, 51–52, 109n13, 203n7, 203n11; registers of, 25–26, 109n13; revival of, 9, 16–17, 22–23; scholarly Yiddish *(perldikn lomdishn yidish)*, 25; songs in, 208; Talmudic yiddish *(talmudishn yidish)*, 12, 24; in United States, 5, 8–14, 18–22
Yiddish Dictionary Committee (YIVO), 11–12
Dos yidishe etnografishe program (life cycle questionnaire), 2, 5–7, 23, 27, 44, 45 fig. 1.1
Yidishe etnografye un folklor (Jewish Ethnography and Folklore)(Rechtman): construction of narrative in, 3–4, 7–8, 23–24; Haykele Twersky and, 30–31; publication of, 12, 14, 15, 16, 17–18, 18–19; reception of, 18–22; scope of, 14, 23–25, 30, 31, 34, 35; as source for *Tsemakh Atlas* (Grade), 22; Ukrainian text used in, 185, 203n6. *See also* An-sky
Yisroel Leybl Navaredok, Reb [Novogrudok], 154, 155, 167n32
Yisroel Meys (great grandson of Besht), 119, 120
Yisroel of Ibnitz, 167n32
Yisroel of Ruzhin, 272
Yitshak Komarner (scribe), 272
Yitskhak-Ayzik, Reb, 71
Yitzhak Isaac Taub of Kaliv, 239n30
YIVO, 11–12, 16
yizker bikher, 7, 202n1
Yoffe, Mordechai, 198, 204n15
Yoffe, Yehuda, 12
Yom Kippur, 63, 64, 109n11, 274
Yosef Yuzpa of Ostroh, 80, 111n41
Yozyl (Jesus), 77, 244
Yudovin, Solomon/Shloyme, 1, 2, 5, 36n3, 42, 43, 46, 53 fig. 1.7. *See also* wood carvings by Solomon Yudovin

zaddekes (righteous woman), 27–28, 76, 119–20, 130, 165n10, 213 zaddikim: behavior of, 118, 120, 143–47, 167n28, 223–24, 231–32, 274; birth of children, 78; blessings from, 121, 167n28, 226–27; confrontation with *Sar Ha-Eysh* [Prince of Fire], 133; deaths of, 71, 73, 85, 86, 121, 132, 272; defiance of Christian authorities by, 69–71, 73–75, 78; in exile, 146–49; exorcism of dybbukim by, 255–57; fasts of, 133; genealogies of, 71, 73; graves of, 26, 71, 86, 110n21, 118, 120, 127, 151; Hasidic zaddik who hears a gentile shepherd boy singing, 223–24, 239n31; as hidden, 121–23, 239n30, 255–57; inscriptions for, 138; *lamed vavnik zaddikim* [Thirty-Six Righteous], 123, 166n15, 189, 198; Liber the Great, Rebbe, 72–75, 110n25, 125–26; martyrdom of, 70–71, 132–33, 191–93, 231; as miracle workers *(poel-yeshues)*, 118, 120, 187–88; peasants' stories of, 183–84; petitions *(kvitlekh)* left on graves of, 33, 114, 117–18, 120, 122; physical appearance of, 73; poverty of, 125; prayer of, 73–74; reactions to the phonograph, 210–11; revelation of, 122; songs of, 215–16; tombs over graves of, 33, 42, 83, 114–15, 116, 151; Torah study of, 132–33; Ukrainian peasants on, 183–84; wills of, 124. *See also* individual headings (e.g., Dovid of Mikolayev (Rebbe))

Zak, Abraham (Avrom), 17
Zakhor (Yerushalmi), 31
Zalkind, Yaakov Meir, 240, 268n1
Zaltsman, Zelke (Mikolayev), 176
Zalyozink, Moshe, 139
zamlers (collectors), 11, 12
Zavadivker, Polly, 56n8
Zborzsher, Velvele [Ze'ev Wolf], 60, 109n4
Zhitlovsky, Chaim, 10, 47, 57n15
Zhitomir, 1, 43, 123, 126–27, 198
Zionism, 4–5, 10
Zipperstein, Seven, 18
Zishe of Anipol, 184–85, 278
Zlotopolyer, Dovid, 232
Zlotshever, Yekhiel Mikhel, 60, 88, 109n4
zodiac, 60, 65, 66, 109n3
Zohar, 166n23, 197, 210, 237n9, 248, 269n4
Zusman, Abele, 85
Zusmans (Ostroh), 77, 85, 111n31
Zwick, Bronya (Binah), 8, 12

NATHANIEL DEUTSCH is Professor of History at the University of California, Santa Cruz. He is author of *The Jewish Dark Continent: Life and Death in the Russian Pale of Settlement* and, with Michael Casper, *A Fortress in Brooklyn: Race, Real Estate, and the Making of Hasidic Williamsburg*, among other books.

NOAH BARRERA is a Yiddish educator and writer. He studied and subsequently taught Yiddish at the YIVO Institute's Uriel Weinreich Summer Program in New York. He coordinated and taught Yiddish language classes at the Workers Circle. He has published numerous Yiddish articles in the Yiddish *Daily Forward* and *Afn Shvel*.

www.ingramcontent.com/pod-product-compliance
Lightning Source LLC
Chambersburg PA
CBHW021344300426
44114CB00012B/1070